CENTRAL STATISTICAL OFFICE

Regional Trends 27

1992 Edition

Editor: TOM GRIFFIN

Associate Editor: PHILIP ROSE

Editorial Staff: STEPHEN DREWELL
DAVE BARAN
COLIN WHITING

London: HMSO

Introduction

This new edition of *Regional Trends* updates and expands the unique description of the regions of the United Kingdom given in previous editions. Its 15 chapters cover a wide range of social, vital, demographic, industrial and economic statistics. To make it easy to understand the differences between regions, information is given in simple and clear tables, maps and charts. A unique feature of *Regional Trends* are the regional profiles (Chapter 1). Each region is profiled with simple text highlighting major regional trends and a few key charts comparing the region to the United Kingdom as a whole.

A great deal of data are included for the 11 standard regions of the United Kingdom, but *Regional Trends* goes further. There is also key information for counties, other sub-regions and individual local authority districts. A comparison is also made between regions of the United Kingdom and those of the other European Community countries.

Although *Regional Trends* is produced as a descriptive brief for government, it is also of interest to a wide variety of others including planners and marketing managers as well as those with general regional interests. The book brings together data from a wide variety of sources and, for many topics, is the only place where data for the whole of the United Kingdom are available in one table.

Coverage and definitions

It is not always possible to give data for more than one year in any table or chart. However, many items are published each year, and trends can be analysed by referring to earlier editions. Due to variations in coverage and definitions, some care may be needed when comparing data from more than one source. Readers should consult the notes and definitions at the end of each chapter. The Central Statistical Office publication, *Social Trends (HMSO)* contains further details on many of the topics covered in this book - generally at national level only.

Diskette versions

For the first time, many of the data series used in this *Regional Trends* are available on computer diskette - please contact the Associate Editor at the address below for further details.

Regional boundaries

Standard statistical regions are used as far as is possible throughout the book. Definitions of these and non-standard regions along with explanatory notes are given in the appendix. Maps of standard regions and counties are given in Chapter 1 and Chapter 14. The United Kingdom consists of England, Wales, Scotland and Northern Ireland. The Isle of Man and the Channel Isles are not part of the United Kingdom.

Contributions

The Editor and Associate Editor wish to thank all those contributors within statistics divisions of government departments and other organisations, without whose help this publication would not be possible. Within the Central Statistical Office the *Regional Trends* production team was: Stephen Drewell, Dave Baran, Colin Whiting, Brian Salerno, Carlton Brown, Richard Adshead, Eloise Critchley, Christine Wilkin, Adeline Fadugba, and Naeema Sharief. Thanks also go to our Graphics Design Unit.

Social and Regional Branch
Central Statistical Office
PO Box 1333
Millbank Tower
Millbank
London
SW1P 4QQ

Symbols and conventions

Reference years
When a choice of years has to be made, the most recent year or run of recent years is shown together with past population census years (1991, 1981 etc.) and sometimes the mid-points between census years (1986 etc.). Occasionally, other years are added to show a peak or trough in the series.

Percentages
Percentages are shown in italics.

Rounding of figures
In tables where figures have been rounded to the nearest final digit, component items may not add to the total shown.

Provisional and estimated data
Occasionally, data are provisional or estimated. To keep footnotes to a minimum, these have not been separately identified. Source departments will be able to advise if revised data are available.

Symbols
    .. = not available   - = negligible (less than half the final digit shown)
    0 = nil   . = not applicable

Non-calendar years.
The following conventions are used:
    1990-91 = financial year (April-March)
    1990/91 = Academic year (September-July) or occasionally some variant
    1990-1991 = 1990 and 1991 combined

Regional Trend 27, © Crown copyright 1992

Contents

4

Chapter 1: Regional Profiles

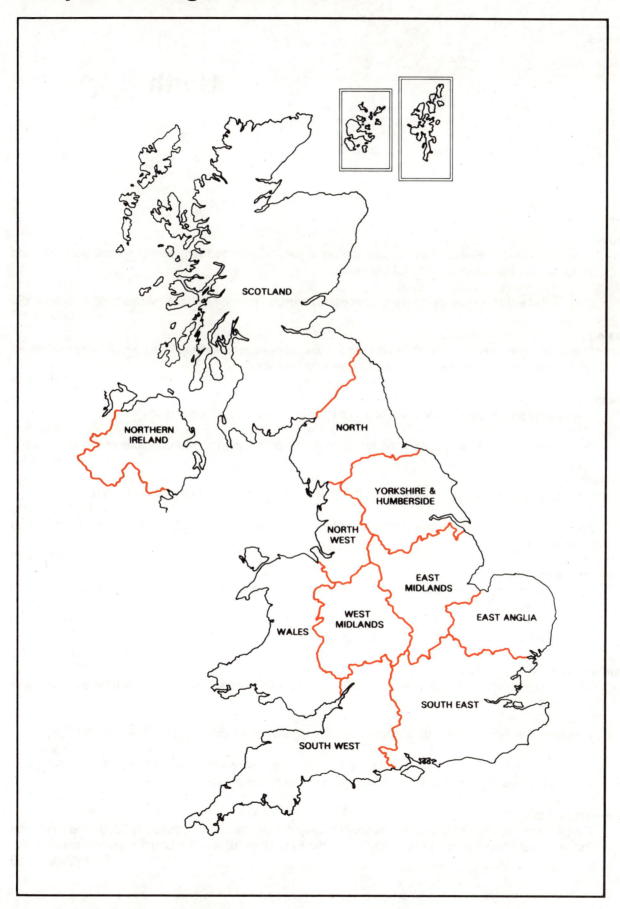

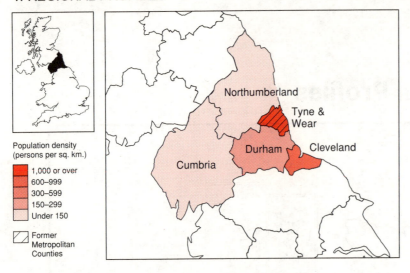

Population density
(persons per sq. km.)

1,000 or over
600–999
300–599
150–299
Under 150

Former
Metropolitan
Counties

North

Population

- The population of the North is falling - the number of people increased in most regions between 1981 and 1990, but the North had a fall of 1.3 per cent.

  (Table 3.1)

- One third of all births in the North are to unmarried mothers - only the North West has a higher proportion.
  (Table 3.16)

Housing

- Owner occupation is lower in the North than in most other regions - although six out of every ten homes were owner occupied in 1990, this was the second lowest rate.

  (Table 4.2)

Education

- The North has the lowest proportion of 16 year-olds continuing their education.

  (Table 5.4)

- *Ils ne comprennent pas* - pupils in the North have one of the poorest performances at GCSE French.
  (Table 5.10)

Employment

- The North still has high unemployment - in 1991, only Northern Ireland had a higher rate.

  (Table 7.16)

- Although very few of the workforce in the North have degrees, apprenticeships remain more common than in most other regions.

  (Table 7.8)

Income and spending

- *Meat and two veg please*. People in the North eat most vegetables per head and they eat an above average amount of meat.

  (Table 8.11)

- A quarter of adults in the North are shareholders - only the South East has more.
  (Chart 8.13)

Crime and justice

- The North has both the highest and the fastest growing crime rates - up by three quarters between 1981 and 1990.

  (Table 9.1)

- *Remember to lock up at night* - the North has the highest crime rates for both burglary and theft.
  (Table 9.1)

- The North has the highest crime rates among the very young (aged between 10 and 13) - around one in every fifty of these youngsters were in trouble with the police in 1990.

  (Table 9.6)

The environment

- *People in the North can breath more easily than they did 20 years ago*. In the early 1970s, the North had the smokiest environment, but by 1989-90 only the East Midlands and the South West had lower levels.
  (Table 11.4)

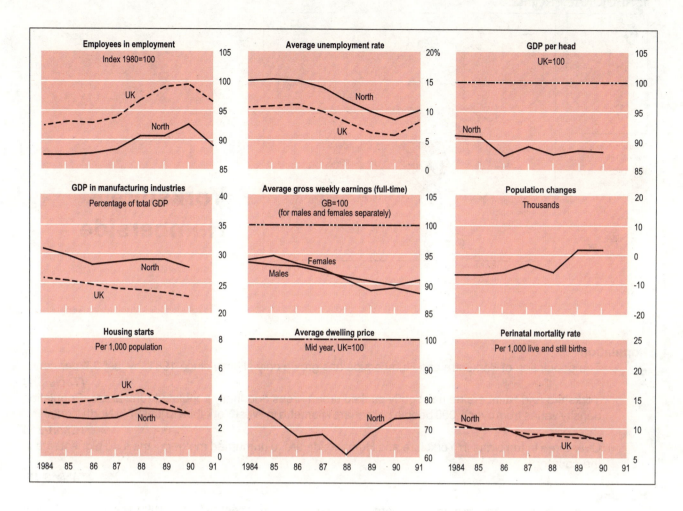

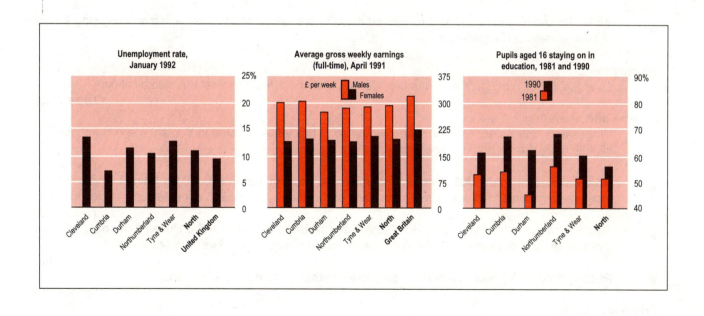

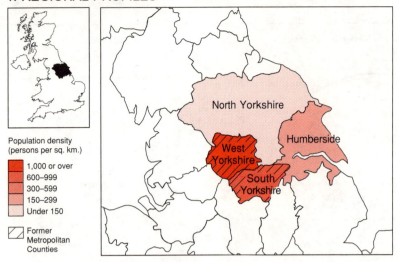

Population density
(persons per sq. km.)

- 1,000 or over
- 600–999
- 300–599
- 150–299
- Under 150

Former Metropolitan Counties

Yorkshire & Humberside

Population

- The population of Yorkshire and Humberside has grown only slightly since 1981, by just 0.7 per cent.
  (Table 3.1)

- Yorkshire and Humberside has tightly packed urban areas and thinly populated rural areas. Population density varies from over 1,000 people per square kilometre in West Yorkshire to just 87 in North Yorkshire.
  (Chart 3.2)

- Over three in ten births in Yorkshire and Humberside are to unmarried mothers - the third highest rate in the country.
  (Table 3.16)

Housing

- House prices in Yorkshire and Humberside increased by 4 per cent between 1990 and 1991 - this was higher than in some other places, with five regions actually having a fall in prices.
  (Table 4.8)

Health

- Yorkshire and Humberside has the heaviest drinkers in England and Wales - with men averaging 9 pints of beer a week and women 2.5.
  (Table 6.10)

Employment

- Over the 1980s, Yorkshire and Humberside was one of the regions most affected by strikes.
  (Table 7.12)

Income and spending

- Wages and salaries account for nearly two-thirds of household income in Yorkshire and Humberside - slightly more than in any other region.
  (Table 8.1)

- Male wage earners in Yorkshire and Humberside earn more money from bonuses, commission and other incentive payments than workers in other parts of the country - over £16 per week on average in 1991.
  (Table 8.3)

- Men's earnings in Yorkshire and Humberside are among the lowest in the United Kingdom. With an average of £287 per week in 1991, only Wales and Northern Ireland fared worse.
  (Table 8.3)

- People in Yorkshire and Humberside eat more fish than people in other regions.
  (Table 8.10)

Crime and justice

- Yorkshire and Humberside had the third highest crime rate in England and Wales in 1990 - with one offence recorded for every ten people.
  (Table 9.1)

- Yorkshire and Humberside has the joint highest crime rate for sexual offences.
  (Table 9.1)

Regional Trends 27, © Crown copyright 1992

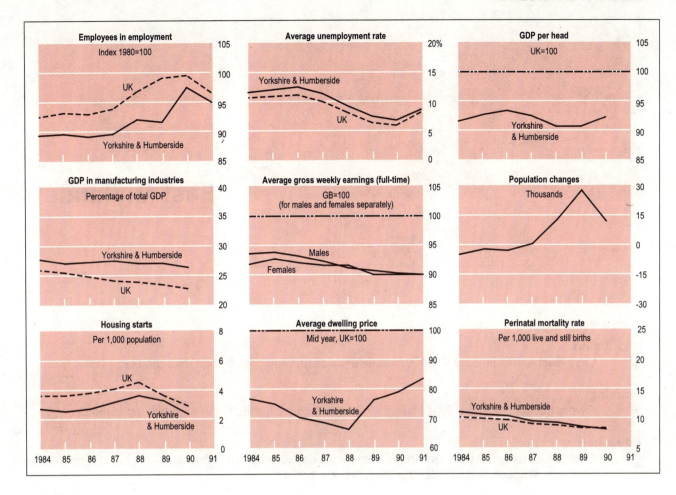

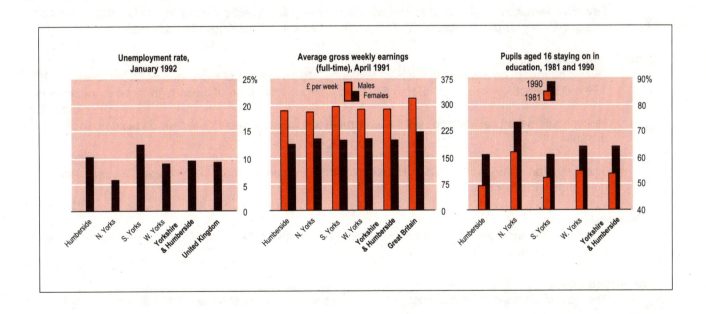

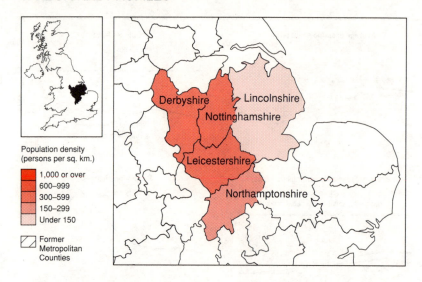

Population density
(persons per sq. km.)

- 1,000 or over
- 600–999
- 300–599
- 150–299
- Under 150

Former
Metropolitan
Counties

East Midlands

Population
- Only East Anglia and the South West have faster growing populations than the East Midlands.

(Table 3.1)

Housing
- Owner occupancy in the East Midlands, at 71 per cent in 1990, is the third highest in the country.

(Table 4.2)

Education
- Over two-thirds of 16 year-olds in the East Midlands continue their education - the highest proportion in England, although both Scotland and Wales fare better.

(Table 5.4)

- *It doesn't add up* - boys in the East Midlands have the poorest performance in GCSE maths - with only a third of leavers achieving a grade A-C in 1989/90.

(Table 5.8)

- Few East Midlands pupils leave school without a recognised qualification - just one in thirteen boys and one in twenty girls did in 1989/90. Only the South West and East Anglia fared better.

(Table 5.7)

Income and spending
- Over a quarter of households in the East Midlands had an income of more than £425 per week in 1989-1990. Only East Anglia and the South East had a larger proportion of these high-income households.

(Table 8.2)

- Households in the East Midlands eat the least meat and meat products - just over 2lb per person per week in 1989-1990.

(Table 8.10)

- *The heat is on in the East Midlands.* Households in the region are more likely to own central heating than households in other regions.

(Table 8.12)

Crime and justice
- The East Midlands has the most serious violent crime rate in the country and the joint highest rate for sexual offences.

(Table 9.1)

The environment
- The East Midlands has the cleanest air in the country - with the least smoke in the atmosphere (joint with the South West).

(Table 11.4)

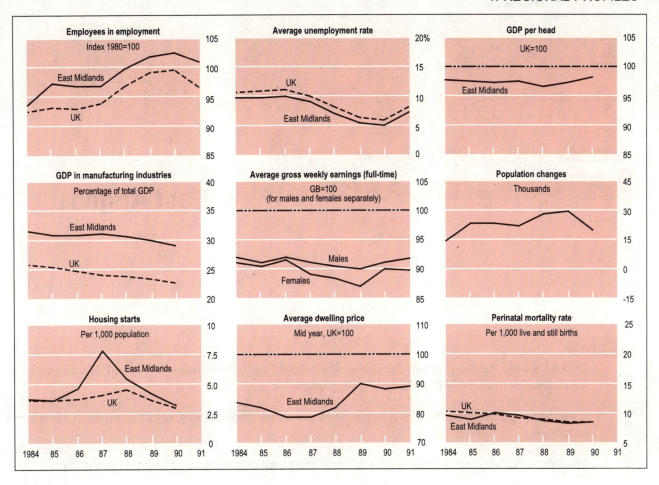

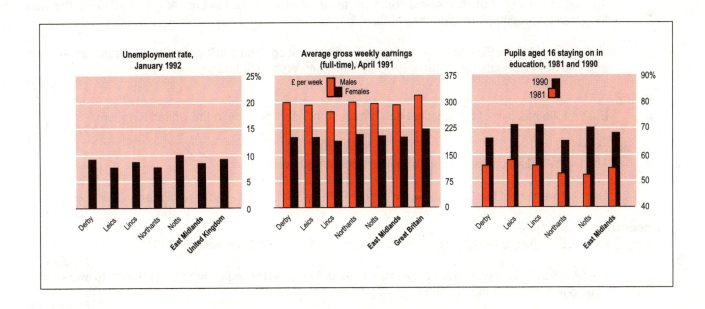

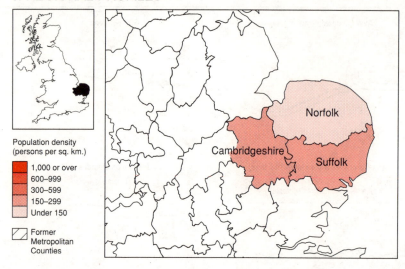

Population density
(persons per sq. km.)

- 1,000 or over
- 600–999
- 300–599
- 150–299
- Under 150

Former
Metropolitan
Counties

East Anglia

Population

● East Anglia has the fastest growing population - up by 8.7 per cent between 1981 and 1990. Despite this, it remains the most thinly populated English region.

(Table 3.1 and Chart 3.2)

● Less than a quarter of births in East Anglia are to unmarried mothers - only Northern Ireland has a lower proportion.

(Table 3.16)

● The infant mortality rate in East Anglia is the second best in the country behind the South West.

(Table 6.2)

Education

● East Anglia provides day care for over a quarter of its toddlers - the second best provision in the country.

(Table 5.2)

● Although 62 per cent of 16 year-old pupils continued their education in East Anglia in 1990/91, this was the smallest proportion outside the North.

(Table 5.4)

● Very few pupils from East Anglia leave school without a recognised qualification - only one in thirteen boys and one in twenty girls did in 1989/90. Only the South West fared better.

(Table 5.7)

Health

● East Anglia has one of the smallest death rates from heart disease in the United Kingdom.

(Table 6.4)

Employment

● The East Anglian unemployment rate is the country's lowest.

(Table 7.16)

● Over 13 per cent of the East Anglian workforce are self-employed - the third highest rate in the country.

(Chart 7.1)

Income and spending

● Men in East Anglia work the longest hours - an average of 42.5 per week in 1991.

(Table 8.3)

● East Anglian bulls appear to keep out of the market. People in the region are the least likely to own shares - just one adult in six did in 1990.

(Chart 8.13)

Crime and justice

● East Anglia has the lowest crime rate in England and Wales, less than 7 offences per 100 population in 1990, and one of the highest clear up rates - almost four out of every ten recorded offences.

(Tables 9.1 and 9.2)

● East Anglia is the region you are least likely to bump into a bobby. In 1990, there were 531 people for every police officer - the highest figure in the country.

(Table 9.14)

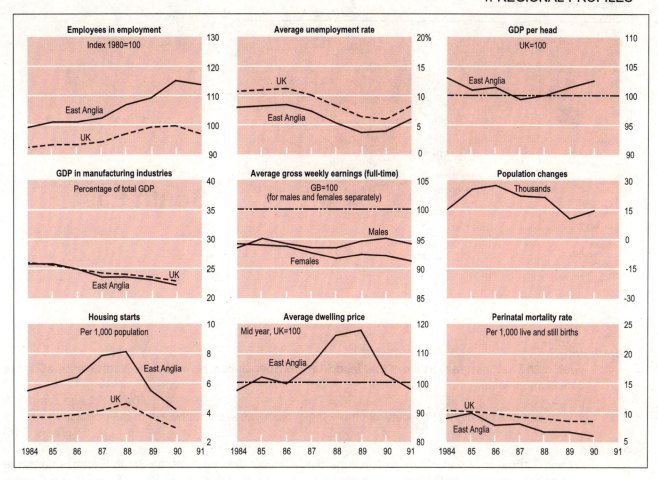

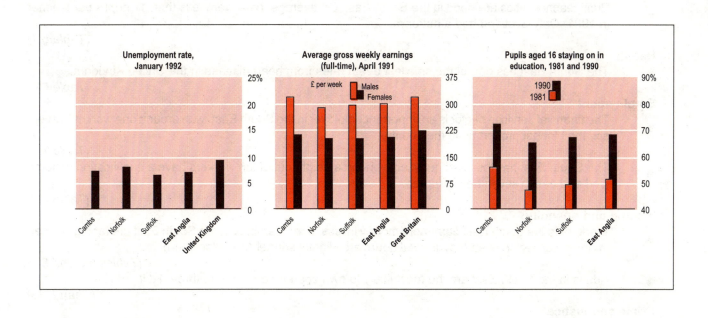

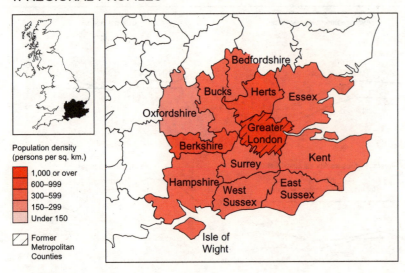

Population density
(persons per sq. km.)

- 1,000 or over
- 600–999
- 300–599
- 150–299
- Under 150

Former
Metropolitan
Counties

South East

Population

- The South East has nearly a third of the United Kingdom population. However, the North West is still more densely populated.

(Table 3.1 and Chart 3.2)

- The region has the highest concentration of ethnic minorities - one in twelve of the population.

(Table 3.15)

Housing

- Owner occupation is particularly high in suburbia. Although the whole of the South East has an owner occupation rate close to the national average, the rate for that part of the South East outside Greater London is, at three quarters, the highest in the country.

(Table 4.2)

Education

- Pupil teacher ratios are good in the South East. On average there were less than 17 pupils per teacher in 1991. Only Scotland had a better rate.

(Table 5.1)

Health

- The South East has one of the smallest death rates from heart disease in the United Kingdom.

(Table 6.4)

Employment

- The financial services sector is an important employer in the South East, with around one worker in every six, the highest proportion in the country.

(Table 7.7)

- The South East has the most qualified workforce - eight out of ten workers have a qualification of some kind and one in seven has a degree.

(Table 7.8)

Income and spending

- Workers in the South East earn more money in less time. Earnings in the South East are far higher than in any other region even though total hours are slightly shorter than elsewhere.

(Tables 8.3 and 8.4)

- Adults in the South East are the most likely to own shares - over one in three did in 1991.

(Chart 8.13)

Crime and justice

- Police in the South East are the least successful at clearing up crime - only one in five recorded offences were cleared up in 1990, substantially lower than elsewhere.

(Table 9.2)

- Crime rates for drug offences are far higher in the South East than in any other region.

(Table 9.8)

Transport

- Two-car families are much more common in the South East. Almost a third of households in the South East outside Greater London have 2 or more cars.

(Table 10.1)

Regional Trends 27, © Crown copyright 1992

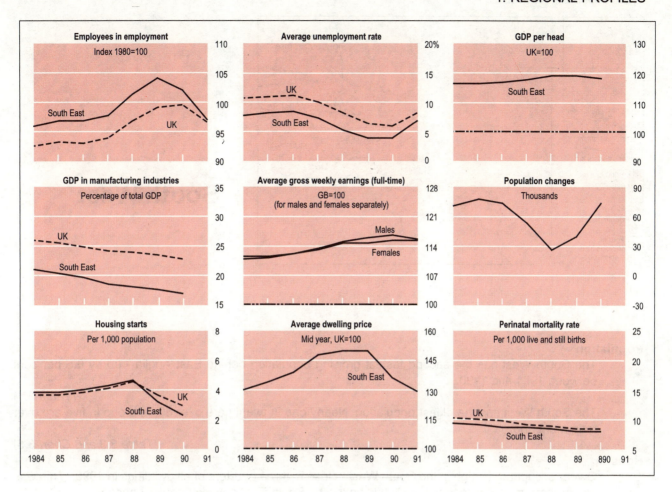

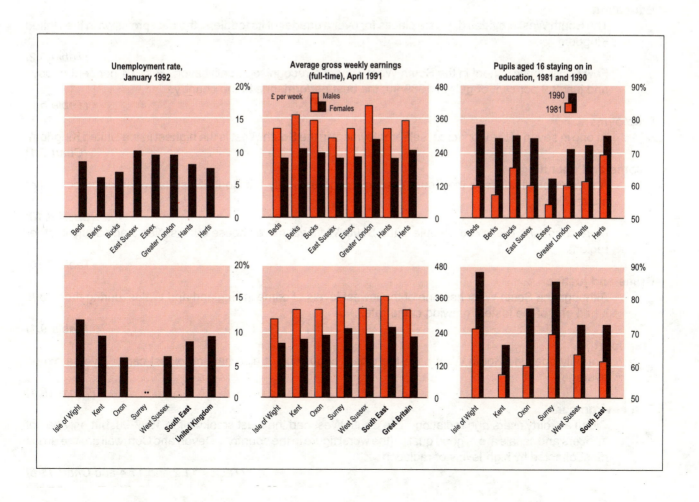

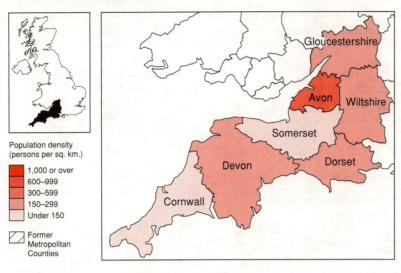

Population density
(persons per sq. km.)

■	1,000 or over
■	600–999
■	300–599
■	150–299
■	Under 150

▨ Former
Metropolitan
Counties

South West

Population

- The South West has the second fastest growing population behind East Anglia - up by 6.5 per cent between 1981 and 1990.

(Table 3.1)

- The South West has the oldest population. Nearly one in twenty are over 80, and one in five are over retirement age.

(Table 3.3 and Chart 3.5)

Housing

- Owner occupancy is high in the South West - close to three quarters of all dwellings in 1990. This was higher than any other region, but slightly below the South East outside Greater London.

(Table 4.2)

Education

- The South West provides day care places for over a quarter of its toddlers, the best provision in the United Kingdom.

(Table 5.2)

- Few pupils leave school in the South West without a recognised qualification - just 5.4 per cent of boys and just 3.9 per cent of girls in 1989/90, the best performance in the country.

(Table 5.7)

Employment

- At one in seven of the workforce, self-employment in the South West is the highest in the United Kingdom.

(Chart 7.1)

Income and spending

- A quarter of all adults in the South West own shares - only the South East has a larger proportion of shareholders.

(Chart 8.13)

- *More cheddar but less cod.* People in the South West eat more cheese but less fish than people in other regions.

(Table 8.10)

Crime and justice

- Although the South West has one of the lowest levels of crime in England and Wales, during the 1980s it had one of the fastest growing crime rates.

(Table 9.1)

Transport

- Not only does the South West have the oldest population, it also has the oldest cars - 7 years old on average.

(Table 10.1)

The environment

- Clean air, dirty rivers and radiation. The South West had the least smoky air in 1989-90, but only half of all rivers and canals are of good quality (the worst figure in the country). Devon and Cornwall are the areas most affected by high levels of radiation.

(Tables 11.2 and 11.4 and Chart 11.6)

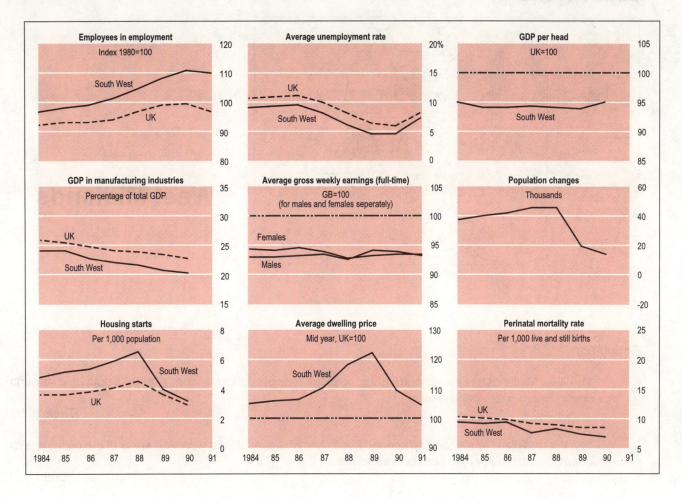

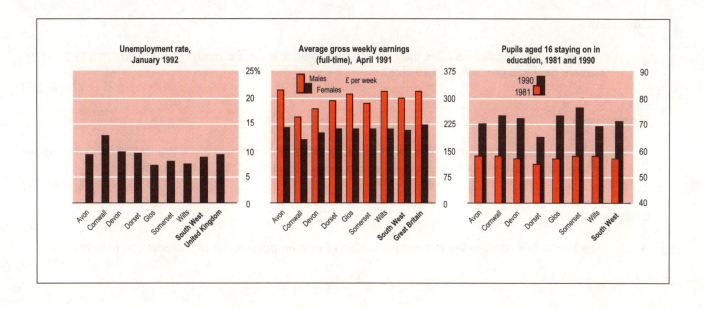

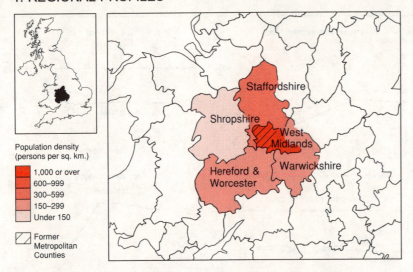

Population density
(persons per sq. km.)

1,000 or over
600–999
300–599
150–299
Under 150

Former
Metropolitan
Counties

West Midlands

Population

- The West Midlands has the second highest concentration of ethnic minorities after the South East - around one in fifteen of the population.

(Table 3.15)

- The West Midlands metropolitan county area is one of the most tightly packed areas of the country, with nearly 3 thousand people per square kilometre.

(Chart 3.2)

- More babies die in the West Midlands than in any other region - one infant under one year old dies for every 100 born.

(Table 6.2)

Education

- Girls in the West Midlands have the poorest performance in GCSE maths - with fewer than three in ten leavers getting a grade A-C in 1989/90.

(Table 5.8)

Employment

- Despite recent decline, manufacturing remains an important employer in the West Midlands, with two out of five male and one out of five female employees - double the rates in the South East.

(Table 7.7)

Crime and justice

- The West Midlands has the highest proportion of women police officers - almost one in seven.

(Table 9.14)

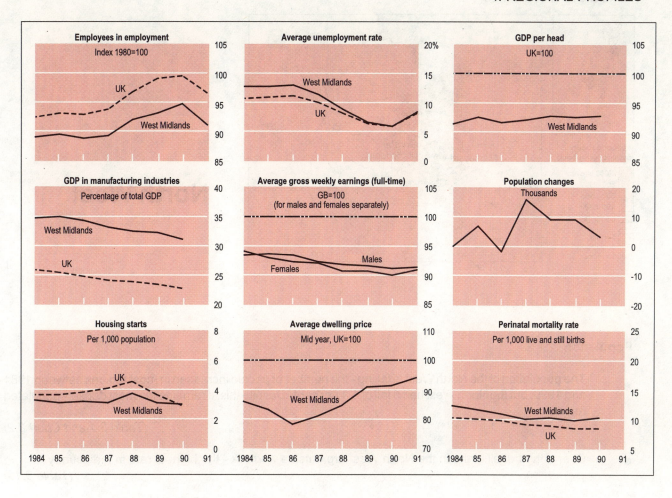

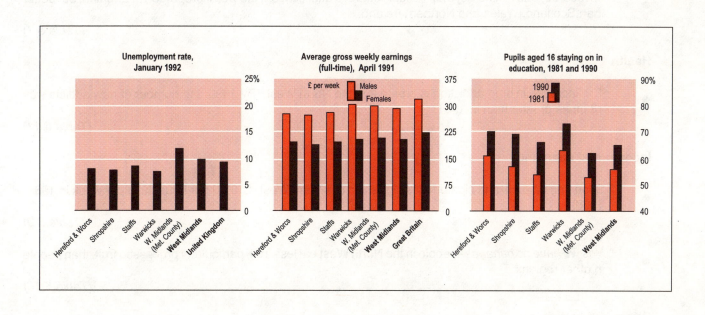

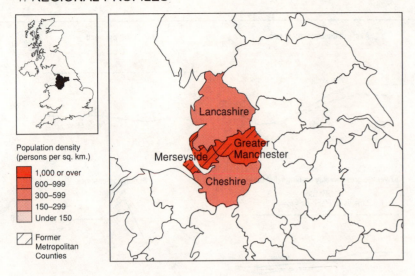

Population density
(persons per sq. km.)

- 1,000 or over
- 600–999
- 300–599
- 150–299
- Under 150

Former Metropolitan Counties

North West

Population

- The population of the North West is falling - the number of people increased in most regions between 1981 and 1990, but the North West had a fall of 1.1 per cent. Despite this, it remains the most densely populated region.

  (Table 3.1 and Chart 3.2)

- Over a third of all births in the North West are outside wedlock - the highest rate in the country.

  (Table 3.16)

Education

- In 1989/90, one in nine boys left school without a qualification, the worst proportion in England, but better than Scotland, Wales and Northern Ireland.

  (Table 5.7)

Health

- The increase in drug addiction is greatest in the North West. By 1990, the number of new addicts was 13 times greater than in 1981.

  (Table 6.11)

Income and spending

- Spending on drink and cigarettes is highest in the North West (£16.80 per household per week in 1989-1990)

  (Table 8.9)

- *Yes we have no bananas* - people in the North West eat less fruit, particularly processed fruit, than people in other regions.

  (Table 8.10)

Crime and justice

- Crime remains a problem in the North West, which had the second worst crime rate in England and Wales in 1990, and one of the worst clear-up rates.

  (Table 9.1 and 9.2)

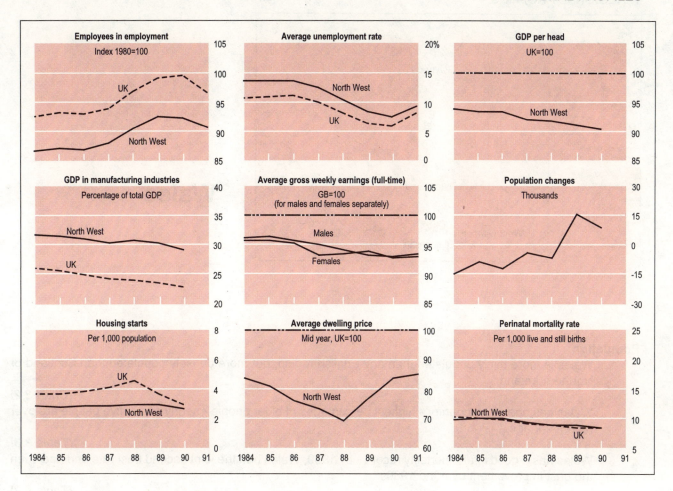

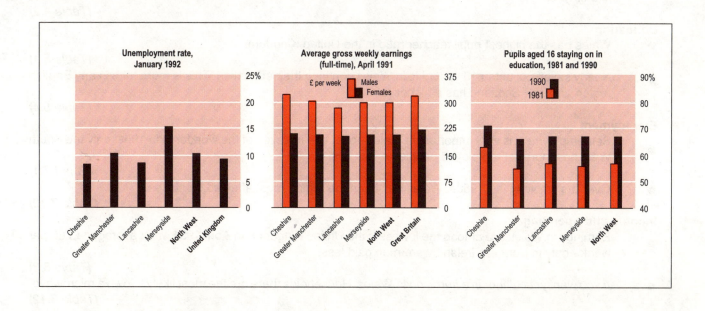

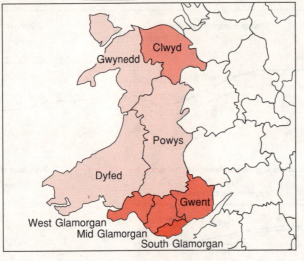

Population density
(persons per sq. km.)

■ 1,000 or over
■ 600–999
■ 300–599
■ 150–299
□ Under 150

▨ Former
Metropolitan
Counties

Wales

Population

● Wales is more thinly populated than any English region, but more densely populated than Scotland or Northern Ireland.

(Chart 3.2)

● Wales has one of the country's highest percentages of older people - nearly one in five people are over retirement age.

(Table 3.3)

● Wales has a good infant mortality record - by 1990, Wales had the joint second best rate and had seen the best improvement over the 1980s.

(Table 6.2)

Housing

● Owner occupancy is high in Wales, at over seven out of ten homes in 1990 - only the South West has a higher rate.

(Table 4.2)

Education

● Wales has the highest pupil/teacher ratio in the United Kingdom.

(Table 5.1)

● Nearly seven out of ten 16 year olds in Wales continue their education. This is more than in any English region and only Scotland has a higher rate.

(Table 5.4)

Employment

● Self-employment is very important in Wales - over one in seven of the workforce in 1991; only the South West has more self-employed people.

(Chart 7.1)

● Over the whole of the 1980s, Wales has been the region most affected by strikes.

(Table 7.12)

Income and spending

● Earnings in Wales are among the lowest in the United Kingdom. In April 1991, men averaged £280 per week - only in Northern Ireland were men paid less.

(Table 8.3)

● *If you want your dinner in a hurry, go to Wales.* Households there are the most likely to own a microwave.

(Table 8.12)

Crime and justice

● The Welsh police are the most successful at clearing up crime - two in every five reported crimes were cleared up in 1990.

(Table 9.2)

 Regional Trends 27, © Crown copyright 1992

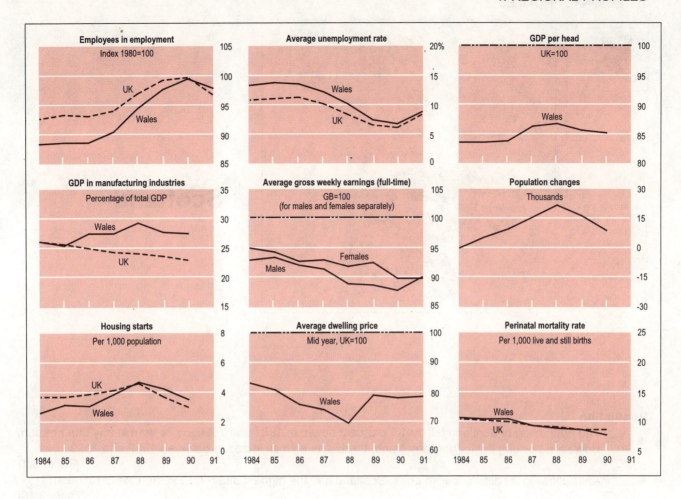

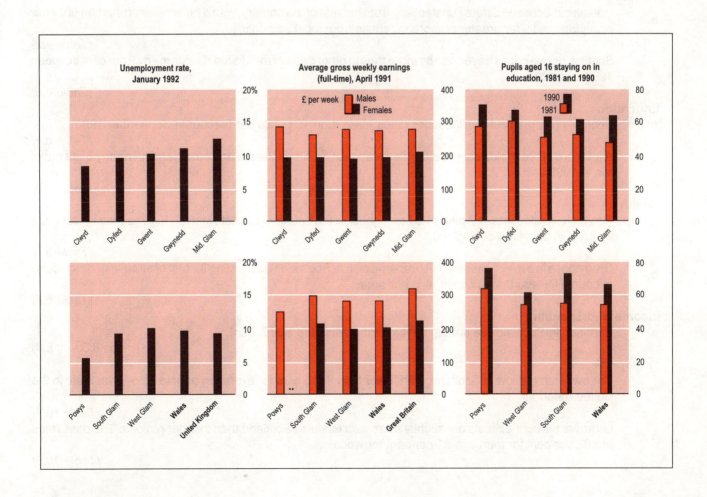

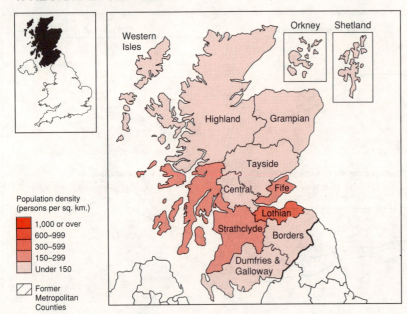

Population density
(persons per sq. km.)

1,000 or over
600–999
300–599
150–299
Under 150

Former
Metropolitan
Counties

Scotland

Population

● The population of Scotland fell by 1.5 per cent between 1981 and 1990, more than in any other region. However, bucking the longer-term trend, there was a small increase between 1989 and 1990.

(Table 3.1)

● After allowing for differences in ages, Scotland has the highest death rate in the United Kingdom.

(Table 3.18)

Housing

● Housing in Scotland differs substantially from the rest of the country, with a far smaller proportion of owner occupiers and a far greater proportion renting from local authorities.

(Table 4.2)

● Scottish house prices have risen by more than in other parts of the United Kingdom - by 9 per cent between 1990 and 1991.

(Table 4.8)

Education

● Scotland has the best pupil/teacher ratios - less than 16 pupils per teacher in September 1990.

(Table 5.1)

● A lot more 16 year-olds continue their education in Scotland than in any other region - nearly eight out of ten in 1990/91.

(Table 5.4)

Health

● The male suicide rate in Scotland is the highest in the country - almost twice as high as the smallest rate which is in the North of England.

(Table 6.4)

● Drug abuse is a major cause of HIV transmission in Scotland - accounting for half of all cases. Drug abuse accounts for less than a fifth in all other areas.

(Table 6.7)

Income and spending

● Earnings in Scotland are among the highest outside the South East.

(Tables 8.3 and 8.4)

Transport

● Car ownership is low in Scotland, with fewer than three cars for every ten people - the lowest rate in the United Kingdom.

(Table 10.1)

● Learners taking their tests are slightly more successful in Scotland than in other regions. The pass rates are 62 per cent for men and 51 per cent for women.

(Table 10.3)

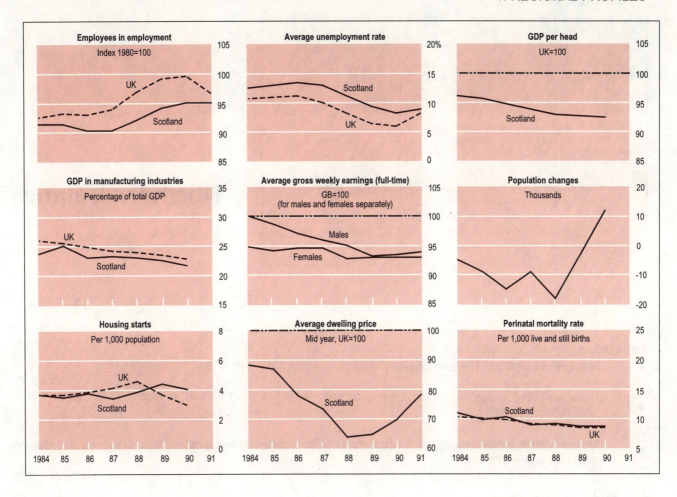

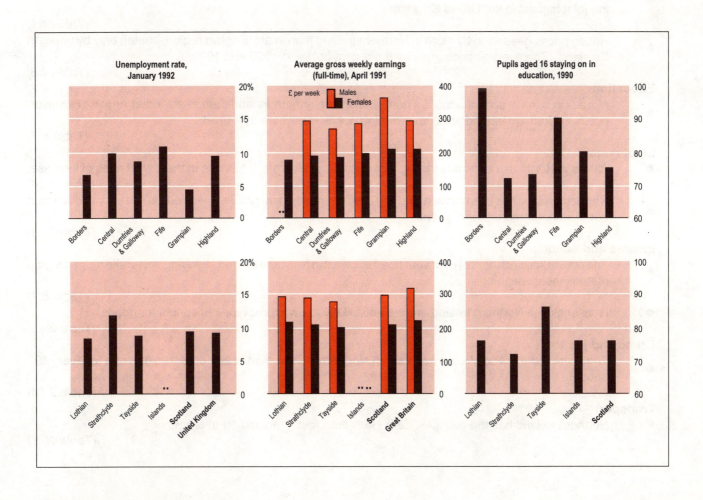

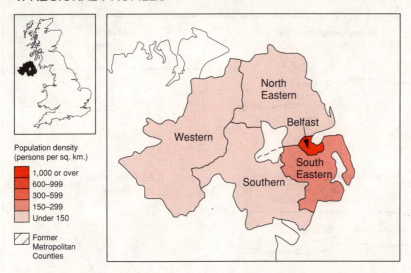

Population density
(persons per sq. km.)

1,000 or over
600–999
300–599
150–299
Under 150

Former
Metropolitan
Counties

Northern Ireland

Population
● Northern Ireland has the youngest population. In 1990, over one in four were under 16.

(Table 3.3)

● Because of the young population, birth rates are high in Northern Ireland, at nearly 17 births per 1,000 population in 1990.

(Table 3.13)

● Northern Ireland has a much lower proportion of births to unmarried mothers than other regions - fewer than one in five in 1990.

(Table 3.16)

Housing
● The stock of homes is growing quickly in Northern Ireland - up by 14 per cent between 1981 and 1990, the joint highest in the United Kingdom.

(Table 4.1)

● House prices have risen by more in Northern Ireland than in any English region, beaten only by prices in Scotland. The average price grew by 8 per cent between 1990 and 1991.

(Table 4.8)

Education
● More pupils leave school without a qualification in Northern Ireland than in any other region. However, pupils in Northern Ireland are outperforming pupils elsewhere at A level.

(Table 5.7)

Employment
● Although Northern Ireland has the highest unemployment rate, it has one of the lowest rates of increase.

(Chart 7.14)

● Northern Ireland has the most serious long term unemployment problem, with one in five unemployed men out of work for more than 5 years.

(Table 7.13)

Income and spending
● The cost of keeping the roof over your head is lowest in Northern Ireland - housing costs take only an eighth of household spending.

(Table 8.9)

● Households in Northern Ireland are the least likely to own most types of consumer goods.

(Table 8.12)

Crime and justice
● There are more police officers per head in Northern Ireland than in any other region - one for every 192 people.

(Table 9.14)

Transport
● Northern Ireland has the youngest cars - less than four years old on average.

(Table 10.1)

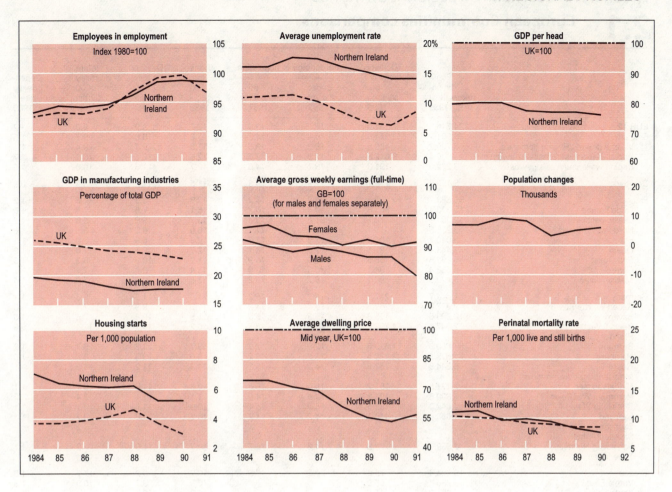

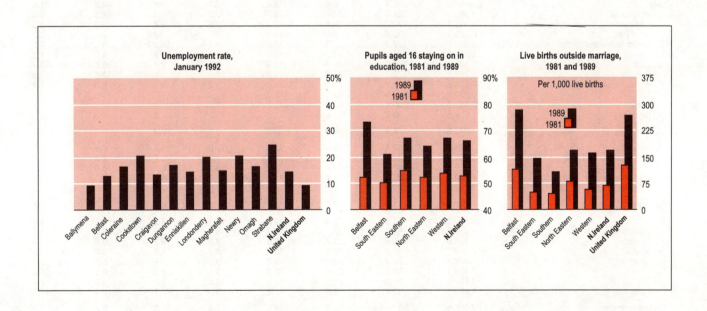

2.1 European Communities comparisons

	Popu-lation[1] (thousands) 1988	Density (persons per sq. km.) 1988	Percentage of population		Births (per 1,000 pop.) 1988	Deaths (per 1,000 pop.) 1988	Infant mortality (per 1,000 births) 1987	Depen-dency rate[1,2] 1989
			Under 15 yrs 1987	65 and over 1987				
EUR 12	324,646.5	144.0	19.0	13.9	12.0	9.9	9.0	1.2
Belgium	9,901.7	324.5	18.4	14.2	12.0	10.6	9.7	1.5
Vlaams gewest/Region flamande	5,709.2	422.5	18.3	13.5	11.5	9.7	9.4	1.5
Region bruxelloise/Brussels gewest	970.4	6,012.5	17.3	17.5	12.9	12.1	10.2	1.7
Region wallonne/Waals gewest	3,222.0	191.3	18.7	14.5	12.7	11.6	10.0	1.6
Denmark	5,129.5	119.1	17.9	15.3	11.5	11.5	8.3	0.8
France	55,883.7	102.7	20.8	13.3	13.8	9.3	7.8	1.2
Ile de France	10,370.4	863.3	20.4	10.7	16.1	7.6	7.8	1.0
Bassin-parisien	10,204.1	70.1	21.8	13.4	13.7	9.6	8.0	1.3
Nord-Pas-de-Calais	3,936.5	317.1	24.4	11.1	16.0	9.5	8.5	1.6
Est	5,040.2	104.9	21.5	11.7	13.9	8.9	8.0	1.3
Ouest	7,443.4	87.5	21.6	14.1	12.7	9.5	7.6	1.2
Sud-Ouest	5,852.6	56.5	18.0	16.9	11.2	10.9	8.3	1.3
Centre-Est	6,556.4	94.1	20.8	13.0	13.4	9.1	7.1	1.2
Mediterranee	6,479.9	96.1	18.7	16.2	12.6	10.6	7.0	1.4
Germany	61,444.7	247.1	14.7	15.2	11.0	11.2	8.3	1.1
Baden-Wurttemberg	9,377.8	262.3	15.4	14.2	11.8	9.9	7.1	1.0
Bayern	10,989.6	155.8	15.3	15.0	11.5	10.8	7.6	1.0
Berlin (West)	2,047.1	4,263.6	13.6	18.5	10.2	14.7	11.4	0.9
Brandenburg	..	..	..	..	..	..	..	..
Bremen	660.3	1,633.6	12.8	17.7	9.7	13.2	9.7	1.2
Hamburg	1,579.3	2,116.5	11.8	18.2	9.6	13.3	8.3	1.0
Hessen	5,544.6	262.6	14.3	15.3	10.4	11.2	6.8	1.1
Mecklenburg-Vorpommern	..	..	..	..	..	..	..	..
Niedersachsen	7,171.5	151.2	15.0	15.6	10.6	11.6	8.1	1.1
Nordrhein-Westfalen	16,800.8	493.2	14.6	14.8	11.1	11.1	9.4	1.2
Rheinland-Pfalz	3,642.3	183.5	15.0	15.4	10.9	11.5	9.1	1.1
Saarland	1,053.6	410.1	14.2	14.7	10.2	11.8	10.7	1.3
Sachsen	..	..	..	..	..	..	..	..
Sachsen-Anhalt	..	..	..	..	..	..	..	..
Schleswig-Holstein	2,559.7	162.8	14.2	15.7	10.7	11.9	7.2	1.1
Thueringen	..	..	..	..	..	..	..	..
Greece	10,004.4	75.8	20.3	13.5	10.7	9.2	11.7	1.5
Voreia Ellada	3,230.7	56.9	..	..	10.9	9.1	10.8	1.3
Kentriki Ellada	2,294.3	42.6	..	..	10.3	10.4	..	1.3
Attiki	3,530.1	927.0	..	..	10.5	8.3	..	1.6
Nisia	949.4	54.4	..	..	12.0	10.4	..	1.5
Ireland	3,538.0	51.4	28.7	10.9	15.3	8.9	7.9	1.6
Italy	57,451.9	190.7	18.4	13.4	10.1	9.4	9.6	1.4
Nord-Ovest	6,230.0	182.8	14.4	16.7	7.3	11.7	8.3	1.3
Lombardia	8,892.7	372.7	16.6	12.9	8.6	9.4	7.9	1.3
Nord Est	6,469.1	162.4	16.8	13.8	8.8	9.8	7.1	1.3
Emilia-Romagna	3,922.7	177.3	13.9	16.9	6.7	11.0	9.2	1.2
Centro	5,814.6	141.3	15.2	16.6	7.8	10.7	8.9	1.3
Lazio	5,146.7	299.2	18.1	12.0	9.8	8.4	10.6	1.4
Campania	5,752.2	423.1	24.2	9.8	14.7	7.8	11.4	1.6
Abruzzi-Molise	1,595.3	104.7	18.5	14.6	10.2	9.5	8.8	1.4
Sud	6,822.3	153.6	22.9	11.2	13.3	7.7	10.5	1.7
Sicilia	5,152.8	200.4	22.2	11.9	13.4	8.6	11.5	1.8
Sardegna	1,653.5	68.6	21.7	11.0	10.2	7.6	6.9	1.6
Luxembourg	373.3	144.3	16.9	13.3	12.3	10.3	9.4	1.4
Netherlands[3]	14,758.6	352.5	18.8	12.3	12.6	8.4	6.5	1.2
Noord-Nederland	1,593.0	144.9	19.5	13.4	11.9	9.2	6.2	1.4
Oost-Nederland	2,999.8	280.9	20.2	11.7	13.2	8.1	6.6	1.3
West-Nederland	6,903.9	602.6	18.1	13.2	12.8	8.8	6.1	1.1
Zuid-Nederland	3,262.0	447.4	18.7	10.5	12.2	7.5	7.5	1.2
Portugal	10,286.2	111.8	22.7	12.4	11.9	9.5	14.2	1.1
Spain	38,809.0	76.9	22.3	12.3	10.7	8.2	9.1	1.6
Noroeste	4,472.8	98.7	20.3	14.4	8.4	9.3	10.7	1.5
Noreste	4,125.6	58.6	20.2	12.6	8.8	8.2	9.9	1.6
Madrid	4,842.3	605.7	23.1	10.6	10.8	6.8	8.6	1.8
Centro	5,468.8	25.4	20.3	14.9	9.9	8.8	8.1	1.7
Este	10,444.1	173.3	21.8	12.4	10.4	8.5	8.3	1.5
Sur	7,989.5	81.0	25.5	10.6	13.5	7.9	9.8	1.8
Canarias	1,465.7	202.4	25.9	8.8	13.2	7.1	8.1	1.6
United Kingdom	57,065.6	233.8	18.9	15.5	13.8	11.3	9.3	1.0
North	3,071.0	199.4	18.9	15.3	13.1	12.3	8.7	1.0
Yorkshire & Humberside	4,912.8	318.6	18.9	15.6	13.7	11.7	9.9	1.0
East Midlands	3,970.3	254.0	18.9	15.0	13.4	11.0	9.3	0.9
East Anglia	2,034.5	161.8	18.9	16.4	13.1	10.9	7.8	0.9
South East	17,344.0	637.1	18.3	15.5	14.2	10.6	9.0	0.9
South West	4,633.9	194.3	17.6	18.1	12.6	11.9	8.5	0.9
West Midlands	5,206.5	400.1	19.3	14.5	14.0	11.0	9.5	1.0
North West	6,363.5	868.0	19.3	15.4	14.2	12.2	9.1	1.0
Wales	2,857.0	137.6	18.9	16.4	13.6	11.9	9.5	1.1
Scotland	5,094.0	64.7	18.9	14.7	13.0	12.2	..	1.0
Northern Ireland	1,578.1	111.8	25.2	12.1	17.6	10.1	..	1.3

1 Definitions of position, employment and unemployment differ from those used in UK tables.
2 Labour force sample survey, 1989.

3 Including 'centraal persoons register'.

(continued)

2.1 *(Continued)*

	Transport accidents (deaths per 100,000 pop.) 1988		Employment[1,2]			Unemployment rate[1] % 1989	Gross domestic product EUR 12 =100 1988[4]	Investment grants committed thousand ECU[5]	
	Total	Road traffic	Agriculture % 1989	Industry % 1989	Services % 1989			EAGGF[6,7] 1988	ERDF[7,8] 1987
EUR 12	..	..	7.1	33.2	59.8	9.0	100	340,298	3,662,376
Belgium	44.0	19.9	3.3	31.4	65.2	8.1	101	11,891	23,513
Vlaams gewest/Region flamande	36.9	19.5	3.4	35.5	61.1	6.1	101	7,951	13,180
Region bruxelloise/Brussels gewest	57.3	12.8	0.1	21.2	78.7	10.4	155	1,166	-
Region wallonne/Waals gewest	52.4	22.7	4.2	26.2	69.6	11.1	84	2,660	10,333
Denmark	15.6	14.5	5.7	27.4	66.9	7.7	109	5,107	17,148
France	18.4	17.8	6.9	30.3	62.8	9.3	108	51,374	316,944
Ile de France	13.1	12.3	0.3	26.6	73.0	7.7	164	617	-
Bassin-parisien	20.7	20.1	9.0	33.6	57.4	9.6	99	3,578	11,019
Nord-Pas-de-Calais	12.2	12.0	4.1	36.1	59.7	12.6	87	537	33,244
Est	17.9	17.2	4.6	38.7	56.7	7.5	99	504	35,189
Ouest	19.9	19.5	12.8	29.1	58.1	9.3	90	2,259	31,290
Sud-Ouest	22.2	21.6	14.2	25.0	60.8	10.0	93	10,741	78,754
Centre-Est	19.1	18.5	6.3	34.8	58.9	8.2	104	4,016	37,596
Mediterranee	21.6	20.6	7.4	22.3	70.4	12.0	94	22,901	44,992
Germany	32.2	12.9	3.9	40.2	56.0	5.5	113	17,027	133,931
Baden-Wurttemberg	30.9	12.8	3.4	46.7	49.9	3.1	119	1,847	479
Bayern	40.6	17.1	7.0	40.5	52.5	3.6	113	4,034	19,579
Berlin (West)	25.1	8.4	0.7	29.4	69.9	6.9	124	..	22,105
Brandenburg	..	..	..	..	..	..	..	..	..
Bremen	36.0	9.7	0.4	32.7	67.0	10.6	146	193	3,876
Hamburg	42.4	8.7	0.3	25.5	74.1	8.5	182	-	-
Hessen	38.2	13.1	2.9	35.9	61.2	4.3	128	2,029	5,814
Mecklenburg-Vorpommern	..	..	..	..	..	..	..	..	..
Niedersachsen	24.8	15.6	6.1	37.5	56.4	7.0	97	5,597	29,885
Nordrhein-Westfalen	28.3	10.1	1.9	43.2	55.0	7.4	109	1,568	19,068
Rheinland-Pfalz	27.6	12.4	4.7	42.5	52.8	4.7	101	1,759	19,189
Saarland	27.7	10.2	1.1	40.4	58.4	8.1	104	-	8,677
Sachsen	..	..	..	..	..	..	..	..	..
Sachsen-Anhalt	..	..	..	..	..	..	..	..	..
Schleswig-Holstein	40.9	13.8	4.2	29.1	66.7	6.4	94	..	5,261
Thueringen	..	..	..	..	..	..	..	..	..
Greece	43.4	20.6	25.3	25.7	48.9	7.5	54	35,845	307,262
Voreia Ellada	..	..	34.2	26.4	39.4	7.2	52	14,346	122,949
Kentriki Ellada	..	..	44.7	20.3	35.0	6.2	54	19,068	81,846
Attiki	..	..	1.5	31.0	67.5	9.4	58		-
Nisia	..	..	34.4	17.6	48.0	3.9	48	2,432	57,075
Ireland	29.9	13.0	15.5	28.8	55.8	17.1	65	20,934	163,451
Italy	38.7	15.1	9.2	32.0	58.8	11.1	104	86,784	992,174
Nord-Ovest	52.0	16.5	7.6	36.8	55.6	7.4	119	6,355	7,159
Lombardia	39.3	20.8	3.5	43.1	53.4	3.9	138	7,650	7,045
Nord Est	50.0	19.6	7.7	37.5	54.7	5.0	117	4,527	5,036
Emilia-Romagna	47.0	23.1	10.3	37.0	52.7	5.2	128	10,218	-
Centro	51.3	17.0	7.5	34.9	57.6	8.1	111	24,708	26,426
Lazio	38.5	15.2	5.4	18.1	76.5	11.1	118	9,609	33,237
Campania	23.1	8.6	12.3	24.8	62.9	22.7	67	7,951	504,391
Abruzzi-Molise	40.4	13.5	15.5	27.9	56.7	11.1	87	4,287	38,029
Sud	29.4	17.5	18.4	22.0	59.6	19.1	68	6,264	146,361
Sicilia	27.7	9.3	14.9	20.4	64.7	22.0	70	3,619	159,322
Sardegna	38.8	15.2	13.3	22.9	63.8	19.3	75	1,596	21,505
Luxembourg	51.2	24.1	3.8	29.2	67.0	1.7	121	67	3,286
Netherlands[3]	23.5	8.9	4.8	26.7	68.5	8.5	103	5,186	20,445
Noord-Nederland	27.7	12.4	7.1	29.3	63.5	10.0	122	-	12,032
Oost-Nederland	24.5	10.1	6.1	29.5	64.4	9.0	85	2,769	-
West-Nederland	23.1	7.1	3.9	21.6	74.5	8.0	110	1,222	-
Zuid-Nederland	21.2	10.0	4.5	34.5	61.0	8.0	94	1,195	8,413
Portugal	44.1	26.9	19.3	34.6	46.0	4.9	54	32,024	388,973
Spain	33.2	16.1	13.2	32.7	54.2	17.4	75	60,978	660,672
Noroeste	41.6	21.3	30.3	27.0	42.7	14.2	69	10,839	92,508
Noreste	33.2	15.9	8.8	39.4	51.7	16.0	88	7,096	5,541
Madrid	25.8	11.1	0.9	30.2	68.9	13.3	86	1,289	-
Centro	32.0	16.0	23.0	29.4	47.6	18.4	64	17,943	217,260
Este	33.4	15.2	6.8	40.2	53.1	14.4	84	12,289	-
Sur	27.3	14.4	16.4	26.2	57.4	25.8	59	10,984	307,790
Canarias	38.2	17.2	9.3	22.8	67.9	22.5	73	539	14,550
United Kingdom	24.3	9.7	2.2	32.6	65.1	7.3	107	13,080	634,523
North	23.6	9.5	2.0	37.0	61.0	11.2	93	208	89,536
Yorkshire & Humberside	23.4	10.4	1.9	36.7	61.4	8.6	96	352	43,750
East Midlands	23.1	10.0	1.8	39.2	59.0	6.2	100	689	3,551
East Anglia	24.1	11.7	4.0	30.5	65.5	4.1	105	2,241	-
South East	21.3	9.0	1.3	27.4	71.3	4.7	130	561	-
South West	22.2	9.9	3.4	30.7	65.8	5.0	102	541	40,145
West Midlands	21.3	9.1	2.5	40.5	57.1	7.4	96	1,004	94,301
North West	23.9	8.3	1.3	34.5	64.3	9.7	99	646	52,964
Wales	28.0	8.6	4.5	33.6	61.9	8.5	89	409	79,278
Scotland	36.6	11.3	3.6	32.6	63.8	10.9	100	4,122	164,844
Northern Ireland	34.5	14.2	5.7	29.3	65.0	17.3	80	2,308	56,421

4 Gross domestic product per head at market prices. Conversion into purchasing power standards.
5 European Currency Units. Country totals include grants to overseas territories and Grants not allocated regionally.
6 EAGF = European Agricultural Guidance and Guarantee Fund, 'Guidance' Section. Figures shown represent direct measures only.
7 Projects covering several regions are presented at national level.
8 ERDF = European Regional Development Fund.

Source: Statistical Office of the European Communities.

EUROPEAN COMMUNITY REGIONS

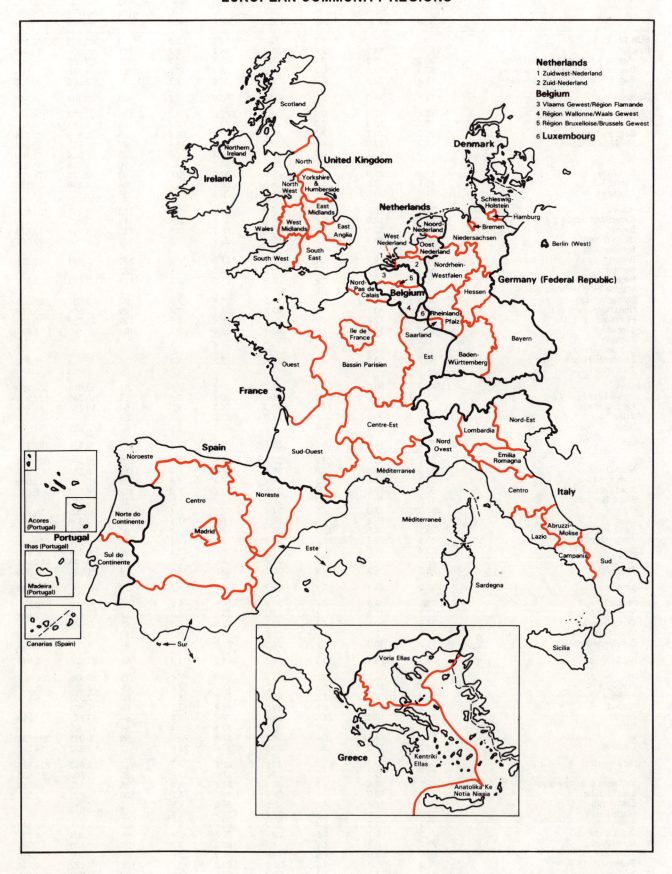

Notes to Chapter 2: European Communities regional statistics

The data appearing in this section are based on information in the statistical yearbook *Regions* produced by the Statistical Office of the European Communities. At the time of going to press, data for the new unified Germany were not available. Data presented cover the former German Federal Republic and West Berlin.

Table 2.1 European Communities comparisons

The *average total population* of a country consists of all persons, national or foreign, who are permanently settled in that country, even if temporarily absent from it.

Employment statistics are derived from the annual Community sample survey on labour forces (LFSS). As the survey is conducted on a sample basis, results relating to small regions should be treated with caution.

Economic activities are broken down in accordance with the General Classification of Economic Activities in the European Communities (NACE): Agriculture (NACE code O), Industry (NACE codes 1 to 5) and Services (NACE codes 6 to 9).

Harmonised unemployment rates are the number of unemployed as a percentage of total labour force. The number of unemployed at national level is calculated on the basis of the 1988 LFSS and is then broken down by regions by means of data on registered unemployed at labour exchanges. The labour force figures are taken directly from the LFSS. Following the recommendations of the International Labour Office, the following concepts have been followed in the presentation of the survey results regarding unemployment and active populations:

1. The unemployed includes people who have no job and are looking for a job, or who have made serious efforts towards finding one and who are immediately available for work.

2. The labour force (active population) comprises those who have a job and the unemployed.

Dependency rates are calculated as the number of non-active persons (total population *minus* labour force) expressed as a percentage of those active.

Financial information is expressed in thousands of ECU (European Currency Units). In the absence of a common system for the conversion of national currencies into ECU, published results are based on the conversion rates applied by the different funds.

The European Agricultural Guidance and Guarantee Fund (EAGGF) contributes (on the basis of its 'guidance' section) to the; 'expenditure financed in order to attain structural adjustments made necessary by the development of the common market or required for the proper working thereof'.

The European Regional Development Fund (ERDF) provides grants dependent on the relative severity of regional imbalances, but; 'regions and areas which may benefit from the Fund shall be limited to those aided areas established by Member States in applying their systems of regional aids'.

Chapter 3: Population

Population change

- East Anglia and the South West are the fastest growing regions. However, between 1981 and 1990 populations fell in the North West, the North and Scotland.

(Table 3.1)

Population density

- *We remain a nation of crowded cities and thinly populated rural areas.* The most densely populated areas are Greater London, the West Midlands and Merseyside. Sparsest are the Highland and Borders areas of Scotland.

(Chart 3.2)

- The United Kingdom is the third most densely populated country in the EC behind the Netherlands and Germany, but England alone is more crowded than these countries.

(Table 2.1)

Age

- Northern Ireland has the youngest population, with one in four aged under 16. The national average is one in five.

(Table 3.3)

- The South West has the oldest population, with one in five over pension age.

(Table 3.3)

Regional movement

- The biggest shift of population is between the South East and the South West. In 1990, 60 thousand people moved from the South East to the South West, with 45 thousand moving the other way.

(Table 3.7)

Births

- Not surprisingly, birth rates are highest in those parts of the country with young populations. In 1990, birth rates were highest in Northern Ireland and lowest in Scotland, East Anglia and the South West.

(Table 3.13)

Deaths

- Death rates are obviously affected by the number of old people. But, after allowing for age structure, Scotland has the highest death rates and East Anglia the lowest.

(Table 3.18)

Births outside marriage

- Over one third of all births in the North West are outside marriage. The rates in the North and Yorkshire and Humberside are also over 30 per cent. The lowest rate is in Northern Ireland, at less than one fifth of all births.

(Table 3.16)

- Nationwide, four out of every five births to mothers aged under 20 are outside marriage. Even in East Anglia and Northern Ireland, where rates are lowest, they are as high as three out of four.

(Table 3.16)

Ethnic minorities

- The highest concentration of ethnic minorities is in the South East - 8.3 per cent of the population - followed by the West Midlands with 6.8 per cent.

(Table 3.15)

3.1 Resident population: by sex

Thousands and percentages

	Population (thousands)				Annual growth rate (percentages)		
	1961	1971	1981	1990	1961-1971	1971-1981	1981-1990
All persons							
United Kingdom	52,807	55,928.0	56,352.0	57,410.6	0.6	0.1	0.2
North	3,113	3,152.1	3,117.4	3,075.4	0.1	-0.1	-0.2
Yorkshire & Humberside	4,677	4,902.3	4,918.4	4,951.9	0.5	-	0.1
East Midlands	3,330	3,651.9	3,852.6	4,018.7	0.9	0.5	0.5
East Anglia	1,489	1,688.1	1,894.7	2,059.0	1.3	1.2	0.9
South East	16,071	17,125.3	17,010.6	17,458.0	0.6	-0.1	0.3
South West	3,712	4,111.8	4,381.3	4,666.5	1.0	0.6	0.7
West Midlands	4,762	5,146.0	5,186.6	5,219.3	0.8	0.1	0.1
North West	6,407	6,634.2	6,459.2	6,388.6	0.3	-0.3	-0.1
England	43,561	46,411.7	46,820.7	47,837.3	0.6	0.1	0.2
Wales	2,635	2,740.3	2,813.4	2,881.4	0.4	0.3	0.3
Scotland	5,184	5,235.6	5,180.2	5,102.4	0.1	-0.1	-0.2
Northern Ireland	1,427	1,540.4	1,537.7	1,589.4	0.8	-	0.4
Males							
United Kingdom	25,528	27,167.3	27,409.2	28,012.8	0.6	0.1	0.2
North	1,506	1,533.2	1,516.8	1,499.9	0.2	-0.1	-0.1
Yorkshire & Humberside	2,262	2,384.9	2,395.0	2,417.0	0.5	-	0.1
East Midlands	1,611	1,797.8	1,894.7	1,981.8	1.1	0.5	0.5
East Anglia	720	838.6	932.5	1,008.1	1.5	1.1	0.9
South East	7,774	8,288.5	8,259.4	8,516.0	0.6	-	0.3
South West	1,796	1,989.9	2,117.2	2,254.0	1.0	0.6	0.7
West Midlands	2,304	2,542.4	2,555.6	2,579.8	1.0	0.1	0.1
North West	3,099	3,193.2	3,124.0	3,111.6	0.3	-0.2	-
England	21,072	22,568.5	22,795.1	23,368.2	0.7	0.1	0.3
Wales	1,275	1,328.5	1,365.0	1,397.4	0.4	0.3	0.3
Scotland	2,485	2,515.7	2,494.9	2,466.8	0.1	-0.1	-0.1
Northern Ireland	696	754.6	754.2	780.4	0.8	-	0.4
Females							
United Kingdom	27,279	28,760.7	28,942.8	29,397.8	0.5	0.1	0.2
North	1,607	1,618.9	1,600.6	1,575.5	0.1	-0.1	-0.2
Yorkshire & Humberside	2,415	2,517.4	2,523.4	2,534.9	0.4	-	0.1
East Midlands	1,719	1,854.1	1,957.9	2,036.8	0.8	0.5	0.4
East Anglia	769	849.5	962.2	1,050.9	1.0	1.3	1.0
South East	8,297	8,836.8	8,751.2	8,942.0	0.6	-0.1	0.2
South West	1,916	2,121.9	2,264.1	2,412.5	1.0	0.7	0.7
West Midlands	2,458	2,603.6	2,631.0	2,639.5	0.6	0.1	-
North West	3,308	3,441.0	3,335.2	3,276.9	0.4	-0.3	-0.2
England	22,489	23,843.2	24,025.6	24,469.1	0.6	0.1	0.2
Wales	1,360	1,411.8	1,448.4	1,484.0	0.4	0.3	0.3
Scotland	2,699	2,719.9	2,685.3	2,635.6	0.1	-0.1	-0.2
Northern Ireland	732	785.8	783.5	809.0	0.7	-	0.4

Source: Office of Population Censuses and Surveys; General Register Offices for Scotland and Northern Ireland

3.2 Population density[1], 1990

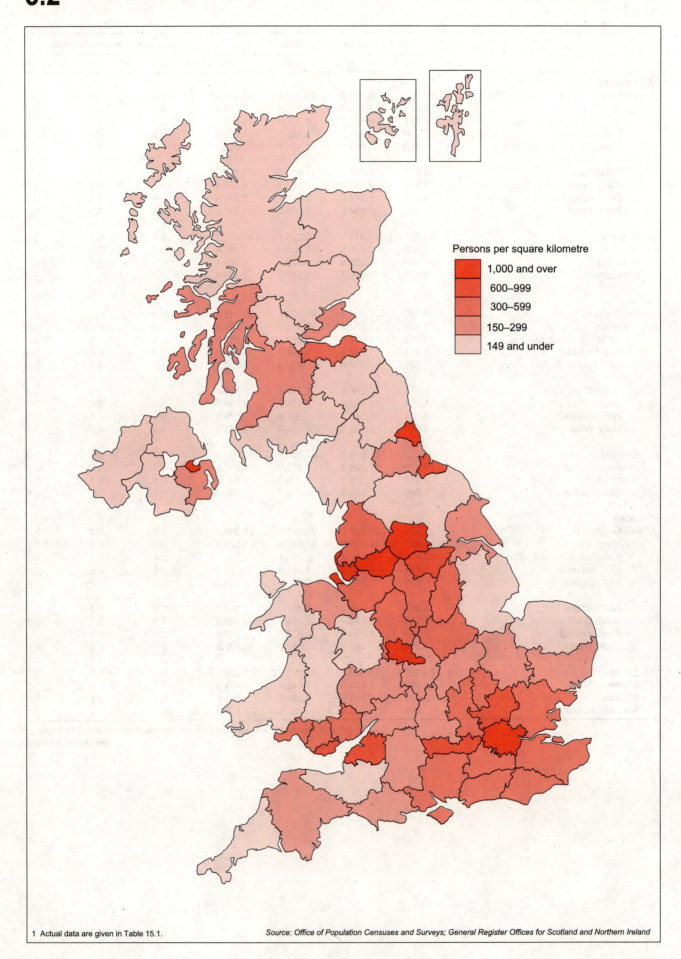

Persons per square kilometre

1,000 and over

600–999

300–599

150–299

149 and under

1 Actual data are given in Table 15.1.

Source: Office of Population Censuses and Surveys; General Register Offices for Scotland and Northern Ireland

3.3 Resident population: by age and sex, 1990

Thousands

	0-4	5-15	16-44	Males 45-64 Females 45-59	Males 65-79 Females 60-79	80 and over	All ages
All persons							
United Kingdom	3,841.1	7,779.9	24,467.6	10,832.1	8,380.8	2,109.1	57,410.6
North	199.4	415.8	1,293.7	599.0	461.7	105.8	3,075.4
Yorkshire & Humberside	331.0	671.9	2,106.2	936.5	725.0	181.4	4,951.9
East Midlands	264.5	544.7	1,728.5	764.3	577.7	139.2	4,018.7
East Anglia	133.5	280.0	860.9	383.4	320.3	80.9	2,059.0
South East	1,178.8	2,295.1	7,577.1	3,258.1	2,479.5	669.4	17,458.0
South West	287.2	598.6	1,909.5	885.2	772.0	214.0	4,666.5
West Midlands	354.7	717.1	2,221.2	1,009.5	746.6	170.2	5,219.3
North West	440.3	881.2	2,711.0	1,204.5	923.0	228.6	6,388.6
England	3,189.4	6,404.4	20,407.9	9,040.4	7,005.8	1,789.4	47,837.3
Wales	190.6	393.9	1,187.1	549.0	452.0	108.8	2,881.4
Scotland	325.9	696.0	2,202.3	975.5	732.7	170.0	5,102.4
Northern Ireland	135.2	285.6	670.3	267.3	190.3	40.8	1,589.4
Males							
United Kingdom	1,967.6	3,991.9	12,362.8	6,091.4	2,965.8	633.2	28,012.8
North	101.9	213.1	653.3	338.8	161.4	31.3	1,499.9
Yorkshire & Humberside	169.1	344.1	1,064.5	529.2	256.6	53.4	2,417.0
East Midlands	135.8	280.2	877.6	434.0	210.7	43.5	1,981.8
East Anglia	68.0	143.5	434.2	217.1	118.8	26.4	1,008.1
South East	602.8	1,177.5	3,818.6	1,828.9	885.8	202.3	8,516.0
South West	147.6	307.6	959.5	494.9	277.7	66.8	2,254.0
West Midlands	182.4	369.6	1,132.1	576.1	267.2	52.3	2,579.8
North West	225.4	451.5	1,372.1	680.1	318.1	64.5	3,111.6
England	1,633.1	3,287.1	10,311.9	5,099.3	2,496.3	540.5	23,368.2
Wales	97.8	202.4	595.9	309.3	159.8	32.2	1,397.4
Scotland	167.2	356.6	1,112.5	536.8	245.6	48.2	2,466.8
Northern Ireland	69.5	145.8	342.6	146.1	64.1	12.3	780.4
Females							
United Kingdom	1,873.5	3,788.0	12,104.8	4,740.7	5,415.0	1,475.9	29,397.8
North	97.5	202.6	640.4	260.3	300.3	74.5	1,575.5
Yorkshire & Humberside	161.9	327.7	1,041.7	407.3	468.4	128.0	2,534.9
East Midlands	128.7	264.5	850.8	330.2	367.0	95.6	2,036.8
East Anglia	65.5	136.5	426.7	166.2	201.5	54.4	1,050.9
South East	575.9	1,117.6	3,758.5	1,429.2	1,593.6	467.1	8,942.0
South West	139.6	291.0	950.0	390.3	494.3	147.2	2,412.5
West Midlands	172.3	347.5	1,089.1	433.3	479.5	117.9	2,639.5
North West	214.9	429.8	1,338.9	524.3	604.9	164.1	3,276.9
England	1,556.3	3,117.3	10,096.0	3,941.1	4,509.6	1,248.9	24,469.1
Wales	92.8	191.5	591.2	239.7	292.2	76.6	1,484.0
Scotland	158.7	339.4	1,089.8	438.7	487.1	121.9	2,635.6
Northern Ireland	65.7	139.7	327.7	121.2	126.1	28.5	809.0

Source: Office of Population Censuses and Surveys; General Register Offices for Scotland and Northern Ireland

3.4 Population aged 17 or under, 1990

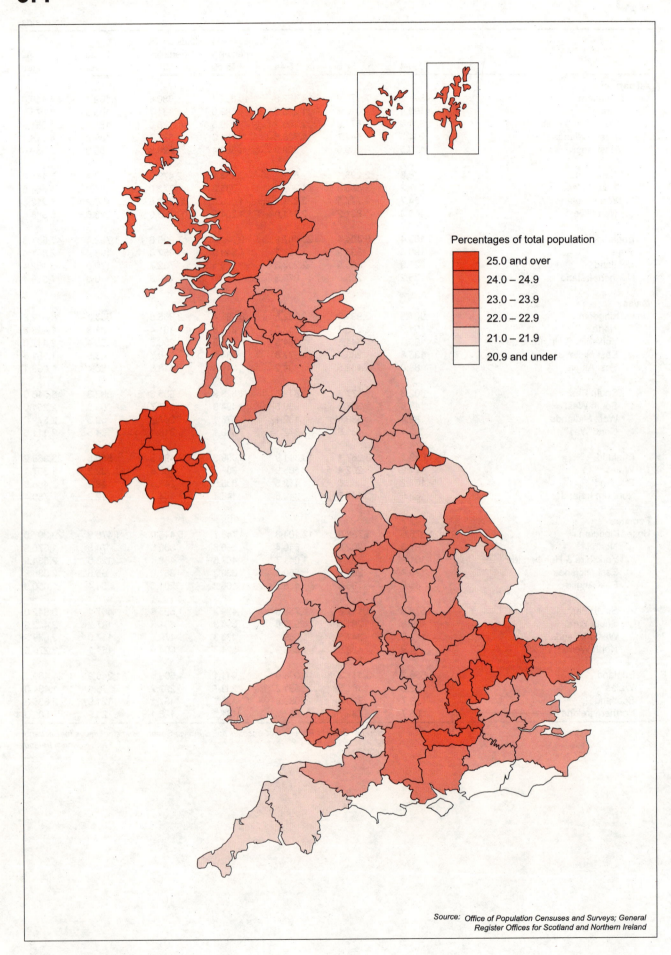

Percentages of total population

- 25.0 and over
- 24.0 – 24.9
- 23.0 – 23.9
- 22.0 – 22.9
- 21.0 – 21.9
- 20.9 and under

Source: Office of Population Censuses and Surveys; General Register Offices for Scotland and Northern Ireland

3.5 Population over retirement age[1], 1990

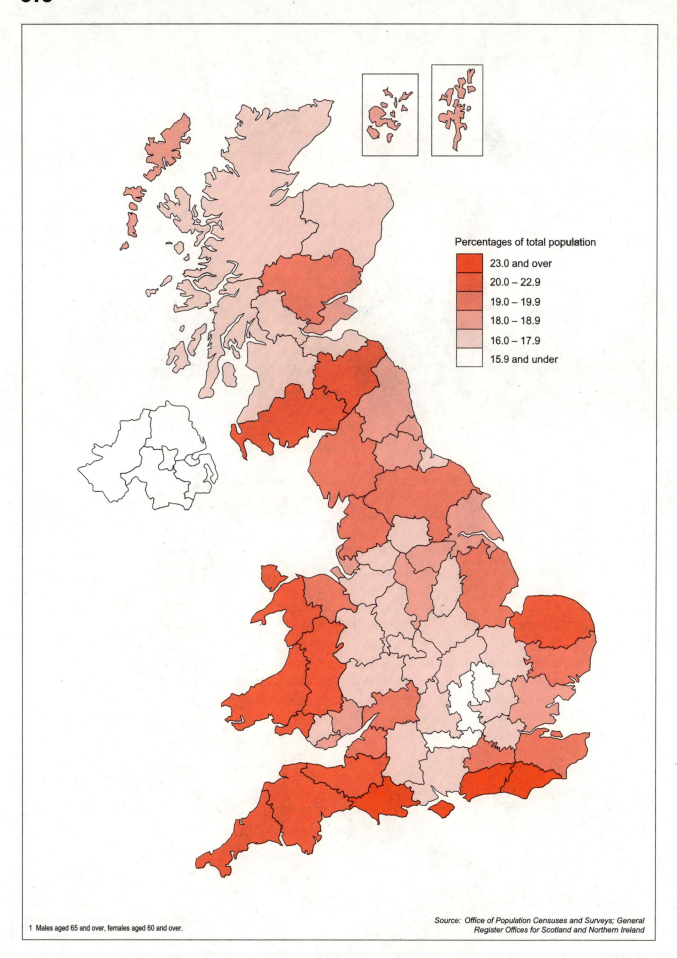

Percentages of total population

- 23.0 and over
- 20.0 – 22.9
- 19.0 – 19.9
- 18.0 – 18.9
- 16.0 – 17.9
- 15.9 and under

1 Males aged 65 and over, females aged 60 and over.

*Source: Office of Population Censuses and Surveys; General
Register Offices for Scotland and Northern Ireland*

3.6 Population growth, mid 1981–1990

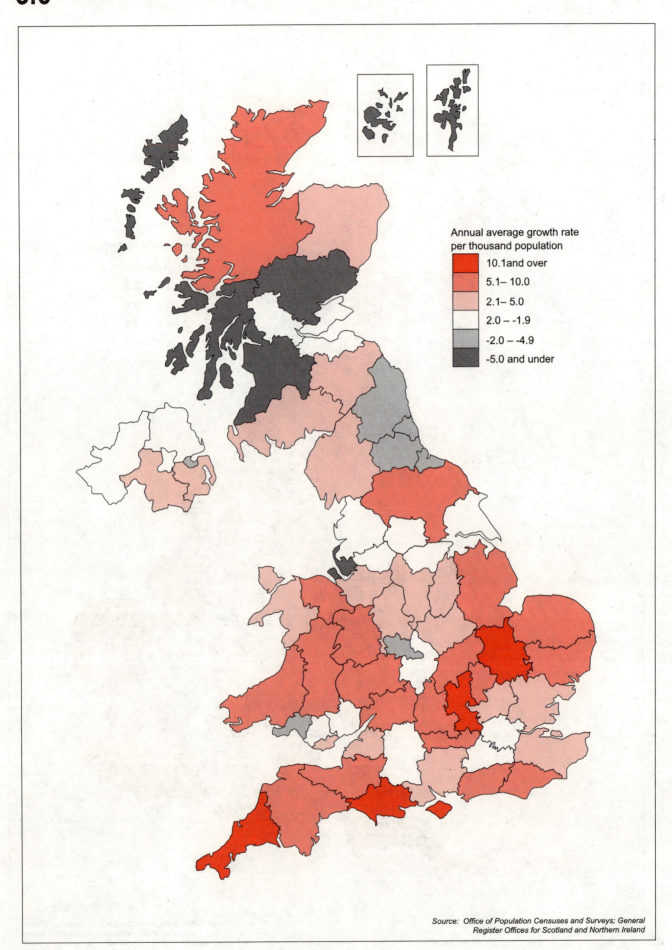

Annual average growth rate
per thousand population

- 10.1 and over
- 5.1– 10.0
- 2.1– 5.0
- 2.0 – -1.9
- -2.0 – -4.9
- -5.0 and under

Source: *Office of Population Censuses and Surveys; General Register Offices for Scotland and Northern Ireland*

3.7 Inter-regional movements[1], 1990

Thousands

Region of destination	United Kingdom	North	Yorkshire & Humberside	East Midlands	East Anglia	South East	South West	West Midlands	North West	Wales	Scotland	Northern Ireland
						Region of origin						
United Kingdom	.	47	78	75	44	248	91	81	94	44	45	13
North	46	.	9	3	2	14	3	3	7	1	4	1
Yorkshire & Humberside	78	9	.	12	3	22	5	6	13	2	4	1
East Midlands	82	3	13	.	6	29	6	11	8	2	3	1
East Anglia	52	2	3	6	.	29	4	3	3	1	2	-
South East	217	14	22	24	20	.	45	25	27	15	19	6
South West	110	3	6	7	4	60	.	12	8	8	4	1
West Midlands	74	3	6	9	2	25	9	.	10	6	2	1
North West	80	6	11	7	2	25	6	9	.	7	5	1
Wales	49	1	2	3	1	16	7	8	9	.	1	-
Scotland	61	6	6	4	3	23	5	4	7	2	.	2
Northern Ireland	12	-	1	1	-	5	1	1	2	-	1	.

1 Based on patients re-registering with NHS doctors in other parts of the UK.

Source: Office of Population Censuses and Surveys; General Register Offices for Scotland and Northern Ireland

3.8 Net inter-regional movements: by age[1], 1990

Thousands

	0-4	5-14	15-24	25-44	Males 45-64 Females 45-59	Males 65-74 Females 60-74	75 and over	All ages
North	-	-	-2	-1	1	-	-	-1
Yorkshire & Humberside	-	-1	1	-1	-	-	-	-
East Midlands	1	1	-	3	1	1	1	6
East Anglia	1	1	-1	3	2	2	1	8
South East	-5	-7	12	-11	-10	-7	-3	-31
Greater London	-7	-7	14	-17	-9	-7	-4	-36
Rest of South East	-	-2	14	4	-6	-4	-	5
South West	1	4	-1	6	4	3	1	18
West Midlands	-	-	-4	-2	-1	-	-	-7
North West	-	-1	-5	-3	-2	-1	-1	-13
England	-2	-4	1	-7	-5	-2	-1	-20
Wales	-	1	-1	1	2	1	-	5
Scotland	2	3	2	6	2	1	-	17
Northern Ireland	-	-	-2	-	-	-	-	-1

1 Based on patients re-registering with NHS doctors in other parts of the UK.

Source: Office of Population Censuses and Surveys; General Register Offices for Scotland and Northern Ireland

3.9　International migration, 1990: inflow

Thousands

	Country of last residence[1]						
		New Commonwealth					
	Old Common-wealth	India, Bangladesh & Pakistan	Other	European Community	USA	Rest of the world	All countries
Region of next residence							
United Kingdom	57	21	38	66	29	56	267
North	1	-	-	2	1	1	5
Yorkshire & Humberside	1	1	3	3	1	2	11
East Midlands	1	1	1	2	-	3	8
East Anglia	3	1	1	7	3	2	15
South East	37	10	22	31	18	36	154
Greater London	22	8	14	13	10	23	89
Rest of South East	15	2	8	19	8	13	65
South West	6	1	2	4	1	2	16
West Midlands	3	3	3	3	-	3	15
North West	2	4	3	9	1	2	20
England	52	20	35	61	26	50	246
Wales	1	-	1	-	-	2	5
Scotland	3	-	1	4	3	3	14
Northern Ireland	1	-	1	1	-	-	3

1 Excluding Irish Republic, Channel Islands and Isle of Man.

Source: International Passenger Survey, Office of Population Censuses and Surveys

3.10　International migration, 1990: outflow

Thousands

	Country of next residence[1]						
		New Commonwealth					
	Old Common-wealth	India, Bangladesh & Pakistan	Other	European Community	USA	Rest of the world	All countries
Region of previous residence							
United Kingdom	59	5	23	59	42	43	231
North	1	-	1	-	1	1	4
Yorkshire & Humberside	3	1	2	1	1	2	10
East Midlands	2	-	1	3	-	2	8
East Anglia	2	-	1	1	5	1	9
South East	31	3	12	33	18	25	121
Greater London	16	2	6	14	7	14	60
Rest of South East	14	-	6	19	10	11	62
South West	6	-	1	9	3	2	21
West Midlands	3	1	2	6	2	2	15
North West	3	-	1	2	1	3	10
England	51	4	20	55	30	38	199
Wales	2	-	1	-	-	1	4
Scotland	5	-	1	3	12	4	25
Northern Ireland	2	-	-	-	-	-	2

1 Excluding Irish Republic, Channel Islands and Isle of Man.

Source: International Passenger Survey, Office of Population Censuses and Surveys

3.11 International migration, 1990: net balance

Thousands

	Country of last or next residence[1]						
	Old Common-wealth	New Commonwealth		European Community	USA	Rest of the world	All countries
		India, Bangladesh & Pakistan	Other				
Region of last or next residence							
United Kingdom	-3	16	15	7	-13	13	36
North	-	-	-1	2	-	-	1
Yorkshire & Humberside	-2	-	2	1	-	-1	1
East Midlands	-1	1	1	-1	-	1	-
East Anglia	1	-	-	6	-2	1	6
South East	6	7	10	-2	1	11	33
Greater London	6	6	8	-1	3	8	30
Rest of South East	-	1	2	-1	-2	2	3
South West	-	1	1	-5	-2	1	-5
West Midlands	-1	2	-	-2	-1	1	-
North West	-1	4	2	7	-	-1	11
England	2	16	15	6	-4	13	47
Wales	-1	-	1	-	-	1	-
Scotland	-2	-	-1	-	-9	-1	-12
Northern Ireland	-1	-	-	1	-	-	-

1 Excluding Irish Republic, Channel Islands and Isle of Man.

Source: International Passenger Survey, Office of Population Censuses and Surveys

3.12 Components of population change, mid-1989 to mid-1990

Thousands

	Resident population mid-1989	Births	Deaths	Net natural change	Net civilian migration and other changes	Total change	Resident population mid-1990
United Kingdom	57,236.2	782.1	664.1	118.0	56.4	174.4	57,410.6
North	3,073.1	39.6	39.1	0.5	1.7	2.3	3,075.4
Yorkshire & Humberside	4,940.4	67.2	59.2	8.0	3.6	11.5	4,951.9
East Midlands	3,999.1	53.8	44.6	9.2	10.4	19.6	4,018.7
East Anglia	2,044.6	26.1	22.7	3.5	11.0	14.4	2,059.0
South East	17,384.2	244.7	187.2	57.5	16.3	73.8	17,458.0
South West	4,652.4	58.5	57.8	0.8	13.3	14.1	4,666.5
West Midlands	5,216.0	73.7	58.2	15.5	-12.1	3.4	5,219.3
North West	6,379.7	90.0	78.7	11.3	-2.4	8.8	6,388.6
England	47,689.4	653.6	547.3	106.3	41.7	147.9	47,837.3
Wales	2,873.1	38.0	35.2	2.8	5.5	8.4	2,881.4
Scotland	5,090.7	64.1	65.5	-1.4	13.1	11.7	5,102.4
Northern Ireland	1,583.0	26.3	16.1	10.2	-3.8	6.4	1,589.4

Source: Office of Population Censuses and Surveys; General Register Offices for Scotland and Northern Ireland

3.13 Live births, deaths and natural increase in population[1]

Thousands and rates

	Thousands					Rate per 1,000 population				
	1961	1971	1981	1986	1990	1961	1971	1981	1986	1990
Live births										
United Kingdom	944.4	901.6	730.8	755.0	798.6	17.9	16.1	13.0	13.3	13.9
North	58.2	52.7	39.8	40.2	40.7	18.7	16.7	12.8	13.1	13.2
Yorkshire & Humberside	83.0	80.2	62.6	65.3	68.9	17.8	16.4	12.7	13.3	13.9
East Midlands	58.7	56.7	49.2	50.3	54.8	17.6	15.5	12.8	12.8	13.6
East Anglia	24.6	26.7	23.7	24.6	26.6	16.5	15.8	12.5	12.3	12.9
South East	275.2	266.4	220.3	230.4	249.6	17.1	15.6	13.0	13.3	14.3
South West	60.5	57.2	50.4	54.5	59.0	16.3	13.9	11.5	12.0	12.6
West Midlands	88.7	88.3	67.5	70.4	75.1	18.6	17.2	13.0	13.6	14.4
North West	117.4	112.0	84.7	87.8	92.3	18.3	16.9	13.1	13.8	14.4
England	766.4	740.1	598.2	623.6	666.9	17.6	15.9	12.8	13.2	13.9
Wales	44.9	43.1	35.8	37.0	38.9	17.0	15.8	12.7	13.1	13.5
Scotland	101.2	86.7	69.1	65.8	66.0	19.5	16.6	13.3	12.9	12.9
Northern Ireland	31.9	31.8	27.3	28.2	26.5	22.4	20.7	17.8	18.0	16.7
Deaths										
United Kingdom[2]	631.8	645.1	658.0	660.7	641.8	12.0	11.5	11.6	11.6	11.2
North	37.1	37.5	38.2	38.0	37.5	11.9	11.9	12.3	12.3	12.2
Yorkshire & Humberside	58.4	58.8	59.1	58.9	56.9	12.5	12.0	12.0	12.0	11.5
East Midlands	37.5	40.2	42.8	43.5	42.9	11.2	11.0	11.2	11.1	10.7
East Anglia	17.3	18.9	21.0	22.0	22.3	11.6	11.2	11.1	11.1	10.8
South East	184.3	190.6	188.6	188.5	180.7	11.5	11.1	11.1	10.9	10.3
South West	46.2	50.7	54.4	56.4	55.7	12.4	12.3	12.5	12.4	11.9
West Midlands	51.8	53.4	56.4	57.7	56.8	10.9	10.4	10.9	11.1	10.9
North West	85.5	82.4	80.4	79.4	76.2	13.3	12.4	12.4	12.5	11.9
England	518.0	532.4	541.0	544.5	528.9	11.9	11.5	11.6	11.5	11.1
Wales	33.7	34.8	35.0	34.7	34.0	12.8	12.7	12.4	12.3	11.8
Scotland	63.9	61.6	63.8	63.5	61.5	12.3	11.8	12.4	12.4	12.1
Northern Ireland	16.1	16.2	16.3	16.1	15.4	11.3	10.6	10.6	10.4	9.7
Natural increase										
United Kingdom	312.6	256.5	72.8	94.3	156.8	5.9	4.6	1.4	1.7	2.7
North	21.1	15.2	1.6	2.2	3.2	6.8	4.1	0.5	0.8	1.0
Yorkshire & Humberside	24.6	21.4	3.5	6.4	12.0	5.3	4.7	0.7	1.3	2.4
East Midlands	21.2	16.5	6.4	6.8	11.9	6.4	5.7	1.6	1.7	3.0
East Anglia	7.3	7.8	2.7	2.6	4.3	4.9	4.7	1.4	1.2	2.1
South East	90.9	75.8	31.7	41.9	69.0	5.6	4.3	1.9	2.4	4.0
South West	14.3	6.5	-4.0	-1.9	3.3	3.9	2.8	-1.0	-0.4	0.7
West Midlands	36.9	34.9	11.1	12.7	18.3	7.7	6.8	2.1	2.5	3.5
North West	31.9	29.6	4.3	8.4	16.1	5.0	4.2	0.7	1.3	2.5
England	248.4	207.7	57.2	79.1	138.0	5.7	4.6	1.2	1.7	2.9
Wales	11.2	8.3	0.8	2.3	4.9	4.2	3.1	0.3	0.8	1.7
Scotland	37.3	25.1	5.3	2.3	4.4	7.2	4.8	0.9	0.5	0.9
Northern Ireland	15.8	15.6	11.0	12.1	11.1	11.1	10.1	6.9	7.6	7.0

1 The data are by region of usual residence. Prior to 1972 births to mothers usually resident outside England and Wales are assigned to region of occurrence; from 1972 onwards such births are not included in the regional figures but in the UK totals only.

2 From 1981 onwards, UK death figures include deaths occurring in England and Wales to non-residents of England and Wales. These numbers are excluded from the data for England and Wales and the standard regions.

Source: Office of Population Censuses and Surveys; General Register Offices for Scotland and Northern Ireland

3.14 Age specific birth rates, 1981 and 1990

Rates

	Under 20	20-24	25-29	30-34	35-39	40 and over	All ages	TPFR[2]
	Live births per 1,000 women in age groups[1]							
1981								
United Kingdom	28	107	130	70	22	5	62	1.81
North	33	118	123	60	19	4	62	1.78
Yorkshire & Humberside	31	117	128	59	18	6	62	1.80
East Midlands	30	113	127	63	19	4	61	1.79
East Anglia	24	115	135	64	17	5	61	1.79
South East	24	92	128	76	25	5	61	1.75
South West	24	103	131	63	18	3	57	1.71
West Midlands	32	108	133	69	20	7	62	1.84
North West	33	111	132	68	23	5	64	1.86
England	28	104	129	69	22	5	61	1.78
Wales	30	121	127	67	21	6	63	1.86
Scotland	31	112	132	66	21	4	63	1.83
Northern Ireland	27	135	173	118	52	13	86	2.59
1990								
United Kingdom	33	91	123	87	31	5	64	1.84
North	43	98	116	73	22	4	62	1.78
Yorkshire & Humberside	42	102	120	75	25	4	64	1.85
East Midlands	35	97	121	78	26	4	63	1.81
East Anglia	28	91	123	78	27	5	61	1.75
South East	25	79	124	101	39	7	65	1.87
South West	25	86	122	85	29	5	60	1.76
West Midlands	39	104	126	84	30	5	67	1.94
North West	44	102	123	83	29	5	67	1.93
England	33	91	123	88	31	5	64	1.84
Wales	39	102	117	80	27	4	64	1.83
Scotland	32	83	117	77	25	4	59	1.67
Northern Ireland	29	100	152	112	49	11	78	2.26

1 The rates for women aged under 20, 40 and over and all ages are based upon the population of women aged 15-19, 40-44 and 15-44 respectively.
2 The Total Period Fertility Rate (TPFR) measures the average number of children which would be born if women were to experience the age-specific fertility rates of the year in question throughout their childbearing life.

Source: Office of Population Censuses and Surveys; General Register Offices for Scotland and Northern Ireland

3.15 Population in private households: by ethnic group, 1988-1990

Thousands and percentages

	West Indian or African	Indian/ Pakistani or Bangladeshi	Other	Total	White (thousands)	All ethnic groups[1] (thousands)	Ethnic minority population as percentage of all ethnic groups
	Ethnic minority groups (thousands)						
Great Britain	597	1,356	671	2,624	51,689	54,823	4.8
North	2	21	12	34	2,978	3,037	1.1
Yorkshire & Humberside	23	143	40	206	4,621	4,870	4.2
East Midlands	21	104	31	156	3,759	3,949	4.0
East Anglia	11	21	22	54	1,951	2,020	2.7
South East	410	625	388	1,423	15,469	17,086	8.3
South West	19	22	38	79	4,451	4,565	1.7
West Midlands	76	233	42	352	4,764	5,158	6.8
North West	26	148	60	234	5,997	6,288	3.7
England	588	1,317	633	2,538	43,990	46,973	5.4
Wales	4	12	16	33	2,780	2,836	1.2
Scotland	5	27	22	53	4,918	5,013	1.1

1 Includes ethnic group not stated.

Source: Labour Force Surveys, Office of Population Censuses and Surveys

3.16 Live births outside marriage: by age of mother, 1981 and 1990

Percentage of all births

	Under 20	20-24	25-29	30-34	35-39	40 and over	All ages
1981							
United Kingdom	45.5	14.5	6.5	6.1	7.8	11.7	12.5
North	50.0	13.2	6.2	5.7	5.1	12.4	13.2
Yorkshire & Humberside	45.8	14.5	6.4	6.9	10.2	11.3	13.5
East Midlands	44.0	14.1	6.1	5.6	12.3	14.5	12.6
East Anglia	34.2	11.6	4.5	7.2	2.7	17.1	9.5
South East	48.4	16.3	7.2	6.3	7.5	13.2	12.6
South West	41.7	11.2	5.5	5.0	6.9	17.0	10.3
West Midlands	45.9	13.8	6.6	5.8	9.5	8.5	12.8
North West	52.3	18.1	7.7	6.7	7.2	11.2	15.5
England	47.2	15.0	6.7	6.2	7.9	12.3	12.9
Wales	40.1	11.8	5.0	6.7	8.0	13.6	11.2
Scotland	39.1	13.7	6.5	6.0	8.9	12.4	12.2
Northern Ireland	33.1	8.0	3.9	3.2	3.4	3.9	7.0
1990							
United Kingdom	80.2	40.6	18.5	14.2	16.4	19.8	27.9
North	85.9	45.2	19.6	14.9	16.5	22.1	32.8
Yorkshire & Humberside	80.1	41.5	18.4	14.9	17.2	22.9	30.6
East Midlands	81.6	39.0	17.1	14.0	16.9	21.6	28.0
East Anglia	74.5	32.0	14.6	12.4	13.3	16.7	22.8
South East	76.8	40.5	19.6	14.7	17.2	20.2	25.9
South West	79.7	35.9	15.9	12.9	16.1	22.2	24.3
West Midlands	77.7	39.8	19.0	14.8	16.5	18.6	29.1
North West	85.3	34.7	18.1	16.0	22.0	19.5	34.4
England	80.2	41.2	19.1	14.6	16.9	20.4	28.3
Wales	81.2	39.5	17.3	14.9	16.2	21.7	29.3
Scotland	80.5	39.8	16.6	12.7	15.2	18.5	27.1
Northern Ireland	76.0	29.4	10.6	7.6	8.3	8.7	18.8

Source: Office of Population Censuses and Surveys; General Register Offices for Scotland and Northern Ireland

3.17 Marriages, 1989

Thousands and percentages

	Total marriages (thousands)	First marriages: sex and age distribution (percentages)						Persons remarrying as a percentage of all marriages	
		Males			Females				
		Under 20	20-24	25 and over	Under 20	20-24	25 and over	Males	Females
United Kingdom	392.0	2.9	38.9	58.2	10.2	50.8	39.0	26.4	25.6
North	20.7	3.5	43.7	52.8	10.6	55.1	34.3	26.0	25.2
Yorkshire & Humberside	35.5	3.6	42.5	53.9	11.7	54.2	34.1	28.7	28.8
East Midlands	28.1	2.8	42.6	54.5	11.5	54.2	34.2	29.0	28.5
East Anglia	14.2	2.8	42.1	55.1	12.5	53.3	34.2	29.9	29.0
South East	118.8	2.2	33.5	64.3	8.7	45.9	45.4	26.0	25.0
South West	32.2	2.2	39.6	58.2	10.1	52.3	37.6	30.0	29.6
West Midlands	35.0	3.6	41.5	54.9	12.1	52.7	35.1	26.1	25.3
North West	42.9	2.8	38.5	58.7	9.4	51.9	38.7	27.3	26.3
England	327.2	2.7	38.3	58.9	10.1	50.5	39.4	27.3	26.5
Wales	19.5	3.4	41.8	54.8	12.2	52.5	35.3	26.7	26.1
Scotland	35.3	3.3	41.7	55.0	9.9	51.7	38.4	23.0	21.9
Northern Ireland	10.0	3.5	42.0	54.5	10.7	51.9	37.3	9.6	8.7

Source: Office of Population Censuses and Surveys; General Register Offices for Scotland and Northern Ireland

3.18 Age-specific death rates: by sex, 1990

Rates and Standardised Mortality Ratios

	Deaths per 1,000 population for specific age groups									SMR[1] (UK = 100)
	0-4	5-14	15-24	25-34	35-44	45-54	55-64	65-74	75 and over	
Males										
United Kingdom	2.2	0.2	0.9	1.0	1.8	4.8	14.8	39.5	109.4	100
North	2.1	0.2	0.8	0.9	1.8	5.3	17.7	45.6	116.1	110
Yorkshire & Humberside	2.5	0.2	0.8	0.8	1.6	4.8	15.5	42.2	112.3	104
East Midlands	2.1	0.2	1.0	0.9	1.6	4.4	14.1	38.3	108.0	97
East Anglia	1.5	0.1	0.8	1.0	1.5	3.7	12.0	32.3	106.0	89
South East	2.1	0.2	0.8	1.0	1.7	4.3	12.6	34.7	102.8	91
South West	1.9	0.2	0.9	0.9	1.7	4.1	12.6	33.8	106.6	92
West Midlands	2.7	0.2	0.8	0.8	1.7	4.7	15.0	42.2	110.9	103
North West	2.2	0.3	0.8	0.9	1.8	5.3	17.3	44.0	116.2	109
England	2.2	0.2	0.8	0.9	1.7	4.5	14.2	38.3	108.0	98
Wales	2.1	0.2	0.7	0.9	1.7	5.0	15.4	42.3	110.8	103
Scotland	2.1	0.3	1.0	1.2	2.2	6.1	17.8	46.2	118.4	114
Northern Ireland	1.9	0.2	0.9	1.2	2.0	5.3	16.3	45.7	119.5	111
Females										
United Kingdom	1.7	0.2	0.3	0.5	1.1	3.0	8.8	22.4	83.1	100
North	1.7	0.2	0.3	0.4	1.2	3.2	10.6	26.9	88.1	110
Yorkshire & Humberside	1.7	0.1	0.3	0.5	1.2	3.1	9.3	23.7	83.5	102
East Midlands	1.8	0.1	0.3	0.4	1.0	2.7	8.4	21.8	82.7	98
East Anglia	1.5	0.2	0.3	0.4	1.0	2.6	6.9	18.7	80.8	93
South East	1.5	0.1	0.3	0.5	1.1	2.7	7.7	19.7	79.0	93
South West	1.4	0.2	0.3	0.4	1.1	2.6	7.2	19.4	79.3	92
West Midlands	2.2	0.1	0.3	0.4	1.2	3.0	8.9	22.5	83.9	101
North West	1.8	0.2	0.2	0.4	1.2	3.4	10.0	25.4	88.4	108
England	1.7	0.1	0.3	0.4	1.1	2.9	8.5	21.8	82.1	98
Wales	1.4	0.2	0.3	0.4	1.0	3.0	9.3	22.7	82.1	99
Scotland	1.5	0.2	0.3	0.5	1.4	3.7	10.9	27.1	90.2	113
Northern Ireland	1.7	0.2	0.3	0.5	1.2	3.4	9.9	24.3	90.1	109

1 Standardised Mortality Ratio, i.e. adjusted for age structure of population.

Source: Office of Population Censuses and Surveys; General Register Offices for Scotland and Northern Ireland

Notes to Chapter 3: Population

Tables 3.1 and 3.3 Resident population

Resident population covers people normally resident in an area. The data include students at 'term-time' addresses and armed forces (both UK Forces and those from other countries) at stationed addresses. Mid-year estimates are based on the Census of Population adjusted for births, deaths, migration into and out of the country and changes in the number of stationed armed forces. The series includes residents who were temporarily outside the country at the time of the census and excludes overseas visitors. In Table 3.1 annual growth rates are shown as geometric averages.

Tables 3.7 and 3.8, Inter-regional migration

Estimates for internal population movements are based on the transfers of NHS doctors' patients between Family Health Services Authorities (FHSAs) in England and Wales and Area Health Boards (AHBs) in Scotland and Northern Ireland. These transfers are recorded at the NHS Central Registers (NHSCRs) in Southport and Edinburgh and at the Central Services Agency in Belfast. The figures shown here have been adjusted to take account of differences in recorded cross-border flows between England and Wales, Scotland, and Northern Ireland.

These figures provide a detailed indicator of population movement within the country, however they should not be regarded as a perfect measure of migration as there is usually some delay between a person moving and registering with a new doctor. Additionally, some moves may not result in a re-registration, that is, individuals may migrate again before registering with a doctor. Conversely, there may be others who move and re-register several times in a year.

The NHSCR at Southport was computerised in early 1991, prior to which a 3-month time lag was assumed between a person moving and their re-registration with an NHS doctor being processed onto the NHSCR. Since computerisation, estimates of internal migration are based on the date of acceptance of the new patient by the FHSA (not previously available), and a one-month time lag assumed. There is thus a discontinuity in the data series, which may have affected figures for the last two quarters of 1990.

Tables 3.9-3.11 International migration

The *International Passenger Survey*, is a continuing sample survey covering the principal air and sea routes between the United Kingdom and overseas excluding routes between the United Kingdom and the Irish Republic. The proportion of passengers sampled in the IPS is currently about 0.2%, although this varies depending on route and time of year. In view of the very small numbers in the sample, estimates of migration, in particular the net migration, are subject to large margins of error.

For demographic purposes a migrant into the United Kingdom is defined as a person who has resided abroad for a year or more and states the intention to stay in the United Kingdom for a year or more; and *vice versa* for a migrant from the United Kingdom. Migrants, defined in this way, are asked an additional group of questions which form the basis of these statistics.

Table 3.13 Vital statistics

Numbers shown are registrations during a calendar year, except for births in England and Wales which are numbers occurring in a calendar year. Crude birth/death rates and natural increase are affected by the age and sex structure of the population. For example, for any given level of fertility and mortality a population with a relatively high proportion of persons in the younger age-groups will have a higher crude birth-rate and a lower crude death-rate and consequently a higher rate of natural increase than a population with a lower proportion of young people.

Table 3.14 Age specific birth rates.

The total period fertility rate is the average number of children which would be born per women if women experienced the age-specific fertility rates of the year in question throughout their childbearing years.

Table 3.18 Standardised mortality ratios

The standardised mortality ratio compares overall mortality in a region with that for the United Kingdom. The ratio expresses the number of deaths in a region as a percentage of the hypothetical number that would have occurred if the region's population had experienced the sex/age-specific rates of the United Kingdom in that year.

Chapter 4: Housing

Stock of dwellings

● The stock of homes is rising fastest in East Anglia and Northern Ireland; both up by 14 per cent between 1981 and 1990.

(Table 4.1)

Owner occupation

● Although owner occupation continues to grow, regional differences range from half of all dwellings in Scotland to three quarters in the South East outside Greater London.

(Table 4.2)

New homes

● Private developers are building more homes per head in Northern Ireland and East Anglia than in other regions.

(Table 4.5)

Council houses

● Rented council houses remain a major feature of Scottish housing; 40 per cent of all dwellings in 1990 - a full 10 percentage points above the next highest region.

(Table 4.2)

House value

● Over half of the total value of United Kingdom housing is in the South East.

(Table 4.6)

House prices

● Between 1990 and 1991, house prices rose fastest in Scotland and Northern Ireland - both by more than 8 per cent.

(Table 4.8)

● Between 1990 and 1991, house prices fell in five regions, with the largest fall in the South East.

(Table 4.8)

Homeless

● Nearly a third of new council tenants in Greater London and a quarter in the West Midlands had been accepted by local authorities as homeless.

(Table 4.11)

4.1 Stock of dwellings[1]

Thousands and percentages

	Thousands					Percentage increase
	1976	1981	1988	1989	1990	1981-1990
United Kingdom	20,599	21,578	22,982	23,194	23,383	8
North	1,169	1,214	1,262	1,271	1,278	5
Yorkshire & Humberside	1,829	1,900	1,986	2,000	2,012	6
East Midlands	1,393	1,484	1,597	1,613	1,628	10
East Anglia	692	755	838	851	864	14
South East	6,236	6,531	7,010	7,078	7,137	9
Greater London	2,640	2,676	2,785	2,802	2,820	5
Rest of South East	3,596	3,854	4,225	4,276	4,317	12
South West	1,613	1,727	1,900	1,925	1,945	13
West Midlands	1,840	1,941	2,052	2,064	2,079	7
North West	2,396	2,466	2,555	2,567	2,579	5
England	17,168	18,018	19,200	19,370	19,522	8
Wales	1,029	1,089	1,148	1,159	1,169	7
Scotland	1,921	1,970	2,084	2,104	2,124	8
Northern Ireland	481	500	550	559	568	14

1 At December.

Source: Department of the Environment; Welsh Office; The Scottish Development Department; Department of the Environment, Northern Ireland

4.2 Stock of dwellings: by tenure

Percentages

	Owner-occupied			Rented from local authority or new town[1,2]			Rented from private owners or with job or business			Rented from housing association		
	1981	1986	1990	1981	1986	1990	1981	1986	1990	1981	1986	1990
United Kingdom	57	62	67	31	27	23	11	8	7	2	2	3
North	48	55	60	39	33	29	10	8	7	3	3	4
Yorkshire & Humberside	57	62	66	31	28	24	10	8	8	1	2	2
East Midlands	60	66	71	27	23	20	11	9	8	1	2	2
East Anglia	59	66	70	25	21	17	14	12	10	2	2	2
South East	59	65	69	26	23	19	12	9	8	3	3	4
Greater London	50	56	61	32	29	25	13	10	8	5	5	5
Rest of South East	65	71	75	23	19	15	11	9	8	2	2	3
South West	64	70	74	21	17	15	13	11	10	2	2	2
West Midlands	58	63	68	31	27	24	9	7	6	2	2	3
North West	60	65	68	29	25	22	9	7	6	2	3	4
England	59	65	69	28	24	21	11	9	8	2	3	3
Wales	63	68	72	27	23	19	9	8	7	1	2	2
Scotland	36	43	51	52	47	40	10	8	6	2	2	3
Northern Ireland	54	61	66	38	33	29	7	5	4	1	1	2

1 Including Scottish Homes, formerly the Scottish Special Housing Association.
2 Northern Ireland Housing Executive in Northern Ireland.

Source: Department of the Environment; Welsh Office; The Scottish Development Department; Department of the Environment, Northern Ireland

4.3 Stock of dwellings: by age, 1990[1]

Percentages

	Pre 1871	1871 -1890	1891 -1918	1919 -1944	1945 -1970	Post 1970
Great Britain	..	14.3 [2]	12.8	19.4	32.0	21.6
North	3.6	7.7	14.5	19.2	35.0	20.1
Yorkshire & Humberside	4.4	8.5	14.9	21.0	32.1	19.1
East Midlands	5.0	7.9	11.6	18.5	32.2	24.8
East Anglia	13.0	6.0	7.5	13.0	30.5	30.1
South East	6.1	8.4	12.5	21.4	30.6	21.0
Greater London	5.4	13.0	17.7	27.5	22.2	14.2
Rest of South East	6.6	5.4	9.1	17.5	36.2	25.4
South West	12.8	6.7	9.6	15.2	30.7	25.3
West Midlands	5.0	6.1	11.0	21.8	35.6	20.6
North West	4.6	10.0	14.0	21.6	30.5	19.3
England	6.3	8.0	12.3	20.1	31.7	21.6
Wales	..	20.9 [2]	16.6	13.1	29.5	19.8
Scotland	2.7	8.0	14.9	16.4	35.7	22.3

1 At end 1990.
2 Includes all pre-1891 dwellings.

Source: Department of the Environment; Welsh Office; The Scottish Development Department

4.4 Renovations: by tenure, 1981 and 1990

Thousands of dwellings

	Grants paid to private owners and tenants[1,2]		Work completed for housing associations		Work completed for local authorities and new towns[1,3,4]	
	1981	1990	1981	1990	1981	1990
United Kingdom	115.7	150.4	..	..	..	323.1
North	4.9	7.7	1.2	0.3	4.1	21.5
Yorkshire & Humberside	7.7	14.5	0.7	0.5	5.0	11.3
East Midlands	7.3	10.4	0.7	0.4	5.6	20.4
East Anglia	3.3	4.6	0.2	0.3	1.2	4.9
South East	20.6	25.3	3.6	6.0	20.1	67.7
Greater London	9.5	10.8	3.3	3.7	13.5	38.4
Rest of South East	11.2	14.5	0.3	2.3	6.7	29.3
South West	6.0	7.6	0.4	1.1	1.9	28.8
West Midlands	7.1	11.7	1.2	0.5	6.4	40.7
North West	12.1	14.9	3.2	1.4	8.5	31.1
England	68.9	96.6	11.2	10.6	52.9	226.5
Wales	7.1	26.5	0.7	0.4	..	11.0
Scotland	15.2	20.5	1.8	0.8	25.3	76.5
Northern Ireland	24.5	6.8	..	..	22.1	9.1

1 Scottish figures are for work approved.
2 English and Welsh grants paid under the *Housing Act 1985* and earlier legislation refer to the number of dwellings whereas grants paid under the *Local Government & Housing Act 1989* refer to the number of grants.
3 Including Scottish Homes, formerly the Scottish Special Housing Association.
4 1990 data for Scottish Homes is not available.

Source: Department of the Environment; Welsh Office; The Scottish Development Department; Department of the Environment, Northern Ireland

4.5 New dwellings[1] completed: by sector

	Thousands				Percentage change	Rate per 1,000 population			
	1981	1988	1989	1990	1981-1990	1981	1988	1989	1990
Private enterprise[2]									
United Kingdom	118.6	205.0	184.9	160.3	*35*	2.1	3.6	3.2	2.8
North	4.9	7.4	8.4	7.2	*47*	1.6	2.4	2.7	2.3
Yorkshire & Humberside	8.5	14.6	12.4	10.2	*20*	1.7	3.0	2.5	2.1
East Midlands	9.5	17.9	14.6	12.9	*36*	2.5	4.5	3.7	3.2
East Anglia	6.6	12.8	11.2	10.4	*58*	3.5	6.3	5.5	5.0
South East	35.0	63.1	56.9	46.3	*32*	2.1	3.6	3.3	2.7
Greater London	4.0	12.0	12.5	12.7	*218*	0.6	1.8	1.9	1.9
Rest of South East	30.9	51.0	44.4	33.6	*9*	3.0	4.8	4.2	3.2
South West	13.9	26.1	20.8	16.4	*18*	3.2	5.6	4.4	3.5
West Midlands	10.3	16.5	12.7	13.2	*28*	2.0	3.2	2.4	2.5
North West	10.3	15.3	14.4	13.5	*31*	1.6	2.4	2.3	2.1
England	98.9	173.8	151.5	130.1	*32*	2.1	3.7	3.2	2.7
Wales	5.1	9.5	9.1	7.7	*51*	1.8	3.3	3.2	2.7
Scotland	11.0	14.2	16.3	16.5	*50*	2.1	2.8	3.2	3.2
Northern Ireland	3.6	7.5	7.9	6.2	*72*	2.3	4.8	5.0	3.9
Housing associations									
United Kingdom	19.4	12.8	13.6	16.8	*-13*	0.3	0.2	0.2	0.3
North	1.1	0.8	1.0	1.0	*-9*	0.4	0.2	0.3	0.3
Yorkshire & Humberside	1.3	1.4	1.4	1.7	*31*	0.3	0.3	0.3	0.3
East Midlands	1.9	0.9	0.7	0.8	*-58*	0.5	0.2	0.2	0.2
East Anglia	1.0	0.6	0.6	0.4	*-60*	0.5	0.3	0.3	0.2
South East	4.7	2.2	2.7	3.8	*-19*	0.3	0.1	0.2	0.2
Greater London	2.0	1.2	1.5	1.9	*-5*	0.3	0.2	0.2	0.3
Rest of South East	2.7	1.0	1.2	1.9	*-30*	0.3	0.1	0.1	0.2
South West	1.2	0.8	0.8	1.2	*0*	0.3	0.2	0.2	0.3
West Midlands	3.0	1.4	1.2	2.1	*-30*	0.6	0.3	0.2	0.4
North West	2.7	2.0	1.3	2.2	*-19*	0.4	0.3	0.2	0.3
England	16.8	10.1	9.6	13.0	*-23*	0.4	0.2	0.2	0.3
Wales	0.5	0.7	1.6	1.7	*240*	0.2	0.2	0.6	0.6
Scotland	1.9	1.3	1.6	1.4	*-26*	0.4	0.3	0.3	0.3
Northern Ireland	0.1	0.7	0.7	0.5	*400*	0.1	0.4	0.4	0.3
Local authorities, new towns and government departments									
United Kingdom	68.6	21.4	19.2	17.7	*-74*	1.2	0.4	0.3	0.3
North	3.3	0.4	0.4	0.2	*-94*	1.1	0.1	0.1	0.1
Yorkshire & Humberside	5.3	1.1	1.3	0.8	*-85*	1.1	0.2	0.3	0.2
East Midlands	3.6	1.3	0.8	0.9	*-75*	0.9	0.3	0.2	0.2
East Anglia	2.2	0.9	1.2	1.3	*-41*	1.1	0.5	0.6	0.6
South East	23.9	7.6	7.2	7.2	*-70*	1.4	0.4	0.4	0.4
Greater London	13.4	1.4	1.3	1.8	*-87*	2.0	0.2	0.2	0.3
Rest of South East	10.5	6.2	5.8	5.4	*-49*	1.0	0.6	0.5	0.5
South West	2.8	2.0	1.8	1.6	*-43*	0.6	0.4	0.4	0.3
West Midlands	5.2	1.2	1.1	1.1	*-79*	1.0	0.2	0.2	0.2
North West	8.6	1.6	0.9	0.8	*-91*	1.3	0.2	0.1	0.1
England	54.9	16.1	14.6	13.9	*-75*	1.2	0.3	0.3	0.3
Wales	3.5	0.8	0.6	0.6	*-83*	1.3	0.3	0.2	0.2
Scotland	7.1	2.8	2.3	2.0	*-72*	1.4	0.6	0.4	0.4
Northern Ireland	3.1	1.7	1.7	1.3	*-58*	2.0	1.1	1.1	0.8

1 Permanent dwellings only ie those with a life expectancy of 60 years or more.
2 Includes private landlords (persons or companies) and owner-occupiers.

Source: Department of the Environment; Welsh Office; The Scottish Development Department; Department of the Environment, Northern Ireland

4.6 Market value[1] of housing stock

£ billion and percentages

	£ billion at end year			Percentage change		
	1976	1981	1987	1976-1981	1981-1987	1976-1987
United Kingdom	162.6	359.1	830.3	121	131	411
North	6.4	13.0	22.4	103	73	250
Yorkshire & Humberside	11.0	24.0	41.5	119	73	278
East Midlands	9.6	20.8	42.6	117	104	344
East Anglia	5.5	12.2	31.1	123	155	469
South East	67.7	149.8	418.6	121	179	519
Greater London	28.1	61.3	181.7	118	196	546
Rest of South East	39.6	88.5	237.0	124	168	499
South West	14.2	32.9	81.4	131	148	472
West Midlands	13.8	29.9	55.3	117	85	302
North West	15.0	33.5	56.5	123	69	277
England	143.1	316.1	749.5	121	137	424
Wales	6.3	13.9	24.4	119	75	284
Scotland	10.4	23.5	46.7	126	99	349
Northern Ireland	2.8	5.6	9.8	102	73	249

1 Market values are values to owners (with tenants in situ where appropriate).

Source: Central Statistical Office

4.7 Housing land and dwelling prices[1], 1981 and 1990

£ and percentages

	Housing land price per hectare (£)[2,3]		Land price per plot as a percentage of new dwelling price		Average new dwelling price[1]		
					(£)		Percentage change
	1981	1990	1981	1990	1981	1990	1981-1990
United Kingdom	..	..	..	..	28,200	76,700	172
North	76,000	216,100	12	15	24,800	67,500	172
Yorkshire & Humberside	61,700	343,800	9	16	25,300	71,900	184
East Midlands	63,200	377,000	11	27	25,100	69,100	175
East Anglia	69,300	524,100	14	45	26,200	69,100	164
South East	203,600	636,500	22	39	33,100	91,800	177
Greater London	391,100	2,194,500	27	33	35,800	94,700	165
Rest of South East	166,400	568,700	20	44	32,800	91,300	178
South West	80,300	186,400	15	13	27,500	74,000	169
West Midlands	123,000	492,600	17	25	26,200	70,600	169
North West	82,700	321,100	13	21	27,100	79,900	195
England	111,800	354,900	16	23	28,500	78,600	176
Wales	32,000	231,500	7	22	25,800	63,100	145
Scotland	..	..	..	..	27,000	63,300	134

1 Purchased with building society mortgages.
2 Private sector housing land.
3 The figures for 1990 are based on a revised methodology. Figures for 1981 have been revised in order to maintain comparability.
4 Some of the figures on land prices are based on less than 50 transactions and are therefore of limited reliability.

Source: Department of the Environment

4.8 Dwelling prices

Indices and £ thousands

| | Index of dwelling prices[1] 1985 = 100 | | | | | | | Building society borrowers average dwelling price, 1991 (£ thousands) | | |
	1981	1985	1987	1988	1989	1990	1991	All	Excluding LA sitting tenants	First time buyers[2]
United Kingdom	74	100	133	167	202	200	196	62.5	64.3	47.1
North	79	100	118	132	170	193	193	46.0	47.8	34.5
Yorkshire & Humberside	78	100	118	139	194	211	220	52.3	53.7	38.6
East Midlands	74	100	124	159	207	207	203	55.7	56.7	41.7
East Anglia	72	100	139	189	221	197	191	61.1	62.0	46.5
South East	..	..	..	..	..	..	..	80.9	82.5	61.8
Greater London	66	100	152	187	203	199	191	85.7	88.9	69.0
Rest of South East	70	100	144	187	216	198	187	79.0	80.2	58.4
South West	74	100	135	181	219	198	192	65.3	66.1	49.5
West Midlands	81	100	125	167	219	223	224	58.7	60.2	44.7
North West	80	100	117	137	184	212	215	53.2	54.8	39.5
England	73	100	135	172	207	203	199	65.3	66.8	49.6
Wales	77	100	118	142	193	201	197	49.0	50.5	38.3
Scotland	74	100	113	122	144	161	175	48.8	53.1	32.9
Northern Ireland	81	100	114	118	124	131	141	35.4	37.2	26.6

1 This mix adjusted index adjusts for the mix of dwellings (by size, type, region, whether new or second-hand) and excludes those bought at non-market prices.
2 Includes LA sitting tenants.

Source: Department of the Environment

4.9 Building societies: mortgage advances and income of borrowers, 1991

| | All borrowers | | | | First time buyers | |
	Number of loans (thousands)	Average recorded income (£ thousand per annum)	Average percentage of price advanced	Percentage of advances over £30,000	Percentage of all loans	Average deposit (£ thousand)
United Kingdom	697	20.5	70	68	47	8.1
North	38	17.2	73	50	43	5.0
Yorkshire & Humberside	65	17.7	70	57	45	5.9
East Midlands	48	18.3	70	66	47	7.2
East Anglia	27	19.9	69	71	46	7.7
South East	215	24.9	69	84	48	11.4
Greater London	59	27.0	70	85	56	14.2
Rest of South East	156	24.2	68	84	44	10.2
South West	64	20.3	67	75	45	8.9
West Midlands	58	19.0	70	71	48	7.6
North West	75	18.2	72	61	49	5.8
England	590	21.0	69	72	47	8.6
Wales	27	17.8	73	56	55	5.6
Scotland	60	19.0	71	51	43	5.9
Northern Ireland	20	16.4	75	30	54	4.3

Source: Department of the Environment

4.10 Sale of local authority dwellings[1]

Percentages

	Percentage of LA stock sold[2]								
	1982-83	1983-84	1984-85	1985-86	1986-87	1987-88	1988-89	1989-90	1990-91
North	4.8	2.2	1.4	1.3	1.3	1.4	2.3	3.3	2.4
Yorkshire & Humberside	3.5	1.7	1.3	1.3	1.3	1.7	2.6	3.9	2.8
East Midlands	5.1	2.8	1.9	2.0	2.2	2.8	4.1	3.3	1.4
Eastern	4.0	3.4	3.1	2.8	3.0	3.6	5.4	2.8	5.3
South East									
Greater London	2.4	1.8	1.8	1.7	1.7	3.0	3.4	3.8	2.5
Rest of South East	3.9	3.9	3.4	2.9	3.2	4.5	6.1	6.7	7.8
South West	4.1	3.3	2.7	2.4	2.6	3.3	5.1	3.4	2.8
West Midlands	3.8	2.8	1.8	1.3	1.6	2.1	3.3	3.6	1.8
North West	3.8	2.7	1.3	1.3	1.3	1.3	1.9	3.1	2.1
England	3.8	2.6	2.0	1.8	1.9	2.6	3.6	3.8	3.1
Wales	5.2	2.8	2.0	1.9	2.3	2.5	4.4	4.9	2.2
Scotland	2.3	2.8	2.3	2.0	2.0	3.1	4.5	4.7	3.3
Northern Ireland	3.2	3.0	2.9	2.3	2.0	1.6	1.9	2.7	2.4

1 Department of the Environment regions.
2 Includes dwellings transferred to housing associations and private developers.

Source: Department of the Environment; The Scottish Office

4.11 Allocation of local authority housing, 1990-91

Percentages and thousands

	Lettings to new tenants (percentages)					Lettings to tenants transferring or exchanging (percentages)	Total lettings (= 100%) (thousands)
	Displaced through slum clearance	Homeless	Keyworkers and other priorities	Ordinary waiting list	On non-secure tenancies[1]		
North	1	13	3	43	1	39	35
Yorkshire & Humberside	1	14	4	38	3	40	52
East Midlands	1	16	2	36	5	40	31
East Anglia	-	16	4	29	4	47	14
South East:							
Greater London	1	31	3	12	19 [2]	34	65
Rest of South East	-	14	2	25	9 [2]	50	62
South West	-	18	2	27	4	49	27
West Midlands	1	23	5	28	3	40	49
North West	1	13	1	47	1	37	66
England	1	18	3	32	6	40	401
Wales	-	10	2	35	.. [3]	52	24

1 As defined in Schedule 1, *Housing Act 1985*.
2 Mainly homeless.
3 Not separately available - included in other categories.

Source: Department of the Environment; Welsh Office

4.12 Homeless households found accommodation by local authorities: by priority need category[1], 1990

	Priority need category (percentages)							All priority need accept-ances (=100%) (numbers)	Total house-holds[2] accepted (numbers)	Accept-ances per thou-sand house-holds
	Households with depen-dent children	House-hold member pregnant	Household member vulnerable due to:				Home-less in emer-gency			
			Old age	Physical handicap	Mental illness	Other reasons				
Great Britain	65	13	5	3	3	8	3	150,589	164,622	7.5
North	65	14	4	3	1	11	2	8,380	9,310	7.7
Yorkshire & Humberside	73	12	4	2	1	6	2	12,330	13,800	7.0
East Midlands	74	14	4	1	1	4	2	8,910	9,810	6.2
East Anglia	65	15	6	3	2	7	2	3,480	3,550	4.4
South East	64	16	6	4	4	4	2	51,480	54,720	7.9
Greater London	61	17	5	5	6	4	2	33,910	36,480	13.2
Rest of South East	70	14	7	3	2	2	2	17,570	18,240	4.4
South West	72	12	7	2	2	3	2	8,380	8,640	4.7
West Midlands	59	14	5	2	1	17	2	15,900	18,290	9.0
North West	63	9	4	4	5	13	2	19,080	22,230	9.0
England	66	14	5	3	3	7	2	127,940	140,350	7.5
Wales[3]	57	7	4	2	1	2	27	8,384	8,670	8.0
Scotland	67	10	5	2	2	12	2	14,265	15,602	7.8

1 Households for whom local authorities accept responsibility to secure permanent accommodation under the *1977 Housing (Homeless Persons)* and *1985 Housing Act and Housing (Scotland) Act 1987*. Priority need is also defined in the Acts.

2 Includes accepted households who were not in priority need.

3 Data published in *Welsh Housing Statistic*s also include non-priority cases given advice and assistance, which are excluded here for comparability with other regions. Data for previous years also excluded priority cases given advice and assistance. The figures include the estimated 2,000 households made homeless in Colwyn as a result of the major flooding incident in February 1990.

Source: Department of the Environment; Welsh Office; The Scottish Office

Notes for Chapter 4: Housing

Tables 4.1-4.3

A dwelling is defined as structurally separate accommodation whose rooms (excluding bathrooms and WCs) are self-contained. The figures include vacant dwellings and temporary dwellings occupied as a normal place of residence. Estimates of the stock in England are based on data from the 1971 and 1981 censuses. Estimates for Wales and Scotland prior to 1981 are based on the 1971 census data and are not strictly comparable with those for later years, which are based on 1981 census data. Northern Ireland stock figures are based on rating lists and Department of the Environment, Northern Ireland estimates. Estimates of the tenure distribution in Table 4.2 are based on the above estimates and certain assumptions regarding the tenure distribution of gains and losses in the housing stock. Estimates for Table 4.3 of the age distribution of the dwelling stock use data from the census reports from 1851 to 1981 together with assumed rates of new construction and demolition (for periods before these were recorded) and further assumptions about the ages of dwellings lost from the housing stock.

Table 4.5 New dwellings completed

A dwelling is defined for the purposes of this table as a building or any part of a building which forms a separate and self-contained set of premises designed to be occupied by a single family. The figures relate to new permanent dwellings only, ie. dwellings with a life expectancy of 60 years or more. A dwelling is counted as completed when it becomes ready for occupation, whether actually occupied or not. Regional figures for local authority housing are of building by authorities in the region and may include dwellings which are situated outside the region. Details of dwellings provided by local housing authorities in England and Wales outside their own area are published quarterly in *Local Housing Statistics* (HMSO).

Table 4.7 Housing land and new dwelling prices

Information on housing land transactions in England and Wales is supplied to the Department of the Environment by the Valuation Office of the Board of Inland Revenue, to whom all property transactions are reported. District valuers provide information on purchases of land known to be intended for housing. Figures in this table are restricted to purchases by the private sector of sites with planning permission for a known number of units (flats or houses). Sites involving less than four units are excluded. Land prices vary widely, according to the quality of site, distance from amenities etc. As a result, average prices tend to fluctuate, especially in regions where there are relatively few transactions. Thus a large increase in the average price between one year and the next will not necessarily be indicative of long-term trends. Some of this volatility can be smoothed out by calculating a weighted index of prices at constant density. The method of calculation of this index is described in *Economic Trends*, No. 244, February 1974 (HMSO).

Data on new house prices are taken from *The Five per cent Sample Survey of Building Society Mortgages* (see notes to Tables 4.8-4.9).

Tables 4.8-4.9 Building societies

Figures in these tables are taken from *The Five per cent Sample Survey of Building Society Mortgages* at completion stage. Full details of the survey are given in *The Five per cent Sample Survey of Building Society Mortgages, CSO Studies in Official Statistics No. 26 1975 (HMSO)*. The income of borrowers is the total recorded income taken into account when the mortgage is granted, but it should be noted that societies' practices vary. Some record the basic income of the main applicant; others record total income from all sources including that of spouse or other joint applicant(s).

Chapter 5: Education

Pupil teacher ratios

- Scotland has the fewest pupils per teacher. The highest rates are in Wales, Northern Ireland and the North West.

(Table 5.1)

- Although Scotland has the smallest overall pupil teacher ratios, there are more toddlers per nursery school teacher than in any other region.

(Table 5.1)

Class sizes

- Since 1981, secondary school class sizes have fallen in every region except the South East.

(Table 5.9)

Day care

- The South West and East Anglia provide day care for a large proportion of their toddlers, both cater for over a quarter of the under fives.

(Table 5.2)

Staying on after 16

- Scotland has the highest proportion of 16-year-olds continuing their education - over three quarters in 1990/91, much higher than elsewhere in the United Kingdom.

(Table 5.4)

Exam results

- Pupils in Northern Ireland outperform other regions at A level - around one in five get 3 or more A levels. This is despite a relatively high proportion (one in five boys and one in ten girls) who leave without any qualifications at all.

(Table 5.7)

- Very few pupils in the South West, East Anglia and the East Midlands leave school without a qualification.

(Table 5.7)

- Girls are far better at English than boys. In 1989/90, even the poorest performance by girls (in Wales, with half getting a GCSE grade A-C) was better than the best performance by boys.

(Table 5.8)

Adult education

- Women are much more likely to take adult education courses than men. In all regions of England and Wales, more than twice as many women enrol on evening adult education courses.

(Table 5.11)

Undergraduates

- In 1989, over 12 thousand students from the North West were studying in Yorkshire and Humberside, and nearly 15 thousand from the South East studied in the South West. These were the largest movements of students between one region and other.

(Table 5.14)

Spending

- The pattern of education authority spending differs between Northern Ireland and the mainland. For example, a much greater proportion goes on capital expenditure and school meals and milk in Northern Ireland.

(Table 5.17)

5.1 Pupils and teachers: by type of school, January 1991[1]

Thousands and numbers

| | | Public sector schools[2] | | | | | |
| | | Primary schools | Secondary schools[3] | | Non-maintained[5] schools | All special schools | All schools |
	All nursery[4] schools		Total	of which comprehensive			
Pupils (thousands)[6]							
United Kingdom	60.3	4,806.6	3,477.1	2,923.7 [7]	603.7	112.6	9,060.3
North	3.7	270.0	203.5	180.0	17.8	6.0	501.0
Yorkshire & Humberside	2.6	410.7	328.2	267.0	31.6	8.9	782.0
East Midlands	1.6	332.7	255.6	218.3	31.6	6.9	628.4
East Anglia	0.6	157.0	126.0	109.8	23.0	2.6	309.2
South East	10.3	1,338.4	957.8	791.1	286.3	36.5	2,629.3
South West	1.5	349.0	266.1	222.3	65.3	8.2	690.1
West Midlands	5.1	466.2	326.9	290.3	45.4	11.9	855.5
North West	5.8	588.8	389.3	367.5	55.0	15.6	1,054.5
England	31.2	3,912.8	2,853.4	2,446.3	556.0	96.6	7,450.0
Wales	2.4	267.7	185.2	183.7	12.1	3.6	471.0
Scotland	22.9	440.6	293.7	293.7	34.6	8.4	800.2
Northern Ireland	3.8	185.5	144.8	..	1.0	4.0	339.1
Teachers (thousands)[6]							
United Kingdom	2.8	218.9	229.2	195.9 [7]	56.4	19.4	526.9
North	0.2	12.1	13.2	12.0	1.5	0.9	27.9
Yorkshire & Humberside	0.1	18.8	21.3	17.8	2.7	1.6	44.5
East Midlands	0.1	14.8	16.9	14.7	3.0	1.2	36.0
East Anglia	..	7.1	7.9	7.0	2.3	0.4	17.7
South East	0.6	61.2	60.7	51.0	27.0	6.3	155.8
South West	0.1	15.6	16.6	14.0	6.7	1.3	40.3
West Midlands	0.2	20.8	21.3	19.3	4.3	1.9	48.5
North West	0.3	25.8	25.6	24.1	4.3	2.8	58.8
England	1.6	176.2	183.5	160.0	51.8	16.4	429.5
Wales	0.1	12.0	12.0	11.9	1.2	0.6	26.0
Scotland	0.9	22.6	24.0	24.0	3.3	1.8	52.7
Northern Ireland	0.2	8.1	9.7	..	0.1	0.6	18.7
Pupils per teacher							
United Kingdom	21.5	22.0	15.2	14.9 [7]	10.7	5.8	17.2
North	19.6	22.3	15.4	15.1	11.6	6.0	17.8
Yorkshire & Humberside	18.4	21.9	15.4	15.0	11.6	5.7	17.6
East Midlands	19.1	22.4	15.1	14.8	10.6	5.7	17.4
East Anglia	19.1	22.3	16.0	15.6	10.2	6.1	17.5
South East	17.6	21.9	15.8	15.6	10.6	5.8	16.9
South West	19.4	22.4	16.0	15.9	9.8	6.4	17.1
West Midlands	24.0	22.4	15.3	15.1	10.6	6.3	17.6
North West	19.1	22.9	15.2	15.2	12.9	5.6	18.0
England	19.1	22.2	15.5	15.3	10.8	5.9	17.3
Wales	20.6	22.3	15.4	15.4	9.8	6.3	18.2
Scotland	25.7	19.5	12.2	12.2	10.4	4.5	15.2
Northern Ireland	24.7	22.8	14.9	..	11.0	6.9	18.1

1 September 1990 for Scotland.
2 For Northern Ireland, all grant-aided schools, including voluntary grammar schools funded by the Department of Education, Northern Ireland.
3 Includes 50 grant maintained schools in England from January 1991.
4 Public sector only for Wales, Scotland and Northern Ireland.
5 Includes assisted schools in Scotland and independent schools in Northern Ireland.
6 Full-time equivalents.
7 Great Britain only.

Source: Department of Education and Science; Welsh Office; The Scottish Office Education Department; Department of Education, Northern Ireland

5.2 Education and day care of children under five: by age and type of day care, 1990

	Under fives in maintained schools[1]				Local authority provided and registered day-care places,[2] March			
	As percentage of population in age group			Total (thousands)	Day nurseries (thousands)	Child-minders (thousands)	Play-groups (thousands)	Total per 100 pop. aged under 5 years
	Aged 2	Aged 3	Aged 4					
United Kingdom	..	*34.2*	*74.8*	695.1	94.4	238.4	493.8	21.7
North	..	..	..	56.7	3.2	10.1	18.8	16.1
Yorkshire & Humberside	..	..	..	76.3	7.9	17.2	35.8	18.6
East Midlands	..	..	..	50.7	6.1	16.4	34.4	21.7
East Anglia	..	..	..	18.1	2.7	9.9	21.7	25.8
South East	..	..	..	156.6	34.3	83.2	162.6	24.1
South West	..	..	..	38.2	5.0	19.8	49.7	26.3
West Midlands	..	..	..	75.6	10.2	20.8	44.1	21.3
North West	..	..	..	105.0	16.2	28.2	44.6	20.4
England	*4.2*	*36.0*	*78.1*	577.2	85.6	205.6	411.6	22.3
Wales	*4.9*	*45.3*	*87.3*	51.6	2.9	9.0	23.6	18.7
Scotland	*0.3*	*18.0*	*46.7*	42.0	5.2 [3]	14.0	44.1	19.4
Northern Ireland	..	*15.4*	*73.7*	24.4	0.7	9.8	14.6	18.4

1 Data at January 1990, ages at 31 August 1989 for England. Data at January 1990, ages at 31 December 1989 for Wales. Data at September 1989, ages at 31 December 1989 for Scotland. Data at January 1991, ages at 31 December 1990 for Northern Ireland.
2 Figures for a few authorities in England have been estimated using the latest available data. Day-care figures for Northern Ireland are the average number of available places during year ending 31 March 1990.
3 Local authority provision only.

Source: Department of Education and Science; Department of Health; Welsh Office; Department of Health and Social Services, Northern Ireland; The Scottish Office Social Work Services Group

5.3 School leavers: by sex and age[1], 1981/82 and 1989/90

Thousands

	Males				Females			
	Aged 15	Aged 16	Aged 17+	All leavers	Aged 15	Aged 16	Aged 17+	All leavers
1981/82								
Great Britain	315.0	53.3	82.7	451.0	291.2	63.3	79.5	434.0
North	19.6	2.0	4.5	26.1	18.4	2.6	4.6	25.6
Yorkshire & Humberside	29.9	3.4	7.5	40.8	27.5	5.0	7.0	39.5
East Midlands	23.2	2.5	5.6	31.3	22.4	2.9	5.3	30.6
East Anglia	11.0	1.4	2.7	15.1	9.9	1.8	2.3	14.0
South East	80.8	19.7	31.7	132.2	74.4	23.8	30.4	128.6
South West	24.7	3.7	7.2	35.6	23.4	4.0	6.7	34.1
West Midlands	33.4	3.9	8.2	45.5	31.0	4.5	7.4	42.9
North West	41.3	4.0	10.2	55.5	38.2	5.2	10.4	53.8
England	263.9	40.7	77.6	382.2	245.2	49.7	74.0	368.9
Wales	15.3	3.6	4.2	23.1	13.3	4.1	4.8	22.1
Scotland	35.7	9.0	0.9	45.7	32.7	9.6	0.7	42.9
1989/90								
Great Britain	219.4	42.4	88.0	349.8	196.7	46.0	89.2	331.9
North	14.1	1.7	4.4	20.2	12.9	1.6	4.9	19.5
Yorkshire & Humberside	21.2	3.5	7.1	31.8	18.6	3.7	6.9	29.2
East Midlands	16.8	2.4	5.9	25.1	15.7	2.2	6.5	24.4
East Anglia	8.3	1.2	3.2	12.7	7.4	1.3	3.3	12.0
South East	55.9	13.3	30.3	99.6	51.7	14.4	29.8	95.8
South West	19.1	2.6	7.6	29.2	17.7	2.7	7.5	27.8
West Midlands	24.2	3.1	8.7	35.9	22.5	3.2	8.1	33.8
North West	28.0	3.7	10.0	41.8	24.7	4.1	10.6	39.4
England	187.5	31.5	77.2	296.2	171.2	33.1	77.6	281.9
Wales[2]	12.4	1.9	4.2	18.5	10.3	2.3	4.6	17.2
Scotland	19.5	9.0	6.6	35.1	15.2	10.6	7.0	32.8

1 Ages at 31 August 1981 and 31 August 1989 respectively for England and Wales. Ages at 31 December 1981 and 31 August 1989 respectively for Scotland.
2 Includes leavers from maintained and independent schools, but not special schools.

Source: Department of Education and Science; Welsh Office; The Scottish Office Education Department

5.4 16 year-olds[1] staying on at school or going to further education, 1981/82 and 1990/91

Thousands and percentages

| | 1981/82 | | | | | 1990/91 | | | | |
	Total (thousands)	Participation in education[2] (percentage)	Staying on at school[2] (thousands)	Going to further education[3] (thousands)		Total (thousands)	Participation in education[2] (percentage)	Staying on at school[2] (thousands)	Going to further education[3] (thousands)	
				Full-time	Part-time[4]				Full-time	Part-time[4]
Region of residence										
Great Britain	..	..	..	..	..	701.2	65.4	233.4	145.7	79.4
North	51.0	51.5	12.1	8.3	5.9	38.2	61.1	10.9	7.3	5.2
Yorkshire & Humberside	78.6	53.8	20.6	13.3	8.4	62.2	63.8	18.7	13.2	7.8
East Midlands	60.6	54.6	14.8	12.2	6.1	50.1	67.7	15.6	11.5	6.8
East Anglia	27.1	50.6	6.9	4.8	2.1	26.4	61.9	8.3	5.2	2.9
South East	243.4	60.8	87.6	42.1	18.3	214.2	63.0	73.1	44.1	17.8
South West	63.2	57.3	17.0	13.7	5.6	59.9	63.0	16.0	15.1	6.7
West Midlands	84.1	55.6	20.9	19.0	6.8	67.6	64.0	19.5	15.1	8.7
North West	105.0	56.7	25.5	21.4	12.6	78.8	66.1	22.8	19.0	10.3
England	713.0	56.9	205.3	134.8	65.7	597.4	63.8	184.8	130.4	66.1
Wales	47.8	58.1	15.1	8.3	4.4	37.2	68.4	13.5	8.9	3.1
Scotland	..	..	..	..	..	66.6	77.7	35.1	6.4	10.2

1 Age at 31 August 1981 and 31 August 1990 for England and Wales, at 31 December 1990 for Scotland.
2 Enrolments at 1 January 1982 and 1 January 1991 respectively for England and Wales. January 1991 estimate for Scotland, excluding privately funded pupils in independent schools and students in tertiary college.
3 Enrolments at 1 November 1981 and 1 November 1990 respectively for England and Wales, at Autumn 1990 for Scotland, plus an estimate for Christmas leavers entering further education. Iincluding students in tertiary colleges.
4 Excludes evening only.

Source: Department of Education and Science; Welsh Office; The Scottish Office Education Department

5.5 School leavers intended destinations, 1981/82 and 1989/90

Percentages and thousands

| | Full-time higher and further education | | | | Employment[1] | | Destination not known | Total leavers (= 100%) (thousands) |
	Degree courses	Teacher training	Other courses	Total	Without qualifications[2]	Total		
1981/82								
North	7.2	0.4	14.4	21.9	9.7	69.1	9.0	51.6
Yorkshire & Humberside	7.6	0.7	16.3	24.6	10.5	67.1	8.3	80.4
East Midlands	7.6	0.4	20.4	28.4	7.9	61.5	10.1	61.9
East Anglia	6.9	0.5	20.5	28.0	8.2	62.9	9.2	29.1
South East	8.6	0.4	20.0	29.0	7.3	59.0	11.9	260.8
South West	7.9	0.3	25.5	33.7	6.5	58.1	8.2	69.7
West Midlands	7.2	0.5	21.6	29.3	10.4	60.0	10.7	88.4
North West	8.5	0.4	18.2	27.1	9.9	60.2	12.7	109.3
England	8.0	0.4	19.7	28.2	8.6	61.1	10.7	751.1
Wales[3]	8.0	1.0	20.0	29.0	19.0	58.0	13.0	45.2
1989/90								
North	10.2	0.9	19.7	30.8	9.2	49.6	19.5	39.7
Yorkshire & Humberside	10.5	0.7	22.6	33.9	8.5	49.1	17.1	61.0
East Midlands	11.5	0.7	23.7	35.9	6.4	46.3	17.8	49.5
East Anglia	9.6	0.6	22.2	32.5	6.2	48.8	18.8	24.6
South East	13.6	0.5	25.4	39.6	7.5	42.9	17.6	195.4
South West	11.8	0.6	31.0	43.4	4.6	42.3	14.3	57.1
West Midlands	11.0	0.6	24.0	35.6	8.1	48.3	16.2	69.7
North West	12.5	0.5	24.0	37.0	9.5	46.6	16.4	81.2
England	12.1	0.6	24.6	37.3	7.6	45.7	17.1	578.1
Wales[3]	11.5	1.5	26.7	39.7	13.7	39.9	20.4	35.7

1 Includes temporary employment pending entry into full-time further education.
2 Without GSCE grades A-G or the GCE/CSE equivalent.
3 Includes leavers from independent schools

Source: Department of Education and Science; Welsh Office

5.6 School leavers[1] actual destinations: Scotland, 1991

Percentages and thousands

	Full-time education	Full-time employment	YTS	Unemployed	Other/ destination unknown	All leavers (= 100%) (thousands)
Leavers with qualifications	32.2	30.4	24.2	7.4	5.8	60.4
Leavers without qualifications[2]	5.6	36.1	33.0	18.9	6.4	7.5
All leavers	29.3	31.0	25.2	8.6	5.9	67.9

1 Leavers from 1989/90.
2 With no SCE O grades 4-5 or equivalent.

Source: The Scottish Office Education Department

5.7 School leavers' examination achievements[1]: by sex, 1989/90

Percentages and thousands

	A levels[3] (or SCE highers)			GCSEs[2] or SCE O/standard (no A levels/SCE highers)				
				Grades A-C[4]		Grades D-G only[6]	No graded	All leavers (= 100%)
	3+ (5+)	2 (3-4)	1 (1-2)	5+[5]	1-4	1+	results[7]	(thousands)
Males								
North	11.0	4.0	3.6	10.4	26.4	34.9	9.8	20.2
Yorkshire & Humberside	13.3	3.9	2.2	11.2	23.8	35.8	9.9	31.8
East Midlands	13.1	4.3	3.9	9.1	26.3	35.6	7.7	25.1
East Anglia	13.6	5.1	3.7	11.9	27.4	30.9	7.4	12.7
South East	16.8	6.4	4.3	11.9	26.7	25.2	8.7	99.6
South West	13.7	5.9	4.2	14.2	27.7	29.0	5.4	29.3
West Midlands	12.9	4.6	3.4	10.3	25.4	34.0	9.4	35.9
North West	15.1	3.6	2.5	12.9	25.2	29.6	11.1	41.8
England	14.6	5.1	3.6	11.6	26.1	30.2	8.8	296.2
Wales[8]	10.1	5.3	4.4	11.8	23.5	28.3	16.6	18.5
Scotland	12.7	10.6	11.0	7.9	23.7	21.8	12.2	35.1
Northern Ireland	17.2	6.1	3.4	9.9	23.8	20.1	19.6 [9]	12.5
Females								
North	12.0	5.8	3.7	14.8	26.9	28.3	8.5	19.5
Yorkshire & Humberside	12.5	4.4	3.2	15.1	28.3	29.5	7.0	29.2
East Midlands	13.5	6.2	3.4	14.3	28.9	28.6	5.1	24.4
East Anglia	15.4	6.4	4.1	18.1	29.0	22.1	5.0	12.0
South East	16.9	7.1	4.3	16.2	28.9	20.5	6.2	95.8
South West	15.2	6.6	3.7	20.6	29.0	21.1	3.9	27.8
West Midlands	12.1	4.8	3.6	15.0	29.7	27.9	6.8	33.8
North West	14.3	4.9	3.8	18.2	28.2	22.7	7.9	39.4
England	14.6	6.0	3.9	16.5	28.7	24.0	6.4	281.9
Wales[8]	12.3	7.3	4.4	13.0	25.9	25.4	11.7	17.2
Scotland	14.6	13.5	15.2	6.9	25.4	15.6	8.9	32.8
Northern Ireland	21.4	7.9	4.1	12.8	25.8	17.1	10.9 [9]	12.0

1 Excludes results in further education.
2 And equivalent grades at GCE and CSE.
3 Two AS levels are counted as equivalent to one A level.
4 Includes GCSE grades A-C, SCE O grades A-C/1-3, SCE standard grades 1-3.
5 Includes leavers with 1 AS level.
6 Includes GCSE grades D-G, SCE O grades D-E/4-5, SCE standard grades 4-7.
7 Includes those pupils with no graded results in GCSE, SCE or A/AS levels. Leavers sitting other examinations (eg Certificate of Education etc) are excluded.
8 Includes leavers from Independent Schools.
9 Includes those who obtained other qualifications such as RSA, BTEC, City and Guilds.

Source: Department of Education and Science; Welsh Office; The Scottish Office Education Department; Department of Education, Northern Ireland

5.8 Percentage of school leavers with GCSE grades[1] A-C: by selected subjects and sex, 1989/90

Percentages and thousands

	English	Mathe-matics[2]	Physics	Geog-raphy	Chemi-stry	History	Biology	Single/ Dual Science	Other Science	Craft Design Tech-nology	French	Total school leavers (thou-sands)
Males												
Great Britain	42.2	37.9	23.0	21.2	18.3	15.3	13.0	..	2.1	..	15.0	349.8
North	35.3	33.9	20.8	20.4	18.3	12.0	10.8	4.6	2.2	17.7	10.7	20.2
Yorkshire & Humberside	37.6	36.0	21.8	19.9	18.9	14.5	11.7	5.0	1.8	17.4	13.2	31.8
East Midlands	37.2	33.5	21.3	18.7	16.2	13.2	11.5	6.0	2.3	14.7	11.8	25.1
East Anglia	37.3	36.2	13.7	19.7	10.8	14.3	8.5	21.5	1.6	20.3	13.9	12.7
South East												
Greater London	41.9	35.3	19.6	16.2	15.4	13.7	12.2	7.1	1.6	17.0	15.0	34.5
Rest of South East	49.4	45.1	24.4	24.3	18.9	18.7	15.7	12.9	2.3	18.8	20.6	65.0
South West	44.3	41.5	24.1	23.9	18.3	17.4	15.1	13.0	4.0	20.3	18.3	29.3
West Midlands	39.3	34.4	22.8	18.8	15.8	14.5	11.8	3.0	2.5	14.0	12.6	35.9
North West	42.7	37.7	24.5	21.8	20.2	16.5	13.0	3.3	1.8	16.1	15.4	41.8
England	42.1	38.1	22.4	20.9	17.6	15.6	12.9	8.1	2.2	17.3	15.5	296.2
Wales	32.8	35.8	20.8	18.9	14.7	11.4	12.4	4.0	2.1	19.7	9.6	18.5
Scotland	47.6	37.0	28.8	25.3	26.0	14.5	14.5	..	1.2	..	15.3	35.1
Females												
Great Britain	56.4	35.6	11.0	17.7	14.6	18.2	20.7	..	1.7	..	24.8	331.9
North	50.5	33.3	10.1	16.9	14.8	17.6	18.7	4.0	1.3	2.8	20.3	19.5
Yorkshire & Humberside	51.1	30.9	8.0	14.7	13.3	17.0	17.1	6.1	1.2	3.1	22.2	29.2
East Midlands	54.1	30.8	9.4	16.7	12.1	16.7	17.1	7.5	1.4	4.2	21.4	24.4
East Anglia	54.6	35.4	7.1	21.4	9.4	17.5	14.1	22.3	2.8	4.8	25.3	12.0
South East												
Greater London	54.1	34.1	11.2	16.0	14.5	17.3	18.9	6.6	1.6	3.5	22.8	31.9
Rest of South East	62.2	40.6	11.7	21.3	14.6	20.0	22.2	12.5	1.6	3.8	29.2	63.9
South West	59.8	39.6	10.4	20.3	13.8	19.5	21.1	13.3	3.9	4.8	28.5	27.8
West Midlands	52.0	28.3	9.5	14.2	12.0	17.4	19.9	3.0	1.7	3.2	21.2	33.8
North West	57.4	35.4	11.3	16.4	15.7	18.6	21.7	4.8	1.3	3.2	24.6	39.4
England	56.2	35.0	10.3	17.7	13.8	18.3	19.8	8.4	1.8	3.6	24.6	281.9
Wales	49.8	33.0	9.4	14.9	11.8	15.9	19.6	3.0	1.7	4.7	20.7	17.2
Scotland	62.0	42.1	18.1	19.0	23.4	18.8	28.7	..	1.0	..	29.0	32.8

1 And equivalent grades at O level A-C, CSE 1, SCE ordinary A-C/1-3 or SCE standard 1-3.
2 Excluding Computer Studies (England).

Source: Department of Education and Science; Welsh Office; The Scottish Office Education Department

5.9 Size of class[1]: by type of school, 1981 and 1991[2]

Numbers

	One teacher classes				All classes[3]			
	Primary		Secondary[4]		Primary		Secondary[4]	
	1981	1991	1981	1991	1981	1991	1981	1991
Great Britain	..	..	..	..	..	26.3	..	19.6
North	24.1	25.9	20.5	20.0	24.7	26.4	21.2	20.9
Yorkshire & Humberside	24.7	25.9	21.3	20.3	25.1	26.4	21.9	20.9
East Midlands	26.0	26.1	21.2	20.0	26.3	26.5	22.0	20.7
East Anglia	24.5	25.5	21.0	20.5	24.9	26.0	22.2	21.3
South East	25.0	26.3	20.5	20.5	25.3	26.7	21.1	21.2
Greater London	23.1	25.8	19.6	20.6	23.5	26.2	20.2	21.2
Rest of South East	26.2	26.6	21.1	20.5	26.6	27.0	21.8	21.1
South West	26.1	26.4	21.7	20.8	26.4	26.7	22.2	21.3
West Midlands	25.1	26.3	20.8	20.3	25.4	26.8	21.3	20.8
North West	26.0	27.2	20.7	20.1	26.2	27.6	21.4	20.8
England	25.2	26.3	20.8	20.3	25.5	26.8	21.5	21.0
Wales	..	..	..	19.5	..	23.1	..	19.2
Scotland	..	..	..	..	23.8	24.7	19.9	18.5

1 Average size of class; maintained schools only.
2 At January 1991 for England, September 1990 for Wales and September 1989 for Scotland.
3 Includes classes where more than one teacher may be present.
4 Includes 50 grant maintained schools in England as at January 1991.

Source: Department of Education and Science; Welsh Office; The Scottish Office Education Department

5.10 Primary and secondary schools in the public sector: by size, 1990/91

Percentages and numbers

	Number of pupils on the register (percentages)								Total number of schools
	Primary schools[1]				Secondary schools[2,3]				
	50 and under	51-100	101-200	201 and over	400 and under	401-800	801-1,000	Over 1,000	(= 100%) (numbers)
United Kingdom	7.9	11.0	27.4	37.1	2.6	7.6	3.2	3.2	28,936
North	6.7	10.6	30.1	34.6	3.8	8.1	2.7	3.3	1,663
Yorkshire & Humberside	5.9	10.2	31.1	33.0	5.9	7.6	2.7	3.5	2,573
East Midlands	8.5	13.4	28.8	32.0	3.0	8.5	2.6	3.2	2,138
East Anglia	10.7	18.3	26.1	28.7	2.4	8.4	2.3	3.1	1,102
South East									
Greater London	..	1.1	28.9	52.7	1.0	8.1	4.6	3.6	2,488
Rest of South East	4.9	11.2	30.7	36.3	2.0	7.9	3.7	3.1	4,912
South West	11.2	18.2	26.5	29.6	1.9	6.3	2.7	3.6	2,403
West Midlands	5.4	8.7	24.2	44.1	2.0	9.3	3.4	3.0	2,553
North West	2.6	5.7	29.9	46.0	0.8	7.6	3.9	3.3	3,112
England	5.6	10.2	28.8	38.3	2.4	7.9	3.3	3.3	22,944
Wales	14.1	15.6	29.7	28.8	0.9	5.4	2.5	3.0	1,947
Scotland	19.3	10.9	18.7	35.8	3.3	6.2	2.8	3.0	2,807
Northern Ireland	14.7	19.3	17.4	29.3	6.1	9.1	2.4	1.7	1,238

1 Includes preparatory departments of grammar schools in Northern Ireland.
2 Includes 50 grant maintained schools in England from January 1991.
3 For Northern Ireland, all grant-aided schools, including voluntary grammar schools funded by the Department of Education, Northern Ireland.

Source: Department of Education and Science; Welsh Office;The Scottish Office Education Department; Department of Education, Northern Ireland

5.11 Enrolments on adult education courses[1]: by age[2] and sex, 1990/91

Thousands

	Persons aged 16-18		Persons aged 19 and over		All persons aged 16 and over		
	Males	Females	Males	Females	Males	Females	Total
Part-time day							
North	0.2	0.2	2.2	12.0	2.3	12.2	14.6
Yorkshire & Humberside	0.6	0.8	6.1	24.6	6.6	25.3	32.0
East Midlands	0.6	0.9	4.1	22.3	4.7	23.2	27.9
East Anglia	0.2	0.3	2.0	11.7	2.2	12.0	14.2
South East	1.6	3.3	52.6	223.9	54.2	227.2	281.5
Greater London	0.6	1.2	30.0	115.2	30.6	116.4	146.9
Rest of South East	1.0	2.1	22.7	108.7	23.7	110.8	134.5
South West	0.3	0.6	5.3	26.5	5.7	27.0	32.7
West Midlands	0.2	0.4	6.2	25.8	6.4	26.2	32.6
North West	0.1	0.2	5.5	21.8	5.6	22.0	27.5
England	3.7	6.6	84.0	368.5	87.7	375.2	462.9
Wales	0.2	0.3	3.9	13.8	4.1	14.0	18.2
Evening only							
North	0.8	1.8	13.6	37.2	14.4	39.0	53.4
Yorkshire & Humberside	1.6	2.8	15.8	36.0	17.4	38.8	56.2
East Midlands	3.1	5.5	19.9	50.4	23.0	55.9	78.9
East Anglia	0.7	1.3	11.9	32.1	12.5	33.3	45.9
South East	4.2	8.4	125.8	287.5	130.0	295.9	425.9
Greater London	1.2	2.3	56.6	124.8	57.8	127.1	184.8
Rest of South East	3.0	6.1	69.2	162.7	72.2	168.9	241.1
South West	1.0	2.2	19.1	49.6	20.1	51.8	71.9
West Midlands	2.4	4.0	21.5	48.4	23.9	52.4	76.3
North West	2.3	3.3	16.9	37.9	19.2	41.2	60.4
England	16.1	29.3	244.4	579.1	260.5	608.4	868.9
Wales	1.2	2.1	13.4	33.2	14.7	35.2	49.9

1 Courses at Adult Education Centres only. Excludes youth clubs, youth centres and courses run by responsible bodies.
2 Age at 31 August 1990.

Source: Department of Education and Science; Welsh Office

5.12 Females as a percentage of all students in public sector and grant-aided establishments of further and higher education, 1981 and 1990

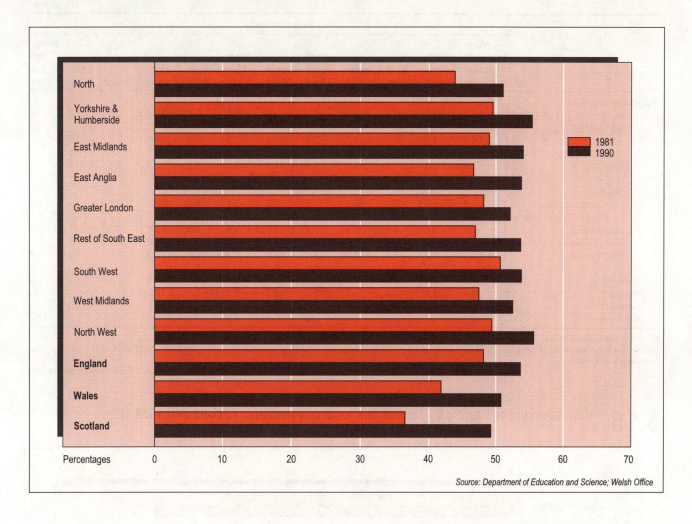

Source: Department of Education and Science; Welsh Office

5.13 New awards[1] to students made at the mandatory rate, 1989/90

Thousands and rates[2]

	At universities		At polytechnics and colleges		Total	
	(thousands)	(rate)	(thousands)	(rate)	(thousands)	(rate)
Great Britain	82.3	97	125.4	148	207.7	246
North	3.5	76	6.2	132	9.7	208
Yorkshire & Humberside	5.9	78	10.4	137	16.3	215
East Midlands	5.1	83	8.2	134	13.3	218
East Anglia	2.8	87	3.2	101	6.0	188
South East						
Greater London	10.9	122	19.0	213	29.9	334
Rest of South East	17.7	105	20.2	120	37.9	226
South West	6.9	98	9.5	135	16.5	234
West Midlands	6.7	81	11.8	143	18.5	224
North West	7.6	78	16.4	169	24.0	247
England	67.1	93	104.9	145	172.0	238
Wales	4.9	109	6.7	150	11.6	259
Scotland[3]	10.3	132	13.8	177	24.1	309

1 Includes mandatory awards, Section 1 (6) awards and Section 2 awards paid at the mandatory rate.
2 The rate is the number of new awards holders per thousand of the relevant age group.
3 The Scottish awards system is not directly comparable with the system in England and Wales.

Source: Department of Education and Science; The Scottish Office Education Department

5.14 Undergraduate students[1]: by region of study and domicile, 1989

Thousands

	Region of study												
	North	York-shire & Humber-side	East Mid-lands	East Anglia	Greater London	Rest of South East	South West	West Mid-lands	North West	Eng-land	Wales	Scot-land[2]	North-ern Ire-land[3]
Region of domicile													
North	9.7	4.4	1.7	0.5	1.8	1.5	0.6	1.5	3.9	25.4	0.5	1.0	-
Yorkshire & Humberside	4.7	16.7	4.2	0.9	3.1	2.8	1.2	3.5	6.3	43.4	1.0	1.0	-
East Midlands	2.2	6.6	8.5	0.9	3.8	3.7	1.7	3.9	4.1	35.3	1.0	0.5	-
East Anglia	0.9	2.0	1.8	1.9	2.8	3.4	1.1	1.3	1.2	16.3	0.5	0.4	-
South East													
Greater London	1.5	3.6	2.6	2.2	39.4	11.3	3.6	3.4	4.4	72.1	1.8	1.3	0.1
Rest of South East	3.5	8.1	7.2	4.2	24.4	33.5	11.0	8.2	7.2	107.2	4.7	2.4	0.1
South West	1.1	2.7	2.5	1.1	6.9	9.1	12.8	3.6	2.8	42.6	3.5	0.7	0.1
West Midlands	1.8	5.4	4.6	0.9	4.8	5.2	3.6	15.5	6.2	48.0	2.8	0.7	0.1
North West	4.1	12.1	4.3	1.2	4.4	4.1	2.1	5.8	26.6	64.5	2.3	1.5	0.1
England	29.4	61.5	37.4	13.8	91.2	74.6	37.6	46.5	62.7	454.8	18.1	11.3	0.6
Wales	0.5	1.5	1.4	0.4	2.7	3.0	2.7	2.3	2.7	17.2	13.0	0.3	-
Scotland	0.7	0.5	0.2	0.3	0.7	0.8	0.4	0.3	0.7	4.6	0.2	61.0	0.1
N. Ireland	0.7	0.7	0.5	0.3	0.9	0.9	0.4	0.6	1.6	6.5	0.3	2.1	13.2

1 Full-time and sandwich course students. Excludes 2,346 students whose place of residence was not known.
2 The region of domicile is not known for students from England studying in Scotland. Therefore, they are shown only in the England total.
3 University students only.

Source: Department of Education and Science; Welsh Office; The Scottish Office Education Department

5.15 Education expenditure[1]: by central and local government, 1981-82 and 1989-90

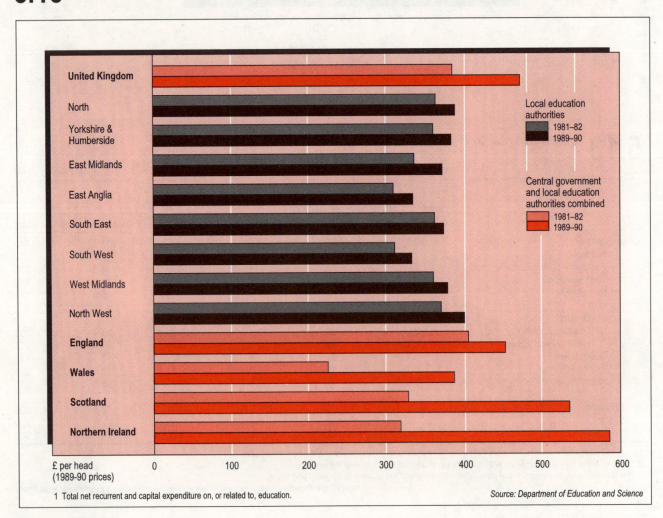

Local education authorities
1981–82
1989–90

Central government and local education authorities combined
1981–82
1989–90

£ per head (1989-90 prices)

0   100   200   300   400   500   600

1 Total net recurrent and capital expenditure on, or related to, education.

Source: Department of Education and Science

5.16 Home students studying in English public sector and grant-aided establishments of further and higher education[1]: by sex and region of residence, 1981[2] and 1990[2]

Thousands

	Full-time sandwich courses		Part-time day students		Evening only		All students	
	Males	Females	Males	Females	Males	Females	Males	Females
Region of residence								
1981								
United Kingdom	237.9	267.5	434.9	230.7	221.1	331.2	893.7	829.4
North	14.3	15.4	32.1	13.3	11.0	16.5	57.4	45.1
Yorkshire & Humberside	23.0	25.5	51.0	28.9	23.5	41.5	97.4	95.9
East Midlands	18.4	21.4	37.2	19.0	19.5	32.2	75.1	72.6
East Anglia	7.5	8.6	14.1	4.7	7.0	11.8	28.7	25.2
South East								
Greater London	34.2	39.1	56.1	34.4	39.4	47.1	129.7	120.6
Rest of South East	48.6	56.2	91.8	46.0	43.5	61.0	183.9	163.1
South West	20.5	23.8	35.1	19.5	19.0	35.1	74.6	78.4
West Midlands	26.9	31.9	49.2	23.4	26.4	37.6	102.5	92.8
North West	34.6	39.3	67.0	40.6	31.2	50.0	132.7	129.9
England[3]	232.7	263.4	433.6	230.5	221.0	331.2	887.3	825.0
Wales	3.8	3.2	1.1	0.2	0.1	0.1	4.9	3.5
Scotland	1.4	0.9	0.2	-	-	-	1.6	0.9
1990								
United Kingdom	342.5	378.3	440.4	421.0	287.2	444.5	1,070.2	1,243.8
North	18.5	20.1	28.5	22.1	16.7	26.3	63.7	68.4
Yorkshire & Humberside	33.6	35.6	50.1	56.4	29.7	50.0	113.4	142.0
East Midlands	26.1	30.4	39.2	37.7	23.6	37.6	88.9	105.8
East Anglia	10.6	12.5	16.0	12.3	10.1	16.8	36.7	41.6
South East								
Greater London	48.8	54.9	52.5	52.6	39.4	52.3	140.6	159.7
Rest of South East	65.7	72.9	85.6	77.1	58.0	89.6	209.4	239.5
South West	31.5	35.1	39.8	37.9	31.2	46.1	102.5	119.0
West Midlands	35.4	40.8	56.4	49.1	36.8	55.9	128.5	145.7
North West	46.8	56.2	68.8	72.1	40.2	68.5	155.8	196.8
England[3]	335.1	371.7	438.6	419.9	286.5	444.1	1,060.1	1,235.8
Wales	5.9	5.2	1.5	0.9	0.5	0.3	7.8	6.4
Scotland	1.6	1.4	0.4	0.1	0.3	0.1	2.2	1.7

1 Excludes students in adult education centres.
2 At November.
3 Includes home students whose place of residence was Northern Ireland, unknown or unclassified.

Source: Department of Education and Science

5.17 Local education authority expenditure, 1989-90

Percentages and £ million

	Nursery and primary schools	Second-ary schools	Special schools	Higher & further educ-ation[1]	Admin-istration & inspe-ction	Other educat-ional services[2]	School meals and milk	Capital expend-iture	Total[3] (= 100%) (£ million)
United Kingdom	29.0	33.5	5.4	17.6	4.7	3.1	2.4	4.2	19,935.6
North	29.8	34.7	5.0	15.5	4.6	2.6	3.3	4.5	1,111.8
Yorkshire & Humberside	29.1	34.2	4.8	17.8	4.1	2.7	2.7	4.6	1,758.7
East Midlands	29.0	36.6	5.0	17.5	3.4	2.1	2.7	3.6	1,383.4
East Anglia	29.3	36.9	4.9	17.7	3.7	1.4	0.4	5.7	635.9
South East	28.3	31.8	6.4	18.5	6.3	2.3	2.0	4.4	6,047.1
South West	27.7	33.6	5.6	19.7	4.5	2.7	2.1	4.1	1,437.7
West Midlands	29.6	34.2	5.4	17.2	4.6	2.6	2.3	4.0	1,838.7
North West	28.5	32.5	6.0	18.8	3.9	2.9	2.7	4.7	2,378.3
England	28.7	33.4	5.7	18.1	4.9	2.5	2.3	4.4	16,591.5
Wales	31.4	33.1	3.2	21.2	3.8	4.5	2.6	0.1	1,027.5
Scotland	32.1	37.4	4.7	10.5	3.0	6.1	2.6	3.7	2,011.0
Northern Ireland	15.6	17.0	3.1	23.2	9.7	12.1	7.3	12.0	305.6

1 Includes awards (fees and maintenance exclusive of parental contributions) to students normally resident within local authority areas prior to going to universities, polytechnics and colleges.
2 Includes school welfare, youth service, transport of pupils and miscellaneous.
3 Excludes loan charges.

Source: Department of Education and Science

Notes to Chapter 5: Education

Table 5.1 Pupils and teachers by type of school

The pupils per teacher ratios take account of full-time teachers and full-time equivalents of part-time teachers. In England and Wales qualified teachers only are included for public sector, nursery and special schools. In Scotland and Northern Ireland all teachers employed in schools, other than in independent schools, are required to be qualified. Part-time pupils are counted as halves except in Scotland where full time equivalence is recorded.

School classifications

Schools are generally classified according to the ages for which they cater, or the type of education they provide. Nursery schools are for children below compulsory age; primary schools consist of infants' schools (for children up to age 7) and junior schools (for children aged 5-11). The norm in Scotland is 7 years of primary education as against 6 years in England, Wales and Northern Ireland. Special schools, both day and boarding, provide education for children with special educational needs who cannot be educated satisfactorily in an ordinary school. Hospital special schools provide education for children spending a period in hospital.

United Kingdom educational establishments may be administered and financed in one of four different ways:

1. Local education authorities are responsible, with the assistance of rate support grant (payable by central government), for financing public sector schools and departments. These cover 'Maintained' in England and Wales, 'Education Authority' in Scotland and 'Controlled' in Northern Ireland. 'Aided' schools in England and Wales receive a grant of eighty five per cent on the governors approved expenditure from central government for capital expenditure on buildings; the running costs are financed by local educational authorities but the schools have a certain amount of autonomy.

2. Assisted schools and departments which are classified as 'Grant-aided' in Scotland and 'Voluntary Grammar' in Northern Ireland are administered and financed by governing bodies which have a substantial degree of autonomy but which receive a grant direct from central government sources. Voluntary Grammar school pupils account for about twenty nine per cent of all secondary school pupils in Northern Ireland.

3. Grant maintained schools. Since 1988 all local education authority maintained secondary, middle and primary schools can apply for Grant Maintained status and receive direct grants from the Department of Education and Science. The governing body of such a school is responsible for all aspects of school management, including the deployment of funds, employment of staff and provision of most of the educational support services staff and pupils. In January 1991 there were 50 Grant Maintained schools in England and Wales.

4. Independent schools and institutions are financed completely by the private sector including individuals, companies and charitable institutions.

Table 5.7 Examination achievements

In 1986 the first phase of the new Standard grade examinations was introduced in Scotland; these examinations will replace the present 'O' grades by 1993. Standard grades are being awarded on an extended 1-7 scale with 'O' grades (previously A-E) being awarded on a comparable 1-5 scale. Standard and 'O' grades 1-3 are equivalent to the previous A-C. SCE Higher grade normally requires one year of study past ordinary/standard grade.

Table 5.10 Primary and secondary schools

Schools in Scotland and Northern Ireland with separate primary and secondary departments have been counted once for each department.

Table 5.16 Further and Higher Education (excluding Universities)

The table includes all students on initial teacher training courses at non-university establishments of Higher and Further Education. Universities (including the Open University), colleges and institutions aided or maintained by government departments (other than those responsible for education) and independent establishments are not covered. Students in England and Wales are counted once only, irrespective of the number of courses for which a student has enroled. In Scotland and Northern Ireland, students continue to be counted once only except if enroled in two or more courses in unrelated subjects. However since October 1975, students in Scotland enroled in SCE and/or GCE courses are counted once only irrespective of the number of levels/grades.

Sandwich courses are those where periods of full-time study are broken by a period (or periods) of associated industrial training or experience, and where the total period (or periods) of full-time study over the whole course averages more than 18 weeks per year.

Part-time day courses are mainly those organised for students released by their employers either for one or two days a week, or for a period (or periods) of block release.

Chapter 6: Health

Infant deaths

- Fewer babies die in the South West, East Anglia and Wales than in other parts of the country. In 1990, infant mortality in these regions was below 7 deaths per 1,000 births compared with almost 10 deaths per 1,000 births in the West Midlands.

  (Table 6.2)

- Fewer very young babies (stillborn or under 1 week old) die in East Anglia - 5.9 deaths per 1,000 births - compared with a high of 10.2 in the West Midlands.

  (Table 6.2)

Visits to the doctors

- Elderly people in the East Midlands are the least likely to consult their doctor, while those in neighbouring West Midlands are the most likely.

  (Table 6.3)

Death rates

- East Anglia, the South East and the South West have the fewest deaths from heart disease while Northern Ireland and Scotland have the most.

  (Table 6.4)

- The suicide rate for men in Scotland is almost twice that in the North of England.

  (Table 6.4)

HIV

- Drug abuse is the major cause of HIV transmission in Scotland, accounting for half of all positive reports. In all other Health Authorities, drug abuse accounts for less than a fifth of cases.

  (Table 6.7)

Vaccination and immunisation of children

- Scotland has the highest rate of vaccination against whooping cough - 86 per cent of children in 1989-90. Wales with 71 per cent has the lowest.

  (Table 6.12)

Drinking

- Yorkshire and Humberside and the North West have the heaviest drinkers in England and Wales. In these regions men average the equivalent of 9 pints of beer a week and women 2.5 pints.

  (Table 6.10)

Prescriptions

- The number of prescriptions issued per person was highest in Wales and lowest in the North West Thames Health Authority.

  (Table 6.17)

Health authority spending

- When the number of people is taken into account, the biggest spending health authority is Scotland (£457 per person) while those in Oxford and Wessex spent less than £300.

  (Table 6.18)

Health service staff

- Wales, Scotland and Northern Ireland all have far more health service staff per head than any English health authority.

  (Table 6.21)

6.1 Population and vital statistics: Health Authority Areas, 1990

Thousands and rates

	Population aged (mid-year estimates) (thousands)				Vital statistics (rates per 1,000)				
	0-14	15-64	65 and over	All ages	Live births[1]	Still-births[2]	Deaths[3]	Perinatal motality[4]	Infant mortality[5]
United Kingdom	10,920.0	37,502.4	8,988.1	57,410.6	64.2	4.8	11.2	8.1	7.9
Northern	579.4	2,013.8	482.2	3,075.4	61.8	4.5	12.2	7.9	7.9
Yorkshire	703.0	2,380.1	572.6	3,655.7	64.8	4.2	11.5	8.0	9.1
Trent	878.9	3,095.7	729.9	4,704.6	62.4	4.5	11.0	8.4	7.8
East Anglia	388.6	1,324.7	345.7	2,059.0	60.6	3.6	10.8	5.9	6.9
North West Thames	661.6	2,336.1	500.9	3,498.6	63.7	4.3	9.5	7.4	6.9
North East Thames	721.4	2,502.3	579.3	3,802.9	67.8	5.4	10.3	8.6	6.9
South East Thames	670.2	2,359.3	628.7	3,658.2	66.4	4.9	10.6	8.2	8.1
South West Thames	530.5	1,945.6	502.5	2,978.6	62.7	3.8	11.0	7.0	6.9
Wessex	533.9	1,896.4	510.0	2,940.3	62.2	4.2	11.4	7.0	7.1
Oxford	508.0	1,716.2	339.7	2,563.9	62.1	4.9	8.7	8.2	7.2
South Western	583.3	2,088.0	590.8	3,262.1	60.1	3.9	11.9	7.1	6.8
West Midlands	1,008.5	3,429.6	781.3	5,219.3	67.1	5.2	10.9	10.2	9.9
Mersey	466.7	1,568.2	367.8	2,402.7	65.1	4.5	11.6	7.9	7.6
North Western	785.0	2,610.6	620.5	4,016.1	68.2	4.9	12.1	8.9	8.5
England	9,018.8	31,266.7	7,551.8	47,837.3	64.3	4.6	11.1	8.1	7.9
Wales	548.2	1,852.9	480.3	2,881.4	63.8	4.6	11.8	7.4	6.9
Scotland	957.2	3,383.8	761.4	5,102.4	58.8	5.3	12.1	8.7	7.7
Northern Ireland	395.8	999.0	194.7	1,589.4	78.0	7.9	9.7	7.6	7.5

1 Per 1,000 women aged 15-44.
2 Per 1,000 live and stillbirths.
3 Per 1,000 population.
4 Stillbirths and deaths of infants under 1 week of age per 1,000 live and stillbirths.
5 Deaths of infants under 1 year of age per 1,000 live births.

Source: Office of Population Censuses and Surveys; General Register Offices for Scotland and Northern Ireland

6.2 Stillbirths, perinatal mortality and infant mortality

Rates

	Stillbirths[1]			Perinatal mortality[2]			Infant mortality[3]		
	1971	1981	1990	1971	1981	1990	1971	1981	1990
United Kingdom	12.6	6.6	4.6	22.6	12.0	8.4	17.9	11.2	7.4
North	13.1	8.0	4.5	23.0	13.2	7.9	18.6	10.7	7.9
Yorkshire & Humberside	12.5	7.8	4.4	22.8	13.2	8.2	19.9	12.1	8.9
East Midlands	11.9	6.2	4.4	22.0	11.4	8.3	18.2	11.0	7.8
East Anglia	10.9	5.5	3.6	20.1	10.2	5.9	15.2	9.8	6.9
South East	11.3	5.9	4.7	20.4	10.7	7.9	15.9	10.4	7.2
South West	11.8	6.3	4.0	20.3	10.8	6.9	16.0	10.4	6.8
West Midlands	13.6	7.0	5.2	23.7	12.9	10.2	17.7	11.7	9.9
North West	14.5	6.7	4.8	25.6	12.4	8.5	19.7	11.2	8.2
England	12.4	6.5	4.6	22.1	11.7	8.1	17.5	10.9	7.9
Wales	14.2	7.3	4.6	24.4	14.1	7.4	18.4	12.6	6.9
Scotland	13.1	6.3	5.3	24.5	11.6	8.7	19.9	11.3	7.7
Northern Ireland	14.3	8.7	4.4	27.2	15.3	7.6	22.7	13.2	7.5

1 Rate per 1,000 live and stillbirths.
2 Stillbirths and deaths under 1 week of age per 1,000 live and still births.
3 Deaths of infants under 1 year of age per 1,000 live births.

Source: Office of Population Censuses and Surveys; General Register Offices for Scotland and Northern Ireland

6.3 Consultations with an NHS general practitioner[1] and reports of long-standing illness: by age, 1990

Percentages

	Persons who consulted an NHS general practitioner						Persons[2] who reported long-standing illness					
	0-4	5-15	16-44	45-64	65 and over	All ages	0-4	5-15	16-44	45-64	65 and over	All ages
Great Britain	24	12	14	16	20	16	13	19	25	46	64	34
North	23	13	15	19	23	17	12	14	25	49	66	35
Yorkshire & Humberside	25	14	17	18	25	19	16	15	27	49	67	36
East Midlands	21	10	14	18	12	14	13	24	25	50	60	34
East Anglia	20	11	14	14	22	16	18	14	28	39	69	36
South East	22	13	14	14	17	15	10	18	25	42	61	33
South West	26	7	14	12	21	14	16	22	26	45	64	36
West Midlands	28	12	15	17	26	18	12	19	22	46	64	32
North West	26	13	15	17	19	16	14	20	23	51	61	34
England	24	12	14	16	19	16	13	19	25	46	63	34
Wales	23	10	15	15	22	16	16	20	28	50	70	37
Scotland	26	10	15	22	25	18	12	18	23	46	65	33

1 In the 14 days before interview.
2 Persons interviewed reporting an illness, disability or infirmity which had troubled them over a period of time.

Source: General Household Survey

6.4 Age adjusted mortality rates[1]: by cause and sex, 1990

Rate per 100,000 population

	Heart disease[2]	Cancer including leu-kaemia	Cerebro-vascular disease	Pneu-monia	Bronchitis, emphy-sema & asthma	Con-genital anomalies	Infectious and parasitic diseases	All accidents, poisonings and violence (except suicide)	Suicide	All other causes	All causes
Males											
United Kingdom	372	301	102	43	21	3	5	37	13	228	1,123
North	418	350	118	42	25	3	4	38	9	237	1,243
Yorkshire & Humberside	398	309	103	41	24	3	5	34	11	239	1,164
East Midlands	361	289	104	35	21	3	5	36	12	228	1,095
East Anglia	323	273	99	33	17	3	4	36	15	199	1,001
South East	320	283	87	38	20	3	5	34	12	221	1,022
South West	340	273	101	32	18	3	4	33	14	210	1,026
West Midlands	383	310	108	38	27	3	6	33	11	240	1,157
North West	418	324	110	46	26	3	5	36	13	248	1,227
England	359	297	99	38	22	3	5	34	12	227	1,096
Wales	401	306	101	39	25	3	6	35	12	231	1,159
Scotland	442	328	129	71	16	3	6	51	17	228	1,290
Northern Ireland	452	291	98	138	21	4	3	49	16	192	1,258
Females											
United Kingdom	321	262	163	70	13	3	5	22	4	251	1,113
North	376	282	177	67	16	2	5	25	4	283	1,236
Yorkshire & Humberside	339	265	164	67	14	2	4	19	3	260	1,135
East Midlands	314	257	158	62	14	3	4	21	4	265	1,099
East Anglia	279	250	154	59	12	4	4	21	3	248	1,032
South East	283	253	144	64	11	3	4	19	4	242	1,025
South West	286	246	155	58	10	3	5	18	4	234	1,019
West Midlands	327	261	176	65	14	3	5	23	3	263	1,140
North West	362	280	174	74	18	3	4	20	3	272	1,209
England	312	260	158	65	13	3	4	20	4	253	1,091
Wales	331	257	168	64	14	2	5	21	3	244	1,110
Scotland	385	285	206	98	10	2	6	34	5	241	1,271
Northern Ireland	390	255	179	189	13	2	4	27	6	194	1,246

1 Deaths at ages under 28 days occuring in England and Wales,can no longer be assigned an underlying cause of death.
2 Excluding acute rheumatic fever.

Source: Office of Population Censuses and Surveys

6.5 Legal abortions[1] to residents: by marital status, age and parity, 1990

Percentages and numbers

	Marital status			Age[2]			Parity[2,3]			Total (= 100%) (numbers)
	Single	Married	Other	Under 20	20-34	35 and over	0	1-3	4 and over	
Great Britain	66.9	21.9	11.2	22.7	66.8	10.5	58.0	37.9	3.2	184,876
Northern	63.6	21.6	14.8	28.2	61.4	10.4	53.2	43.1	3.0	7,289
Yorkshire	65.1	21.6	13.2	26.7	63.0	10.3	55.2	40.4	3.5	10,221
Trent	65.1	23.0	11.9	26.6	63.6	9.8	56.7	39.1	2.8	12,509
East Anglia	62.8	26.3	10.8	26.6	62.0	11.3	57.6	37.4	2.6	5,112
North West Thames	69.1	21.8	9.1	15.3	73.5	11.2	63.3	33.0	2.5	18,465
North East Thames	68.2	22.0	9.8	16.8	73.5	9.7	58.1	36.6	3.9	22,015
South East Thames	70.5	19.5	10.0	18.0	72.3	9.7	58.6	37.2	3.4	16,748
South West Thames	68.1	20.8	11.1	18.1	70.0	11.9	64.5	32.3	2.3	11,778
Wessex	64.4	22.2	13.4	27.3	61.2	11.5	61.4	35.5	2.7	8,002
Oxford	65.2	24.6	10.2	23.6	64.3	12.1	61.0	35.1	2.7	8,074
South Western	64.9	21.2	13.8	26.0	63.5	10.5	60.2	35.8	2.5	7,903
West Midlands	65.9	23.8	10.3	25.7	63.7	10.6	54.3	40.8	4.4	18,380
Mersey	68.2	19.1	12.7	25.0	64.3	10.7	54.4	41.6	2.8	7,520
North Western	67.6	20.2	12.2	25.3	65.0	9.7	53.8	41.7	3.5	12,444
England	67.0	21.8	11.2	22.3	67.2	10.5	58.2	37.6	3.2	166,460
Wales	63.0	24.2	12.8	25.6	61.9	12.5	53.4	42.9	3.5	7,440
Scotland	68.3	20.8	10.9	26.7	63.8	9.4	58.6	38.8	2.5	10,976

1 Carried out in Great Britain.
2 Percentages may not add up to 100 because of cases where age or parity was not known. In Great Britain there were 12 and 1,763 cases where age and parity were not stated.
3 Number of previous live and still births.

Source: Office of Population Censuses and Surveys; Scottish Health Service Common Services Agency

6.6 Notifications of selected infectious diseases, 1981 and 1990

Numbers

	Whooping cough		Measles		Tuberculosis		Malaria		Acute meningitis[1]	
	1981	1990	1981	1990	1981	1990	1981	1990	1981	1990
United Kingdom	21,459	16,862	61,747	15,641	9,086	5,898	1,328	1,565	1,597	2,946
North	1,144	1,530	5,789	1,489	428	205	12	21	50	146
Yorkshire & Humberside	1,964	2,029	6,852	1,812	745	537	107	140	266	344
East Midlands	931	936	4,091	954	587	404	107	116	53	163
East Anglia	573	508	1,632	363	114	97	9	22	28	76
South East	7,422	3,983	10,687	3,475	3,365	2,119	503	872	478	727
South West	1,494	1,281	3,061	886	394	173	43	56	98	232
West Midlands	2,429	1,457	3,453	1,678	1,022	732	423	148	105	262
North West	2,379	2,401	12,854	2,046	1,148	743	52	94	231	419
England	18,336	14,125	48,419	12,703	7,803	5,010	1,256	1,469	1,309	2,369
Wales	1,059	1,161	4,556	598	325	194	12	24	84	203
Scotland	1,385	1,291	4,698	2,006	799	563	60	68	173	216
Northern Ireland	679	285	4,074	334	159	131	0	4	31	158

1 Scotland figures are for meningococcal infection.

Source: Office of Population Censuses and Surveys; Scottish Health Service Common Services Agency; Department of Health and Social Services, Northern Ireland

6.7 Exposure category of HIV-1 antibody positive reports: cumulative totals to 31 December 1991

Numbers

	Between men	Sexual Intercourse			Injecting drug use[1]			Blood[2]	Other[3]/Undetermined			Cumulative total
		Between men and women										
		Male	Female	Unknown	Male	Female	Unknown		Male	Female	Unknown	
United Kingdom	9,954	858	949	14	1,694	693	30	1,422	907	222	85	16,828
Northern	164	25	14	-	48	11	1	97	10	-	-	370
Yorkshire	226	35	36	-	36	20	-	74	11	2	-	440
Trent	225	35	23	-	44	15	-	77	4	7	-	430
East Anglia	103	24	10	-	33	13	-	40	8	3	-	234
North West Thames	3,912	141	205	-	313	101	2	84	206	52	16	5,032
North East Thames	1,848	178	193	10	145	82	2	181	261	29	22	2,951
South East Thames	1,218	96	108	1	152	64	-	145	74	18	1	1,877
South West Thames	282	57	64	1	39	11	-	33	61	10	1	559
Wessex	222	16	21	-	33	8	-	41	13	5	3	362
Oxford	193	26	39	1	46	14	-	119	7	1	-	446
South Western	220	30	27	-	40	6	-	32	6	3	-	364
West Midlands	252	27	33	-	27	5	-	158	48	9	-	559
Mersey	99	11	6	-	10	9	-	46	13	1	-	195
North Western	451	40	22	-	48	24	-	124	6	3	-	718
England	9,415	741	801	13	1,014	383	5	1,251	728	143	43	14,537
Wales	127	28	20	-	10	2	-	62	10	-	-	259
Scotland	365	82	118	1	668	305	25	91	167	79	42	1,943
Northern Ireland	47	7	10	-	2	3	-	18	2	-	-	89

1 Includes 139 male drug users who also had sexual intercourse with other men.
2 Blood/blood factor and tissue recipients.
3 Includes mother to infant transmission.

Source: Public Health Laboratory Service, Communicable Disease Surveillance Centre;
Communicable Diseases (Scotland) Unit.

6.8 Exposure category of AIDS cases: cumulative totals to 31 December 1991

Numbers

	Between men	Sexual intercourse		Injecting drug use[1]		Blood[2]	Other[3]/Undetermined		Cumulative total since 1982
		Between men and women							
		Male	Female	Male	Female		Male	Female	
United Kingdom	4,197	277	165	259	69	366	79	39	5,451
Northern	48	9	1	1	-	35	2	-	96
Yorkshire	77	12	2	5	2	33	3	2	136
Trent	72	10	2	2	2	13	-	3	104
East Anglia	47	7	2	1	1	10	-	-	68
North West Thames	1,822	65	36	62	10	28	21	5	2,049
North East Thames	812	40	45	41	13	53	12	12	1,028
South East Thames	447	33	23	36	9	41	7	4	600
South West Thames	144	26	14	5	1	10	10	2	212
Wessex	82	5	3	6	-	17	3	2	118
Oxford	62	7	7	8	2	30	5	-	121
South Western	86	8	1	6	-	13	2	1	117
West Midlands	90	7	8	4	1	9	3	1	123
Mersey	46	3	3	2	-	16	-	1	71
North Western	164	14	7	10	2	15	2	2	216
England	3,999	246	154	189	43	323	70	35	5,059
Wales	45	8	3	3	1	18	3	-	81
Scotland	135	19	6	67	25	24	5	4	285
Northern Ireland	18	4	2	-	-	1	1	-	26

1 Includes 83 male drug users who also had sexual intercourse with other men.
2 Blood/blood factor and tissue recipients.
3 Includes mother to infant transmissions.

Source: Public Health Laboratory Service, Communicable Disease Surveillance Centre;
Communicable Diseases (Scotland) Unit

6.9 Cigarette smoking amongst persons aged 16 and over

Percentages

	1976	1978	1980	1982	1984	1986	1988	1990
Great Britain	42	40	39	35	34	33	32	30
North	45	41	41	41	36	35	36	32
Yorkshire & Humberside	40	39	40	35	39	34	32	29
East Midlands	41	39	39	33	31	31	32	28
East Anglia	39	38	36	30	24	31	29	26
South East	39	39	38	34	33	32	31	29
South West	40	39	34	34	30	29	28	27
West Midlands	43	39	37	35	33	34	29	29
North West	46	43	43	36	35	35	33	33
England	41	40	39	35	33	32	31	29
Wales	41	40	42	35	37	31	31	31
Scotland	46	45	44	42	39	36	37	34

Source: General Household Survey

6.10 Consumption of alcohol: by sex, 1978 and 1989[1]

Units of alcohol per person per week[2]

	Males		Females		Total		Standardised total[3]	
	1978	1989[1]	1978	1989[1]	1978	1989[1]	1978	1989[1]
North	21.6	14.4	3.5	4.0	11.6	8.7	11.8	8.9
Yorkshire & Humberside	15.4	18.9	3.6	5.3	9.7	11.2	9.1	11.6
East Midlands	11.2	13.4	2.1	4.1	6.4	8.5	6.3	8.4
East Anglia	9.6	11.4	3.2	3.1	6.2	7.2	6.2	7.0
South East	15.6	13.0	4.7	4.6	9.7	8.5	9.8	8.5
Greater London	14.7	13.4	4.1	4.8	9.2	8.7	9.1	8.8
Rest of South East	16.3	12.8	5.2	4.5	10.1	8.4	10.4	8.4
South West	12.7	12.4	3.4	4.4	7.3	8.3	7.7	8.1
West Midlands	15.7	13.6	5.3	3.6	10.2	8.4	10.2	8.3
North West	17.4	17.6	3.9	5.5	10.2	11.5	10.2	11.2
England	15.5	14.2	4.2	4.5	9.4	9.1	9.5	9.1
Wales	15.7	15.5	5.0	4.2	11.0	9.0	10.0	9.4

1 The combined results of the 1987 and 1989 ad hoc surveys of drinking in England and Wales.
2 Average number of units consumed in the seven days before interview by persons aged 18 and over.
3 Consumption total if ratio of men to women in region was made equal to the ratio of men to women in England and Wales as a whole.

Source: Drinking in England and Wales in the late 1980s, *Office of Population Censuses and Surveys*

6.11 New addicts notified: by type of drug, 1990

Numbers

	Heroin	Methadone	Dipipanone	Cocaine	Morphine	Other drugs	Total[1]
United Kingdom	5,819	1,469	154	633	296	135	6,923
North	81	12	2	13	6	3	102
Yorkshire & Humberside	247	46	6	26	19	11	299
East Midlands	146	49	3	13	12	6	182
East Anglia	124	44	8	12	7	15	168
South East	2,385	541	47	347	94	31	2,836
Greater London	1,864	345	12	256	62	10	2,120
Rest of South East	521	196	35	91	32	21	716
South West	324	94	6	57	19	12	394
West Midlands	268	44	8	20	21	13	308
North West	1,853	390	12	124	56	12	1,958
England	5,428	1,220	92	612	234	103	6,247
Wales	66	55	4	8	18	17	137
Scotland	319	192	58	13	41	8	525
Northern Ireland	6	2	-	-	3	7	14

1 As an addict can be reported as addicted to more than one notifiable drug, the figures for individual drugs cannot be added together to produce this total.

Source: Home Office

6.12 Vaccination and immunisation of children

Percentages

	Children born in first year stated and vaccinated by end of second year									
	Diphtheria		Whooping cough		Poliomyelitis		Tetanus		Measles[2]	
	1979 1981	1988 1989-90[1]	1979 1981	1988 1989-90[1]	1979 1981	1988 1989-90[1]	1979 1981	1988 1989-90[1]	1979 1981	1988 1989-90[1]
Great Britain	..	89	..	79	..	89	..	89	..	85
Northern	81	90	41	79	82	90	81	90	58	86
Yorkshire	83	89	49	79	84	89	83	89	60	86
Trent	87	88	52	80	87	88	88	88	60	85
East Anglia	87	92	56	83	87	92	87	92	69	88
North West Thames	82	86	48	78	80	86	82	86	52	80
North East Thames	78	83	43	74	77	83	78	83	45	79
South East Thames	83	89	48	80	82	89	83	89	50	82
South West Thames	87	89	51	80	84	88	87	89	56	81
Wessex	88	93	49	83	88	93	88	93	65	88
Oxford	87	92	56	84	87	92	87	92	68	89
South Western	85	94	47	83	85	94	85	94	62	92
West Midlands	80	86	41	74	81	86	80	86	49	82
Mersey	78	89	36	75	78	89	78	89	49	84
North Western	79	90	34	74	79	89	79	90	45	84
England	83	89	46	78	82	89	83	89	55	84
Wales	78	90	26	71	78	91	78	90	35	81
Scotland	80	94	54	86	82	94	80	94	54	91

1 Figures for England include children vaccinated who had reached the age of two during the period 1 April 1989 - 31 March 1990; figures for Wales are for 1990; figures for Scotland relate to children born in 1988 and vaccinated by 31 December 1990.
2 Measles, mumps and rubella (MMR) in Scotland.

Source: Department of Health; Welsh Office; Scottish Health Service

6.13 Children removed to a place of safety[1]: by age, 1989-90 and 1990-91

Numbers

	1989-90				1990-91			
	Aged 0-4	Aged 5-15	Aged 16 and over	Total	Aged 0-4	Aged 5-15	Aged 16 and over	Total
North	124	206	5	335	124	148	5	277
Yorkshire & Humberside	429	484	29	942	451	520	19	990
East Midlands	247	204	11	462	296	200	1	497
East Anglia	106	95	7	208	99	78	4	181
South East	1,029	1,432	123	2,584	916	1,458	123	2,497
South West	235	248	12	495	216	219	14	449
West Midlands	334	412	23	769	347	351	27	725
North West	625	785	49	1,459	540	640	48	1,228
England	3,129	3,866	259	7,254	2,989	3,614	241	6,844
Wales	144	160	9	313	160	132	8	300

1 This table only includes cases where the local authority was responsible for removal to a place of safety or where the local authority makes provision for a child removed by the authority of some other body or person. Some figures have been estimated.

Source: Department of Health; Welsh Office

6.14 NHS hospitals: number of beds, waiting lists and patient flow, 1981 and 1990-91

	Available beds (rate[1])	Occupied beds (rate[1])	Average length of stay (days)	Discharges and deaths[2] (rate[1])	In-patient treatment Persons awaiting in-hospital treatment[3] (rate[1])	Persons waiting over a year as a percentage of total[4]	Day cases (rate[1])	Total out -patient attend- ances[5] (rate[1])
1981								
Northern	7.8	6.1	17.6	127.0	11.2	24.4	18.0	767.0
Yorkshire	8.0	6.5	18.3	129.3	10.7	22.4	17.4	734.0
Trent	6.7	5.3	17.5	111.1	12.3	34.3	13.3	665.7
East Anglia	6.9	5.5	17.2	115.9	12.3	23.9	17.9	632.2
North West Thames	7.8	6.5	19.6	121.1	12.3	24.1	12.8	824.3
North East Thames	7.6	6.3	18.2	126.7	13.8	24.7	12.6	926.4
South East Thames	7.6	6.2	17.5	128.8	12.8	26.4	12.6	895.7
South West Thames	8.6	7.3	24.3	110.1	12.8	26.4	9.8	706.1
Wessex	6.7	5.4	17.1	116.3	14.9	29.2	15.9	614.9
Oxford	5.7	4.5	14.2	115.3	13.8	34.1	10.2	605.2
South Western	7.8	6.3	19.4	118.8	14.5	31.6	14.0	603.8
West Midlands	6.8	5.5	17.9	112.4	15.2	37.5	12.5	670.3
Mersey	8.6	7.0	21.1	122.0	13.4	31.6	22.2	792.5
North Western	7.6	6.2	16.4	137.6	14.8	31.2	21.9	827.8
England[6]	7.5	6.1	18.1	123.0	13.4	29.2	15.2	759.7
Wales	8.2	6.5	17.7	133.3	11.8	26.4	13.2	697.3
Scotland	11.3	9.4	22.4	152.3	13.2	..	19.0	801.6
Northern Ireland	11.1	8.8	12.5	162.1	13.9	31.4	6.3	745.8
1990-91[2]								
Northern	6.6	..	..	173.8	12.3	16.0	30.6	821.8
Yorkshire	5.6	..	..	169.7	14.0	17.0	27.8	756.7
Trent	4.9	..	..	152.9	13.1	18.0	19.1	724.2
East Anglia	5.2	..	..	153.4	17.2	23.0	21.9	697.0
North West Thames	5.1	..	..	129.1	12.8	27.0	24.2	705.5
North East Thames	5.4	..	..	158.1	17.3	30.0	24.8	864.1
South East Thames	4.7	..	..	148.4	16.9	28.0	23.6	808.6
South West Thames	5.6	..	..	129.2	13.4	28.0	24.5	667.6
Wessex	4.7	..	..	153.1	14.5	23.0	25.9	638.2
Oxford	3.9	..	..	132.4	13.5	26.0	17.2	594.8
South Western	5.4	..	..	156.3	15.9	24.0	24.0	601.0
West Midlands	5.1	..	..	158.6	13.8	23.0	25.3	721.7
Mersey	5.5	..	..	167.5	12.3	9.0	35.2	817.6
North Western	6.0	..	..	182.7	16.9	24.0	38.2	867.1
England[6]	5.3	..	..	157.3	14.8	23.0	26.4	755.3
Wales	6.7	5.1	11.2	167.4	17.1	24.3	35.2	805.3
Scotland	9.9	8.1	16.5	178.8	11.9	12.7	39.9	891.3
Northern Ireland	8.5	6.6	14.0	171.6	17.0	31.9	31.3	818.7

1 Rate per 1,000 population.
2 Data for England and the English regions for discharges and deaths in 1990-91 are not strictly comparable with 1981, nor with data for Wales, Scotland and Northern Ireland.
3 Includes cases when an admission has been reserved. Excludes expectant mothers booked for confinement, planned cases i.e. patients who have deferred admission for personal reasons, or whose condition does not require attention until a later date, patients already occupying hospital beds but awaiting transfer to another department or hospital and by day cases.
4 Patients waiting for non-urgent admissions as a percentage of all waiting list cases.
5 At consultant clinics, excludes accident and emergency admissions.
6 Includes Special Health Authorities which are not allocated regionally.

Source: Department of Health; Welsh Office; Scottish Health Service Common Services Agency; Department of Health and Social Services, Northern Ireland

6.15 NHS hospitals out-patients[1]: by sector, 1990-91

Rates

	Acute specialties		Psychiatric		Accident and emergency		Obstetrics		Others	
	New out-patients[2]	Attend-ances[3]	New out-patients[2]	Attend-ances[3]	New out-patients[2]	Attend-ances[3]	New out-patients[4]	Attend-ances[3]	New out-patients[2]	Attend-ances[3]
United Kingdom	162.6	4.0	4.7	7.8	236.2	1.2	68.0	4.3	2.4	8.0
Northern	174.2	4.0	5.0	7.6	235.0	1.3	66.4	4.7	2.2	7.9
Yorkshire	149.5	4.2	3.6	9.7	234.6	1.2	66.6	4.9	2.7	8.0
Trent	149.1	4.1	3.5	8.7	197.5	1.3	58.7	4.1	3.1	10.4
East Anglia	147.1	4.0	4.7	6.5	163.2	1.2	65.7	3.8	2.5	9.9
North West Thames	149.0	3.9	6.3	6.2	242.1	1.2	70.5	3.8	3.8	5.7
North East Thames	180.9	4.1	4.6	7.2	266.9	1.2	63.4	5.2	3.3	5.9
South East Thames	176.1	3.9	5.0	7.2	265.4	1.2	66.2	4.4	2.1	7.3
South West Thames	142.4	3.7	4.4	10.2	209.1	1.2	81.0	3.2	4.1	9.0
Wessex	137.3	4.0	3.1	8.1	190.1	1.2	75.8	3.0	1.7	6.1
Oxford	133.4	3.9	4.0	6.9	175.8	1.2	52.2	3.8	0.9	9.8
South Western	141.7	3.7	3.8	7.1	219.6	1.3	54.9	3.1	1.3	5.9
West Midlands	140.7	4.3	3.6	8.6	251.3	1.2	65.0	4.5	1.9	11.5
Mersey	162.5	4.2	4.8	8.6	284.3	1.2	73.2	4.7	2.1	9.2
North Western	170.2	4.2	4.6	9.7	275.3	1.2	74.6	5.5	3.3	7.3
England[5]	156.5	4.1	4.4	8.0	234.2	1.2	67.0	4.3	2.5	8.1
Wales	168.7	4.0	4.7	7.6	240.5	1.3	72.7	4.6	2.7	10.0
Scotland	212.4	3.6	7.5	7.2	234.9	1.2	70.2	4.2	0.9	3.6
Northern Ireland	175.7	3.9	5.6	6.4	292.6	1.4	82.2	4.8	1.0	4.8

1 Figures for England, Wales and Scotland include clinics held outside of hospitals (eg at health centres) by hospital based consultants.
2 Rate per 1,000 population. Figures for England and Scotland are for consultant outpatient clinics only.
3 Out-patient attendances per new out-patient.
4 Rate per 1,000 females aged 15-44. Figures for England and Scotland are for consultant outpatient clinics only.
5 Includes Special Health Authorities which are not allocated regionally.

Source: Department of Health; Welsh Office; Scottish Health Service Common Services Agency; Department of Health and Social Services, Northern Ireland

6.16 Elderly persons in residential accommodation[1]: by type of accommodation, 1986 and 1990

Numbers and rates

	Total number of residents aged 65 and over		Residents in local authority staffed homes (rates[2])		Residents in registered voluntary homes (rates[2])		Residents in registered private homes (rates[2])	
	1986	1990	1986	1990	1986	1990	1986	1990
Great Britain	230,500	264,964	14.1	11.9	3.6	3.6	9.9	14.7
North	12,409	15,250	18.8	15.5	1.6	2.0	6.9	14.3
Yorkshire & Humberside	21,020	25,134	17.5	15.0	1.3	1.7	9.4	15.7
East Midlands	14,365	16,834	14.4	12.0	2.3	2.3	8.5	13.3
East Anglia	9,225	10,360	13.5	11.2	3.3	2.7	12.5	16.4
South East	71,295	78,067	12.4	10.4	5.2	4.9	9.7	13.4
South West	28,247	32,598	12.0	10.2	3.5	3.6	19.7	24.5
West Midlands	18,319	22,288	14.2	11.9	2.2	2.4	8.9	14.4
North West	29,502	35,327	16.1	13.0	3.3	3.8	11.4	19.0
England[3]	204,382	235,858	14.2	11.9	3.5	3.5	10.8	15.9
Wales	11,992	13,562	15.7	13.3	2.0	1.8	9.0	13.4
Scotland	14,126	15,544	11.7	11.1	5.4	5.4	1.8	3.9

1 Including residents in homes for the elderly whose age is not known.
2 Rate per 1,000 population aged 65 and over.
3 Figures for 1990 are not strictly comparable with those for 1986.

Source: Department of Health; Welsh Office; The Scottish Office

6.17 Pharmaceutical services[1], 1981 and 1990

	Number of prescriptions written (millions)		Percentage of prescriptions exempt[2] from charges		Number of prescriptions per person[3]		Average net ingredient cost[4] (£ per person)		Average net ingredient cost[4] (£ per prescription)	
	1981	1990	1981	1990	1981	1990	1981	1990	1981	1990
United Kingdom	370.1	446.7	74.9	84.5	6.6	7.8	18.50	44.67	2.79	5.73
Northern	21.6	25.9	75.7	86.2	7.0	8.6	20.79	49.80	2.95	5.82
Yorkshire	23.5	28.9	75.9	85.3	6.9	8.4	18.95	46.60	2.74	5.52
Trent	28.6	35.8	74.8	84.7	6.6	8.0	17.93	44.60	2.74	5.55
East Anglia	8.9	11.3	74.5	81.8	6.4	7.4	19.20	45.00	2.98	6.12
North West Thames	21.8	23.9	69.9	80.1	5.6	5.9	15.59	35.60	2.79	6.01
North East Thames	24.1	27.4	72.7	83.1	6.2	6.8	16.50	39.30	2.65	5.79
South East Thames	23.1	27.0	79.1	83.2	6.3	7.0	17.61	40.40	2.81	5.78
South West Thames	17.9	19.8	72.8	80.1	5.9	6.4	16.74	39.70	2.85	6.23
Wessex	16.6	20.4	79.2	82.1	6.9	7.4	18.96	45.10	2.93	6.10
Oxford	12.1	14.7	70.9	78.0	5.6	6.2	16.71	39.70	2.99	6.38
South Western	19.4	23.5	76.0	83.3	6.5	7.5	18.76	44.60	2.87	5.98
West Midlands	33.4	41.3	74.6	84.8	6.6	8.0	17.87	44.60	2.72	5.57
Mersey	18.1	22.6	77.3	87.8	7.2	9.1	18.80	50.20	2.61	5.49
North Western	30.9	38.0	76.8	86.6	7.5	9.3	20.11	50.30	2.66	5.43
England	300.0	360.5	74.6	83.9	6.5	7.6	18.10	43.80	2.78	5.77
Wales	23.4	28.3	79.0	88.9	8.6	10.1	23.03	54.32	2.67	5.36
Scotland	34.0	42.5	73.2	84.6	6.2	7.9	18.22	45.15	2.93	5.73
Northern Ireland	12.7	15.4	79.3	90.5	8.1	9.5	23.50	52.90	2.88	5.60

1 Figures relate to NHS prescriptions dispensed by retail chemists, drug stores and appliance contractors. Prescriptions for medicines dispensed by dispensing doctors are excluded.
2 Includes prescriptions for which prepayment certificates have been purchased.
3 Based on persons on the NHS prescribing list.
4 Net ingredient cost is the cost of medicines before any discounts and does not include any dispensing costs or fees.

Source: Department of Health; Welsh Office; Scottish Health Service Common Services Agency; Department of Health and Social Services, Northern Ireland

6.18 Health authorities expenditure[1]: by function 1990-91

£ per head

	Head quarters administration	Hospital services		Community health services		Other sevices[2] (revenue expenditure)	Capital expenditure	Total expenditure
		Diagnosis and treatment	Support services	Diagnosis and treatment	Support services			
United Kingdom	16.86	176.54	67.33	35.00	6.10	19.76	31.78	353.36
Northern	14.94	172.12	58.35	34.18	4.46	18.81	26.38	329.23
Yorkshire	15.96	161.68	54.62	33.30	4.85	18.99	29.42	318.83
Trent	11.88	155.08	53.48	33.32	4.76	18.46	31.51	308.50
East Anglia	15.13	159.55	53.45	31.84	3.76	18.00	26.72	308.44
North West Thames	17.01	175.62	62.32	36.61	7.01	16.62	38.25	353.45
North East Thames	18.43	205.34	73.73	38.89	7.05	17.66	31.57	392.67
South East Thames	19.78	178.00	64.73	40.58	7.89	21.56	26.64	359.17
South West Thames	17.52	164.87	66.04	35.80	5.72	32.39	26.73	349.08
Wessex	14.53	146.74	53.98	34.79	5.24	15.48	28.86	299.61
Oxford	12.62	136.05	49.21	31.45	4.31	14.30	22.87	270.81
South Western	14.46	156.34	52.05	36.72	5.66	21.17	33.42	319.84
West Midlands	15.71	159.47	59.13	33.65	5.49	15.88	31.84	321.17
Mersey	14.30	176.72	57.48	35.20	5.44	24.52	32.06	345.72
North Western	16.56	176.51	58.28	39.45	5.73	18.99	31.84	347.37
England[3]	16.03	170.86	59.95	35.61	5.62	19.42	31.04	338.54
Wales	16.54	189.79	70.30	36.01	6.05	19.76	34.34	372.80
Scotland	20.93	212.09	125.02	30.78	8.10	23.94	35.81	456.70
Northern Ireland	29.30	209.28	98.78	28.24	14.24	16.51	36.18	432.55

1 Excluding Family Practitioner Services.
2 Includes ambulance services, mass radiography (except in Northern Ireland), blood transfusion and emergency bed services.
3 Includes figures for London post-graduate teaching hospitals, which are not allocated regionally.

Source: Department of Health; Welsh Office; Management Executive, the NHS in Scotland; Department of Health and Social Services, Northern Ireland

6.19 General practitioners: numbers and list sizes, 1990

Numbers and percentages

| | | General Medical Practitioners (at 1 October) | | | | | General Dental Practitioners (at 30 September) | |
| | Number of unrestricted principals | List size | | | | | Number of general prac- tioners[1] | Persons[2] per dentist |
		Average list size	Percentage under 1,500	Percentage between 1,500-1,999	Percentage between 2,000-2,499	Percentage 2,500 and over		
United Kingdom	31,566	1,894	17	43	30	9	18,589	3,088
Northern	1,639	1,912	15	47	31	7	869	3,539
Yorkshire	1,953	1,922	11	48	33	6	1,094	3,342
Trent	2,402	1,979	13	39	34	12	1,218	3,887
East Anglia	1,112	1,824	16	56	25	3	605	3,403
North West Thames	1,998	2,003	13	42	30	16	1,512	2,294
North East Thames	2,050	2,030	13	38	34	15	1,226	3,058
South East Thames	1,947	1,995	15	33	39	13	1,341	2,728
South West Thames	1,576	1,980	10	44	35	10	1,240	2,357
Wessex	1,591	1,841	14	54	28	4	949	3,053
Oxford	1,357	1,931	11	47	36	6	826	3,104
South Western	1,980	1,713	23	55	20	2	1,209	2,851
West Midlands	2,736	1,980	13	39	36	12	1,395	3,741
Mersey	1,249	1,998	11	42	35	12	764	3,145
North Western	2,032	2,006	11	38	39	12	1,232	3,235
England	25,622	1,942	14	43	33	10	15,480	3,090
Wales	1,635	1,813	19	52	23	6	837	3,443
Scotland	3,384	1,592	36	53	10	1	1,694	3,012
Northern Ireland	925	1,814	38	16	18	28	578	2,750

1 Includes assistants and trainees
2 Based on mid-1990 estimates of population.

Source: Department of Health; Welsh Office; Scottish Health Service Common Services Agency; Department of Health and Social Services, Northern Ireland

6.20 Primary health care nursing services: by category of staff[1]

Whole-time equivalents

| | Community psychiatric nurses | | | Midwives | | | Health visitors[2] | | | District nurses[3] | | |
	1981	1986	1990	1981	1986	1990	1981	1986	1990	1981	1986	1990
Northern	60	158	196	221	253	244	618	691	690	1,039	1,162	1,157
Yorkshire	68	199	268	260	323	348	688	743	824	1,104	1,106	1,165
Trent	100	260	331	442	475	479	860	956	1,011	1,386	1,524	1,610
East Anglia	50	106	144	194	218	211	328	375	358	550	587	558
North West Thames	69	168	202	174	230	248	732	810	790	896	989	1,079
North East Thames	97	137	282	240	279	273	648	739	772	988	1,011	1,182
South East Thames	36	208	277	231	316	328	687	834	746	1,236	1,241	1,205
South West Thames	134	209	264	168	206	189	661	639	653	973	966	965
Wessex	83	176	209	165	222	238	554	608	639	798	910	900
Oxford	71	122	173	168	191	178	462	563	561	738	692	698
South Western	95	147	314	134	217	279	608	680	685	932	970	1,052
West Midlands	53	255	373	419	489	463	1,005	1,118	1,105	1,602	1,570	1,611
Mersey	90	156	215	217	244	232	486	502	516	756	800	829
North Western	78	228	344	373	466	472	909	1,173	1,124	1,527	1,638	1,726
England[4]	1,083	2,532	3,598	3,406	4,127	4,201	9,244	10,430	10,473	14,523	15,187	15,736
Wales	80	142	..	193	249	..	559	615	..	1,244	1,230	..
Scotland	..	..	98	143	187	208	1,488	1,598	1,646	2,318	2,450	2,359
Northern Ireland	..	96	129	57	117	146	440	468	495	637	602	639

1 Agency nurses and midwives are excluded.
2 Includes health visitors in both the community and school health services (except that in Scotland, health visitors in schools are excluded from 1990), HV fieldwork teachers, TB visitors with HV certificates, dual/triple posts (HV/DN/ Mid) and bank health visitors. Excludes HV students.
3 Includes district nurse practical work teachers, SRN, SSEN, and SEN assisting district nurses, dual posts (DN/Mid) and bank district nurses. Excludes DN students.
4 England totals include staff in Special Health Authorities for London post-graduate teaching hospitals.

Source: Department of Health; Welsh Office; Scottish Health Service Common Services Agency; Department of Health and Social Services, Northern Ireland

6.21 Health Service staff[1]

Thousands and rates

	Total whole-time equivalents (thousands)			Rate per 10,000 population		
	1981	1986	1990	1981	1986	1990
United Kingdom	1,083.8	1,069.1	1,041.6	192.1	188.0	181.4
Northern	56.4	56.2	55.9	181.1	182.5	181.9
Yorkshire	65.2	62.9	62.1	181.5	174.6	169.8
Trent	77.5	78.3	80.1	168.8	169.1	170.3
East Anglia	31.2	32.2	33.6	164.5	161.6	163.0
North West Thames[2]	65.7	58.6	55.9	189.7	167.9	137.7
North East Thames[2]	72.6	72.4	71.4	196.4	192.5	187.9
South East Thames[2]	71.4	65.5	65.1	198.5	181.0	177.9
South West Thames[2]	55.1	49.1	46.2	182.2	165.6	155.2
Wessex	45.7	46.4	47.4	166.2	161.3	162.3
Oxford	36.2	35.6	36.3	155.6	143.7	141.7
South Western	56.4	55.9	55.9	184.3	175.9	171.2
West Midlands	88.6	88.8	89.0	170.9	171.4	170.4
Mersey	47.3	45.1	43.1	192.6	187.0	179.5
North Western	78.1	77.9	74.8	193.3	195.1	186.3
England[3]	861.0	841.8	817.2	183.9	178.1	170.8
Wales	57.2	60.0	61.9	203.6	213.0	214.9
Scotland	126.9	128.8	123.5	244.9	251.6	242.0
Northern Ireland	38.7	38.5	39.0	256.4	246.0	245.3

1 Includes Family Practitioner Committee Service.
2 London ambulance service staff have been apportioned between the four Thames regions on the basis of population.
3 England totals include staff in Special Health Authorities for London post-graduate teaching hospitals. Dental Estimates Board, Prescription Pricing Authority and Other Statutory Authorities (eg Public Health Laboratory Service and Health Education Authority) are included for 1990. Hence figures for 1990 are not strictly comparable with those for earlier years.

Source: Department of Health; Welsh Office; Scottish Health Service Common Services Agency: Department of Health and Social Services, Northern Ireland

Notes to Chapter 6: Health

For most of the tables in this section, figures for the Regional Health Authority areas of England, as opposed to standard regions, are given. The areas covered by the Regional Health Authorities are shown in a map at the end of this book, definitions appear in *Health and Personal Social Services Statistics for England, 1982, (HMSO)*. In Scotland and Northern Ireland procedures may differ slightly from those used in England and Wales; reference is made to these differences in footnotes to the tables.

Table 6.11 Drug addicts notified

Figures relate to notifications under the Misuse of Drugs (Notification of and Supply to Addicts) Regulations 1973, which require doctors to send to the Chief Medical Officer at the Home Office, particulars of persons whom they consider to be addicted to any of 14 controlled drugs.

Tables 6.14 and 6.15 NHS hospitals

Figures for average daily *occupied beds* are obtained by dividing the total of the daily numbers of in-patients for the year by the number of days in the year. An in-patient for this purpose is a person who has gone through the full admission procedure. Average daily *available beds* are the average number of staffed beds available during the year.

A *day case* is a person who comes for investigation, treatment or operation under clinical supervision on a planned non-resident basis and who occupies a bed.

For 1990-91 the English rates for discharges and deaths are based on 'finished consultant episodes (FCE)'. This is a completed period of care of a patient using a bed, under one consultant, in a particular District/Special Health Authority. A patient transferring from one consultant to another in the same hospital is counted as a FCE, but a patient transferring from one hospital to another in the same district without changing consultant is excluded. Healthy live born babies are included. English data for 1981 and all data for Wales, Scotland and Northern Ireland are based on a system which counts a patient transferring from one hospital to another, with the same consultant, as a discharge and excludes new born babies.

Acute specialities are all specialities except geriatrics, younger disabled, GP maternity, obstetrics, mental handicap and mental illness. In Scotland it comprises speciality groups: acute specialities; supra-area and special categories (excluding accident and emergency).

The *medical specialities* are General medicine, Paediatrics, Infectious diseases, Thoracic medicine, Dermatology, Neurology, Cardiology, Rehabilitation, Genito-urinary medicine and Rheumatology, plus other specialist units of Anaesthetics, Audiological medicine, Child assessment unit, Clinical neurological physiology, Clinical pharmacology and therapeutics, Clinical physiology, Coronary care, Endocrinology, Gastroenterology, Haematology, Intensive care unit, Medical oncology, Nephology, Spinal injuries unit, Tropical medicine and Terminal care unit.

The *surgical specialties* are General surgery, Ear, nose and throat, Traumatic and orthopaedic, Ophthalmology, Radiotherapy, Urology, Plastic surgery, Thoracic surgery, Oral surgery, Orthodontics, Neurosurgery, Gynaecology, Pre-convalescent, Burns unit, Cardiac surgery, Paediatric surgery and Restorative dentistry.

The *psychiatric specialties* are Mental Illness, Mental Handicap, Psychogeriatrics, Child Psychiatry, Adolescent Psychiatry and Forensic Psychiatry. In Scotland it comprises speciality groups: Psychiatric specialities and mental handicap. In Scotland others comprises long-stay speciality group (geriatric assessment and long-stay and young chronic sick).

An out-patient is defined as a person attending an out-patients' department for treatment or advice. A new out-patient is one whose first attendance of a continuous series (or single attendance where relevant) at a clinical out-patient department for the same course of treatment falls within the period under review. Each out-patient attendance of a course or series is included in the year in which the attendance occurred. Persons attending more than one department are counted in each department.

Table 6.18 Health Authority expenditure

The functional analysis is derived from the Authorities' annual accounts. Brief details of the expenditure covered by the headings are as follows:-

Headquarters Administration: the expenditure incurred in administering the health service at regional and district levels including office accommodation costs, etc.

Hospital and Community Health Services: 'support services' include administration and clerical services at unit level, medical records, staff training, transport, catering, laundry and other domestic services, heating, maintenance of buildings, plant, grounds, general estate management and other miscellaneous services.

Other Services (Revenue Expenditure): These include the Ambulance, Blood Transfusion, Mass Radiography (except in Northern Ireland where this service is costed under hospital services: diagnosis and treatment) and Emergency Bed services, the cost of maintaining health service patients in hospitals and homes outside the Service, and Community Health Councils which were introduced on 1 April 1974 as part of the reorganised NHS.

Capital Expenditure: shows the cost of building and improvements to health service properties, the initial equipment of these buildings and the purchase of sites. It also includes the replacement of certain major items of equipment. In Northern Ireland the figure includes expenditure on capital works incurred by the Department of Health and Social Services, but not the cost of salaries of professional and technical staff engaged on these projects.

In Northern Ireland from October 1973, hospital, family practitioner, community health and personal social services have been provided by four Health and Social Services Boards as part of an integrated service. Estimates have been made of the costs attributable to headquarters administration in respect of the administration of health care services only. In Northern Ireland Headquarters Administration includes both Health Board and Unit of Management Expenditure on health care services.

Table 6.21 Health Authority Staff

Whole-time equivalents are the number of whole-time staff plus the total hours or sessions per week contracted by part-time divided by the number of hours or sessions in the appropriate standard working week.

The NHS main staff groups are nursing and midwifery, professional and technical, professions allied to medicine, scientific and professional, maintenance, ancillary, administrative and clerical, ambulance, medical and dental and other practitioners.

England totals include staff in Special Health Authorities for London post graduate teaching hospitals, Dental Estimates Board, Prescription Pricing Authority and Family Practitioner Committees (directly employed staff only). From 1987 other statutory Authorities are included, eg Public Health Laboratory Service, amounting to almost 3,000 whole-time equivalents.

Medical and dental staff included are those holding permanent paid (whole-time, part-time and part-time sessional) and/or honourary appointments in NHS hospitals and Community Health Services. Figures now include clinical assistants and hospital practitioners; these were excluded in the overall figure in previous years. Pharmacists in General Pharmaceutical Services are excluded. Occasional sessional staff in Community Health Medical and Dental Services for whom no whole-time equivalent is collected are not included. The whole-time equivalent of staff holding appointments with more than one region is included in the appropriate region. FHSA staff includes EMP's, EDP's, Opticians and ancillary staff.

Chapter 7: Employment

Self employment

- Self employment is highest in the South West, Wales and East Anglia where around one in seven of the workforce are self employed.

(Chart 7.1)

Employees

- The public administration sector is the biggest employer in Northern Ireland - with nearly a third of all male and over half of all female employees, much higher than in any other region.

(Table 7.7)

- The financial sector is a much more important employer in the South East than elsewhere, around one person in every six works in this sector.

(Table 7.7)

- Despite recent decline, manufacturing remains an important employer in the West Midlands - with two out of five male and one out of five female employees, double the rates in the South East.

(Table 7.7)

Qualifications of the workforce

- The South East has the most qualified workforce. Eight out of every ten have a qualification of some kind - indeed, one in seven are educated to degree level.

(Table 7.8)

Absence from work due to illness

- Sickness absence from work is highest in Wales, Scotland and the North and lowest in East Anglia.

(Table 7.11)

Unemployment

- In the main, those areas with low levels of unemployment have the largest increases in unemployment and those with high levels have the smallest increases.

(Chart 7.14)

Long term unemployment

- Long term unemployment is much more serious in Northern Ireland, where one in five unemployed men have been out of work for more than 5 years. This compares with only one in twenty for the United Kingdom as a whole and one in forty for the South East, the South West and East Anglia.

(Table 7.13)

Youth Training

- Around a quarter of youngsters leaving YT schemes in 1990/91 in the Northern and London regions were unemployed when they were surveyed later.

(Table 7.23)

7.1   The civilian workforce, 1991[1]

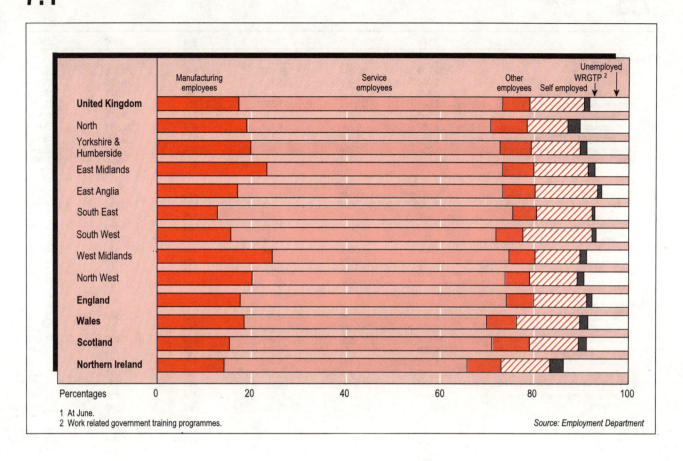

1 At June.
2 Work related government training programmes.

Source: Employment Department

7.2   Civilian labour force: by age, 1991 and 2001

Percentages and thousands

	1991 (Estimates)					2001 (Projections)				
	(percentages aged)					(percentages aged)				
	16-24	25-44	Females 45-59 Males 45-64	Females 60+ Males 65+	All ages (= 100%) (thou-sands)	16-24	25-44	Females 45-59 Males 45-64	Females 60+ Males 65+	All ages (= 100%) (thou-sands)
United Kingdom	20.0	49.0	28.2	2.9	28,772	16.4	49.7	31.4	2.6	29,577
North	19.3	51.2	27.4	2.0	1,458	15.7	51.7	30.7	1.9	1,444
Yorkshire & Humberside	20.2	49.6	28.1	2.2	2,446	16.3	49.8	32.0	1.9	2,495
East Midlands	19.2	49.6	28.7	2.5	2,074	15.0	50.5	32.2	2.3	2,182
East Anglia	19.4	47.9	29.3	3.4	1,043	15.9	48.8	32.4	2.9	1,138
South East	19.7	48.4	28.3	3.6	9,080	16.3	49.3	31.3	3.1	9,398
Greater London	19.7	49.9	27.2	3.2	3,452	16.2	51.5	29.8	2.6	3,499
Rest of South East	19.7	47.5	29.0	3.8	5,629	16.4	48.1	32.1	3.4	5,899
South West	19.5	48.0	29.1	3.4	2,354	16.1	48.7	32.2	3.0	2,534
West Midlands	20.2	48.4	28.9	2.5	2,656	16.6	48.6	32.5	2.3	2,671
North West	20.1	50.0	27.4	2.4	3,141	16.6	49.8	31.3	2.2	3,139
England	19.7	48.9	28.3	3.0	24,251	16.2	49.5	31.7	2.6	25,001
Wales	20.5	49.7	27.5	2.3	1,343	17.1	51.0	29.8	2.1	1,393
Scotland	21.2	49.0	27.3	2.5	2,488	16.8	50.0	30.7	2.4	2,454
Northern Ireland	22.1	49.0	26.7	2.3	690	18.7	51.5	27.9	2.0	730

Source: Labour Force Survey, Employment Department

7.3 Employment structure of the civilian workforce: by sex

Thousands

	1976	1979	1981	1986	1990	1991
United Kingdom						
Civilian workforce	25,766	26,374	26,533	27,475	28,175	27,971
Males	15,944	15,967	16,100	16,081	15,998	15,919
Females	9,822	10,408	10,433	11,394	12,177	12,051
Employees in employment	22,548	23,173	21,892	21,387	22,898	22,234
Males	13,396	13,487	12,562	11,744	12,071	11,599
Females	9,152	9,686	9,331	9,644	10,827	10,635
Self-employed (with or without employees)	1,952	1,906	2,119	2,633	3,298	3,143
Unemployed (males and females)	1,266	1,296	2,521	3,229	1,556	2,241
WRGTP[1]	.	.	.	226	423	352
North						
Civilian workforce	1,442	1,438	1,398	1,418	1,389	1,371
Males	912	883	860	840	794	783
Females	530	555	538	578	595	588
Employees in employment	1,255	1,248	1,122	1,061	1,112	1,079
Males	769	741	654	585	590	566
Females	486	506	468	476	522	513
Self-employed (with or without employees)	87	77	84	105	115	115
Unemployed (males and females)	100	114	192	232	117	141
WRGTP[1]	.	.	.	20	45	36
Yorkshire & Humberside						
Civilian workforce	2,239	2,259	2,253	2,312	2,382	2,360
Males	1,404	1,385	1,387	1,363	1,351	1,338
Females	834	875	866	949	1,031	1,022
Employees in employment	1,968	2,011	1,852	1,762	1,928	1,881
Males	1,191	1,195	1,083	970	1,017	978
Females	777	815	768	792	911	902
Self-employed (with or without employees)	162	134	164	216	255	238
Unemployed (males and females)	109	115	237	312	151	203
WRGTP[1]	.	.	.	22	48	38
East Midlands						
Civilian workforce	1,690	1,742	1,767	1,873	1,923	1,945
Males	1,054	1,065	1,084	1,101	1,096	1,103
Females	636	677	683	772	827	841
Employees in employment	1,497	1,555	1,467	1,490	1,579	1,556
Males	900	914	855	831	839	814
Females	597	641	613	659	740	742
Self-employed (with or without employees)	122	116	144	167	221	225
Unemployed (males and females)	71	71	155	199	92	139
WRGTP[1]	.	.	.	17	31	25
East Anglia						
Civilian workforce	776	812	829	910	1,003	1,003
Males	489	504	517	540	569	577
Females	287	309	313	370	435	426
Employees in employment	669	702	681	717	815	807
Males	405	417	400	402	433	428
Females	265	285	281	314	382	379
Self-employed (with or without employees)	75	79	87	105	145	132
Unemployed (males and females)	32	31	61	81	34	57
WRGTP[1]	.	.	.	7	9	7
South East						
Civilian workforce	8,168	8,381	8,511	8,967	9,221	9,009
Males	4,984	5,031	5,110	5,174	5,193	5,089
Females	3,184	3,351	3,400	3,794	4,029	3,919
Employees in employment	7,247	7,473	7,263	7,255	7,642	7,263
Males	4,243	4,295	4,135	3,968	4,004	3,772
Females	3,004	3,178	3,128	3,287	3,638	3,491
Self-employed (with or without employees)	631	651	700	904	1,170	1,063
Unemployed (males and females)	290	258	548	772	342	628
WRGTP[1]	.	.	.	36	67	55
South West						
Civilian workforce	1,777	1,835	1,924	2,048	2,207	2,253
Males	1,107	1,097	1,175	1,191	1,238	1,271
Females	670	738	749	857	969	982
Employees in employment	1,514	1,598	1,541	1,579	1,780	1,755
Males	894	921	883	862	925	903
Females	619	677	658	717	855	852
Self-employed (with or without employees)	169	146	227	256	315	323
Unemployed (males and females)	94	91	156	196	85	153
WRGTP[1]	.	.	.	17	27	22

(continued)

7.3 *(continued)*

Thousands

	1976	1979	1981	1986	1990	1991
West Midlands						
Civilian workforce	2,466	2,502	2,512	2,519	2,566	2,502
Males	1,550	1,547	1,549	1,506	1,485	1,449
Females	917	955	963	1,014	1,081	1,053
Employees in employment	2,186	2,241	2,051	1,961	2,101	2,010
Males	1,325	1,338	1,199	1,110	1,147	1,080
Females	861	903	852	852	954	930
Self-employed (with or without employees)	160	141	170	187	277	239
Unemployed (males and females)	120	120	291	342	144	216
WRGTP[1]	.	.	.	30	44	37
North West						
Civilian workforce	3,035	3,077	3,038	3,037	3,021	3,025
Males	1,843	1,834	1,815	1,758	1,714	1,723
Females	1,191	1,242	1,223	1,279	1,307	1,302
Employees in employment	2,638	2,676	2,466	2,295	2,437	2,396
Males	1,543	1,539	1,391	1,234	1,281	1,249
Females	1,095	1,137	1,075	1,061	1,155	1,147
Self-employed (with or without employees)	209	214	217	267	306	303
Unemployed (males and females)	188	187	355	444	223	281
WRGTP[1]	.	.	.	31	55	45
England						
Civilian workforce	21,593	22,046	22,232	23,085	23,712	23,468
Males	13,344	13,347	13,497	13,473	13,438	13,334
Females	8,249	8,700	8,734	9,613	10,274	10,134
Employees in employment	18,973	19,503	18,444	18,120	19,394	18,746
Males	11,270	11,360	10,600	9,962	10,236	9,791
Females	7,703	8,143	7,845	8,158	9,158	8,956
Self-employed (with or without employees)	1,615	1,558	1,793	2,207	2,805	2,638
Unemployed (males and females)	1,005	985	1,994	2,578	1,188	1,818
WRGTP[1]	.	.	.	180	326	266
Wales						
Civilian workforce	1,188	1,237	1,200	1,228	1,289	1,288
Males	764	773	748	745	750	744
Females	424	464	453	483	540	543
Employees in employment	995	1,033	939	887	998	983
Males	612	618	551	494	527	509
Females	383	415	389	393	471	474
Self-employed (with or without employees)	122	124	115	154	184	174
Unemployed (males and females)	71	80	146	174	79	110
WRGTP[1]	.	.	.	13	28	21
Scotland						
Civilian workforce	2,361	2,431	2,434	2,460	2,461	2,494
Males	1,439	1,448	1,447	1,441	1,394	1,421
Females	922	983	986	1,018	1,067	1,074
Employees in employment	2,071	2,102	2,002	1,879	1,977	1,980
Males	1,210	1,205	1,128	1,021	1,034	1,031
Females	861	897	874	858	943	949
Self-employed (with or without employees)	151	160	149	205	234	254
Unemployed (males and females)	139	168	283	351	194	216
WRGTP[1]	.	.	.	24	56	45
Northern Ireland						
Civilian workforce	624	661	667	696	713	721
Males	397	399	407	417	417	421
Females	227	261	259	279	296	299
Employees in employment	509	535	507	501	530	525
Males	304	304	283	267	274	269
Females	205	231	224	235	256	256
Self-employed (with or without employees)	64	64	61	60	76	77
Unemployed (males and females)	51	62	98	126	95	98
WRGTP[1]	.	.	.	8	13	20

1 Work Related Government Training Programmes.

Source: Employment Department

7.4 Civilian labour force: by sex

Thousands

	Estimates									Projec-tions
	1971	1979	1981	1984[1]	1984[1]	1988	1989	1990	1991	2001
Males										
United Kingdom	15,965	15,999	16,038	15,866	15,929	16,198	16,331	16,374	16,300	16,420
North	894	896	893	848	850	851	848	841	826	798
Yorkshire & Humberside	1,401	1,403	1,399	1,364	1,368	1,365	1,387	1,400	1,396	1,391
East Midlands	1,070	1,121	1,125	1,115	1,125	1,148	1,179	1,169	1,185	1,221
East Anglia	479	526	529	544	545	569	576	589	585	628
South East	4,982	4,909	4,957	4,996	5,011	5,125	5,125	5,133	5,109	5,188
Greater London	..	..	2,008	1,956	1,986	1,965	1,976	1,990	1,933	1,921
Rest of South East	..	..	2,949	3,040	3,026	3,160	3,148	3,143	3,176	3,267
South West	1,118	1,170	1,189	1,191	1,199	1,270	1,295	1,291	1,309	1,382
West Midlands	1,546	1,531	1,512	1,471	1,476	1,524	1,536	1,550	1,537	1,513
North West	1,881	1,820	1,825	1,773	1,776	1,783	1,798	1,803	1,784	1,743
England	13,371	13,376	13,429	13,302	13,351	13,635	13,742	13,776	13,731	13,865
Wales	766	780	766	743	746	751	767	767	763	775
Scotland	1,426	1,453	1,449	1,433	1,441	1,414	1,418	1,424	1,402	1,361
Northern Ireland	402	390	395	388	391	398	403	407	404	420
Females										
United Kingdom	9,534	10,647	10,845	11,202	11,320	12,017	12,422	12,526	12,472	13,157
North	500	573	584	592	597	627	643	630	632	645
Yorkshire & Humberside	813	918	947	961	969	1,005	1,031	1,050	1,050	1,103
East Midlands	615	710	740	784	785	842	898	903	889	961
East Anglia	258	333	351	368	373	453	456	476	457	510
South East	3,156	3,323	3,414	3,621	3,662	3,823	3,941	3,987	3,971	4,210
Greater London	..	..	1,437	1,453	1,473	1,467	1,521	1,538	1,519	1,578
Rest of South East	..	..	1,977	2,167	2,189	2,357	2,420	2,449	2,453	2,632
South West	634	784	800	866	880	993	1,028	1,023	1,045	1,152
West Midlands	906	998	1,000	999	1,014	1,078	1,118	1,130	1,119	1,158
North West	1,176	1,269	1,281	1,255	1,271	1,348	1,371	1,355	1,356	1,396
England	8,059	8,909	9,117	9,446	9,551	10,170	10,487	10,553	10,520	11,136
Wales	396	473	483	510	511	530	577	585	580	618
Scotland	877	1,031	998	994	1,004	1,051	1,083	1,103	1,086	1,093
Northern Ireland	202	234	247	251	255	267	276	285	286	309
All persons										
United Kingdom	25,499	26,646	26,883	27,068	27,249	28,215	28,753	28,900	28,772	29,577
North	1,394	1,469	1,477	1,440	1,447	1,478	1,491	1,471	1,458	1,444
Yorkshire & Humberside	2,214	2,321	2,346	2,325	2,338	2,370	2,418	2,450	2,446	2,495
East Midlands	1,685	1,831	1,865	1,900	1,909	1,991	2,078	2,072	2,074	2,182
East Anglia	737	859	880	913	918	1,022	1,032	1,064	1,043	1,138
South East	8,138	8,232	8,371	8,617	8,673	8,948	9,066	9,119	9,080	9,398
Greater London	..	..	3,445	3,410	3,459	3,432	3,497	3,528	3,452	3,499
Rest of South East	..	..	4,926	5,207	5,214	5,517	5,568	5,592	5,629	5,899
South West	1,752	1,954	1,989	2,057	2,079	2,263	2,323	2,314	2,354	2,534
West Midlands	2,452	2,530	2,512	2,470	2,490	2,602	2,653	2,680	2,656	2,671
North West	3,058	3,089	3,105	3,028	3,047	3,132	3,169	3,158	3,141	3,139
England	21,430	22,284	22,546	22,748	22,902	23,805	24,229	24,329	24,251	25,001
Wales	1,162	1,253	1,248	1,253	1,257	1,280	1,344	1,352	1,343	1,393
Scotland	2,303	2,484	2,447	2,428	2,445	2,465	2,501	2,527	2,488	2,454
Northern Ireland	603	625	642	640	646	664	679	693	690	730

1 GB labour force definitions up to 1984, ILO definitions from 1984.

Source: Labour Force Survey, Employment Department

7.5 Households: by economic status of head[1], spring 1991

Percentages and thousands

	Economically active									
	In Employment									
	Employees				On government employment or training prog-rammes	All in employ-ment	Unem-ployed	All eco-nomically active	Economi-cally inactive	Number of house-holds (= 100%) (thou-sands)
	Full-time[2]	Part-time[2]	All em-ployees[3]	Self employed						
United Kingdom	60.7	3.5	64.2	14.2	0.6	79.0	6.8	85.8	14.2	16,221
North	58.1	3.8	61.9	9.0	1.1	72.0	8.0	80.1	19.9	893
Yorkshire & Humberside	60.9	4.0	64.9	12.2	..	77.9	6.9	84.7	15.3	1,400
East Midlands	64.6	3.1	67.7	13.4	..	81.7	6.6	88.3	11.7	1,155
East Anglia	62.7	3.6	66.2	16.6	..	83.3	5.1	88.5	11.5	579
South East	63.3	3.1	66.4	16.2	0.4	83.1	5.7	88.8	11.2	4,986
Greater London	59.4	2.9	62.3	15.5	0.6	78.4	7.2	85.6	14.4	1,990
Rest of South East	65.9	3.3	69.2	16.7	..	86.2	4.7	90.9	9.1	2,995
South West	57.6	4.2	61.9	19.7	..	82.3	6.2	88.5	11.5	1,280
West Midlands	62.0	2.8	64.8	12.4	0.7	77.9	8.2	86.1	13.9	1,491
North West	57.8	3.9	61.8	12.4	..	74.7	7.7	82.4	17.6	1,814
England	61.4	3.5	64.9	14.5	0.5	80.0	6.6	86.6	13.4	13,599
Wales	55.8	3.4	59.1	13.5	..	73.3	7.1	80.4	19.6	778
Scotland	59.0	4.3	63.3	10.8	0.7	74.8	7.1	82.0	18.0	1,466
Northern Ireland	51.4	2.8	54.3	16.3	..	71.4	10.9	82.3	17.7	378

1 Heads aged 16-59/64.
2 Respondents' self-assessment.
3 Includes those not stating whether full-time or part-time.

Source: Labour Force Survey, Employment Department

7.6 Persons with a second job, 1981 and 1990

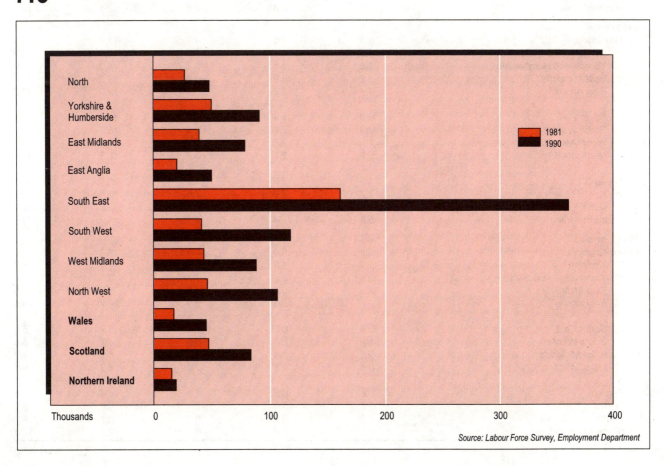

Source: Labour Force Survey, Employment Department

7.7 Employees in employment: by Standard Industrial Classification and sex, 1981 and 1991[1]

Percentages and thousands

	Agriculture, forestry, fishing (0)	Energy and water supply (1)	Metals, minerals and chemicals (2)	Metal goods, engineering and vehicles industries (3)	Other manufacturing (4)
1981 Males					
United Kingdom	2.2	4.9	5.9	18.4	10.9
North	1.8	9.6	10.8	19.0	8.7
Yorkshire & Humberside	2.0	9.9	9.9	15.4	12.6
East Midlands	2.8	10.0	5.6	20.6	14.8
East Anglia	6.7	2.5	3.7	15.7	13.3
South East	1.2	2.4	3.2	16.2	9.5
South West	4.1	2.7	3.8	18.6	11.2
West Midlands	1.7	3.9	8.3	32.4	9.1
North West	0.9	3.9	7.5	19.8	14.1
England	1.9	4.6	5.8	19.2	11.0
Wales	3.3	10.1	11.3	13.6	7.2
Scotland	3.4	5.7	5.0	15.5	11.1
Northern Ireland	5.6	3.1	3.9	11.3	13.6
1981 Females					
United Kingdom	1.0	1.0	2.1	6.5	10.6
North	0.4	1.3	2.4	6.0	10.1
Yorkshire & Humberside	0.9	1.2	2.7	4.8	14.8
East Midlands	1.5	1.1	2.6	5.9	21.1
East Anglia	3.9	0.6	1.2	5.6	12.7
South East	0.8	0.9	1.8	6.6	7.2
South West	1.5	0.9	1.3	5.5	8.5
West Midlands	1.0	1.0	4.0	13.3	8.5
North West	0.4	1.0	2.6	6.2	13.0
England	1.0	1.0	2.3	6.9	10.5
Wales	1.1	1.4	2.2	6.1	8.0
Scotland	0.7	1.0	1.2	4.6	11.9
Northern Ireland	1.5	0.6	0.6	3.4	14.4
1991 Males					
United Kingdom	1.8	3.1	4.4	14.6	10.1
North	1.6	5.4	7.5	16.5	9.8
Yorkshire & Humberside	1.8	4.6	6.9	14.0	13.3
East Midlands	2.2	4.9	5.6	16.7	14.6
East Anglia	4.4	2.2	3.0	12.7	12.2
South East	0.9	1.9	2.5	11.4	7.6
South West	3.3	2.4	2.9	15.7	10.0
West Midlands	1.6	2.5	6.1	25.1	9.5
North West	0.9	2.7	5.7	16.6	12.3
England	1.6	2.9	4.4	15.0	10.1
Wales	3.2	3.9	7.6	14.2	9.5
Scotland	2.3	4.9	2.9	12.0	10.2
Northern Ireland	5.9	2.4	3.1	9.3	12.0
1991 Females					
United Kingdom	0.7	0.8	1.5	4.3	7.9
North	0.4	1.0	1.6	4.3	7.7
Yorkshire & Humberside	0.6	0.8	1.7	3.3	10.5
East Midlands	1.0	0.8	1.8	4.2	14.6
East Anglia	2.4	0.6	0.9	4.1	8.6
South East	0.6	0.7	1.3	3.9	5.0
South West	1.2	0.8	0.9	4.2	5.6
West Midlands	0.8	0.8	2.7	8.1	7.8
North West	0.4	0.8	2.0	4.3	9.1
England	0.8	0.8	1.5	4.4	7.5
Wales	0.8	0.8	1.6	5.4	9.9
Scotland	0.5	0.9	0.9	3.1	9.3
Northern Ireland	1.3	0.4	0.7	2.4	11.3

(continued)

Regional Trends 27, © Crown copyright 1992

7.7 (continued)

Percentages and thousands

	Construction (5)	Distribution, hotels and catering, repairs (6)	Transport and commun- ication (7)	Banking, fina- nce, insurance, business servi- ces & leasing (8)	Public administration and other services (9)	All industries and services (= 100%) (thousands)
1981 Males						
United Kingdom	8.1	15.2	9.1	7.2	18.1	12,562
North	9.8	11.7	7.8	4.4	16.3	654
Yorkshire & Humberside	8.2	13.9	8.0	4.8	15.2	1,083
East Midlands	6.8	13.9	6.7	4.5	14.3	855
East Anglia	8.7	16.8	9.1	5.8	17.8	400
South East	7.3	17.3	11.6	10.9	20.5	4,135
South West	8.2	17.7	8.0	6.4	19.3	883
West Midlands	6.8	13.0	5.8	5.1	13.9	1,199
North West	8.0	14.1	9.2	6.0	16.5	1,391
England	7.6	15.4	9.2	7.5	17.7	10,600
Wales	9.1	12.6	8.2	4.8	19.9	551
Scotland	11.4	13.9	9.4	5.7	18.8	1,128
Northern Ireland	9.3	14.3	5.9	4.8	28.0	283
1981 Females						
United Kingdom	1.2	24.3	3.0	9.0	41.3	9,331
North	1.1	28.4	2.2	6.3	41.7	468
Yorkshire & Humberside	1.2	25.6	2.3	6.9	39.6	768
East Midlands	1.0	22.2	2.7	6.2	35.8	613
East Anglia	1.2	24.7	2.7	7.9	39.5	281
South East	1.4	23.1	4.1	12.5	41.6	3,128
South West	1.2	28.8	2.4	8.6	41.3	658
West Midlands	1.2	22.9	2.3	7.4	38.5	852
North West	1.1	24.5	2.5	7.8	40.9	1,075
England	1.2	24.3	3.1	9.4	40.4	7,845
Wales	1.1	24.8	2.2	6.0	47.3	389
Scotland	1.4	26.1	2.6	7.4	43.1	874
Northern Ireland	0.9	17.3	1.7	5.8	53.9	224
1991 Males						
United Kingdom	7.1	18.2	8.9	11.4	20.4	11,599
North	9.9	14.6	8.3	7.3	19.1	566
Yorkshire & Humberside	7.9	18.4	8.5	7.7	17.0	978
East Midlands	6.2	19.5	7.3	7.3	15.7	814
East Anglia	6.6	19.8	10.9	8.5	19.9	428
South East	6.2	19.7	10.6	16.7	22.5	3,772
South West	6.3	20.7	7.4	10.0	21.5	903
West Midlands	6.6	15.8	7.5	8.3	16.9	1,080
North West	6.9	17.7	8.5	10.2	18.5	1,249
England	6.7	18.7	9.1	11.7	19.9	9,791
Wales	7.2	14.8	8.5	9.6	21.7	509
Scotland	10.1	16.2	8.7	10.3	22.5	1,031
Northern Ireland	7.5	16.6	6.0	6.2	30.9	269
1991 Females						
United Kingdom	1.3	24.2	2.9	12.9	43.5	10,635
North	1.2	26.0	2.3	9.0	46.6	513
Yorkshire & Humberside	1.2	26.0	2.4	10.0	43.6	902
East Midlands	1.4	24.8	2.7	9.6	39.2	742
East Anglia	1.2	26.2	3.4	9.9	42.8	379
South East	1.4	22.2	4.0	17.7	43.2	3,491
South West	1.3	28.2	2.3	12.6	42.9	852
West Midlands	1.3	22.7	2.4	11.9	41.6	930
North West	1.3	24.5	2.7	11.7	43.3	1,147
England	1.4	24.1	3.1	13.5	42.9	8,956
Wales	1.1	24.0	2.1	8.8	45.7	474
Scotland	1.4	26.1	2.3	10.5	45.0	949
Northern Ireland	1.2	20.0	1.7	7.2	53.9	256

1 At June.

Source: Employment Department

7.8 Educational qualifications[1] of the workforce[2], 1991

Percentages and thousands

	Degree or equivalent	Higher education below degree	GCE A level or equivalent	Appren-ticeship	GCE O level or equivalent	CSE below grade 1	Other qualifi-cations[3]	No quali-fication	Total[4] (=100%) (thous-ands)
United Kingdom	9.7	6.5	20.3	7.3	18.8	4.1	6.2	26.4	27,776
North	6.9	6.4	18.8	11.3	17.7	5.2	6.6	26.4	1,425
Yorkshire & Humberside	7.7	6.7	19.1	8.3	17.6	4.0	6.6	29.1	2,385
East Midlands	8.9	5.7	20.2	7.6	16.1	5.3	7.0	28.4	2,010
East Anglia	8.0	6.2	19.5	6.9	19.6	5.4	6.7	26.7	1,014
South East	13.6	6.1	20.5	5.4	20.4	4.2	6.7	22.4	8,688
Greater London	16.4	5.2	19.9	4.6	17.9	3.4	7.4	24.5	3,305
Rest of South East	11.9	6.6	20.9	5.9	21.9	4.6	6.3	21.0	5,383
South West	8.2	7.5	20.8	6.6	21.9	4.9	6.2	23.4	2,264
West Midlands	7.0	5.5	19.1	5.4	17.8	4.7	6.8	32.9	2,565
North West	8.3	6.7	19.7	7.7	19.5	4.6	5.4	27.3	3,038
England	10.0	6.3	20.0	6.7	19.3	4.5	6.5	25.9	23,389
Wales	7.5	6.4	18.1	8.1	20.5	4.5	4.9	29.1	1,306
Scotland	7.7	8.3	25.5	11.1	14.3	..	3.8	28.5	2,408
Northern Ireland	8.6	6.1	16.0	12.3	16.6	2.8	4.9	32.2	673

1 Figures relate to the highest qualification achieved.
2 Economically active persons aged 16-59/64.
3 Includes YTS certificate.
4 Includes those who did not know or did not state their qualifications.

Source: Labour Force Survey, Employment Department

7.9 Population aged 16 and over: by occupational grouping, spring 1991

Percentages and thousands

	In employment												Number of persons (=100%) (thous-ands)
	Employees												
	Managerial & administrators	Associate prof-essional & tech-nical	Clerical & secr-eterial	Craft and similar	Personal and prot-ective services	Sales	Plant & machine oper-ative	Other	Self-emp-loyed	All in employ-ment[1]	Unem-ployed	Economic-ally inactive	
United Kingdom	6.2	4.6	4.3	8.8	6.4	4.9	4.2	5.3	7.6	58.2	5.3	36.5	45,048
North	4.4	4.4	3.6	7.2	7.4	4.8	4.0	6.0	4.9	53.5	6.5	40.0	2,423
Yorkshire & Humberside	5.3	4.1	3.9	8.1	7.6	4.7	4.0	6.7	6.6	57.3	5.2	37.5	3,899
East Midlands	6.7	4.9	4.0	8.0	8.3	4.1	3.9	6.5	7.7	60.0	4.7	35.3	3,183
East Anglia	6.5	4.2	4.4	7.8	6.6	5.8	4.1	6.2	8.5	60.3	4.1	35.6	1,631
South East	8.3	5.5	5.2	10.5	4.8	4.9	4.4	3.7	8.5	60.9	4.8	34.3	13,716
South West	5.7	4.0	3.9	8.7	5.4	5.4	4.6	4.2	10.7	58.3	4.8	36.9	3,716
West Midlands	5.6	4.0	3.6	8.2	7.9	4.6	4.2	7.4	6.7	58.2	6.0	35.8	4,098
North West	5.5	4.4	4.3	8.8	6.5	4.8	4.0	6.0	6.6	56.5	6.0	37.6	4,986
England	6.6	4.7	4.4	9.0	6.3	4.8	4.2	5.3	7.8	58.8	5.2	36.0	37,651
Wales	4.5	4.0	3.4	7.6	6.4	5.3	3.9	5.7	7.1	53.2	5.5	41.3	2,278
Scotland	4.4	4.3	4.5	7.8	7.3	5.8	3.9	5.5	5.6	56.4	5.7	37.9	3,975
Northern Ireland	3.7	4.4	3.3	8.0	6.5	4.0	3.5	4.4	7.5	52.9	7.2	39.9	1,145

1 Includes those on government employment or training programmes, employment status not stated and occupation not stated/inadequately described.

Source: Labour Force Survey, Employment Department

7.10 Economic activity rates[1]: by sex

Percentages

	Estimates										Projec- tions
	1981	1984[2]	1984[2]	1985	1986	1987	1988	1989	1990	1991	2001
Males											
United Kingdom	76.5	74.2	74.5	74.9	74.2	74.2	74.3	74.6	74.5	73.9	72.9
North	76.9	72.4	72.5	72.1	71.9	72.4	72.1	71.7	71.0	70.1	68.7
Yorkshire & Humberside	76.6	73.6	73.8	74.7	72.9	72.6	72.4	73.0	73.6	73.3	72.1
East Midlands	77.8	75.2	75.9	74.1	75.4	74.9	74.4	75.7	74.7	75.3	74.2
East Anglia	73.8	73.0	73.2	72.2	71.5	72.5	72.5	72.8	73.9	72.6	71.8
South East	77.3	76.3	76.6	76.3	75.7	75.5	76.6	76.4	76.2	75.7	75.0
Greater London	77.6	75.4	76.6	76.5	75.8	75.5	75.8	76.1	76.3	74.4	74.7
Rest of South East	77.2	76.9	76.6	76.2	75.6	75.5	77.1	76.5	76.1	76.5	75.2
South West	72.2	69.9	70.4	71.0	71.0	71.2	71.1	72.1	71.8	71.9	71.0
West Midlands	78.0	74.5	74.7	75.5	75.0	75.7	75.5	75.8	76.4	75.7	73.8
North West	77.0	74.1	74.2	74.8	73.9	73.8	73.7	74.0	74.1	73.5	73.4
England	76.7	74.4	74.7	75.3	74.6	74.7	74.8	75.1	74.9	74.4	72.7
Wales	73.3	70.3	70.6	69.4	69.0	67.7	68.9	70.1	69.9	69.0	67.7
Scotland	76.9	74.8	75.2	73.8	73.0	73.2	73.1	73.2	73.3	72.6	70.9
Northern Ireland	76.5	73.2	73.8	73.1	73.5	72.5	72.6	73.2	72.1	71.3	70.7
Females											
United Kingdom	47.5	48.3	48.8	49.3	49.7	50.4	51.0	52.6	52.8	52.5	55.0
North	46.3	46.6	47.0	45.6	47.4	49.0	49.2	50.4	49.3	49.7	51.7
Yorkshire & Humberside	47.7	47.9	48.2	48.4	49.2	49.9	49.4	50.4	51.3	51.4	53.9
East Midlands	48.4	50.1	50.1	49.8	51.5	50.6	51.9	54.9	54.9	53.8	55.8
East Anglia	46.3	46.7	47.3	48.9	49.0	50.3	54.0	54.1	56.0	53.4	55.6
South East	48.8	50.9	51.5	51.3	51.4	52.3	52.9	54.4	55.0	54.7	57.6
Greater London	50.1	50.9	51.6	52.2	50.7	51.9	51.8	53.7	54.3	53.9	57.9
Rest of South East	47.9	51.0	51.5	50.7	51.8	52.5	53.6	54.9	55.5	55.3	57.5
South West	44.0	46.1	46.8	48.2	47.4	50.3	50.4	52.0	51.6	52.2	54.7
West Midlands	48.8	48.1	48.8	49.3	50.7	50.2	50.9	52.7	53.3	52.7	54.5
North West	48.9	47.8	48.4	49.6	49.3	50.4	51.2	52.0	51.5	51.7	54.1
England	47.9	48.9	49.4	50.0	50.3	51.2	51.7	53.2	53.4	53.1	55.6
Wales	42.2	44.0	44.1	43.3	45.1	43.8	44.5	48.2	48.7	48.1	50.8
Scotland	47.4	46.8	47.3	48.0	47.7	48.5	49.3	50.8	51.6	51.2	52.6
Northern Ireland	43.5	43.3	43.8	43.1	44.9	44.4	44.7	46.0	47.4	47.4	49.6

1 Percentage of the home population aged 16 or over who are in the civilian labour force.
2 GB labour force definitions up to 1984, ILO definitions from 1984.

Source: Labour Force Survey, Employment Department

7.11 Employees absent from work owing to sickness[1]: by sex

Percentages

	1984			1986			1991		
	Males	Females	All persons	Males	Females	All persons	Males	Females	All persons
United Kingdom	4.4	5.1	4.7	4.2	4.9	4.5	4.0	5.6	4.8
North	5.7	4.0	5.0	4.5	5.0	4.7	4.3	6.4	5.3
Yorkshire & Humberside	4.2	4.2	4.2	3.8	4.3	4.0	4.2	4.8	4.5
East Midlands	4.3	4.9	4.5	4.6	4.6	4.6	3.8	5.9	4.7
East Anglia	4.3	4.8	4.5	3.4	5.9	4.4	3.1	4.3	3.7
South East	4.4	5.3	4.8	4.2	5.1	4.6	3.7	5.1	4.4
South West	4.5	4.9	4.7	4.1	5.0	4.5	4.0	5.7	4.8
West Midlands	4.4	5.3	4.8	4.6	4.6	4.6	4.0	6.7	5.2
North West	5.0	6.1	5.5	4.2	5.2	4.6	4.3	5.7	5.0
England	4.5	5.1	4.8	4.2	5.0	4.5	3.9	5.5	4.7
Wales	4.2	4.3	4.2	3.4	5.1	4.2	4.9	6.0	5.5
Scotland	3.8	4.7	4.2	3.9	4.6	4.2	4.1	6.7	5.3
Northern Ireland	4.9	5.8	5.3	3.7	4.9	4.2	4.3	5.7	5.0

1 At least one day away from work during the week before interview.

Source: Labour Force Survey, Employment Department

7.12 Days lost due to industrial disputes

Thousands and rates[1]

	1981		1984		1986		1990		Annual average 1980-1990	
	Thou-sands	Rate[1]	Thou-sands	Rate[1]	Thou-sands	Rate[1]	Thou-sands	Rate[1]	Thou-sands	Rate[1]
United Kingdom	4,266	195	27,135	1,278	1,920	89	1,903	83	6,730	307
North	341	304	4,211	3,976	233	220	78	70	893	816
Yorkshire & Humberside	449	242	9,354	5,291	250	142	89	46	1,541	846
East Midlands	116	79	2,908	2,015	60	40	33	21	494	330
East Anglia	80	117	87	124	28	39	26	32	64	88
South East	843	116	1,522	212	298	41	523	69	853	116
South West	171	111	393	255	62	39	22	13	147	92
West Midlands	613	299	1,368	696	180	92	183	87	485	240
North West	692	281	1,381	603	390	170	720	298	676	283
England	3,305	179	21,224	1,182	1,501	83	1,678	87	5,153	278
Wales	292	311	3,527	3,981	78	88	84	91	827	889
Scotland	599	299	2,333	1,227	312	166	122	62	692	357
Northern Ireland	69	136	52	105	30	60	18	35	58	114

1 Days lost per 1,000 employees.

Source: Employment Department

7.13 Unemployed claimants: by duration and sex, 1992[1]

Percentages and numbers

	2 weeks or less	Over 2 and up to 8 weeks	Over 8 and up to 13 weeks	Over 13 and up to 26 weeks	Over 26 weeks up to 1 year	Over 1 and up to 2 years	Over 2 and up to 3 years	Over 3 and up to 5 years	Over 5 years	Total (= 100%) (numbers)
Males										
United Kingdom	5.8	13.8	10.0	18.1	22.2	17.0	4.7	3.3	5.0	2,045,371
North	4.9	13.8	9.7	17.5	20.3	17.8	5.4	4.2	6.4	123,461
Yorkshire & Humberside	5.6	13.6	9.6	17.9	21.8	17.3	5.3	3.7	5.2	180,725
East Midlands	6.2	15.0	10.5	18.1	21.9	16.9	4.6	2.9	3.9	128,208
East Anglia	7.4	17.1	11.8	18.8	21.1	15.8	3.9	1.7	2.4	54,899
South East	6.4	13.8	10.5	19.2	24.6	17.0	3.8	2.1	2.5	592,310
South West	6.7	15.8	11.4	19.4	22.5	16.3	3.6	1.9	2.4	152,408
West Midlands	5.5	13.1	9.6	17.8	23.8	17.3	4.6	3.1	5.2	197,400
North West	5.5	13.1	9.5	17.2	20.9	17.6	5.6	4.3	6.3	249,966
England	6.0	14.0	10.2	18.4	22.8	17.1	4.5	2.9	4.1	1,679,377
Wales	5.5	13.6	10.4	18.5	21.7	18.5	4.7	3.1	3.9	101,149
Scotland	5.3	14.5	9.9	17.2	20.0	16.1	5.3	4.7	7.0	184,108
Northern Ireland	3.1	8.2	6.3	13.0	15.6	16.0	7.5	8.4	21.7	80,737
Females										
United Kingdom	9.2	15.8	11.3	21.0	21.6	12.1	3.1	2.5	3.4	628,493
North	8.7	15.5	10.6	20.8	20.7	12.8	3.7	2.8	4.4	34,535
Yorkshire & Humberside	8.9	16.3	10.5	20.3	21.5	12.2	3.3	2.9	4.0	52,365
East Midlands	9.7	16.0	11.0	20.7	22.1	11.7	3.0	2.3	3.5	40,264
East Anglia	11.6	18.0	12.9	20.6	20.3	10.9	2.3	1.4	2.1	18,208
South East	9.2	15.2	11.5	22.4	23.3	12.1	2.6	1.6	2.0	191,914
South West	10.5	16.8	13.2	21.5	20.4	11.1	2.4	1.8	2.3	48,921
West Midlands	8.7	15.0	10.4	20.8	23.0	12.6	3.1	2.4	4.0	61,392
North West	9.0	16.0	10.8	20.2	20.5	12.6	3.8	3.1	4.0	71,990
England	9.3	15.7	11.3	21.3	22.1	12.1	3.0	2.2	3.0	519,589
Wales	9.6	17.6	12.5	21.5	19.7	11.3	2.8	2.3	2.8	27,606
Scotland	9.3	17.0	12.1	18.7	20.0	11.7	3.5	3.4	4.3	57,243
Northern Ireland	6.7	11.4	8.0	19.2	18.3	13.4	5.6	6.5	10.8	24,055

1 At January.

Source: Employment Department

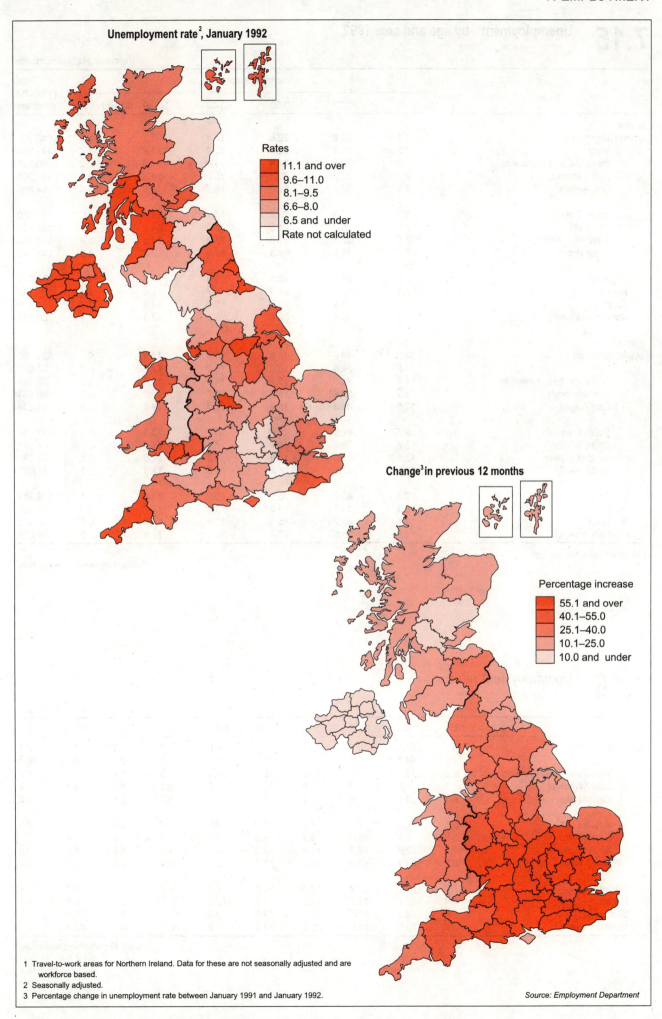

Unemployment rate [2]**, January 1992**

Rates

- 11.1 and over
- 9.6–11.0
- 8.1–9.5
- 6.6–8.0
- 6.5 and under
- Rate not calculated

Change [3] **in previous 12 months**

Percentage increase

- 55.1 and over
- 40.1–55.0
- 25.1–40.0
- 10.1–25.0
- 10.0 and under

1 Travel-to-work areas for Northern Ireland. Data for these are not seasonally adjusted and are
    workforce based.
2 Seasonally adjusted.
3 Percentage change in unemployment rate between January 1991 and January 1992.

Source: Employment Department

7.15 Unemployment[1]: by age and sex, 1992

Percentages and numbers

	Under 20	20-29	30-39	40-49	50-59	60 and over	Total (= 100%) numbers
			Percentage aged				
Males							
United Kingdom	7.1	38.2	22.6	15.8	13.7	2.6	2,045,371
North	7.9	38.9	22.4	15.2	13.8	1.7	123,461
Yorkshire & Humberside	7.9	39.5	21.4	15.0	14.0	2.2	180,725
East Midlands	7.7	37.7	21.4	15.9	14.3	3.1	128,208
East Anglia	7.8	36.1	21.0	16.7	14.5	3.8	54,899
South East	5.9	37.3	23.9	16.1	13.6	3.2	592,310
South West	7.0	36.2	21.6	17.5	14.6	3.2	152,408
West Midlands	7.5	37.5	21.6	15.5	14.5	3.4	197,400
North West	7.7	40.5	22.3	14.9	12.7	1.9	249,966
England	7.0	38.0	22.5	15.8	13.8	2.8	1,679,377
Wales	7.9	40.1	22.9	15.7	12.0	1.4	101,149
Scotland	7.4	39.5	22.4	15.3	13.8	1.7	184,108
Northern Ireland	6.6	35.8	25.1	18.1	12.9	1.4	80,737
Females							
United Kingdom	13.0	40.6	16.6	15.8	13.9	0.1	628,493
North	15.5	39.6	16.0	15.2	13.7	0.1	34,535
Yorkshire & Humberside	14.8	41.0	15.7	14.9	13.5	0.1	52,365
East Midlands	13.8	39.9	16.2	16.2	13.9	0.1	40,264
East Anglia	13.6	38.8	15.7	17.8	14.1	0.1	18,208
South East	10.7	41.6	18.0	16.1	13.5	0.1	191,914
South West	12.7	38.9	16.1	17.9	14.3	0.1	48,921
West Midlands	13.5	40.0	15.8	15.9	14.6	0.1	61,392
North West	14.8	41.6	15.2	14.5	13.8	0.1	71,990
England	12.8	40.7	16.6	15.9	13.8	0.1	519,589
Wales	15.3	40.1	16.0	15.8	12.7	0.0	27,606
Scotland	13.1	40.2	16.5	15.4	14.8	0.1	57,243
Northern Ireland	12.5	38.8	18.3	15.3	14.8	0.3	24,055

1 Unadjusted figures.

Source: Employment Department

7.16 Unemployment rates

Percentages

	1981	1983	1984	1985	1986	1987	1988	1989	1990	1991
United Kingdom	8.1	10.5	10.7	10.9	11.1	10.0	8.1	6.3	5.8	8.1
North	11.7	14.6	15.2	15.4	15.3	14.1	11.9	9.9	8.7	10.4
Yorkshire & Humberside	8.8	11.4	11.7	12.0	12.5	11.3	9.3	7.4	6.7	8.7
East Midlands	7.4	9.5	9.8	9.8	10.0	9.0	7.1	5.4	5.1	7.2
East Anglia	6.3	8.0	7.9	8.1	8.5	7.3	5.2	3.6	3.7	5.8
South East	5.5	7.5	7.8	8.1	8.3	7.2	5.4	3.9	4.0	7.0
South West	6.8	8.7	9.0	9.3	9.5	8.1	6.2	4.5	4.4	7.1
West Midlands	10.0	12.9	12.7	12.8	12.9	11.4	8.9	6.6	5.9	8.6
North West	10.2	13.3	13.6	13.7	13.7	12.5	10.4	8.5	7.7	9.4
England	7.7	10.0	10.2	10.4	10.6	9.4	7.4	5.6	5.3	8.4
Wales	10.4	12.9	13.2	13.6	13.5	12.0	9.8	7.3	6.6	8.7
Scotland	9.9	12.3	12.6	12.9	13.3	13.0	11.2	9.3	8.1	8.7
Northern Ireland	12.7	15.5	15.9	15.9	17.2	17.0	15.6	14.6	13.4	13.7

Source: Employment Department

7.17 Vacancies[1] at jobcentres

Thousands

	1981	1983	1984	1985	1986	1987	1988	1989	1990	1991
United Kingdom	91.1	137.3	150.2	162.1	188.8	235.4	248.7	219.5	173.7	118.0
North	4.0	5.9	6.6	7.8	9.8	12.0	11.4	10.7	10.7	6.6
Yorkshire & Humberside	5.3	8.7	8.2	8.7	11.3	15.6	15.5	13.3	11.7	7.9
East Midlands	5.5	8.0	8.1	9.0	10.3	12.2	13.8	12.9	10.5	7.1
East Anglia	3.6	5.1	5.4	5.8	6.2	8.0	9.7	8.3	5.4	3.2
South East	34.0	50.8	59.4	62.3	70.8	90.7	95.1	71.7	47.6	28.8
South West	7.7	12.7	13.6	16.1	18.1	19.7	20.4	18.5	13.9	9.9
West Midlands	5.9	9.6	10.7	12.2	15.4	21.1	24.1	20.5	14.6	8.2
North West	7.9	13.3	14.5	16.0	19.0	24.2	23.9	24.4	21.1	15.8
England	73.9	114.0	126.5	137.9	161.0	203.3	213.7	180.3	135.4	87.4
Wales	4.9	6.8	7.3	8.0	9.5	11.1	12.1	13.8	12.2	8.2
Scotland	11.6	15.3	14.8	14.6	16.3	18.8	20.0	21.7	21.6	18.3
Northern Ireland	0.7	1.2	1.5	1.6	2.0	2.2	2.8	3.7	4.5	4.1

1 Vacancies remaining unfilled, seasonally adjusted annual averages.

Source: Employment Department

7.18 Restart counselling, 1990-91

Thousands and percentages

	Number invited to interview (thousands)	Number of interviews conducted[1] (thousands)	Interviews resulting in an offer of help		Interviews where the offer of help was taken up	
			(thousands)	(percentages)	(thousands)	(percentages)
Great Britain	1,690.0	1,888.4	1,568.5	83	1,314.1	70
Northern	127.1	142.6	120.2	84	81.1	57
Yorkshire & Humberside	176.6	185.0	150.8	82	114.4	62
East Midlands & Eastern	140.5	144.7	117.2	81	100.8	70
London & South East	393.1	448.9	378.3	84	358.4	80
South West	83.8	93.5	73.5	79	59.6	64
West Midlands	151.3	167.8	140.2	84	116.7	70
North West	290.0	313.3	265.9	85	213.1	68
England	1,362.4	1,495.8	1,246.1	83	1,044.2	70
Wales	91.5	114.7	91.6	80	77.7	68
Scotland	236.0	277.8	230.9	83	192.2	69

1 This is the number of interviews held, as one person may be interviewed more than once, the figure may be higher than the number of people contacted.

Source: Employment Department

7.19 Business enterprise training[1], 1990-91

Numbers

	Training in business skills	Improving employer investment	Information for firms about training	Innovative training solutions	Other
Northern	3,307	129	1,154	13	27
North West	1,227	77	165	35	54
East Midlands and Eastern	1,035	30	110	6	30
West Midlands	1,776	55	1,517	0	353

1 Responsibility for business and enterprise training and support moved from Employment Department Area Offices to Training and Enterprise Councils throughout 1990-91. These figures should be used in conjunction with the Business Growth Training figures in table 7.23.

Source: Employment Department

7.20 Business growth training[1], 1990-91

Numbers

	Better business and training plans[2]	Business skills seminars[3]	Using consultants to manage change[4]	Tackling skills needs[4,5]	Innovative training solutions[4,6]
Great Britain	30,835	62,587	1,042	196	88
Yorkshire and Humberside	..	4,008	87	12	11
East Midlands and Eastern	..	6,494	165	11	11
London	..	16,945	123	10	9
South East	..	5,866	77	8	9
South West	..	3,453	87	12	7
West Midlands	..	4,821	168	5	6
North West	..	8,758	94	5	6
Wales	..	2,351	56	16	4
Scotland	..	8,286	185	8	13

1 Responsibility for business and enterprise training and support moved from Employment Department Area Offices to Training and Enterprise Councils throughout 1990-91. These figures should be used in conjunction with the Business Enterprise Training figures in table 7.22.
2 Number of kits issued.
3 Comprises Firm Start, Growth Programmes, Graduate Enterprise Programmes and Business Enterprise Programmes, 1,605 of which are managed through Employment Department Head Office.
4 Number of projects.
5 Great Britain total includes 109 projects managed through Employment Department Head Office.
6 Great Britain total includes 12 projects managed through Employment Department Head Office.

Source: Employment Department

7.21 Employment training[1]: by total starts[2], 1990-91

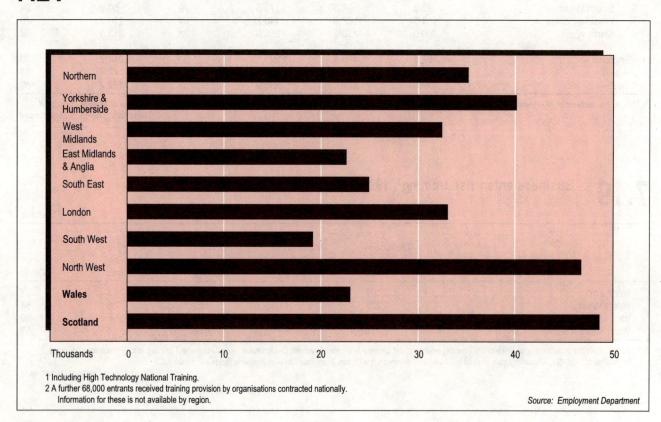

1 Including High Technology National Training.
2 A further 68,000 entrants received training provision by organisations contracted nationally. Information for these is not available by region.

Source: Employment Department

7.22

Youth training scheme: by total starts[1,2], 1990- 91

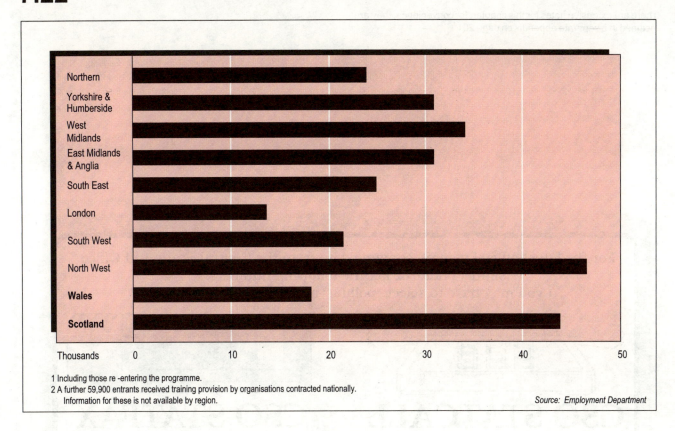

1 Including those re -entering the programme.
2 A further 59,900 entrants received training provision by organisations contracted nationally.
  Information for these is not available by region.

Source: Employment Department

7.23

Youth Training leavers[1], 1990-91

Percentages and thousands

	Status three/six months after leaving (percentages)					Gained qualificat-ion during training (percen-tages)	Replies received (= 100%) (thou-sands)[4]	All entrants (thou-sands)[5]
	Full-time and part-time work[2]	Different YT scheme	Full-time course at college/ training centre	Unem-ployed	Other[3]			
Great Britain[6]	56.8	10.2	5.6	20.1	7.3	38.0	122	348
Northern	47.1	15.4	5.0	24.3	8.2	32.7	10	24
Yorkshire & Humberside	54.8	11.0	5.4	21.2	7.6	35.2	14	31
West Midlands	58.5	9.8	5.9	18.6	7.2	39.4	13	34
East Midlands & East	63.1	7.8	6.1	16.4	6.6	41.5	15	31
South East	62.6	5.3	7.2	17.9	7.1	45.9	9	25
London	51.6	7.1	7.5	26.0	7.9	32.9	4	14
South West	63.6	7.3	6.1	16.5	6.5	47.2	8	22
North West	55.3	10.3	6.0	20.9	7.6	37.8	16	47
England	57.5	9.6	5.9	19.8	7.4	38.8	88	226
Wales	53.1	10.3	5.4	22.5	8.6	32.9	7	18
Scotland	52.9	14.2	4.7	21.9	6.3	36.4	18	44

1 Leavers before October 1990 followed up after three months. October to December 1990 leavers followed up in June 1991. Leavers after December 1990
  followed up after six months.
2 Includes those leavers in self-employment.
3 Includes those not answered.
4 Great Britain and England totals include replies received for which no regional breakdown is avaliable.
5 All entrants includes those re-entering YT.
6 National Providers Unit trainees are included in Great Britain totals but cannot be allocated to regions.

Source: Employment Department

There are extensive notes for this chapter, for convenience, they are included in a separate appendix on page 201.

For the latest official macro-economic data from the Central Statistical Office simply phone or fax the following numbers
(you may have to select "polling" mode on your fax machine)

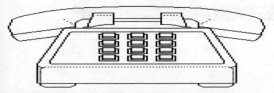

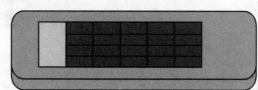

CSO STATCALL
0839 3383 PLUS ..

CSO STATFAX
0336 4160 PLUS ..

Retail prices index	37
Monthly trade figures	38
Balance of payments	39
PSBR	40
Index of production	41
Producer prices	42
Retail sales index	43
Credit business	44
Gross domestic product	45
and for forthcoming economic release dates	46

Calls are charged at 36p per minute cheap rate; 48p per minute at all other times

CSO   Great George Street London SWIP 3AQ

Chapter 8: Income and Spending

Wages and hours

- Workers in the South East earn more in less time. Wages in the South East are far higher than in any other region even though total hours are slightly shorter than elsewhere.

(Tables 8.3 and 8.4)

Tax

- Taxpayers in the South East pay higher rates of tax than elsewhere - in 1989-90 they paid an average of nearly 18 per cent in income tax. This was a full 4 percentage points above taxpayers in the North (who paid the lowest rate).

(Table 8.8)

Government spending

- Government spending on cash benefits per head is highest in Northern Ireland and lowest in East Anglia.

(Table 8.7)

Household spending

- The cost of keeping the roof over your head is lowest in Northern Ireland - housing costs account for only an eighth of total household spending. In East Anglia, the South East, and the West Midlands housing takes around a fifth of spending.

(Table 8.9)

- People in the South East spend more on leisure than in any other region. A seventh of household spending goes on leisure compared with just under a tenth in Northern Ireland.

(Table 8.9)

Consumption

- *Butchers do good business in Scotland* where spending on meat (especially beef) and meat products is higher than in other regions. But, fishmongers should thrive in Yorkshire and Humberside where they eat the most fish.

(Table 8.10)

Consumer goods

- People in the South East have more luxury goods than in other regions - the region has the highest ownership rates for dishwashers, telephones and video recorders.

(Table 8.12)

- Microwave ownership is highest in Wales.

(Table 8.12)

Share ownership

- Share ownership is highest in the South East with over a third of adults owning shares and lowest in East Anglia (16 per cent of adults).

(Chart 8.13)

8.1 Household income: by source, 1980-1981 and 1989-1990

	Percentage of average gross weekly household income						Average gross weekly household income[2](£) (= 100%)	Number of households in sample
	Wages and salaries	Self employ-ment	Invest-ments	Annuities and pensions[1]	Social security benefits[2]	Other income		
1980-1981[3]								
United Kingdom	69.5	5.8	3.5	2.9	12.6	5.7	157.80	14,469
North	71.0	4.0	2.2	2.9	16.2	3.7	140.24	927
Yorkshire & Humberside	70.1	4.3	2.5	2.5	15.9	4.7	135.01	1,306
East Midlands	71.8	5.8	2.8	2.4	11.8	5.4	148.63	950
East Anglia	67.8	7.2	3.7	2.9	12.4	6.0	151.65	518
South East	70.8	6.0	4.0	2.9	9.5	6.8	183.44	4,291
South West	60.8	7.2	5.8	4.4	14.2	7.6	149.06	1,090
West Midlands	71.2	4.9	3.2	2.5	12.0	6.2	155.31	1,316
North West	69.3	5.7	2.9	2.6	13.7	5.8	155.42	1,670
England	69.7	5.7	3.6	2.9	12.0	6.1	160.70	12,068
Wales	65.7	6.6	2.9	3.8	16.6	4.4	143.81	825
Scotland	70.5	7.2	2.7	2.7	13.9	3.0	146.79	1,312
Northern Ireland	64.8	6.0	2.1	1.9	22.0	3.2	122.53	264
1989-1990[3]								
United Kingdom	62.8	9.8	5.1	4.7	10.6	6.9	319.36	14,456
North	62.5	8.2	3.5	4.3	15.4	6.1	265.62	847
Yorkshire & Humberside	64.8	6.3	4.7	4.7	13.5	6.0	263.52	1,289
East Midlands	63.7	8.1	4.8	5.6	10.8	7.1	311.67	1,023
East Anglia	61.3	10.3	6.5	5.6	9.4	7.0	325.08	560
South East	64.1	11.3	5.8	4.2	7.4	7.3	395.42	4,233
South West	58.2	12.2	5.9	6.3	9.6	7.8	317.36	1,260
West Midlands	64.3	8.0	4.3	4.0	11.8	7.6	295.87	1,347
North West	63.6	8.4	4.4	4.2	12.4	6.9	289.75	1,609
England	63.3	9.8	5.2	4.6	10.0	7.1	329.06	12,168
Wales	53.2	11.6	5.7	6.3	16.9	6.2	263.08	725
Scotland	63.7	8.8	4.5	4.8	13.3	4.8	277.48	1,300
Northern Ireland	57.5	10.2	2.9	2.8	19.4	7.2	232.69	263

1 Excluding social security benefits.
2 The figures cannot be compared directly between years. Following the introduction of the Housing Benefit Scheme in 1982, changes were made to the calculation of household income and housing expenditure.
3 Averages for the two calendar years taken together.

Source: Family Expenditure Survey, Central Statistical Office

8.2 Distribution of household income, 1989-1990

	Percentage of households in each weekly income group								Average income £ per week		Number of house-holds in sample (=100%)
	Under 60	60 but under 80	80 but under 125	125 but under 175	175 but under 225	225 but under 325	325 but under 425	425 and over	Per house-hold	Per person	
United Kingdom	8.3	5.8	11.5	9.4	8.6	16.7	13.9	25.7	319.4	128.1	14,456
North	11.2	7.3	14.4	10.9	7.8	16.4	13.9	18.1	265.6	103.3	847
Yorkshire & Humberside	10.3	6.5	13.3	9.9	9.9	18.4	14.7	17.1	263.5	105.1	1,289
East Midlands	6.7	5.2	12.1	10.0	7.9	17.8	14.6	25.7	311.7	121.9	1,023
East Anglia	5.7	5.7	9.3	10.2	9.1	15.5	17.1	27.3	325.1	133.2	560
South East	6.6	4.6	9.3	7.2	7.4	14.9	14.5	35.5	395.4	161.4	4,233
South West	5.5	5.3	9.0	10.6	10.4	18.5	15.7	25.0	317.4	130.1	1,260
West Midlands	9.5	4.6	14.0	9.2	9.1	17.5	12.3	23.8	295.9	118.4	1,347
North West	8.7	7.0	11.6	10.3	8.9	18.0	13.9	21.7	289.7	115.7	1,609
England	7.8	5.5	11.1	9.1	8.5	16.7	14.4	26.9	329.1	132.4	12,168
Wales	9.4	7.6	15.3	13.4	8.7	17.4	10.3	17.9	263.1	104.9	725
Scotland	11.3	7.1	12.9	9.6	9.1	16.9	12.5	20.5	277.5	112.0	1,300
Northern Ireland	15.6	8.4	14.8	14.1	8.4	13.7	8.7	16.3	232.7	81.2	263

Source: Family Expenditure Survey, Central Statistical Office

8.3 Average weekly earnings and hours for men[1], 1991[2]

	Average gross weekly earnings							Percentage of employees who received overtime pay	Average weekly hours	
		of which			Percentage earning under				Total including overtime (hours)	Overtime (hours)
	Total (£)	Overtime pay (£)	PBR[3] etc pay (£)	Shift etc premium pay (£)	£200	£270	£360			
All full-time men										
Great Britain	318.9	22.5	13.6	5.7	22.4	47.7	72.0	35.4	41.5	3.3
North	289.3	25.0	15.5	7.6	25.4	52.9	78.4	37.7	42.1	3.7
Tyne & Wear	288.1	24.7	13.8	5.9	26.1	55.7	78.0	..	41.8	3.7
Yorkshire & Humberside	286.6	23.5	16.2	5.5	27.5	54.5	79.2	37.9	41.9	3.6
South Yorkshire	294.7	20.8	19.9	6.5	24.1	51.6	77.9	..	41.4	3.2
West Yorkshire	285.7	23.4	15.6	4.7	29.0	55.8	79.7	..	41.7	3.6
East Midlands	292.6	25.1	15.5	5.3	25.6	53.8	78.4	38.3	42.2	3.8
East Anglia	300.2	24.4	13.5	5.4	24.9	52.1	76.2	38.8	42.5	3.8
South East	368.7	21.4	13.4	5.0	15.4	37.0	61.6	32.4	40.9	2.9
Greater London	408.7	20.5	14.2	5.3	11.7	30.9	54.9	29.4	40.2	2.7
South West	297.1	20.4	10.2	5.1	25.6	51.6	75.7	35.7	41.1	3.0
West Midlands	291.1	20.8	15.6	5.3	25.2	54.2	78.7	36.0	41.5	3.2
West Midlands (MC)	298.0	20.1	14.4	5.9	22.4	51.9	77.3	..	41.2	3.0
North West	300.3	23.3	13.1	6.8	24.5	51.1	75.1	36.2	41.5	3.4
Greater Manchester	300.4	21.5	14.0	5.8	24.9	51.4	74.8	..	41.3	3.2
Merseyside	299.2	26.4	11.9	8.5	24.4	51.8	75.4	..	41.6	3.5
England	322.8	22.3	13.9	5.5	21.6	46.8	71.3	35.2	41.4	3.2
Wales	280.1	22.2	13.4	6.9	28.6	56.7	81.0	36.6	41.7	3.4
Scotland	299.5	23.9	11.4	6.8	27.1	52.1	74.5	36.9	42.1	3.5
Northern Ireland	272.4	25.9	8.4	4.7	37.0	59.3	78.1	35.8	41.9	3.7
Full-time manual men										
Great Britain	253.1	35.3	15.1	9.2	31.6	65.3	88.0	52.1	44.4	5.3
North	251.8	36.6	18.4	10.8	31.6	65.4	88.8	50.1	44.3	5.4
Yorkshire & Humberside	245.3	35.0	20.1	8.2	34.8	67.8	89.7	52.6	44.3	5.3
East Midlands	248.0	38.0	18.8	8.3	33.0	67.4	88.5	54.3	44.8	5.7
East Anglia	251.2	37.6	14.3	8.7	32.6	66.7	89.3	57.5	45.3	5.9
South East	272.4	37.5	11.9	9.2	24.5	56.8	83.6	52.7	44.6	5.4
South West	235.1	30.8	10.3	8.2	37.6	72.3	91.9	52.2	43.9	4.8
West Midlands	243.0	31.2	18.3	8.4	32.4	69.6	91.6	50.7	43.8	4.8
North West	249.8	35.2	14.0	11.2	32.5	67.3	88.8	51.6	44.2	5.2
England	254.2	35.5	15.1	9.1	30.7	64.7	87.9	52.5	44.4	5.3
Wales	239.3	31.5	16.7	10.3	36.8	69.9	90.9	48.0	44.0	4.9
Scotland	251.1	35.5	14.1	9.2	36.8	68.6	87.2	51.4	45.1	5.4
Northern Ireland	214.8	27.8	10.5	6.6	52.2	79.3	93.1	43.8	43.1	4.3
Full-time non-manual men										
Great Britain	375.7	11.4	12.4	2.6	14.5	32.4	58.1	21.0	38.7	1.4
North	336.0	10.5	11.9	3.5	17.6	37.3	65.4	22.2	39.1	1.4
Yorkshire & Humberside	334.7	10.1	11.8	2.2	18.9	39.1	66.8	20.7	38.7	1.3
East Midlands	343.2	10.4	11.7	2.0	17.2	38.4	66.9	20.2	39.0	1.4
East Anglia	349.4	11.1	12.6	2.2	17.1	37.4	63.0	20.1	39.3	1.5
South East	425.0	12.0	14.2	2.6	10.1	25.4	48.8	20.5	38.5	1.4
South West	347.9	11.8	10.1	2.4	15.7	34.6	62.4	22.2	38.6	1.4
West Midlands	343.1	9.6	12.6	2.0	17.4	37.5	64.8	20.0	38.7	1.2
North West	348.0	12.1	12.1	2.6	17.0	35.8	62.2	21.6	38.7	1.5
England	380.0	11.3	12.9	2.5	14.1	31.8	57.4	20.8	38.7	1.4
Wales	328.8	11.0	9.3	2.9	18.9	40.9	69.2	22.9	38.8	1.4
Scotland	349.4	12.0	8.7	4.2	17.2	35.2	61.5	21.9	38.7	1.4
Northern Ireland	331.2	23.9	6.3	2.7	21.5	38.9	62.8	27.7	40.5	3.0

1 Data relate to full-time men on adult rates whose pay for the survey pay-period was not affected by absence.
2 At April.
3 PBR ETC. pay is payments-by-results, bonuses, commission and other incentive payments.

Source: New Earnings Survey, Employment Department; Department of Economic Development, Northern Ireland

8.4 Average weekly earnings and hours for women[1], 1991[2]

		Average gross weekly earnings						Percentage of employees	Average weekly hours	
		of which						who received overtime pay	Total including overtime (hours)	Overtime (hours)
	Total (£)	Overtime pay (£)	PBR[3] etc pay (£)	Shift etc premium pay (£)	Percentage earning under					
					£150	£200	£270			
All full-time women										
Great Britain	222.4	5.3	4.5	2.8	24.7	51.8	74.7	18.6	37.4	0.8
North	196.4	3.7	3.9	4.0	34.2	63.8	82.8	15.3	37.6	0.6
Tyne & Wear	203.6	3.9	3.4	3.5	30.3	61.4	81.9	..	37.3	0.6
Yorkshire & Humberside	200.2	5.3	4.6	2.9	32.9	60.8	81.7	18.9	37.4	0.9
South Yorkshire	199.6	4.3	3.8	3.2	30.5	59.8	81.8	..	37.2	0.7
West Yorkshire	204.1	5.8	5.7	2.7	31.6	59.2	80.3	..	37.3	0.9
East Midlands	199.4	5.3	7.0	2.9	32.3	62.0	82.5	20.1	37.7	0.9
East Anglia	202.7	5.4	3.1	2.4	30.9	60.6	82.0	22.0	37.9	0.9
South East	256.1	6.1	4.5	2.4	13.9	36.4	64.2	19.2	37.2	0.8
Greater London	284.9	6.5	5.1	2.3	8.0	24.4	54.3	18.9	37.0	0.8
South West	207.7	4.6	3.1	3.0	28.3	58.8	79.3	18.9	37.3	0.7
West Midlands	202.2	4.6	5.7	2.3	30.8	61.9	81.5	17.7	37.4	0.8
West Midlands (MC)	208.1	5.2	5.3	2.5	27.0	58.9	80.0	..	37.5	0.9
North West	206.8	4.9	4.6	2.8	28.9	59.0	79.3	17.3	37.2	0.8
Greater Manchester	206.5	5.1	4.8	2.1	29.1	58.8	78.6	..	37.0	0.8
Merseyside	208.3	5.8	4.7	4.1	26.7	56.7	81.3	..	37.3	0.8
England	225.2	5.4	4.6	2.7	23.7	50.5	73.9	18.7	37.3	0.8
Wales	199.1	4.0	3.9	3.5	32.6	61.6	80.9	16.2	37.4	0.7
Scotland	206.5	5.1	3.3	4.1	29.7	59.7	79.1	18.8	37.4	0.8
Northern Ireland	201.7	4.0	5.6	4.4	36.9	59.0	76.3	12.9	37.8	0.7
Full-time manual women										
Great Britain	159.2	8.6	10.0	4.6	52.1	80.9	95.0	25.5	39.7	1.6
North	150.4	5.1	11.6	5.8	59.9	83.5	95.7	17.8	39.0	1.0
Yorkshire & Humberside	149.1	9.1	11.6	4.0	60.7	87.2	96.6	25.8	39.6	1.7
East Midlands	149.4	8.2	18.7	3.5	58.2	86.3	97.3	27.4	39.8	1.7
East Anglia	155.2	8.9	6.2	3.7	55.3	83.6	95.7	28.6	40.2	1.8
South East	180.4	10.3	4.8	5.1	38.8	69.4	90.0	28.2	39.9	1.9
South West	149.5	7.6	6.6	4.7	57.7	86.9	97.3	26.6	39.7	1.5
West Midlands	150.2	6.8	15.4	3.3	55.3	86.0	98.4	23.4	39.6	1.5
North West	153.6	8.2	12.3	3.8	55.8	84.1	96.4	23.6	39.5	1.5
England	160.5	8.6	10.1	4.3	51.4	80.3	94.7	25.8	39.7	1.6
Wales	153.3	9.0	10.6	7.4	56.7	82.3	96.4	24.0	40.1	1.8
Scotland	151.3	8.3	9.3	5.2	55.8	85.7	97.0	23.5	39.9	1.6
Northern Ireland	140.2	4.5	15.5	5.0	68.7	89.7	96.9	17.9	38.8	0.9
Full-time non-manual women										
Great Britain	236.8	4.5	3.2	2.5	18.4	45.2	70.1	17.1	36.8	0.6
North	209.5	3.3	1.7	3.4	26.9	58.1	79.1	14.6	37.2	0.5
Yorkshire & Humberside	214.2	4.2	2.7	2.5	25.3	53.6	77.6	17.0	36.8	0.6
East Midlands	217.5	4.3	2.7	2.7	22.9	53.2	77.1	17.4	37.0	0.6
East Anglia	215.0	4.5	2.3	2.1	24.6	54.6	78.4	20.3	37.3	0.7
South East	268.6	5.4	4.5	2.0	9.8	31.0	60.0	17.7	36.8	0.7
South West	219.5	3.9	2.4	2.6	22.3	53.1	75.7	17.4	36.8	0.6
West Midlands	217.0	3.9	2.9	2.0	23.8	55.1	76.7	16.0	36.8	0.6
North West	219.2	4.1	2.8	2.6	22.6	53.2	75.3	15.9	36.6	0.6
England	239.6	4.7	3.4	2.3	17.6	43.9	69.3	17.1	36.8	0.6
Wales	212.8	2.5	1.9	2.3	25.4	55.5	76.2	13.9	36.6	0.4
Scotland	220.5	4.3	1.8	3.8	23.0	53.1	74.5	17.6	36.7	0.6
Northern Ireland	220.3	3.8	2.6	4.2	27.3	49.8	70.1	11.4	37.5	0.6

1 Data relate to full-time women on adult rates whose pay for the survey pay-period was not affected by absence.
2 At April.
3 PBR etc. pay is payments-by-results, bonuses, commission and other incentive payments.

Source: New Earnings Survey, Employment Department; Department of Economic Development, Northern Ireland

8.5 Average weekly earnings[1]: by Standard Industrial Classification and sex, 1991[2]

£ per week

	All industries and services (Divisions 0 to 9)		Agriculture, forestry & fishing (Division 0)		Energy & water supply industries (Division 1)		All manufacturing industries (Divisions 2 to 4)	
	Males	Females	Males	Females	Males	Females	Males	Females
Great Britain	318.9	222.4	214.2	164.3	385.4	255.4	308.1	192.9
North	289.3	196.4	..	..	340.1	227.0	292.8	175.0
Yorkshire & Humberside	286.6	200.2	218.2	..	347.5	221.7	282.2	169.7
East Midlands	292.6	199.4	222.6	..	344.8	..	286.9	171.2
East Anglia	300.2	202.7	..	..	339.3	..	304.0	191.3
South East	368.7	256.1	217.1	..	437.2	294.2	354.5	234.3
South West	297.1	207.7	..	..	385.4	..	297.8	187.2
West Midlands	291.1	202.2	..	..	335.7	234.9	286.6	174.6
North West	300.3	206.8	..	..	361.2	239.2	302.4	179.5
England	322.8	225.2	215.6	159.3	376.4	256.0	310.4	195.8
Wales	280.1	199.1	..	..	348.4	..	287.1	176.6
Scotland	299.5	206.5	208.6	..	452.8	267.4	293.2	173.5
Northern Ireland	267.9	198.4	146.3	..	320.6	..	244.9	151.3

	Manufacture of metals, mineral products & chemicals (Division 2)		Metal goods, engineering & vehicle industries (Division 3)		Other manufacturing industries (Division 4)		Construction (Division 5)	
	Males	Females	Males	Females	Males	Females	Males	Females
Great Britain	316.3	211.7	311.6	197.8	298.7	184.6	294.9	195.5
North	318.8	..	297.3	184.7	264.8	162.7	275.0	..
Yorkshire & Humberside	305.7	183.8	274.0	178.6	276.4	161.6	269.5	..
East Midlands	297.0	187.2	293.2	180.8	274.9	165.5	289.6	..
East Anglia	306.8	..	311.0	..	296.4	188.4	287.4	..
South East	373.2	253.4	349.6	224.8	355.3	236.3	352.3	221.6
South West	290.0	184.4	312.0	194.2	278.7	182.8	272.5	..
West Midlands	279.9	171.2	289.1	177.9	284.8	172.0	271.7	..
North West	329.1	203.6	306.6	189.5	282.3	166.5	280.0	..
England	319.4	212.9	312.8	199.3	302.4	188.4	301.4	199.2
Wales	300.2	208.4	296.2	185.9	261.1	161.0	244.6	..
Scotland	298.3	..	304.1	187.4	278.4	164.2	276.2	..
Northern Ireland	263.9	153.4	267.4	187.3	220.2	140.2	217.4	..

	Distribution, hotels & catering, repairs (Division 6)		Transport and communication (Division 7)		Banking, finance, insurance, business services & leasing (Division 8)		Other services (Division 9)	
	Males	Females	Males	Females	Males	Females	Males	Females
Great Britain	264.3	174.1	302.7	229.8	412.8	244.7	327.3	242.9
North	238.8	147.2	265.9	193.2	311.5	182.7	312.9	222.2
Yorkshire & Humberside	249.7	156.9	274.1	193.9	323.9	203.3	305.5	231.2
East Midlands	254.8	164.9	272.1	195.2	..	203.4	309.1	232.5
East Anglia	251.9	166.5	297.9	204.5	361.8	200.3	316.0	235.3
South East	296.3	204.6	341.6	256.6	486.1	289.2	353.9	263.4
South West	243.5	156.3	268.7	213.5	350.4	210.1	316.2	233.7
West Midlands	252.0	154.3	268.9	205.8	346.4	202.8	318.3	238.2
North West	248.6	163.0	279.7	196.7	341.9	204.5	319.2	235.8
England	268.5	177.2	306.6	232.5	423.2	249.7	330.7	245.1
Wales	220.8	137.5	263.9	..	301.9	189.9	299.5	225.4
Scotland	235.9	158.1	278.7	206.2	326.2	201.3	313.7	233.6
Northern Ireland	198.3	126.6	253.7	211.2	291.9	214.0	322.3	229.0

1 Full-time employees paid on adult rates whose pay was not affected by absence.
2 At April.

Source: New Earnings Survey, Employment Department; Department of Economic Development, Northern Ireland

8.6 Distribution of income liable to assessment for tax, 1989-90

Percentages and thousands

	Percentage of tax units in each income range							Tax units with incomes of £3,000 or more (= 100%)
	£3,000-£4,999	£5,000-£7,499	£7,500-£9,999	£10,000-£14,999	£15,000-£19,999	£20,000-£29,999	£30,000 and over	(thousands)
United Kingdom[1]	12.9	16.1	15.1	22.9	14.5	11.7	6.8	23,200
North	12.8	17.6	17.7	23.4	14.1	10.8	3.7	1,140
Yorkshire & Humberside	16.0	16.3	13.6	24.1	14.6	10.4	5.0	1,930
East Midlands	12.6	17.1	14.7	23.1	14.5	12.2	5.9	1,560
East Anglia	10.3	18.5	15.0	23.7	14.7	11.7	6.1	860
South East	11.3	13.9	13.6	23.1	14.9	13.1	10.1	7,450
South West	11.6	18.4	17.5	22.4	13.6	11.0	5.5	1,830
West Midlands	12.0	17.5	15.5	24.0	14.5	11.1	5.5	2,010
North West	15.7	17.6	15.4	21.9	13.9	10.5	5.0	2,440
England[1]	12.5	16.0	14.8	23.2	14.6	11.8	7.1	19,400
Wales	15.5	16.0	16.2	23.0	15.7	8.9	4.7	1,050
Scotland	14.5	15.7	16.4	21.8	14.0	12.1	5.4	2,200
Northern Ireland	16.0	20.9	17.6	17.0	11.8	11.6	5.1	522

1 Figures for United Kingdom and England include members of HM Forces, the Merchant Navy and a few civil servants, mainly serving overseas, who cannot be allocated to regions.

Source: Survey of Personal Incomes, Board of Inland Revenue

8.7 Estimated government expenditure on certain cash benefits[1], 1989-90

£ million and £ per head

	National insurance benefits								Total benefits as stated[2]
	Retirement pension	Sickness and invalidity	Widow's	Unemployment	Disablement	Income support	Child benefit	War pensions	
£ million									
United Kingdom	20,558	4,208	862	765	477	8,053	4,718	641	40,281
North	1,083	323	47	61	55	510	256	39	2,376
Yorkshire & Humberside	1,803	427	73	64	54	678	414	54	3,567
East Midlands	1,374	262	56	42	29	478	337	38	2,618
East Anglia	738	80	28	22	16	176	163	20	1,243
South East	6,497	831	248	178	92	2,171	1,368	197	11,581
South West	1,915	257	67	62	26	509	360	57	3,252
West Midlands	1,715	365	77	58	49	793	449	44	3,551
North West	2,333	593	97	94	67	1,083	548	81	4,897
England	17,457	3,138	693	583	388	6,399	3,896	530	33,084
Wales	958	350	45	45	32	442	236	36	2,143
Scotland	1,689	553	92	106	43	834	406	63	3,786
Northern Ireland	453	168	32	31	14	378	180	12	1,268
£ per head[3]									
United Kingdom	359.2	73.5	15.1	13.4	8.3	140.7	82.4	11.2	703.8
North	352.5	105.1	15.4	20.0	18.0	166.1	83.4	12.7	773.2
Yorkshire & Humberside	365.0	86.4	14.8	13.0	10.9	137.2	83.8	10.9	722.2
East Midlands	343.6	65.6	14.0	10.6	7.2	119.6	84.4	9.6	654.6
East Anglia	360.9	39.1	13.5	10.9	7.8	86.3	79.6	9.7	607.7
South East	373.7	47.8	14.3	10.2	5.3	124.9	78.7	11.3	666.2
South West	411.6	55.2	14.4	13.3	5.6	109.3	77.4	12.2	699.0
West Midlands	328.7	69.9	14.7	11.2	9.4	152.1	86.2	8.5	680.7
North West	365.6	92.9	15.3	14.8	10.5	169.8	85.9	12.7	767.5
England	366.1	65.8	14.5	12.2	8.1	134.2	81.7	11.1	693.7
Wales	333.5	121.7	15.6	15.5	11.1	153.9	82.1	12.5	745.9
Scotland	331.8	108.7	18.1	20.8	8.5	163.9	79.7	12.3	743.6
Northern Ireland	286.3	106.1	19.9	19.7	8.7	239.1	113.8	7.7	801.3

1 The quality of these estimates varies between benefits. For some of them, including retirement pension, the regional breakdown in Great Britain is based solely on population estimates. Because of changes in method, the estimates might not be entirely consistent with those published for previous years.
2 The benefits covered do not account for the total value of social security benefits paid.
3 Based on mid-1989 population estimates.

Source: Department of Social Security; Department of Social Security, Northern Ireland

8.8 Income tax payable, 1989-90

	Basic rate		Tax in excess of basic rate		Total payable (£ million)	Total annual income (£ million)	Average rate of tax pay-able (%)	Average amount of tax pay-able (£)
	Number of tax units (thousands)	Amount (£ million)	Number of tax units (thousands)	Amount (£ million)				
United Kingdom[1]	21,500	49,500	1,510	3,910	53,400	333,000	16.0	2,490
North	1,040	1,940	31	57	2,000	14,300	13.9	1,920
Yorkshire & Humberside	1,740	3,530	88	209	3,740	25,600	14.6	2,150
East Midlands	1,420	3,120	94	214	3,340	21,800	15.3	2,350
East Anglia	808	1,780	44	131	1,910	12,200	15.7	2,370
South East	7,030	19,700	740	2,130	21,900	122,000	17.9	3,110
South West	1,670	3,680	101	308	3,990	25,400	15.7	2,390
West Midlands	1,870	3,880	96	215	4,100	27,300	15.0	2,200
North West	2,230	4,510	117	283	4,790	31,900	15.0	2,150
England[1]	18,000	42,600	1,320	3,560	46,200	283,000	16.3	2,560
Wales	933	1,870	44	104	1,970	13,600	14.5	2,120
Scotland	2,050	4,120	112	191	4,310	29,400	14.7	2,100
Northern Ireland	480	944	30	58	1,000	6,720	14.9	2,090

1 Figures for United Kingdom and England include members of HM Forces, the Merchant Navy and a few civil servants, mainly serving overseas, who cannot be allocated to regions. Also included are those who are liable to tax in the United Kingdom, but are resident overseas.

Source: Board of Inland Revenue

8.9 Household expenditure: by commodity and service, 1989-1990

£ per week and percentages

	Housing	Fuel, light & power	Food	Alcohol and tobacco	Clothing and footwear	House-hold goods and services	Motoring and fares	Leisure goods and services	Miscellan-eous and personal goods and services	Average house-hold expend-iture	Average expend-iture per person
£ per week											
United Kingdom	42.2	10.8	43.2	14.6	15.6	31.1	37.8	30.6	10.1	236.1	94.7
North	34.2	10.4	40.6	15.3	13.9	26.7	31.8	23.9	8.1	204.4	79.5
Yorkshire & Humberside	32.7	10.7	39.4	14.9	14.8	27.5	32.1	26.6	9.5	208.2	83.0
East Midlands	43.4	10.8	42.8	15.3	15.7	29.2	41.2	30.1	10.4	239.0	93.5
East Anglia	46.2	10.7	43.7	11.9	12.8	30.1	36.1	30.1	9.7	231.1	94.7
South East	51.9	10.7	47.5	14.2	17.5	36.9	41.5	37.7	12.1	269.8	110.1
South West	44.8	10.9	42.3	13.2	13.8	30.6	40.4	32.3	10.3	238.5	97.8
West Midlands	43.5	10.3	41.6	13.1	14.5	29.6	39.8	26.3	8.7	227.3	91.0
North West	38.9	10.8	41.1	16.8	15.1	29.5	38.3	28.7	9.5	228.6	91.3
England	44.3	10.7	43.5	14.4	15.5	31.8	38.8	31.6	10.4	241.0	97.0
Wales	33.3	11.6	40.0	14.4	14.6	29.2	33.4	26.5	9.0	211.9	84.5
Scotland	30.7	11.2	42.0	16.3	16.9	26.9	31.4	26.5	8.9	210.7	85.0
Northern Ireland	26.3	14.2	43.8	11.7	17.1	26.0	35.7	20.0	7.7	202.6	70.6
As a percentage of average weekly household expenditure											
United Kingdom	*17.9*	*4.6*	*18.3*	*6.2*	*6.6*	*13.2*	*16.0*	*13.0*	*4.3*	*100.0*	
North	*16.7*	*5.1*	*19.6*	*7.5*	*6.8*	*13.1*	*15.6*	*11.7*	*4.0*	*100.0*	
Yorkshire & Humberside	*15.7*	*5.1*	*18.9*	*7.2*	*7.1*	*13.2*	*15.4*	*12.8*	*4.6*	*100.0*	
East Midlands	*18.2*	*4.5*	*17.9*	*6.4*	*6.6*	*12.2*	*17.2*	*12.6*	*4.3*	*100.0*	
East Anglia	*20.0*	*4.6*	*18.9*	*5.1*	*5.5*	*13.0*	*15.6*	*13.0*	*4.2*	*100.0*	
South East	*19.2*	*4.0*	*17.6*	*5.3*	*6.5*	*13.7*	*15.4*	*14.0*	*4.5*	*100.0*	
South West	*18.8*	*4.6*	*17.7*	*5.5*	*5.8*	*12.8*	*17.0*	*13.5*	*4.3*	*100.0*	
West Midlands	*19.1*	*4.5*	*18.3*	*5.8*	*6.4*	*13.0*	*17.5*	*11.6*	*3.8*	*100.0*	
North West	*17.0*	*4.7*	*18.0*	*7.3*	*6.6*	*12.9*	*16.8*	*12.6*	*4.1*	*100.0*	
England	*18.4*	*4.4*	*18.1*	*6.0*	*6.4*	*13.2*	*16.1*	*13.1*	*4.3*	*100.0*	
Wales	*15.7*	*5.5*	*18.9*	*6.8*	*6.9*	*13.8*	*15.8*	*12.5*	*4.2*	*100.0*	
Scotland	*14.6*	*5.3*	*20.0*	*7.7*	*8.0*	*12.7*	*14.9*	*12.6*	*4.2*	*100.0*	
Northern Ireland	*13.0*	*7.0*	*21.6*	*5.8*	*8.4*	*12.8*	*17.6*	*9.9*	*3.8*	*100.0*	

Source: Family Expenditure Survey, Central Statistical Office

8.10 Household consumption of, and expenditure on, main foods, 1989-1990

Quantity and pence per person per week

	Liquid and processed milk and cream		Cheese		Butter		Margarine	
	Pints	Pence	Ounces	Pence	Ounces	Pence	Ounces	Pence
Great Britain	3.9	124.3	4.0	40.7	1.7	11.4	3.3	9.9
North	3.8	116.7	3.8	36.3	1.7	12.0	4.0	11.1
Yorkshire & Humberside	3.9	123.1	3.7	35.8	1.3	9.3	4.1	11.6
East Midlands	4.2	136.4	4.6	44.7	1.4	9.3	3.1	9.6
East Anglia/South East	3.9	131.7	4.3	45.4	1.8	11.9	2.8	8.6
South West	4.1	125.2	4.7	47.5	1.9	12.4	3.2	9.1
West Midlands	3.8	117.6	3.9	37.8	1.3	9.0	3.9	11.0
North West	3.7	120.1	3.6	34.7	1.5	10.1	3.6	11.0
England	3.9	126.0	4.1	41.2	1.6	10.8	3.4	9.9
Wales	3.9	115.9	3.4	33.0	1.9	12.6	3.3	10.6
Scotland	3.9	113.1	4.0	40.8	2.3	16.3	3.1	9.6

	Eggs		Meat and meat products		Fish		Fresh and other fruit	
	Number	Pence	Ounces	Pence	Ounces	Pence	Ounces	Pence
Great Britain	2.2	18.6	35.0	332.6	5.1	64.9	32.0	91.9
North	2.9	22.3	36.7	320.9	5.5	65.2	29.2	81.9
Yorkshire & Humberside	2.5	19.5	36.2	326.7	6.1	76.9	29.5	79.4
East Midlands	2.1	16.7	33.7	316.5	5.1	63.7	31.7	87.9
East Anglia/South East	2.0	18.4	34.0	341.8	5.3	71.3	38.6	116.2
South West	2.4	18.9	34.1	313.1	4.6	56.8	35.3	98.1
West Midlands	2.1	16.6	37.0	324.1	4.9	59.5	27.0	72.6
North West	2.2	17.5	35.2	327.8	4.9	59.2	26.0	72.6
England	2.2	18.3	34.9	329.4	5.2	66.3	32.7	93.8
Wales	2.1	18.1	35.1	324.4	5.0	58.7	27.6	79.5
Scotland	2.7	21.7	35.8	369.0	4.6	54.6	27.8	81.5

	Potatoes		Other vegetables & vegetable products[1]		Bread		Flour	
	Ounces	Pence	Ounces	Pence	Ounces	Pence	Ounces	Pence
Great Britain	35.4	26.4	45.5	136.6	28.8	68.2	3.2	3.6
North	40.0	25.9	46.5	127.5	31.9	71.8	4.8	5.5
Yorkshire & Humberside	36.6	25.4	47.0	133.4	28.7	68.9	4.8	5.0
East Midlands	34.4	25.1	47.5	141.9	27.9	65.2	3.1	3.4
East Anglia/South East	28.2	25.3	47.3	152.5	25.2	63.8	3.4	3.9
South West	37.5	24.3	48.6	138.0	27.8	65.6	3.9	4.3
West Midlands	38.1	24.8	45.4	131.5	31.8	67.6	2.5	2.8
North West	39.0	29.8	40.4	121.0	29.6	70.3	1.9	2.1
England	34.2	25.9	46.1	138.9	28.0	66.7	3.4	3.7
Wales	42.4	29.5	43.9	125.1	32.0	71.9	2.6	2.9
Scotland	41.4	28.9	41.4	121.3	34.4	80.6	2.4	2.7

	Cakes and biscuits		Sugar & preserves		Coffee		Tea	
	Ounces	Pence	Ounces	Pence	Ounces	Pence	Ounces	Pence
Great Britain	8.9	58.6	8.0	17.9	0.6	20.9	1.6	19.1
North	9.1	59.1	8.8	19.6	0.7	24.1	1.6	19.3
Yorkshire & Humberside	9.3	59.4	7.7	17.1	0.7	22.7	1.6	19.6
East Midlands	8.4	55.2	7.5	16.4	0.6	20.6	1.5	17.3
East Anglia/South East	8.7	59.2	7.2	17.1	0.7	20.5	1.5	17.8
South West	9.8	62.4	8.7	19.9	0.7	21.9	1.5	18.6
West Midlands	8.3	54.0	9.1	18.6	0.6	19.5	1.6	19.3
North West	8.9	57.1	7.6	16.5	0.6	18.7	1.7	20.2
England	8.9	58.3	7.9	17.6	0.6	20.8	1.5	18.7
Wales	7.9	52.0	8.5	19.4	0.5	16.5	1.8	22.6
Scotland	9.4	65.4	8.8	19.5	0.7	24.1	1.7	20.9

1 Including tomatoes and potato products.

Source: National Food Survey, Ministry of Agriculture, Fisheries and Food

8.11 Household consumption of food, by selected foods, 1980-1981 and 1989-1990

Ounces per person per week[1]

	Liquid & processed milk & cream		Meat and meat products		Vegetables & vegetable products[2]		Fresh and other fruit		Bread		Fish	
	1980-1981	1989-1990	1980-1981	1989-1990	1980-1981	1989-1990	1980-1981	1989-1990	1980-1981	1989-1990	1980-1981	1989-1990
Great Britain	4.5	3.9	39.8	35.0	86.0	80.9	28.0	32.0	31.2	28.8	4.9	5.1
North	4.2	3.8	42.3	36.7	91.7	86.4	21.8	29.2	35.5	31.9	5.6	5.5
Yorkshire & Humberside	4.2	3.9	37.6	36.2	85.9	83.6	22.0	29.5	31.4	28.7	5.4	6.1
East Midlands	4.7	4.2	37.6	33.7	86.8	81.9	25.3	31.7	32.5	27.9	5.0	5.1
East Anglia/South East	4.5	3.9	40.2	34.0	84.4	75.5	33.6	38.6	27.4	25.2	4.7	5.3
South West	4.6	4.1	38.2	34.1	88.0	86.2	30.6	35.3	30.6	27.8	4.1	4.6
West Midlands	4.6	3.8	40.0	37.0	84.3	83.6	26.2	27.0	31.5	31.8	5.0	4.9
North West	4.5	3.7	41.4	35.2	87.8	79.4	24.0	26.0	34.3	29.6	4.6	4.9
England	4.5	3.9	39.8	34.9	86.1	80.3	28.3	32.7	30.6	28.0	4.9	5.2
Wales	4.8	3.9	38.5	35.1	97.9	86.3	26.8	27.6	34.4	32.0	5.1	5.0
Scotland	4.6	3.9	40.4	35.8	78.2	82.8	25.4	27.8	35.2	34.4	4.8	4.6

1 Except equivalent pints of milk and cream.
2 Including tomatoes, fresh potatoes and potato products.

Source: National Food Survey, Ministry of Agriculture, Fisheries and Food

8.12 Households with selected durable goods, 1980-1981 and 1989-1990

Percentages and numbers

Percentage of households in sample having

	Microwave oven	Washing machine	Tumble drier	Dish-washer	Refrig-erator[1]	Deep freezer[1]	Tele-phone	Television Black & white only	Television Colour	Video	Home comp-uter	Central heating	Total no. of house-holds in samples
1980-1981													
Great Britain	..	77	22	4	93	47	73	24	73	..	..	58	23,726
North	..	88	19	1	89	42	64	22	76	..	..	64	1,433
Yorkshire & Humberside	..	84	24	2	89	40	68	24	73	..	..	52	2,179
East Midlands	..	84	22	3	93	45	73	22	75	..	..	65	1,597
East Anglia	..	80	27	5	92	59	73	23	75	..	..	68	847
South East	..	69	23	6	96	55	80	25	68	..	..	62	7,304
South West	..	72	22	5	93	54	72	26	70	..	..	57	1,818
West Midlands	..	77	21	2	91	42	71	27	70	..	..	54	2,259
North West	..	77	21	2	92	40	71	26	72	..	..	54	2,818
England	..	76	22	4	93	48	74	25	72	..	..	59	20,256
Wales	..	81	23	2	91	50	67	27	71	..	..	52	1,161
Scotland	..	83	24	3	91	39	74	21	76	..	..	51	2,309
Northern Ireland	..	70	..	..	85	..	57	91		..	..	37	1,175
1989-1990													
Great Britain	48	86	45	12	..	80	87	5	93	62	20	79	19,708
North	46	90	41	7	..	74	79	7	92	60	21	86	1,168
Yorkshire & Humberside	49	88	43	8	..	77	83	6	92	59	18	73	1,781
East Midlands	48	90	46	11	..	81	86	5	94	63	21	86	1,448
East Anglia	46	86	45	13	..	81	89	5	93	54	18	81	754
South East	50	84	47	17	..	84	92	4	94	65	21	84	5,930
South West	49	85	48	15	..	84	89	5	94	59	20	76	1,658
West Midlands	48	86	45	11	..	78	85	7	92	62	20	76	1,845
North West	49	85	43	9	..	79	84	6	93	62	20	72	2,264
England	49	86	45	13	..	81	88	5	93	62	20	80	16,848
Wales	54	88	44	8	..	82	84	5	93	62	19	78	1,059
Scotland	42	91	47	10	..	73	84	4	94	60	18	74	1,801
Northern Ireland	32	83	36	9	98	63	77	8	89	44	12	76	6,233

1 Fridge freezers are attributed to both Refrigerator and Deep freezer.

Source: Office of Population Censuses and Surveys; General Household Survey; Northern Ireland Department of Finance and Personnel, Family Expenditure Surveys, Continuous Household Surveys

8.13 Adults owning shares or mutual funds (unit trusts), 1991

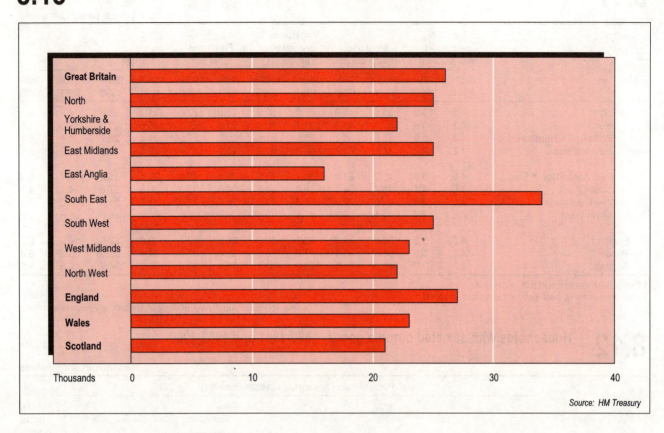

Thousands

Source: HM Treasury

There are extensive notes for this chapter, for convenience, they are
included in a separate appendix on page 202.

All The Latest Statistics
from the
Central Statistical Office

0839-338-PLUS

Retail Price Index 337
Monthly Trade Figures 338
Balance of Payments (quarterly) 339
Public Sector Borrowing Requirement 340
Index of Output of the Production Industries 341
Producer Prices 342
Retail Sales 343
Credit Business 344
Gross Dometic Product 345

CSO

STATCALL

**Calls charged at 33p per minute cheap rate,
44p per minute at all other times**

Chapter 9: Crime and Justice

Crime rates

- In England and Wales, crime is highest in the North, the North West and Yorkshire and Humberside - all with at least one offence per year recorded for every ten people.

  (Table 9.1)

- Although the South West has one of the lowest levels of crime in England and Wales, during the 1980s it had one of the fastest growing crime rates.

  (Table 9.1)

- In 1990, the highest rate for burglary was in the North and the highest for sexual offences in the East Midlands and Yorkshire and Humberside.

  (Table 9.1)

Clear-up rates

- The Welsh police are the most successful at clearing up crime. Crime clear-up rates are highest in Wales where two in five of all reported crimes are cleared up and lowest in the South East where only one in five is cleared up.

  (Table 9.2)

Young offenders

- Crime rates for young offenders are highest in the North and Yorkshire and Humberside.

  (Table 9.6)

Drugs

- Drug offences are increasing in all regions. In 1990, rates were far higher in the South East than in any other region, but since 1981 the biggest increases have been in Scotland, the West Midlands and the North West.

  (Table 9.8)

Sentences

- Those found guilty at the Crown Court are slightly more likely to be jailed in Northern Ireland and East Anglia than in other regions. They are least likely to lose their freedom in the South West and Yorkshire and Humberside.

  (Table 9.9)

Breath tests

- More breath tests are being carried out in every region, but much lower percentages were positive in 1990 than in 1981.

  (Table 9.12)

- Nine out of ten drivers breathalysed in East Anglia and the East Midlands were under the limit.

  (Table 9.12)

Police manpower

- In Northern Ireland, there is one police officer for every 193 people. At the other end of the scale, in East Anglia there is only one officer for every 531 people.

  (Table 9.14)

- The West Midlands has the highest proportion of women officers -almost one in seven. Northern Ireland has the lowest at one in twelve.

  (Table 9.14)

Regional Trends 27, © Crown copyright 1992

9.1 Notifiable offences recorded by the police: by offence group, 1981 and 1990

Rates per 100,000 population and percentages

	Violence against the person	Sexual offences	Burglary	Robbery	Theft and handling stolen goods	Fraud and forgery	Criminal damage	Other[1]	Total[1]
1981									
North	229	36	1,861	16	3,612	155	894	10	6,813
Yorkshire & Humberside	245	46	1,608	20	3,192	140	854	18	6,122
East Midlands	265	49	1,327	19	3,160	192	746	20	5,780
East Anglia	155	38	879	11	2,750	143	510	23	4,510
South East	177	36	1,370	75	3,444	263	815	20	6,200
South West	149	36	868	14	2,507	198	508	13	4,293
West Midlands	231	43	1,566	34	3,012	137	773	15	5,810
North West	217	41	1,937	37	3,615	298	890	23	7,057
England	203	40	1,457	43	3,265	217	783	18	6,026
Wales	187	31	1,284	13	2,643	179	711	10	5,057
Scotland[2]	154	40	1,847	81	3,882	414	1,191	271	7,880
Northern Ireland[3]	154	21	1,338	178	1,660	170	343	82	3,946
1990									
North	399	54	2,939	30	5,932	262	2,227	50	11,892
Yorkshire & Humberside	433	67	2,474	41	5,188	232	1,508	56	10,000
East Midlands	465	67	1,754	40	4,827	223	1,418	50	8,844
East Anglia	301	55	1,372	21	3,743	226	924	56	6,697
South East	352	61	1,829	121	4,696	352	1,415	70	8,896
South West	304	54	1,538	33	4,052	358	984	50	7,374
West Midlands	387	51	2,006	68	4,271	194	1,278	50	8,304
North West	311	47	2,459	71	5,015	315	1,756	82	10,056
England	364	58	2,017	75	4,730	296	1,445	62	9,047
Wales	381	52	1,570	16	4,130	233	1,549	47	7,979
Scotland[2]	266	64	1,994	91	5,001	491	1,694	901	10,502
Northern Ireland[3]	212	50	932	103	1,841	263	139	60	3,599
Percentage increase 1981-1990									
North	*75*	*48*	*58*	*91*	*64*	*68*	*149*	*394*	*75*
Yorkshire & Humberside	*77*	*48*	*54*	*111*	*63*	*66*	*76*	*213*	*63*
East Midlands	*75*	*38*	*32*	*103*	*53*	*16*	*90*	*148*	*53*
East Anglia	*94*	*46*	*56*	*80*	*36*	*59*	*81*	*139*	*49*
South East	*99*	*68*	*34*	*62*	*36*	*34*	*74*	*254*	*43*
South West	*104*	*48*	*77*	*138*	*62*	*81*	*94*	*290*	*72*
West Midlands	*67*	*19*	*28*	*100*	*42*	*42*	*65*	*238*	*43*
North West	*44*	*17*	*27*	*94*	*39*	*6*	*97*	*250*	*42*
England	*80*	*46*	*38*	*76*	*45*	*36*	*84*	*239*	*50*
Wales	*104*	*69*	*22*	*26*	*56*	*30*	*118*	*350*	*58*
Scotland[2]	*73*	*57*	*8*	*13*	*29*	*19*	*42*	*233*	*33*
Northern Ireland[3]	*38*	*138*	*-30*	*-42*	*11*	*55*	*-59*	*-27*	*-9*

1 Includes, from January 1983, offences of trafficking in controlled drugs.
2 Figures for Scotland are not comparable with those for England, Wales and Northern Ireland because of the differences in the legal system, recording practices and classification.
3 Excludes criminal damage valued at £400 or less in 1990.

Source: Home Office; The Scottish Office Home and Health Department; Northern Ireland Office

9.2 Percentage of notifiable offences cleared up by the police[1]: by offence group, 1990

Percentages

	Violence against the person	Sexual offences	Burglary	Robbery	Theft and handling stolen goods	Fraud and forgery	Criminal damage	Drugs[2]	Other	Total
North	78	84	34	37	34	64	32	99	99	36
Yorkshire & Humberside	84	84	30	39	37	71	25	98	94	37
East Midlands	80	81	31	39	34	58	23	90	94	36
East Anglia	86	86	30	48	37	67	27	98	96	38
South East	67	64	13	18	20	47	14	99	92	21
South West	85	85	21	39	28	77	26	102	101	32
West Midlands	82	75	33	43	37	54	24	100	97	37
North West	76	81	34	31	36	82	27	97	98	38
England	76	75	25	26	29	60	21	98	95	31
Wales	88	95	33	58	39	71	27	102	101	40
Scotland[3]	82	79	16	28	24	69	20	..	97	32
Northern Ireland	62	92	22	18	36	74	36	92	69	38

1 Some percentages may be greater than 100, as offences cleared-up in current year may have been initially recorded in an earlier year.
2 Trafficking in controlled drugs only for England and Wales.
3 Figures for Scotland are not comparable with those for England, Wales and Northern Ireland because of the differences in the legal system, recording practices and classification.

Source: Home Office; The Scottish Office Home and Health Department: Northern Ireland Office

9.3 Notifiable offences recorded by the police and proportion cleared up, 1990

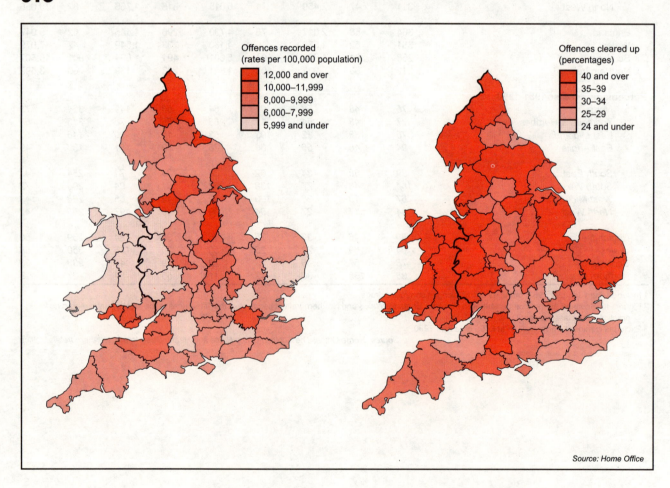

Offences recorded
(rates per 100,000 population)
- 12,000 and over
- 10,000–11,999
- 8,000–9,999
- 6,000–7,999
- 5,999 and under

Offences cleared up
(percentages)
- 40 and over
- 35–39
- 30–34
- 25–29
- 24 and under

Source: Home Office

9.4 Percentage of offences resulting in a police caution[1,2]: by offence and age, 1990

Percentages

	Violence against the person	Sexual offences	Burglary	Robbery	Theft and handling stolen goods	Fraud and forgery	Criminal damage	Drugs	Other indictable offences	Summary offences[3]	Total indict-able[4]
Persons aged under 17											
North	65	70	56	27	84	82	63	88	50	71	75
Yorkshire &											
Humberside	71	77	63	20	85	76	63	88	55	76	77
East Midlands	71	86	64	33	86	79	65	82	50	73	77
East Anglia	73	66	72	56	86	63	70	96	24	80	81
South East	70	81	64	30	87	86	75	88	57	77	80
South West	60	85	66	42	85	77	85	74	57	62	79
West Midlands	69	87	73	51	89	87	60	82	56	73	81
North West	66	76	63	26	82	79	74	87	40	73	75
England	68	80	64	34	86	82	71	87	51	74	78
Wales	64	78	66	41	83	71	65	75	28	71	75
Persons aged 17 and over											
North	8	22	2	-	22	11	8	24	5	7	15
Yorkshire &											
Humberside	20	29	5	1	27	15	5	28	7	8	19
East Midlands	22	34	7	1	28	16	7	37	16	9	21
East Anglia	17	40	7	2	25	11	4	31	9	9	19
South East	19	21	6	1	28	15	13	50	8	26	25
South West	15	28	7	1	30	14	36	21	30	8	23
West Midlands	11	19	4	3	22	14	4	22	7	6	15
North West	13	29	4	-	24	15	13	35	3	10	18
England	16	25	5	1	16	15	11	41	9	15	21
Wales	6	16	3	-	13	5	5	17	19	8	10

1 Persons who on admission of guilt were given formal oral cautions by the police.
2 Those cautioned as a percentage of persons found guilty or cautioned.
3 Excluding motoring offences to which written warnings were issued.
4 Excluding motoring offences.

Source: Home Office

9.5 Operations in which firearms were issued to the police and offences recorded by the police in which firearms were reported to have been used, 1984 and 1990

Numbers

	1984						1990					
	Operations in which firearms were issued to the police	Offences involving firearms					Operations in which firearms were issued to the police	Offences involving firearms				
		Armed robb-eries	Violence against the person	Criminal damage	Other[1]	Total		Armed robb-eries	Violence against the person	Criminal damage	Other[1]	Total
Great Britain	2,835	2,224	3,029	3,967	509	9,729	2,925	4,185	2,905	4,104	663	11,857
North	38	26	211	288	4	529	229	154	192	343	15	704
Yorkshire & Humberside	161	61	338	412	21	832	239	258	287	791	33	1,369
East Midlands	34	24	214	455	5	698	54	87	223	467	19	796
East Anglia	38	19	55	131	5	210	85	71	83	192	15	361
South East	2,083	1,605	861	779	72	3,317	1,798	2,508	889	789	134	4,320
South West	91	22	103	94	3	222	131	89	115	86	10	300
West Midlands	42	167	355	627	13	1,162	117	200	279	446	24	949
North West	161	156	410	422	17	1,005	179	531	361	239	56	1,187
England	2,648	2,080	2,547	3,208	140	7,975	2,832	3,898	2,429	3,353	306	9,986
Wales	19	18	172	209	2	401	42	41	149	191	6	387
Scotland[2]	168	126	310	550	367	1,353	51	246	327	560	351	1,484

1 Mainly burglary, sexual offences, theft and public order offences.
2 Scottish figures are for offences recorded by the police in which firearms were alleged to be involved. Figures for violence against the person include petty assault. Additionally, figures are for occasions (not operations) in which firearms were issued to the police.

Source: Home Office; The Scottish Office Home and Health Department

9.6 Young offenders found guilty or cautioned: by type of offence and age, 1981 and 1990

Rate per 100,000 population

	1981						1990					
	Violence against the person	Sexual off-ences	Burglary, robbery and theft[1]	Drugs off-ences	Other indict-able off-ences	All indict-able off-ences	Violence against the person	Sexual off-ences	Burglary, robbery and theft[1]	Drugs off-ences	Other indict-able off-ences	All indict-able off-ences
Age 10-13												
North	91	12	2,485	-	113	2,701	93	13	1,834	2	83	2,026
Yorkshire & Humberside	77	28	2,240	-	89	2,431	114	30	1,621	4	69	1,838
East Midlands	98	21	1,893	-	95	2,107	90	22	1,110	1	62	1,286
East Anglia	50	17	2,265	-	79	2,412	50	10	835	2	86	984
South East	40	7	1,400	-	56	1,502	49	9	785	7	57	908
South West	41	13	1,337	-	71	1,463	40	11	636	1	60	748
West Midlands	72	22	1,892	-	81	2,067	89	25	1,484	5	93	1,696
North West	67	12	2,258	-	61	2,397	88	17	1,395	8	70	1,578
England	61	14	1,819	-	73	1,967	72	16	1,122	5	68	1,282
Wales	62	14	1,770	-	95	1,941	67	17	1,268	3	141	1,497
Age 14-16												
North	415	60	5,108	4	221	5,808	647	55	4,515	73	293	5,583
Yorkshire & Humberside	425	92	4,470	5	176	5,168	665	123	4,485	60	215	5,548
East Midlands	460	105	4,085	3	186	4,839	737	120	3,647	49	209	4,756
East Anglia	323	64	3,335	23	156	3,901	418	53	3,118	129	245	3,963
South East	332	50	3,358	20	165	3,925	388	48	2,670	213	205	3,524
South West	316	58	2,999	9	133	3,515	324	51	2,308	42	236	2,961
West Midlands	372	89	3,883	6	150	4,500	635	78	4,018	77	307	5,113
North West	421	53	4,707	15	200	5,396	584	79	3,881	240	325	5,109
England	374	66	3,871	13	172	4,495	481	66	3,161	135	230	4,324
Wales	331	48	4,094	14	214	4,701	520	81	3,817	59	381	4,858
Age 17-20												
North	516	46	3,516	70	201	4,349	632	59	3,191	168	451	4,500
Yorkshire & Humberside	527	75	3,207	56	230	4,095	714	73	3,158	255	509	4,710
East Midlands	595	96	2,689	57	234	3,670	736	87	2,757	165	524	4,269
East Anglia	429	62	2,338	124	218	3,171	515	48	2,595	287	457	3,902
South East	473	40	2,824	166	241	3,744	401	39	2,294	746	410	3,890
South West	427	63	2,423	119	194	3,226	481	49	2,315	218	362	3,425
West Midlands	529	75	2,757	51	255	3,667	696	67	2,808	224	668	4,463
North West	533	41	3,623	100	299	4,598	548	50	3,176	652	812	5,236
England	500	56	2,947	111	241	3,855	540	54	2,666	470	511	4,242
Wales	461	55	3,159	101	261	4,037	699	45	2,763	234	732	4,473

1 Includes handling, fraud and forgery.

Source: Home Office

9.7 Seizures of controlled drugs: by type of drug, 1990

Number of seizures

	Class A drugs				Class B drugs		
	Heroin	Cocaine	LSD	All class A drugs[1]	Cannabis	Ampheta -mines	All class B drugs[1]
United Kingdom[2]	2,593	1,805	1,859	7,153	52,856	4,629	55,634
North	44	7	116	193	1,072	131	1,146
Yorkshire & Humberside	99	26	129	286	2,453	246	2,598
East Midlands	13	25	54	112	1,266	136	1,345
East Anglia	49	15	59	151	1,540	148	1,614
South East	1,160	1,176	729	3,369	21,131	1,900	22,297
South West	52	21	94	216	2,620	329	2,800
West Midlands	60	18	84	194	3,027	194	3,130
North West	664	83	281	1,156	5,671	813	6,149
England	2,442	1,764	1,637	6,555	45,312	4,055	47,743
Wales	37	14	40	170	2,042	212	2,149
Scotland	114	25	172	412	5,317	355	5,552
Northern Ireland	-	2	10	16	185	7	190

1 Since a seizure may involve more than one type of drug, and drugs other than those listed are included, figures for individual drugs cannot be added together to produce totals.

2 Seizures of drugs made by Custom and Excise are included against each country but not counted against each region.

Source: Home Office

9.8 Persons found guilty, cautioned or dealt with by compounding[1] for drug offences: by selected offences, 1981 and 1990

Rate per 100,000 population

	1981				1990			
	Trafficking offences[2]	Unlawful production of cannabis	Unlawful possession	All offences[3]	Trafficking offences[2,4]	Unlawful production of cannabis	Unlawful possession	All offences[3,4]
United Kingdom	5	3	25	31	12	1	69	78
North	2	2	17	19	5	1	30	32
Yorkshire & Humberside	3	3	15	18	6	1	45	49
East Midlands	2	2	16	18	5	1	30	33
East Anglia	5	5	32	36	11	3	59	65
South East	12	4	45	57	8	1	116	124
South West	3	4	27	30	4	1	41	43
West Midlands	3	2	12	15	5	1	42	45
North West	3	2	24	27	11	1	71	81
England	6	3	28	34	12	1	73	83
Wales	2	5	24	28	9	2	52	59
Scotland	1	1	15	17	12	-	58	66
Northern Ireland	1	1	5	6	2	-	8	9

1 HM Customs and Excise cases dealt with by the payment of a penalty in lieu of prosecution. Compounding was only introduced in 1982; 1981 figures therefore relate only to persons found guilty or cautioned.

2 Unlawful import or export, unlawful production of drugs other than cannabis, unlawful supply and possession with intent to supply unlawfully.

3 As the same person may be found guilty, cautioned, or dealt with by compounding for more than one offence, figures for individual types of offences cannot be added together to produce totals.

4 Persons dealt with by Customs and Excise are included against each country but are not counted against each region.

Source: Home Office

9.9 Persons[1] found guilty of indictable[2] and summary offences[3]: by court and type of sentence, 1990

	Result as a percentage of number of persons sentenced								Total found guilty	
	Prob- ation order	Super- vision or care order	Fine	Fully sus- pended sentence	Immed- iate custodial sentence[4]	Absolute or condit- ional discharge	Comm- unity service order	Other- wise dealt with	Rate[5]	Number of persons (= 100%)
Crown Court: indictable offences										
North	14	1	8	14	42	6	14	2	1.8	4,704
Yorkshire & Humberside	13	1	7	14	39	6	17	3	2.1	8,980
East Midlands	10	1	7	16	47	5	12	3	1.7	5,985
East Anglia	11	1	8	16	48	4	10	2	1.2	2,171
South East	11	-	11	17	42	5	11	2	1.9	29,148
South West	15	-	9	16	39	4	14	2	1.0	4,255
West Midlands	11	1	7	15	45	6	13	2	2.0	9,106
North West	13	1	6	15	45	6	13	2	2.1	11,888
England	12	1	8	16	43	5	13	2	1.8	76,237
Wales	12	1	6	16	44	5	13	4	1.6	4,026
Northern Ireland	7	-	3	29	48	..	..	13	1.0	1,256
Magistrates' Courts: indictable offences										
North	11	3	44	2	5	24	7	5	6.4	17,274
Yorkshire & Humberside	9	2	46	3	4	21	8	6	6.2	26,797
East Midlands	10	2	46	2	4	24	6	7	5.8	20,237
East Anglia	9	1	52	2	4	21	7	4	5.5	9,871
South East	9	2	52	3	4	20	6	4	5.1	76,942
South West	11	2	51	3	5	18	7	3	4.8	19,791
West Midlands	9	2	49	3	5	22	6	4	6.4	28,980
North West	10	2	46	3	5	23	6	5	7.3	40,647
England	10	2	49	3	5	21	6	4	5.8	240,539
Wales	8	2	53	2	4	23	5	3	7.5	18,873
Northern Ireland	9	-	34	16	15	..	..	26	6.1	8,064
Magistrates' Courts: summary offences										
North	1	-	89	-	1	6	1	1	13.5	36,141
Yorkshire & Humberside	1	-	90	1	1	5	1	1	12.2	52,465
East Midlands	1	-	90	1	1	5	1	2	9.8	34,417
East Anglia	1	-	93	-	-	4	1	1	8.1	14,579
South East	1	-	91	1	1	5	1	1	9.4	142,871
South West	1	-	91	-	1	4	1	1	8.1	33,281
West Midlands	1	-	90	1	1	5	1	1	9.8	44,185
North West	1	-	90	-	1	5	1	1	12.1	66,765
England	1	-	90	1	1	5	1	1	10.2	424,704
Wales	1	-	91	-	1	4	1	1	14.5	36,398
Northern Ireland	2	-	65	6	4	..	..	23	3.2	4,293

1 The *Criminal Law Act 1977* does not apply in Northern Ireland, hence figures are not directly comparable with England and Wales. Companies etc. are included for Northern Ireland.
2 Includes indictable motoring offences.
3 Excludes summary motoring offences.
4 Includes Young Offender Institutions, partly suspended and unsuspended imprisonment.
5 Rate per 1,000 population aged 10 and over.

Source: Home Office; Northern Ireland Office

9.10 Persons[1] against whom charge proved at courts in Scotland: by sentence, 1990

Numbers

	Absolute discharge	Admonished /cautioned	Probation	Fine	Immediate custodial sentence	Otherwise dealt with	Total
High court[2]							
Crimes	8	12	21	6	574	24	645
Offences	6	12	2	12	32	-	64
Sheriff courts: solemn procedure[2]							
Crimes	2	46	167	281	1,171	379	2,046
Offences	2	12	20	139	197	66	436
Sheriff courts: summary procedures[3]							
Crimes	83	2,437	2,264	14,941	5,857	3,656	29,238
Offences	161	3,773	799	42,971	2,505	1,571	51,780
District courts[3]							
Crimes	54	1,706	437	12,923	1,603	371	17,094
Offences	273	4,713	163	60,940	517	98	66,704

1 Including companies.
2 Trial by judge and jury.
3 Trial by judge(s) alone.

Source: The Scottish Office Home and Health Department

9.11 Prosecutions for motoring and motor vehicle offences[1]: by selected offence groups, 1981 and 1990

Percentages and thousands

	Driving etc. after consuming alcohol or drugs	Careless, reckless driving etc.	Licence, insurance and record keeping offences	Vehicle test and condition offences	Neglecting traffic signs, pedestrian rights etc.	Obstruc- tion, waiting and parking offences	Speed limit offences	Total number of offences[2] (= 100%) (thousands)
1981								
United Kingdom	4	7	33	13	7	4	14	2,608
North	4	7	37	17	5	3	10	140
Yorkshire & Humberside	3	8	37	16	6	4	10	240
East Midlands	3	8	37	17	6	2	11	212
East Anglia	4	8	36	16	4	4	13	74
South East	4	6	32	15	8	5	10	780
South West	3	8	31	16	7	5	14	213
West Midlands	3	7	38	16	5	3	13	266
North West	4	8	34	14	7	4	12	323
England	4	7	34	16	7	4	11	2,247
Wales	4	8	36	17	7	4	9	137
Scotland	9	10	31	14	5	4	19	148
Northern Ireland	8	22	23	4	2	2	21	24
1990								
United Kingdom	6	6	46	15	3	2	9	2,248
North	6	4	48	17	2	1	8	132
Yorkshire & Humberside	6	6	45	13	3	1	9	198
East Midlands	5	6	49	15	3	1	8	179
East Anglia	5	5	47	14	3	1	12	78
South East	7	5	46	14	3	3	8	592
South West	5	4	48	16	2	2	11	207
West Midlands	6	6	47	16	4	1	7	246
North West	5	6	48	16	4	1	9	320
England[3]	6	5	47	15	3	2	9	1,953
Wales[3]	6	6	51	17	3	1	5	146
Scotland	9	11	36	11	3	3	16	120
Northern Ireland	10	20	20	9	3	4	26	29

1 A person can be prosecuted for more than one offence at the same time. England and Wales figures cover offences dealt with at magistrates' courts.
2 The total includes other offences which are not shown separately.
3 In England and Wales, comparison of 1990 figures with 1981 is affected by the extension of fixed penalty notices to further offences in 1986.

Source: Home Office; The Scottish Office Home and Health Department; Northern Ireland Office

9.12 Breath testing and average court fines for driving etc. after consuming alcohol or drugs, 1981 and 1990

	1981		1990[1]		
	Total breath tests (thousands)	Percentage of positive tests	Total breath tests (thousands)	Percentage of positive tests	Average fine[2] (£)
North	10.9	40	32.6	19	162
Yorkshire & Humberside	14.0	46	37.8	26	245
East Midlands	21.0	18	73.8	10	237
East Anglia	8.5	25	34.0	10	248
South East	54.2	44	235.3	14	262
South West	15.1	35	38.4	22	261
West Midlands	15.2	37	41.6	24	246
North West	25.0	41	51.2	20	230
England	163.9	38	544.9	16	245
Wales	13.5	33	51.7	12	208
Scotland	..	..	..	..	216
Northern Ireland	2.5	44	2.6	32	87

1 The introduction of a new breath test form in England and Wales in 1987 was associated with improvements in the comprehensiveness of reporting of breath tests.
2 Average of fines imposed at Magistrates' Courts for offences for which a fine was the principal sentence.

Source: Home Office; The Scottish Office Home and Health Department; Northern Ireland Office

9.13 Sentencing at court for all offences: by length of sentence imposed for principal offence, 1981[1] and 1990

Percentages and numbers

	1981[1]				1990				
	Length of sentence			Number of persons[2] sentenced to immediate imprisonment (= 100%)	Length of sentence			Number of persons[2] sentenced to immediate imprisonment (= 100%)
	One year or less	Over 1 year up to 2 years	Over 2 years up to 4 years	Over 4 years		One year or less	Over 1 year up to 2 years	Over 2 years up to 4 years	Over 4 years	
United Kingdom	..	..	..	..	51,308	73	14	8	5	51,831
North	82	11	5	2	2,425	69	15	11	5	2,182
Yorkshire & Humberside	80	12	6	2	4,086	69	16	10	5	3,924
East Midlands	78	14	6	3	2,885	72	16	8	4	3,167
East Anglia	82	9	6	3	1,262	71	16	9	4	1,305
South East	77	13	7	3	16,610	66	16	10	8	15,173
South West	82	10	6	2	2,843	76	14	7	3	2,552
West Midlands	76	14	7	3	3,977	69	18	8	5	4,531
North West	83	10	5	2	6,420	73	15	8	4	6,485
England	79	12	7	3	40,508	69	16	9	6	39,319
Wales	78	13	7	2	1,825	73	15	7	4	2,051
Scotland[3]	91	5	2	2	7,060	90	4	4	3	8,483
Northern Ireland	69	12	8	11	1,915	77	7	7	9	1,978

1 Figures for 1981 do not include summary motoring offences.
2 Persons aged 21 and over.
3 Figures for Scotland include motor vehicle offences.

Source: Home Office; Scottish Office Home and Health Department; Northern Ireland Office

9.14   Police manpower: by type, 1990[1]

| | Regular police | | | | Special constables, civilian staff and cadets (rates per 1,000 regular police) | | | |
	Number	Population per officer[2]	Hectares per officer	Percentage of women officers	Special con-stables[3]	Civilian staff[4]	Cadets	Traffic wardens (numbers)
United Kingdom	149,164	384	163	*11.0*	119	348	3	5,507
North	7,729	398	199	*9.7*	132	337	1	244
Yorkshire & Humberside	11,828	418	130	*10.5*	130	327	3	360
East Midlands	8,384	477	186	*10.0*	202	326	-	298
East Anglia	3,848	531	327	*9.5*	207	346	5	125
South East								
Metropolitan Police	28,278	255	7	*12.5*	48	484	6	1,436
City of London	815	5	-	*11.3*	69	341	-	78
Other forces in S.E.	20,510	427	123	*11.8*	142	321	2	780
South West	9,721	479	245	*9.9*	219	327	2	411
West Midlands	12,361	422	105	*13.4*	178	338	5	384
North West	17,099	373	43	*11.9*	84	319	-	523
England	120,573	396	108	*11.5*	126	364	3	4,639
Wales	6,517	441	319	*9.2*	114	320	1	169
Scotland	13,841	369	557	*9.1*	129	226	3	547
Northern Ireland	8,233	193	173	*8.6*	.	339	.	152

1 At 31 December.
2 Based on mid-1989 population estimates.
3 Total number enrolled.
4 Part-time staff counted as half full-time.

Source: Home Office; The Scottish Office Home and Health Department; Northern Ireland Office

Notes to Chapter 9: Crime and Justice

There are complex legal and administrative differences between the legal systems in England and Wales, Scotland and Northern Ireland, which make simple comparisons difficult.

Table 9.1-9.10

The figures are compiled from police returns to the Home Office, The Scottish Home and Health Department and Northern Ireland Office. Figures for notifiable offenses recorded by the police in England and Wales for 1980 onward are not comparable with those for earlier years given in earlier volumes because of new counting rules introduced at the beginning of 1980.

Indictable offences cover those offences which must or may be tried by jury in the Crown Court and include the more serious offences. Summary offences are those for which a defendant would normally be tried at a magistrate's court and are generally less serious - the majority of motoring offences fall into this category. In Northern Ireland *non-indictable offences* are dealt with at a magistrate's court. Some indictable offences can also be dealt with there. In Scotland the term 'crimes' is used for the more serious criminal acts (roughly equivalent to indictable offences); the less serious are termed 'offences'. The majority of cases are tried summarily (without a jury) in the Sheriff or District court, while the most serious cases are tried in the High Court or the Sheriff court under solemn procedure (with a jury).

Cautions - if a person admits to committing an offence he may be given a formal police caution by, or on the instruction of, a senior police officer as an alternative to court proceedings. The figures exclude informal warnings given by the police, written warnings issued for motoring offences and warnings given by non-police bodies e.g a department store in the case of shoplifting. In Scotland warnings may be given by the Procurator Fiscal.

In April 1979 a new Crown Court system was introduced in Northern Ireland. Prior to this date the County Courts and Assizes system was equivalent to the Crown Court in England and Wales.

Table 9.2 and Chart 9.3 Clear-up rates

Offences recorded by the police as having been cleared up include offences for which persons have been charged or cautioned, those admitted and taken into consideration when persons are tried for other offences, and those admitted by prisoners who have been sentenced for other offences.

There is considerable variation by police forces in the way in which these different categories of clear-up are used. As a measure of police performance the clear-up rate has its limitations and it is not necessarily well correlated with other measures.

Table 9.7 Seizure of controlled drugs

The figures in this table, which are compiled from returns to the Home Office, relate to seizures made by police, officials of HM Customs and Excise and other bodies such as the Port of London Authority, and to drugs controlled under the Misuse of Drugs Act 1971. The Act divides drugs into three categories according to their harmfulness. A full list of drugs in each category is given in Schedule 2 to the Misuse of Drugs Act 1971, as amended by Orders in Council.

Table 9.9 Persons found guilty

On 29 March 1982 under section 47 of the Criminal Law Act 1977, courts in England and Wales were given power to partly suspend certain sentences of imprisonment. As a result, the term 'suspended sentence' is now known as 'fully suspended sentence' and 'immediate custody' includes partly suspended sentences as well as unsuspended sentences of imprisonment and sentence to a young offender institution.

Table 9.11 Prosecutions for motoring offenses

The introduction of the extended fixed penalty system on 1 October 1986 reduced the number of offences dealt with by prosecution, as many of the more minor offences were dealt with by fixed penalty notice instead.

Chapter 10: Transport

Cars

- Car ownership is highest in East Anglia and the South East outside Greater London (420 cars per 1,000 population) and lowest in Scotland (294 cars per 1,000 population).

(Table 10.1)

- Two car families are much more common in the South East. Almost a third of all households in the South East outside Greater London have 2 or more cars - twice the rate in Yorkshire and Humberside and the North.

(Table 10.1)

- The age of people and their cars go hand in hand. The South West, the region with the oldest population, also has the oldest cars - on average much older than those in Northern Ireland, the region with the youngest population.

(Tables 10.1 and 3.3)

Driving tests

- Learners taking their tests are slightly more successful in Scotland than in other regions. The pass rates are 62 per cent for men and 51 per cent for women.

(Table 10.3)

Road accidents

- Allowing for the distances travelled, fatal and serious accidents on major British roads are lowest in the South West and highest in Scotland.

(Table 10.5)

- People in East Anglia are almost twice as likely to be involved in a fatal or serious road accident as those in the North West.

(Table 10.5)

Freight Traffic

- Around three-quarters of goods carried on the roads in England and Wales start and end their journey in the same region.

(Table 10.7)

- In all regions, the vast majority of freight moved overland is moved by road - as much as 98 per cent in East Anglia and the South East. Even the smallest figure, in Yorkshire and Humberside, is 83 per cent.

(Table 10.7 and 10.8)

Air Traffic

- Domestic air travel has increased substantially in Yorkshire and Humberside, the West Midlands, the North West and Northern Ireland. The number of passengers more than doubled between 1981 and 1990.

(Table 10.10)

Regional Trends 27, © Crown copyright 1992

10.1 Cars[1] and car ownership, 1981 and 1990

	1981					1990				
	Percentage of house-holds with regular use of			Cars per 1,000 pop.	Average vehicle age (years)	Percentage of house-holds with regular use of			Cars per 1,000 pop.	Average vehicle age (years)
	No car	One car only	Two or more cars			No car	One car only	Two or more cars		
United Kingdom[2]	39	45	15	281	6.1	33	44	23	361	5.9
North	48	41	10	227	5.4	42	43	16	295	5.6
Yorkshire & Humberside	46	43	12	245	5.5	38	46	16	323	5.5
East Midlands	37	47	15	273	6.0	31	44	25	351	6.0
East Anglia	31	51	18	321	6.3	26	47	26	420	6.1
South East	36	46	19	316	6.3	28	44	28	396	6.1
Greater London	45	42	14	287	6.1	38	42	19	355	6.0
Rest of South East	30	48	22	336	6.4	23	45	32	420	6.2
South West	31	51	18	329	4.1	25	48	27	410	6.9
West Midlands	38	46	16	290	6.0	35	42	23	386	5.9
North West	45	42	13	250	5.7	37	44	19	338	5.6
England	39	45	16	288	6.1	32	44	24	372	6.0
Wales	38	47	15	271	6.3	30	49	21	346	6.3
Scotland	49	40	11	217	5.0	42	41	17	294	5.2
Northern Ireland	40	46	14	237	..	34	47	19	302	3.8

1 Includes cars and light vans normally available to the household.
2 Excludes Northern Ireland in 1981.

Source: Department of Transport; Department of Finance and Personnel, Northern Ireland

10.2 Cars[1]: by year of first registration, 1991[2]

Percentages and thousands

	Year of registration									Total (= 100%) (thousands)
	Before 1977	1977 -1978	1979 -1980	1981 -1982	1983 -1984	1985 -1986	1987 -1988	1989 -1990	1991	
Great Britain[3]	3.1	2.6	6.2	10.2	14.7	16.4	19.2	20.1	7.5	20,252
North	1.8	1.9	5.2	9.6	14.6	16.9	20.3	21.9	7.6	920
Yorkshire & Humberside	1.9	1.9	5.2	9.4	14.2	16.9	20.6	22.3	7.5	1,606
East Midlands	2.9	2.6	6.4	10.6	15.1	16.8	19.3	19.2	7.3	1,409
East Anglia	3.3	2.9	6.7	10.6	15.1	16.4	18.9	18.9	7.2	864
South East	3.7	2.9	6.5	10.4	14.7	16.3	18.9	19.2	7.4	6,827
Greater London	3.6	2.9	6.7	10.5	14.4	15.6	18.1	19.8	8.5	2,356
Rest of South East	3.7	2.8	6.4	10.3	14.9	16.7	19.3	18.9	6.9	4,471
South West	4.9	3.7	7.8	11.6	15.9	16.5	17.4	16.2	6.0	1,923
West Midlands	3.1	2.7	6.3	9.9	14.0	15.5	18.3	21.2	8.9	2,039
North West	2.2	2.1	5.7	9.9	14.3	16.3	19.5	22.2	7.7	2,146
England	3.2	2.7	6.4	10.4	14.7	16.4	19.0	19.9	7.5	17,734
Wales	2.9	2.7	6.7	11.0	15.6	17.1	20.0	18.2	5.9	986
Scotland	1.3	1.2	3.9	8.7	14.6	16.8	20.6	23.8	9.0	1,526

1 Cars in all taxation classes.
2 At 31 December 1991.
3 Totals include 6,000 vehicles where the county of the registered keeper is unknown.

Source: Annual Vehicle Census, Department of Transport

10.3 Private motoring driving tests: by sex, 1981 and 1990

Thousands and percentages

	1981				1990			
	Tests conducted (thousands)		Percentage passes		Tests conducted (thousands)		Percentage passes	
	Males	Females	Males	Females	Males	Females	Males	Females
Great Britain	1,032.5	998.9	53	42	877.1	1,095.5	58	48
North	61.2	51.0	51	39	37.2	46.1	61	49
Yorkshire & Humberside	88.1	79.8	52	41	76.7	95.9	55	45
East Midlands	90.9	88.4	52	40	59.0	77.5	59	47
Eastern	51.6	53.2	53	40	55.6	67.2	60	50
South East	93.7	92.2	53	43	98.9	126.8	58	48
Greater London	214.4	225.7	53	43	164.4	206.4	56	45
South West	76.5	75.4	57	45	73.2	86.9	61	50
West Midlands	102.0	91.4	53	43	85.6	105.3	58	46
North West	124.6	122.9	54	43	116.5	149.6	60	49
England	903.1	880.0	53	42	767.1	961.7	59	48
Wales	40.6	37.5	53	43	36.0	44.4	57	48
Scotland	88.7	81.3	52	42	73.1	89.3	62	51

Source: Department of Transport

10.4 Surfaced road lengths: by type of road

Percentages and thousand kilometres

	Motorway[1]	Other trunk[2]	Principal[3]	Non-principal	Unclassified	All roads
Percentage increase 1976-1991						
United Kingdom	41	..	7	3	12	8
North	4	-2	8	4	11	8
Yorkshire & Humberside	40	-19	10	0	13	8
East Midlands	15	-2	8	4	14	9
East Anglia	.	14	5	3	10	7
South East	82	-3	4	2	13	9
South West	12	-20	13	5	12	8
West Midlands	68	-19	6	4	11	7
North West	11	-34	19	1	9	7
England	40	-10	8	3	12	8
Wales	172	-2	9	2	14	8
Scotland	32	-6	4	2	13	6
Northern Ireland[4]	3	..	1	0	7	4
1991[5] (thousand kilometres)						
United Kingdom	3.14	12.36	37.91	118.41	212.38	384.20
North	0.15	0.78	2.00	6.96	13.26	23.15
Yorkshire & Humberside	0.31	0.75	2.55	7.21	18.15	28.98
East Midlands	0.18	1.21	2.74	9.53	14.97	28.64
East Anglia	0.02	0.85	1.63	8.19	9.60	20.30
South East	0.88	1.77	6.98	17.38	42.95	69.97
South West	0.30	1.10	4.24	17.96	24.72	48.31
West Midlands	0.38	0.90	2.69	9.11	16.83	29.90
North West	0.44	0.51	2.57	4.49	17.62	25.62
England	2.68	7.87	25.41	80.82	158.09	274.87
Wales	0.12	1.58	2.62	12.51	16.54	33.36
Scotland	0.23	2.91	7.67	17.49	23.52	51.82
Northern Ireland[4]	0.11	..	2.21	7.59	14.24	24.16

1 Motorway lengths show mainline lengths of trunk motorways only.
2 All purpose roads which together with motorways comprise the national system of through routes.
3 Non-trunk roads of regional and urban importance including local authority motorways.
4 Northern Ireland Class I roads are shown as principal roads. Class II and III roads are shown as non-principal roads.
5 At 1 April.

Source: Department of Transport

10.5 Fatal and serious road accidents, 1981 and 1990

Numbers and rates

	1981			1990			
	Total	Per 100,000 population	Per 100,000 vehicles	Total	Per 100,000 population	Per 100,000 vehicle kms[1]	Per 100,000 vehicles
United Kingdom	70,539 [2]	125 [2]	357.2 [2]	57,194	100	0.011 [3]	226.8
North	3,002	96	340.6	2,550	83	0.010	231.0
Yorkshire & Humberside	6,032	123	384.7	5,004	101	0.012	250.8
East Midlands	5,822	151	426.4	4,075	101	0.011	231.8
East Anglia	2,931	185	359.0	2,878	140	0.012	262.4
South East	21,474	126	325.4	18,565	106	0.013	225.6
South West	7,176	164	386.0	4,496	96	0.008	187.1
West Midlands	6,832	132	365.6	5,141	98	0.010	209.3
North West	5,765	89	285.9	4,818	75	0.009	187.8
England	59,034	126	347.8	47,527	99	0.011	219.6
Wales	3,426	122	366.8	2,435	85	0.010	199.3
Scotland	7,875	152	563.8	5,730	112	0.013	316.4
Northern Ireland	204	13	46.7	1,502	95	..	276.6

1 Major roads only.
2 Not including Northern Ireland serious accidents.
3 Great Britain only.

Source: Department of Transport

10.6 Public expenditure on roads, 1989-90

£ million

	Motorways and trunk roads				Local roads			
	New construction and improvement	Maintenance	Public lighting	Total	New construction and improvement	Maintenance	Public lighting	Total[1]
North	59.3	..	0.8	..	48.6	74.5	14.9	139.9
Yorkshire & Humberside	30.2	..	2.0	..	69.4	107.5	18.1	195.7
East Midlands	88.0	..	1.6	..	39.9	80.3	13.5	134.2
East Anglia	58.4	..	2.6	..	32.6	49.8	5.6	88.2
South East	332.6	..	5.1	..	345.9	388.0	55.0	792.3
South West	92.2	..	1.2	..	67.9	116.1	15.4	200.5
West Midlands	213.5	..	2.0	..	80.4	98.5	18.5	198.8
North West	62.7	..	5.9	..	101.4	112.2	29.0	243.5
England	936.8	..	21.4	..	786.1	1,027.4	169.9	1,993.1
Wales	101.4	29.9	2.4	133.7	60.1	86.1	11.3	157.9

1 Includes technical surveys.

Source: Department of Transport; Welsh Office

10.7 Road haulage[1], 1990

Percentages and million tonnes

Loading region	Unloading region (percentages)											Total loaded (=100%) (million tonnes)
	North	York-shire & Humber-side	East Mid-lands	East Anglia	South East	South West	West Mid-lands	North West	Wales	Scot-land	North-ern Ireland	
Loading region												
United Kingdom	6	10	9	5	23	8	10	11	5	10	2	1,687
North	72	8	2	1	2	-	2	7	1	6	-	104
Yorkshire & Humberside	6	71	6	1	3	1	3	7	1	2	-	180
East Midlands	1	7	61	6	9	1	7	7	1	1	-	167
East Anglia	1	2	4	70	15	1	2	2	1	-	-	89
South East	-	1	2	3	86	3	2	2	1	-	-	377
South West	-	1	1	1	11	76	4	1	3	-	-	131
West Midlands	1	2	7	1	6	2	72	5	3	1	-	164
North West	4	6	3	1	4	1	5	71	3	2	-	181
Wales	1	1	2	1	4	5	5	7	73	-	-	95
Scotland	3	1	1	-	1	-	1	2	-	92	-	160
Northern Ireland	-	-	-	-	-	-	-	-	-	-	98	41

1 Traffic carried by UK registered vehicles only. International road haulage is considered to be loaded/unloaded at the port of entry/exit.

Source: Department of Transport

10.8 Rail freight traffic, 1990

Percentages and million tonnes

Loading region	Unloading region (percentages)											Total loaded (=100%) (million tonnes)
	North	Yorkshire & Hum-berside	East Mid-lands	East Anglia	South East	South West	West Mid-lands	North West	Eng-land	Wales	Scot-land	
Loading region												
Great Britain	7.0	24.3	15.6	2.1	16.7	1.8	8.0	7.7	83.2	9.9	6.9	137.6
North	46.4	30.9	5.3	0.5	1.0	2.2	6.9	2.9	96.2	0.9	3.0	14.2
Yorkshire & Humberside	2.3	72.8	12.3	0.3	4.3	0.3	3.9	1.5	97.8	1.0	1.2	36.1
East Midlands	0.1	4.6	55.0	3.8	17.1	0.2	10.6	8.3	99.7	0.1	0.2	28.2
East Anglia	3.0	9.6	7.9	12.5	19.6	1.5	7.0	17.3	78.3	7.7	14.0	2.0
South East	0.4	4.9	0.1	3.4	68.5	2.3	5.3	8.7	93.5	2.5	4.0	8.6
South West	8.7	0.3	0.1	1.0	71.0	11.9	2.0	1.6	96.5	1.1	2.3	9.9
West Midlands	1.8	1.5	0.7	1.1	20.5	0.3	53.1	18.0	97.1	1.4	1.6	6.4
North West	8.1	3.8	1.6	3.8	7.6	2.1	12.5	51.5	90.9	4.9	4.2	8.2
England	8.1	29.1	18.5	2.0	19.2	1.8	9.3	8.7	96.7	1.3	1.9	113.6
Wales	0.2	1.9	0.1	1.1	6.4	1.7	2.3	3.6	17.3	81.5	1.2	14.2
Scotland	4.0	1.9	3.9	5.2	3.3	1.1	1.3	1.7	22.5	5.2	72.3	9.8

Source: Department of Transport

10.9 Freight traffic through seaports[1], 1990

Million tonnes

	Inward					Outward					Total goods handled
	Liquid bulk	Dry bulk	Container and ro-ro	Semi-bulk and con- ventional	Total inward	Liquid bulk	Dry bulk	Container and ro-ro	Semi-bulk and con- ventional	Total outward	
United Kingdom	121.9	87.4	48.1	20.9	278.3	133.6	31.1	38.5	10.3	213.5	491.8
North	6.3	11.2	1.2	1.2	20.0	22.4	8.4	1.0	1.3	33.1	53.0
Yorkshire & Humberside	21.4	13.2	5.3	3.5	43.5	8.7	2.6	3.3	1.7	16.4	59.8
East Midlands	-	0.3	0.2	0.8	1.4	-	0.5	0.1	-	0.6	1.9
East Anglia	1.2	1.7	10.9	1.0	14.8	0.1	1.3	8.6	1.3	11.2	26.0
South East	41.2	30.5	19.1	6.9	97.7	15.5	3.8	14.2	0.6	34.1	131.7
South West	3.3	3.1	0.9	1.0	8.3	0.9	3.6	0.7	0.1	5.3	13.5
West Midlands	0.0	0.0	0.0	0.0	0.0	0.0	0.0	0.0	0.0	0.0	0.0
North West	15.1	4.5	2.8	1.6	24.0	5.2	1.9	3.9	0.2	11.2	35.2
England	88.4	64.5	40.5	16.0	209.5	52.7	22.1	31.8	5.2	111.7	321.1
Wales	22.7	12.5	1.1	1.7	37.9	14.2	1.8	1.4	1.0	18.5	56.4
Scotland	6.9	6.6	2.1	2.8	18.4	66.4	6.3	2.4	4.0	79.1	97.6
Northern Ireland	3.9	3.8	4.4	0.4	12.5	0.3	0.9	2.9	0.1	4.2	16.7

1 Foreign and domestic traffic.

Source: Department of Transport

10.10 Commercial air transport, 1981 and 1990

Thousands and tonnes

	1981					1990				
	Passengers (thousands)			Freight (tonnes)	Mail (tonnes)	Passengers (thousands)			Freight (tonnes)	Mail (tonnes)
	Inter- national	Domestic	Total[1]			Inter- national	Domestic	Total[1]		
United Kingdom	43,732	14,039	58,979	723,707	104,463	77,408	25,009	104,135	1,193,050	172,166
North	631	551	1,246	1,397	1,046	1,046	852	1,993	915	2,409
Yorkshire & Humberside	163	214	411	351	2	442	527	1,019	695	0
East Midlands	518	221	747	3,555	1,761	882	398	1,284	11,116	9,401
East Anglia	77	79	160	840	422	122	114	249	341	834
South East	34,578	5,287	40,386	611,490	70,976	58,893	9,654	69,045	994,347	97,807
South West[2]	221	322	554	615	1,807	803	547	1,427	2,231	4,134
West Midlands	1,105	388	1,560	2,641	345	2,688	821	3,647	22,006	999
North West	3,812	1,480	5,466	43,369	13,048	8,269	3,021	11,651	89,885	22,828
England	41,104	8,542	50,530	664,258	89,407	73,145	15,934	90,315	1,121,536	138,412
Wales	232	65	331	472	689	545	49	626	2,371	857
Scotland	2,214	4,205	6,698	44,425	10,971	3,267	6,595	10,300	43,622	24,682
Northern Ireland	182	1,227	1,420	14,552	3,396	451	2,431	2,894	25,521	8,215

1 Includes passengers in transit, i.e. arriving at and leaving the airport by air.
2 Includes Bournemouth (Hurn) Airport which was included in the South East in Regional Trends editions prior to 1986 (No. 21).

Source: Civil Aviation Authority

Notes to Chapter 10: Transport

Table 10.6 Road accidents

An *accident* is one involving personal injury occurring on the public highway (including footways) in which a road vehicle is involved and which becomes known to the police within 30 days. The vehicle need not be moving and it need not be in collision with anything.

Persons killed are those who sustained injuries which caused death less than 30 days after the accident.

A *serious injury* is one for which a person is detained in hospital as an in-patient, or any of the following injuries whether or not they are detained in hospital: fractures, concussion, internal injuries, crushing, severe cuts and lacerations, severe general shock requiring medical treatment, injuries causing death 30 or more days after the accident.

There are many reasons why *accident rates* vary between regions. For example, an area that 'imports' large numbers of visitors or commuters will have a relatively high proportion of accidents related to vehicles or drivers from outside the area. A rural area with low population density but high road mileage can be expected, other things being equal, to have lower than average accident rates.

Table 10.9 Freight traffic through seaports

Figures are based on returns made by port authorities to the Department of Transport and cover all ports in the United Kingdom grouped by region. *Domestic* traffic refers to traffic through the ports of the United Kingdom to and from all parts of the United Kingdom, Isle of Man and the Channel Islands.

Traffic to and from off-shore oil installations, landings, of sea-dredged aggregates and material shipped for dumping at sea are also included. Non-oil traffic with United Kingdom off-shore installations is included under 'semi-bulk and conventional traffic'.

Further information, and definitions of the traffic classification used, can be found in *Port Statistics 1988* (Department of Transport/British Ports Federation).

Chapter 11: Environment

Rivers and canals

●   Northumbrian and Welsh water areas continue to have the cleanest rivers and canals in England and Wales - over four fifths of them are of good quality. In the South West and Severn Trent areas only half are good quality. Almost all rivers, lochs and canals in Scotland are of good quality.

(Table 11.2)

Air pollution

●   In the early 1970s, the North had the smokiest environment, but has subsequently cleaned up its act - by 1989-90 only the East Midlands and the South West had lower levels.

(Table 11.4)

Acid rain

●   The strongest acid rain falls chiefly in the Eastern regions of the country. However, because it rains more in the hilly Western parts, more acid actually reaches the soil there.

(Chart 11.5)

Radiation

●   Devon and Cornwall are the areas most affected by high levels of radiation. Average levels of both indoor radon and outdoor gamma ray radiation are much higher than in other parts of the country.

(Chart 11.6)

11.1 Water pollution incidents and prosecutions: by type of pollution, 1990[1]

Numbers

	Industrial		Sewage/sewerage		Farm		Other		Total	
	Incidents	Prosecu-tions[2]	Incidents	Prosecu-tions[2]	Incidents	Prosecu-tions[2]	Incidents	Prosecu-tions[2]	Incidents	Prosecu-tions[2]
North West	860	58	968	4	630	50	1,713	0	4,171	112
Northumbrian	365	17	477	4	65	5	338	0	1,245	26
Severn Trent	2,243	28	424	32	271	26	3,143	9	6,081	95
Yorkshire	771	31	737	13	305	27	768	0	2,581	71
Anglian	833	12	362	3	179	10	273	4	1,647	29
Thames	1,507	36	765	13	58	4	1,111	2	3,441	55
Southern	656	10	487	7	84	5	562	1	1,789	23
Wessex	437	5	218	8	226	14	603	0	1,484	27
South West	688	14	656	12	782	40	832	5	2,958	71
Welsh	388	26	717	14	547	40	1,094	5	2,746	85
England & Wales	8,748	237	5,811	110	3,147	221	10,437	26	28,143	594

1 The NRA regional boundaries are based on river catchment areas and not county borders.
2 Prosecutions relate to pollution incidents occurring in 1990 for which prosecutions had been taken up to 31 April 1992. A number of prosecutions for 1990 incidents are still pending and hence are not included in the figures.

Source: National Rivers Authority

11.2 Rivers and canals: by quality, 1985 and 1990[1]

Percentages and kilometres

	1985					1990				
	Quality (percentages)				Total length (= 100%)	Quality (percentages)				Total length (= 100%)
	Good	Fair	Poor	Bad	kms	Good	Fair	Poor	Bad	kms
North West	59	21	16	5	5,900	55	26	15	4	5,900
Northumbrian	88	9	2	1	2,780	86	11	3	0	2,790
Severn Trent	51	36	12	1	6,150	52	37	10	1	6,670
Yorkshire	74	13	9	3	6,040	70	15	12	3	6,030
Anglian	58	33	9	0	4,450	57	36	8	0	4,450
Thames	64	29	6	0	3,810	61	32	7	0	3,740
Southern	76	22	3	0	1,990	69	23	7	1	2,230
Wessex	62	31	6	1	2,550	60	34	5	1	2,700
South West	66	27	6	1	2,970	51	30	17	1	3,070
Welsh	81	13	6	1	4,760	84	9	6	1	4,800
England & Wales	66	24	9	2	41,390	64	25	9	2	42,380

1 In some cases estimates of river quality have been based upon financial years and/or more than one year's data.

Source: National Rivers Authority

11.3 Water abstractions from surface water and ground water: by purpose, 1990

Megalitres per day and percentages

| | Water supply[1] | Agriculture | | Industry | | Total quantity abstracted | Percentage of total abstract-ions that were from groundwater |
		Spray irriga-tion[2]	Other	EGC[3]	Other[4]		
North West	1,883	4	4	161	734	2,787	16
Northumbria	1,060	1	0	0	38	1,098	9
Severn Trent	2,421	68	9	2,991	451	5,940	20
Yorkshire	1,498	24	15	662	351	2,551	13
Anglian	1,928	213	18	2	295	2,456	43
Thames	3,827	14	12	111	167	4,131	39
Southern	1,621	29	9	0	1,184	2,843	50
Wessex	798	12	20	0	137	967	51
South West	630	6	29	210	128	1,003	9
Welsh	2,671	7	11	8,475	310	11,474	1
England & Wales	18,336	378	129	12,612	3,795	35,249	20

1 Water supply (ie piped mains water) includes abstractions by water services companies, water supply companies and small private abstactors.
2 Includes small amounts for non-agricultural spray irrigation.
3 Electricity Generating Companies.
4 Excludes tidal water and water used for water power and fish farming.

Source: National Rivers Authority

11.4 Atmospheric pollution, 1971-72 and 1989-90

| | Smoke | | | Sulphur dioxide | | | |
| | Micrograms per cubic metre | | Percentage change 1971-72 to 1989-90 | Micrograms per cubic metre | | Percentage change 1971-72 to 1989-90 | Total sites[1] (numbers) |
	1971-72	1989-90		1971-72	1989-90		
United Kingdom	61	12	*-80*	114	35	*-69*	48
North	83	10	*-88*	94	26	*-72*	4
Yorkshire & Humberside	78	12	*-85*	158	38	*-76*	3
East Midlands	50	8	*-84*	105	45	*-57*	3
East Anglia	61	10	*-84*	65	18	*-72*	1
South East:							
Greater London	41	10	*-76*	190	37	*-81*	5
Rest of South East	35	10	*-71*	79	35	*-56*	5
South West	35	8	*-77*	73	22	*-70*	3
West Midlands	78	15	*-81*	117	44	*-62*	4
North West	82	15	*-82*	150	41	*-73*	11
England	63	11	*-83*	125	36	*-71*	39
Wales	45	10	*-78*	72	26	*-64*	4
Scotland	48	13	*-73*	63	30	*-52*	4
Northern Ireland	79	37	*-53*	87	63	*-28*	1

1 The number of monitoring sites changes from year to year as sites cease, start or even restart monitoring. The number of sites given is the number that were operational in both years. For some regions, the number of sites is small and great care should be taken in interpreting trends.

Source: Warren Spring Laboratory

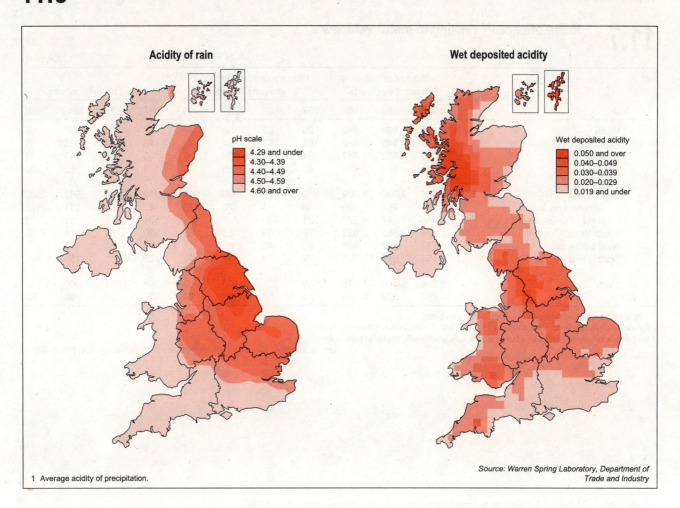

Acidity of rain

Wet deposited acidity

pH scale
- 4.29 and under
- 4.30–4.39
- 4.40–4.49
- 4.50–4.59
- 4.60 and over

Wet deposited acidity
- 0.050 and over
- 0.040–0.049
- 0.030–0.039
- 0.020–0.029
- 0.019 and under

1 Average acidity of precipitation.

Source: Warren Spring Laboratory, Department of Trade and Industry

11.6 Radiation dose rates

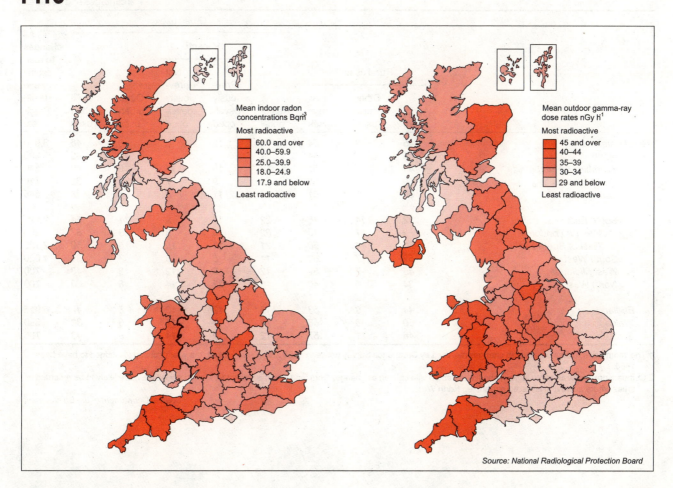

Mean indoor radon
concentrations Bqm^3

Most radioactive
- 60.0 and over
- 40.0–59.9
- 25.0–39.9
- 18.0–24.9
- 17.9 and below

Least radioactive

Mean outdoor gamma-ray
dose rates nGy h^{-1}

Most radioactive
- 45 and over
- 40–44
- 35–39
- 30–34
- 29 and below

Least radioactive

Source: National Radiological Protection Board

11.7 Noise offences[1,2] relating to motor vehicles

Numbers

	Findings of guilt at Magistrates' Courts			Written warnings issued for alleged offences[3]				Fixed penalty notices			
	1987	1988	1989	1987	1988	1989	1990	1987	1988	1989	1990
North	356	198	240	80	63	59	49	64	56	59	56
Yorkshire & Humberside	399	446	452	154	93	94	71	145	101	95	91
East Midlands	835	682	747	184	235	208	182	55	73	92	41
East Anglia	488	386	410	45	27	35	22	133	147	160	206
South East	1,925	2,008	1,809	370	296	548	547	616	430	589	525
Greater London	367	261	230	49	47	322	175	42	53	101	122
Rest of South East	1,558	1,747	1,579	321	249	226	372	574	377	488	403
South West	575	569	623	76	68	85	55	100	64	118	89
West Midlands	512	542	498	63	42	44	11	215	155	138	127
North West	454	619	596	77	79	87	72	228	155	158	127
England	5,544	5,450	5,375	1,049	903	1,160	1,009	1,556	1,181	1,409	1,262
Wales	487	558	509	53	58	56	84	127	89	66	69

1 Offences relating to excessive noise while using a vehicle.
2 Excludes alleged offences dealt with by Vehicle Defect Registration Schemes(VDRS).
3 Written warnings may be issued by the police instead of instituting court proceedings.

Source: Offences Relating to Motor Vehicles, England and Wales, *Home Office*

11.8 Land changing to residential use: by previous use, 1986[1]

Percentages and hectares

	Rural uses				Urban uses				All changes to residential use (= 100%) (hectares)
						Vacant[2]			
	Agriculture	Other rural uses	All rural uses	Residential	Previously developed	Not previously developed	Other urban uses	All urban uses	
Great Britain	45	9	54	15	12	10	8	46	8,010
North	45	10	54	11	13	11	11	46	280
Yorkshire & Humberside	43	7	51	12	16	14	8	49	540
East Midlands	60	8	68	11	9	7	5	32	710
East Anglia	56	6	61	15	11	8	5	39	545
South East	32	14	46	22	12	9	11	54	2,420
Greater London	2	11	13	32	18	3	33	87	290
Rest of South East	36	14	50	21	11	10	8	50	2,125
South West	62	7	69	11	5	8	7	31	1,020
West Midlands	45	7	52	12	16	12	8	48	700
North West	34	5	40	16	22	14	8	60	700
England	44	9	53	16	12	10	8	47	6,915
Wales	60	8	68	9	7	11	6	32	390
Scotland	46	11	57	12	9	14	8	43	705

1 The information relates only to map changes recorded by Ordanance Survey between 1985 and 1990 for which the year of change is judged to have been 1986.
2 Comparisons between some regions should be treated with caution as changes from land which is vacant for a short period are more likely to be recorded in areas where surveying is more frequent (eg North West).

Source: Department of the Environment

11.9   Land changing to urban use: by previous use, 1986[1]

Percentages and thousand hectares

	Rural uses	Urban uses		All changes to urban land use (= 100%) (thousand hectares)
		Previously developed	Vacant and not previously developed	
Great Britain	49	43	8	16.0
North	37	56	7	0.8
Yorkshire & Humberside	41	50	9	1.2
East Midlands	62	33	5	1.2
East Anglia	60	33	8	0.9
South East	44	49	7	4.4
Greater London	15	82	3	0.8
Rest of South East	50	43	8	3.6
South West	67	27	6	1.7
West Midlands	47	45	8	1.4
North West	37	53	10	1.6
England	48	44	7	13.3
Wales	59	34	6	1.1
Scotland	51	39	10	1.6

1 The information relates only to map changes recorded by Ordanance Survey between 1985 and 1990 for which the year of change is judged to have been 1986.

Source: Department of the Environment

Chart 11.5 Acidity of rain and wet deposited acidity

The pH scale indicates the acidity/alkalinity of a substance. A neutral substance has a value of 7.0; values lower than 7.0 indicate an acid substance, the lower the value the greater the acidity. The scale is logarithmic; rain of pH 4.0 is ten times more acidic than rain of pH 5.0.

For the latest official macro-economic data from the Central Statistical Office
simply phone or fax the following numbers
(you may have to select "polling" mode on your fax machine)

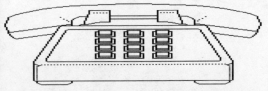

CSO STATCALL
0839   3383   PLUS ..

CSO STATFAX
0336   4160   PLUS ..

Retail prices index	37
Monthly trade figures	38
Balance of payments	39
PSBR	40
Index of production	41
Producer prices	42
Retail sales index	43
Credit business	44
Gross domestic product	45
and for forthcoming economic release dates	46

Calls are charged at 36p per minute cheap rate; 48p per minute at all other times

CSO   Great George Street London SWIP 3AQ

Regional Trend 27, © Crown copyright 1992

12.1 Gross domestic product, factor cost: current prices

	1981	1982	1983	1984	1985	1986	1987	1988	1989	1990
£ million										
United Kingdom	218,755	238,231	261,083	280,052	306,716	326,182	358,297	397,292	436,180	477,747
North	10,720	11,468	12,459	12,981	14,258	15,136	16,854	18,464	20,439	22,243
Yorkshire & Humberside	16,627	18,176	19,775	20,702	23,174	25,702	27,828	30,547	33,704	37,448
East Midlands	13,696	15,026	16,284	17,460	19,378	21,364	23,602	26,268	29,213	32,368
East Anglia	6,706	7,520	8,188	9,215	10,098	11,317	12,302	13,938	15,578	17,312
South East	72,655	77,988	86,269	91,754	101,862	113,350	125,253	141,337	155,484	169,398
South West	14,985	16,662	18,304	19,533	21,584	23,991	26,587	29,865	32,834	36,300
West Midlands	17,265	18,695	20,375	21,807	24,444	26,646	29,363	33,105	36,290	39,727
North West	22,349	24,274	26,238	27,695	30,359	33,438	36,037	40,110	43,727	47,412
England	175,003	189,810	207,890	221,148	245,157	270,944	297,827	333,634	367,268	402,207
Wales	8,639	9,550	10,449	10,807	11,926	13,247	14,998	16,948	18,443	20,053
Scotland	18,349	20,030	21,874	22,799	25,014	27,208	29,481	32,434	35,482	38,738
Northern Ireland	4,431	4,868	5,325	5,652	6,306	6,996	7,441	8,243	9,097	9,821
United Kingdom less Continental Shelf and statistical discrepancy	206,422	224,257	245,538	260,406	288,403	318,394	349,746	391,259	430,290	470,820
Continental Shelf	11,589	13,465	15,792	19,111	18,457	8,471	9,565	6,919	6,524	6,767
Statistical discrepancy (income adjustment)	744	509	-247	535	-144	-683	-1,014	-886	-634	160
As a percentage of United Kingdom *less* **Continental Shelf and statistical discrepancy**										
United Kingdom	*100.0*	*100.0*	*100.0*	*100.0*	*100.0*	*100.0*	*100.0*	*100.0*	*100.0*	*100.0*
North	*5.2*	*5.1*	*5.1*	*5.0*	*4.9*	*4.8*	*4.8*	*4.7*	*4.7*	*4.7*
Yorkshire & Humberside	*8.1*	*8.1*	*8.1*	*7.9*	*8.0*	*8.1*	*8.0*	*7.8*	*7.8*	*8.0*
East Midlands	*6.6*	*6.7*	*6.6*	*6.7*	*6.7*	*6.7*	*6.7*	*6.7*	*6.8*	*6.9*
East Anglia	*3.2*	*3.4*	*3.3*	*3.5*	*3.5*	*3.6*	*3.5*	*3.6*	*3.6*	*3.7*
South East	*35.2*	*34.8*	*35.1*	*35.2*	*35.3*	*35.6*	*35.8*	*36.1*	*36.1*	*36.0*
South West	*7.3*	*7.4*	*7.5*	*7.5*	*7.5*	*7.5*	*7.6*	*7.6*	*7.6*	*7.7*
West Midlands	*8.4*	*8.3*	*8.3*	*8.4*	*8.5*	*8.4*	*8.4*	*8.5*	*8.4*	*8.4*
North West	*10.8*	*10.8*	*10.7*	*10.6*	*10.5*	*10.5*	*10.3*	*10.3*	*10.2*	*10.1*
England	*84.8*	*84.6*	*84.7*	*84.9*	*85.0*	*85.1*	*85.2*	*85.3*	*85.4*	*85.4*
Wales	*4.2*	*4.3*	*4.3*	*4.2*	*4.1*	*4.2*	*4.3*	*4.3*	*4.3*	*4.3*
Scotland	*8.9*	*8.9*	*8.9*	*8.8*	*8.7*	*8.5*	*8.4*	*8.3*	*8.2*	*8.2*
Northern Ireland	*2.1*	*2.2*	*2.2*	*2.2*	*2.2*	*2.2*	*2.1*	*2.1*	*2.1*	*2.1*
£ per head										
United Kingdom less Continental Shelf and statistical discrepancy	3,663	3,983	4,358	4,612	5,094	5,609	6,143	6,856	7,518	8,201
North	3,439	3,691	4,019	4,197	4,620	4,914	5,478	6,012	6,651	7,233
Yorkshire & Humberside	3,381	3,702	4,028	4,221	4,727	5,246	5,679	6,218	6,822	7,562
East Midlands	3,555	3,901	4,219	4,507	4,972	5,450	5,987	6,616	7,305	8,054
East Anglia	3,539	3,934	4,254	4,751	5,140	5,683	6,109	6,851	7,619	8,408
South East	4,271	4,586	5,062	5,362	5,925	6,565	7,233	8,149	8,944	9,703
South West	3,420	3,789	4,137	4,379	4,796	5,281	5,794	6,445	7,057	7,779
West Midlands	3,329	3,609	3,936	4,213	4,716	5,143	5,649	6,358	6,957	7,611
North West	3,460	3,774	4,093	4,330	4,754	5,246	5,657	6,303	6,854	7,421
England	3,738	4,056	4,438	4,710	5,204	5,734	6,282	7,019	7,701	8,408
Wales	3,071	3,403	3,721	3,850	4,241	4,696	5,288	5,932	6,419	6,960
Scotland	3,542	3,877	4,247	4,431	4,870	5,313	5,767	6,367	6,970	7,592
Northern Ireland	2,882	3,165	3,450	3,646	4,048	4,465	4,724	5,223	5,747	6,181
£ per head, United Kingdom *less* **Continental Shelf and statistical discrepancy = 100**										
United Kingdom	100.0	100.0	100.0	100.0	100.0	100.0	100.0	100.0	100.0	100.0
North	93.9	92.7	92.2	91.0	90.7	87.6	89.2	87.7	88.5	88.2
Yorkshire & Humberside	92.3	92.9	92.4	91.5	92.8	93.5	92.4	90.7	90.7	92.2
East Midlands	97.0	97.9	96.8	97.7	97.6	97.2	97.5	96.5	97.2	98.2
East Anglia	96.6	98.8	97.6	103.0	100.9	101.3	99.4	99.9	101.3	102.5
South East	116.6	115.1	116.2	116.2	116.3	117.0	117.7	118.9	119.0	118.3
South West	93.4	95.1	94.9	94.9	94.1	94.1	94.3	94.0	93.9	94.9
West Midlands	90.9	90.6	90.3	91.4	92.6	91.7	92.0	92.7	92.5	92.8
North West	94.5	94.8	93.9	93.9	93.3	93.5	92.1	91.9	91.2	90.5
England	102.0	101.8	101.8	102.1	102.2	102.2	102.3	102.4	102.4	102.5
Wales	83.8	85.4	85.4	83.5	83.3	83.7	86.1	86.5	85.4	84.9
Scotland	96.7	97.3	97.5	96.1	95.6	94.7	93.9	92.9	92.7	92.6
Northern Ireland	78.7	79.5	79.2	79.0	79.5	79.6	76.9	76.2	76.4	75.4

Source: Central Statistical Office

12.2 Gross domestic product by industry groups, factor cost: current prices

£ million

	1987	1988	1989	1990	1987	1988	1989	1990
	North				**Yorkshire & Humberside**			
Agriculture, forestry and fishing	277	297	338	322	554	517	601	600
Energy and water supply	1,105	1,161	1,226	1,315	2,002	1,993	1,969	2,114
Manufacturing	4,839	5,357	5,943	6,171	7,612	8,260	9,139	9,882
Minerals, metals and chemicals[1]	1,698	2,006	2,126	..	1,998	2,188	2,391	..
Metal goods, engineering, vehicles	1,576	1,652	1,917	..	2,340	2,625	3,132	..
Other manufacturing industries	1,565	1,699	1,900	..	3,274	3,447	3,615	..
Construction	1,187	1,385	1,644	1,825	1,841	2,226	2,598	2,959
Distribution, hotels and catering; repairs	2,082	2,294	2,561	2,935	4,131	4,773	5,297	5,964
Transport and communication	1,073	1,143	1,310	1,483	1,874	2,019	2,218	2,501
Financial & business services, etc[2]	1,780	1,870	2,255	2,433	3,096	3,217	4,019	4,659
Ownership of dwellings	911	992	1,059	1,282	1,407	1,498	1,602	1,931
Public administration and defence[3]	1,067	1,152	1,204	1,372	1,700	1,905	1,975	2,170
Education and health services	1,897	2,101	2,326	2,498	2,928	3,258	3,590	3,944
Other services	1,178	1,299	1,302	1,374	1,728	2,019	2,182	2,339
Adjustment for financial services	-541	-588	-728	-766	-1,046	-1,138	-1,487	-1,617
Total	16,854	18,463	20,439	22,243	27,828	30,547	33,704	37,448
	East Midlands				**East Anglia**			
Agriculture, forestry and fishing	697	598	732	787	718	666	764	767
Energy and water supply	1,702	1,789	1,784	1,833	326	357	390	443
Manufacturing	7,360	8,043	8,730	9,371	2,865	3,270	3,562	3,831
Minerals, metals and chemicals[1]	1,201	1,413	1,523	..	420	485	483	..
Metal goods, engineering, vehicles	2,622	2,902	3,233	..	993	1,186	1,359	..
Other manufacturing industries	3,537	3,728	3,974	..	1,453	1,599	1,719	..
Construction	1,565	1,936	2,221	2,461	988	1,178	1,350	1,513
Distribution, hotels and catering; repairs	3,215	3,717	4,243	4,795	1,806	2,121	2,367	2,731
Transport and communication	1,363	1,521	1,694	1,907	1,058	1,171	1,278	1,440
Financial & business services, etc[2]	2,418	2,759	3,498	3,948	1,596	1,861	2,304	2,473
Ownership of dwellings	1,231	1,410	1,623	2,038	752	831	918	1,142
Public administration and defence[3]	1,639	1,705	1,827	2,039	861	902	980	1,084
Education and health services	1,936	2,324	2,521	2,782	1,138	1,337	1,477	1,643
Other services	1,217	1,264	1,396	1,501	730	860	1,001	1,077
Adjustment for financial services	-740	-799	-1,055	-1,094	-535	-617	-814	-832
Total	23,602	26,268	29,213	32,368	12,302	13,938	15,578	17,312
	South East				**Greater London**			
Agriculture, forestry and fishing	984	911	1,006	1,094	49	48	53	59
Energy and water supply	3,419	3,453	3,662	4,252	1,350	1,328	1,424	1,717
Manufacturing	23,202	25,263	27,268	28,642	7,532	8,154	8,852	9,239
Minerals, metals and chemicals[1]	3,870	4,302	4,553	..	989	1,154	1,319	..
Metal goods, engineering, vehicles	10,387	11,365	12,321	..	2,763	3,025	3,178	..
Other manufacturing industries	8,945	9,596	10,395	..	3,780	3,975	4,355	..
Construction	8,368	10,144	11,322	12,567	2,695	3,189	3,550	4,099
Distribution, hotels and catering; repairs	18,181	21,180	23,317	25,081	7,850	8,841	9,541	10,272
Transport and communication	10,925	12,129	13,229	14,315	5,457	6,004	6,361	6,805
Financial & business services, etc[2]	31,592	36,573	43,262	46,478	16,922	19,199	22,844	24,312
Ownership of dwellings	8,507	9,507	10,150	12,466	3,736	4,185	4,379	5,529
Public administration and defence[3]	8,480	9,209	9,907	10,975	3,148	3,447	3,769	4,185
Education and health services	10,530	11,675	12,630	13,615	4,944	5,319	5,779	6,228
Other services	9,521	10,879	12,060	12,860	4,733	5,223	5,818	6,184
Adjustment for financial services	-8,459	-9,587	-12,330	-12,948	-5,512	-6,177	-7,765	-7,932
Total	125,253	141,338	155,484	169,396	52,905	58,759	64,605	70,698
	Rest of South East				**South West**			
Agriculture, forestry and fishing	936	863	954	1,035	674	711	817	768
Energy and water supply	2,069	2,125	2,238	2,535	954	1,006	1,103	1,349
Manufacturing	15,670	17,109	18,417	19,403	5,838	6,462	6,808	7,375
Minerals, metals and chemicals[1]	2,881	3,148	3,234	..	784	865	913	..
Metal goods, engineering, vehicles	7,625	8,340	9,143	..	2,698	3,126	3,225	..
Other manufacturing industries	5,165	5,621	6,040	..	2,356	2,471	2,669	..
Construction	5,673	6,955	7,772	8,468	2,197	2,628	2,999	3,215
Distribution, hotels and catering; repairs	10,331	12,339	13,776	14,808	4,117	4,844	5,460	5,909
Transport and communication	5,468	6,125	6,868	7,509	1,653	1,894	2,003	2,218
Financial & business services, etc[2]	14,670	17,374	20,418	22,166	4,105	4,669	5,713	6,135
Ownership of dwellings	4,772	5,322	5,772	6,937	1,752	1,930	2,050	2,593
Public administration and defence[3]	5,332	5,763	6,138	6,790	2,568	2,773	2,989	3,381
Education and health services	5,586	6,357	6,851	7,387	2,484	2,790	3,054	3,451
Other services	4,788	5,656	6,241	6,676	1,701	1,845	2,062	2,216
Adjustment for financial services	-2,947	-3,410	-4,566	-5,016	-1,455	-1,687	-2,225	-2,311
Total	72,348	82,579	90,879	98,699	26,587	29,865	32,834	36,300

See footnotes on next page.

12.2 (continued)

£ million

West Midlands / North West

	1987	1988	1989	1990	1987	1988	1989	1990
	West Midlands				**North West**			
Agriculture, forestry and fishing	475	487	527	550	297	310	344	338
Energy and water supply	1,168	1,220	1,179	1,258	1,580	1,548	1,571	1,711
Manufacturing	9,718	10,754	11,697	12,364	10,936	12,327	13,245	13,816
Minerals, metals and chemicals[1]	1,571	1,849	1,981	..	2,499	2,848	2,831	..
Metal goods, engineering, vehicles	5,599	6,122	6,617	..	4,151	4,839	5,603	..
Other manufacturing industries	2,547	2,783	3,100	..	4,286	4,640	4,811	..
Construction	1,869	2,296	2,593	2,919	2,172	2,588	2,917	3,255
Distribution, hotels and catering; repairs	4,066	4,792	5,286	5,846	5,118	5,806	6,293	7,282
Transport and communication	1,664	1,923	2,110	2,276	2,608	2,888	3,127	3,319
Financial & business services, etc[2]	3,720	4,135	4,946	5,361	4,750	5,162	6,445	6,991
Ownership of dwellings	1,866	2,072	2,304	2,769	2,265	2,405	2,606	3,055
Public administration and defence[3]	1,620	1,695	1,819	2,012	2,300	2,445	2,459	2,561
Education and health services	2,627	2,989	3,362	3,819	3,444	3,874	4,273	4,697
Other services	1,665	1,951	2,043	2,207	2,197	2,543	2,770	2,871
Adjustment for financial services	-1,095	-1,210	-1,575	-1,653	-1,630	-1,786	-2,322	-2,481
Total	29,363	33,105	36,290	39,727	36,037	40,110	43,727	47,412

England / Wales

	1987	1988	1989	1990	1987	1988	1989	1990
	England				**Wales**			
Agriculture, forestry and fishing	4,675	4,497	5,128	5,225	367	387	402	415
Energy and water supply	12,256	12,528	12,884	14,275	1,252	1,100	1,055	1,096
Manufacturing	72,370	79,737	86,393	91,450	4,092	4,935	5,092	5,472
Minerals, metals and chemicals[1]	14,040	15,957	16,801	..	1,617	1,958	1,943	..
Metal goods, engineering, vehicles	30,367	33,817	37,408	..	1,288	1,596	1,730	..
Other manufacturing industries	27,963	29,964	32,184	..	1,186	1,381	1,419	..
Construction	20,188	24,381	27,643	30,713	924	1,082	1,302	1,458
Distribution, hotels and catering; repairs	42,715	49,527	54,824	60,542	1,920	2,209	2,525	2,765
Transport and communication	22,219	24,689	26,968	29,460	882	988	1,118	1,281
Financial & business services, etc[2]	53,057	60,246	72,444	78,478	1,526	1,652	1,990	2,147
Ownership of dwellings	18,692	20,644	22,312	27,277	717	875	981	1,271
Public administration and defence[3]	20,235	21,788	23,159	25,594	1,237	1,401	1,416	1,609
Education and health services	26,984	30,349	33,233	36,450	1,656	1,833	2,073	2,129
Other services	19,937	22,661	24,816	26,444	881	982	1,137	1,133
Adjustment for financial services	-15,502	-17,411	-22,536	-23,702	-456	-495	-647	-723
Total	297,827	333,634	367,268	402,207	14,998	16,948	18,443	20,053

Scotland / Northern Ireland

	1987	1988	1989	1990	1987	1988	1989	1990
	Scotland				**Northern Ireland**			
Agriculture, forestry and fishing	916	887	1,004	1,074	340	379	431	388
Energy and water supply	1,536	1,696	1,705	1,849	292	299	306	347
Manufacturing	6,797	7,415	7,935	8,345	1,330	1,417	1,596	1,728
Minerals, metals and chemicals[1]	1,191	1,350	1,438	..	175	212	249	..
Metal goods, engineering, vehicles	2,486	2,669	3,044	..	314	375	375	..
Other manufacturing industries	3,121	3,395	3,452	..	840	829	972	..
Construction	2,154	2,467	2,758	3,178	503	582	662	735
Distribution, hotels and catering; repairs	3,980	4,526	4,875	5,529	1,003	1,116	1,206	1,314
Transport and communication	2,313	2,581	2,719	2,808	378	427	457	482
Financial & business services, etc[2]	4,012	4,237	5,075	5,503	791	886	1,052	1,132
Ownership of dwellings	1,233	1,325	1,444	1,699	372	411	417	472
Public administration and defence[3]	2,427	2,663	2,764	2,924	1,084	1,206	1,283	1,397
Education and health services	3,433	3,824	4,487	5,156	1,063	1,164	1,301	1,408
Other services	2,037	2,319	2,603	2,636	524	612	717	770
Adjustment for financial services	-1,358	-1,506	-1,887	-1,962	-239	-256	-330	-352
Total	29,481	32,434	35,482	38,738	7,441	8,243	9,097	9,821

United Kingdom

	1987	1988	1989	1990
Agriculture, forestry and fishing	6,299	6,149	6,965	7,102
Energy and water supply	15,336	15,623	15,950	17,567
Continental shelf	9,565	6,919	6,524	6,767
Manufacturing	84,589	93,504	101,015	106,995
Minerals, metals and chemicals[1]	17,023	19,478	20,431	..
Metal goods, engineering, vehicles	34,456	38,457	42,557	..
Other manufacturing industries	33,110	35,569	38,027	..
Construction	23,769	28,512	32,365	36,085
Distribution, hotels and catering; repairs	49,618	57,378	63,429	70,151
Transport and communication	25,792	28,684	31,262	34,031
Financial & business services, etc[2]	59,386	67,021	80,561	87,260
Ownership of dwellings	21,013	23,255	25,154	30,719
Public administration and defence[3]	24,984	27,058	28,622	31,524
Education and health services	33,136	37,170	41,094	45,143
Other services	23,379	26,573	29,274	30,983
Adjustment for financial services	-17,555	-19,668	-25,401	-26,740
Statistical discrepancy (income adjustment)	-1,014	-886	-634	160
Total	358,297	397,292	436,180	477,747

1 Extraction of minerals and ores other than fuels, manufacturing of metals, mineral products.
2 Banking, finance, insurance, business services and leasing.
3 Public administration, national defence and compulsory social security.

Source: Central Statistical Office

12.3 Gross domestic product per head as a percentage of the UK average[1]

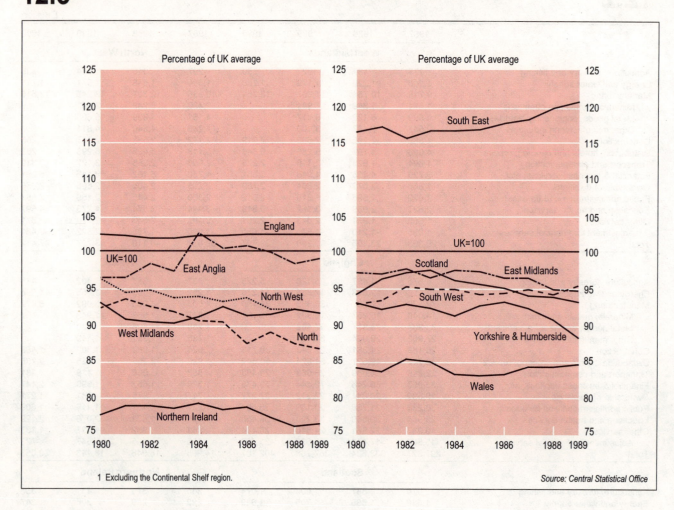

1 Excluding the Continental Shelf region.

Source: Central Statistical Office

12.4 Total personal income

	£ million				£ per head				£ per head index UK = 100
	1986	1988	1989	1990	1986	1988	1989	1990	1990
United Kingdom	332,473	398,728	441,040	493,089	5,857	6,987	7,706	8,589	100.0
North	16,249	18,813	20,593	22,908	5,275	6,126	6,701	7,449	86.7
Yorkshire & Humberside	26,955	31,451	34,846	39,714	5,502	6,402	7,053	8,020	93.4
East Midlands	22,117	26,428	29,702	33,641	5,642	6,657	7,427	8,371	97.5
East Anglia	11,573	14,233	15,859	17,978	5,811	6,996	7,757	8,731	101.7
South East	116,203	142,436	157,267	174,345	6,731	8,212	9,047	9,987	116.3
Greater London	48,489	57,450	64,715	..	7,157	8,530	9,578	..	..
Rest of South East	67,713	84,986	92,553	..	6,455	8,011	8,709	..	..
South West	26,894	31,835	35,316	40,349	5,920	6,870	7,591	8,647	100.7
West Midlands	27,578	33,584	36,817	41,539	5,323	6,450	7,058	7,959	92.7
North West	34,384	40,621	44,736	49,727	5,394	6,383	7,012	7,784	90.6
England	281,954	339,402	375,136	420,200	5,967	7,140	7,866	8,784	102.3
Wales	13,993	16,891	18,879	20,849	4,960	5,912	6,571	7,236	84.2
Scotland	28,829	33,275	36,893	40,941	5,629	6,532	7,247	8,024	93.4
Northern Ireland	7,697	9,161	10,132	11,099	4,913	5,805	6,401	6,985	81.3

Source: Central Statistical Office

12.5 Personal disposable income[1]

	£ million				£ per head				£ per head index UK = 100
	1986	1988	1989[2]	1990[2]	1986	1988	1989[2]	1990[2]	1990
United Kingdom	263,594	315,983	351,438	384,814	4,644	5,537	6,140	6,703	100.0
North	13,045	15,237	16,742	18,206	4,235	4,962	5,448	5,920	88.3
Yorkshire & Humberside	21,568	25,167	28,116	31,559	4,402	5,123	5,691	6,373	95.1
East Midlands	17,424	20,823	23,606	26,200	4,445	5,245	5,903	6,520	97.3
East Anglia	9,102	11,238	12,608	13,986	4,570	5,524	6,166	6,793	101.3
South East	91,288	111,262	123,620	133,560	5,288	6,415	7,111	7,650	114.1
Greater London	39,074	46,365	53,223	..	5,767	6,884	7,877	..	..
Rest of South East	52,213	64,897	70,396	..	4,978	6,117	6,624	..	..
South West	21,499	25,339	28,254	31,632	4,732	5,468	6,073	6,779	101.1
West Midlands	21,931	26,659	29,481	32,531	4,233	5,120	5,652	6,233	93.0
North West	27,211	32,413	35,992	39,049	4,269	5,093	5,642	6,112	91.2
England	223,069	268,137	298,417	326,723	4,721	5,641	6,258	6,830	101.9
Wales	11,280	13,752	15,522	16,790	3,999	4,814	5,403	5,827	86.9
Scotland	22,905	26,534	29,070	32,093	4,473	5,209	5,710	6,290	93.8
Northern Ireland	6,341	7,559	8,429	9,208	4,047	4,790	5,325	5,795	86.5

1 Total personal income less United Kingdom taxes on income, national insurance etc. contributions, community charge, net current transfers abroad and miscellaneous current transfers.

2 Figures are not comparable with earlier years due to the introduction of the community charge in 1989 for Scotland and 1990 for England and Wales.

Source: Central Statistical Office

12.6 Consumers' expenditure: by broad function, 1990

	£ million						£ per head index UK = 100
	Food, drink and tobacco	Housing and fuel	Other	Consumers' expenditure in the UK[1]	Total consumers' expenditure[2]	£ per head	
United Kingdom	72,398	62,264	203,365	338,027	349,421	6,086	100.0
North	3,630	2,769	8,577	14,976	15,832	5,148	84.6
Yorkshire & Humberside	5,819	4,375	14,812	25,007	26,335	5,318	87.4
East Midlands	5,109	4,339	12,782	22,231	23,202	5,773	94.9
East Anglia	2,480	2,387	7,478	12,345	12,602	6,121	100.6
South East	23,054	22,950	76,577	122,581	124,412	7,126	117.1
Greater London	9,642	9,755	33,785	53,182	52,590	7,740	127.2
Rest of South East	13,411	13,196	42,792	69,399	71,822	6,735	110.7
South West	5,914	5,472	16,814	28,200	29,014	6,218	102.2
West Midlands	6,245	5,536	16,114	27,895	29,282	5,610	92.2
North West	8,146	6,498	20,414	35,058	36,537	5,719	94.0
England	60,396	54,327	173,570	288,293	297,216	6,213	102.1
Wales	3,474	2,676	8,648	14,799	15,515	5,384	88.5
Scotland	6,751	4,034	16,629	27,415	28,605	5,606	92.1
Northern Ireland[3]	1,776	1,226	4,519	7,521	8,085	5,088	83.6

1 Expenditure by UK households and foreign residents in the UK.

2 Expenditure by UK consumers, including private non-profit-making bodies serving persons and UK households abroad but excluding expenditure in the UK by foreign residents in the UK.

3 The community charge operates in Great Britain, but domestic rates continue in Northern Ireland. Thus Northern Ireland figures are not comparable with those for Great Britain.

Source: Central Statistical Office

12.7 Consumers' expenditure

	1981	1984	1985	1986	1987	1988	1989[1]	1990[1]
£ million								
United Kingdom	155,412	199,425	217,618	241,275	264,879	298,795	326,489	349,421
North	7,847	9,458	10,362	11,683	12,580	13,865	15,103	15,832
Yorkshire & Humberside	12,071	15,499	16,718	18,272	20,162	22,879	25,123	26,335
East Midlands	9,972	12,769	13,609	14,779	16,311	18,613	21,138	23,202
East Anglia	4,969	6,655	7,530	8,530	9,275	10,575	11,674	12,602
South East	53,933	70,863	77,991	87,113	95,384	107,173	116,248	124,412
South West	12,015	15,441	17,188	19,601	22,039	24,753	26,806	29,014
West Midlands	13,476	16,776	17,963	19,598	21,667	24,770	27,546	29,282
North West	17,113	21,148	22,692	25,321	28,162	31,688	34,566	36,537
England	131,396	168,610	184,053	204,896	225,580	254,316	278,205	297,216
Wales	7,066	8,815	9,814	10,643	11,416	12,943	14,361	15,515
Scotland	13,443	17,616	18,887	20,238	21,930	24,790	26,488	28,605
Northern Ireland	3,508	4,385	4,864	5,499	5,953	6,746	7,435	8,085
As a percentage of United Kingdom								
United Kingdom	*100.0*	*100.0*	*100.0*	*100.0*	*100.0*	*100.0*	*100.0*	*100.0*
North	*5.0*	*4.7*	*4.8*	*4.8*	*4.7*	*4.6*	*4.6*	*4.5*
Yorkshire & Humberside	*7.8*	*7.8*	*7.7*	*7.6*	*7.6*	*7.7*	*7.7*	*7.5*
East Midlands	*6.4*	*6.4*	*6.3*	*6.1*	*6.2*	*6.2*	*6.5*	*6.6*
East Anglia	*3.2*	*3.3*	*3.5*	*3.5*	*3.5*	*3.5*	*3.6*	*3.6*
South East	*34.7*	*35.5*	*35.8*	*36.1*	*36.0*	*35.9*	*35.6*	*35.6*
South West	*7.7*	*7.7*	*7.9*	*8.1*	*8.3*	*8.3*	*8.2*	*8.3*
West Midlands	*8.7*	*8.4*	*8.3*	*8.1*	*8.2*	*8.3*	*8.4*	*8.4*
North West	*11.0*	*10.6*	*10.4*	*10.5*	*10.6*	*10.6*	*10.6*	*10.5*
England	*84.5*	*84.5*	*84.6*	*84.9*	*85.2*	*85.1*	*85.2*	*85.1*
Wales	*4.5*	*4.4*	*4.5*	*4.4*	*4.3*	*4.3*	*4.4*	*4.4*
Scotland	*8.6*	*8.8*	*8.7*	*8.4*	*8.3*	*8.3*	*8.1*	*8.2*
Northern Ireland	*2.3*	*2.2*	*2.2*	*2.3*	*2.2*	*2.3*	*2.3*	*2.3*
£ per head								
United Kingdom	2,758	3,532	3,844	4,251	4,653	5,236	5,704	6,086
North	2,517	3,058	3,358	3,793	4,089	4,515	4,915	5,148
Yorkshire & Humberside	2,454	3,160	3,410	3,729	4,115	4,657	5,085	5,318
East Midlands	2,588	3,296	3,492	3,770	4,137	4,688	5,286	5,773
East Anglia	2,622	3,431	3,833	4,283	4,606	5,198	5,709	6,121
South East	3,171	4,130	4,537	5,046	5,508	6,180	6,687	7,126
South West	2,742	3,461	3,819	4,314	4,803	5,342	5,762	6,218
West Midlands	2,598	3,241	3,466	3,783	4,169	4,758	5,281	5,610
North West	2,649	3,307	3,553	3,972	4,421	4,980	5,418	5,719
England	2,806	3,591	3,907	4,336	4,758	5,350	5,834	6,213
Wales	2,511	3,140	3,490	3,773	4,025	4,530	4,998	5,384
Scotland	2,595	3,423	3,677	3,952	4,290	4,866	5,203	5,606
Northern Ireland	2,281	2,828	3,122	3,509	3,779	4,275	4,697	5,088
£ per head, United Kingdom = 100								
United Kingdom	100.0	100.0	100.0	100.0	100.0	100.0	100.0	100.0
North	91.3	86.6	87.4	89.2	87.9	86.2	86.2	84.6
Yorkshire & Humberside	89.0	89.5	88.7	87.7	88.4	88.9	89.2	87.4
East Midlands	93.9	93.3	90.8	88.7	88.9	89.5	92.7	94.9
East Anglia	95.1	97.1	99.7	100.8	99.0	99.3	100.1	100.6
South East	115.0	116.9	118.0	118.7	118.4	118.0	117.2	117.1
South West	99.4	98.0	99.4	101.5	103.2	102.0	101.0	102.2
West Midlands	94.2	91.8	90.2	89.0	89.6	90.9	92.6	92.2
North West	96.1	93.6	92.4	93.5	95.0	95.1	95.0	94.0
England	101.8	101.7	101.6	102.0	102.3	102.2	102.3	102.1
Wales	91.1	88.9	90.8	88.8	86.5	86.5	87.6	88.5
Scotland	94.1	96.9	95.7	93.0	92.2	92.9	91.2	92.1
Northern Ireland	82.7	80.1	81.2	82.6	81.2	81.6	82.3	83.6

1 Figures are not comparable with earlier years due to the introduction of the community charge in 1989 in Scotland and 1990 in England and Wales.

Source: Central Statistical Office

12.8 Factor incomes in the gross domestic product, factor cost: current prices

£ million

	Income from employment	Income from self-employment	Gross trading profits and surpluses	Less stock appreciation	Rent[1]	Gross domestic product
1987						
United Kingdom	229,532	39,383	66,042	4,725	29,079	358,297
North	11,331	1,387	3,110	272	1,298	16,854
Yorkshire & Humberside	18,331	2,967	4,995	412	1,947	27,828
East Midlands	15,374	2,786	4,141	348	1,648	23,602
East Anglia	7,479	2,051	1,933	164	1,003	12,302
South East	82,710	14,397	17,910	1,443	11,680	125,253
South West	17,210	3,860	3,540	358	2,336	26,587
West Midlands	19,234	2,997	5,195	474	2,411	29,363
North West	23,798	3,199	6,596	535	2,978	36,037
England	195,468	33,644	47,420	4,007	25,301	297,827
Wales	9,269	1,658	3,217	207	1,061	14,998
Scotland	19,872	2,999	4,881	407	2,135	29,481
Northern Ireland	4,922	1,082	942	88	582	7,441
Continental Shelf	0	0	9,581	16	0	9,565
Statistical discrepancy (income adjustment)	..	..	..	..	..	-1,014
1988						
United Kingdom	255,357	44,835	71,272	6,212	32,926	397,292
North	12,198	1,537	3,638	352	1,442	18,464
Yorkshire & Humberside	19,972	3,312	5,675	544	2,132	30,547
East Midlands	16,887	3,119	4,825	464	1,901	26,268
East Anglia	8,532	2,246	2,257	229	1,132	13,938
South East	93,346	16,453	19,995	1,876	13,419	141,337
South West	19,156	4,497	4,081	495	2,627	29,865
West Midlands	21,597	3,462	5,959	641	2,727	33,105
North West	26,177	3,702	7,666	685	3,250	40,110
England	217,865	38,329	54,096	5,286	28,630	333,634
Wales	10,235	1,966	3,766	304	1,285	16,948
Scotland	21,853	3,264	5,503	541	2,355	32,434
Northern Ireland	5,404	1,276	1,043	135	656	8,243
Continental Shelf	0	0	6,864	-55	0	6,919
Statistical discrepancy (income adjustment)	..	..	..	..	..	-886
1989						
United Kingdom	283,585	51,605	72,820	7,292	36,096	436,180
North	13,490	1,833	3,950	377	1,543	20,439
Yorkshire & Humberside	22,089	3,957	6,004	638	2,291	33,704
East Midlands	18,911	3,746	4,861	524	2,219	29,213
East Anglia	9,634	2,551	2,375	266	1,283	15,578
South East	104,377	18,400	20,330	2,207	14,584	155,484
South West	21,204	5,311	4,044	570	2,844	32,834
West Midlands	23,816	3,972	6,112	671	3,061	36,290
North West	28,678	4,227	8,098	839	3,563	43,727
England	242,200	43,997	55,774	6,092	31,389	367,268
Wales	11,349	2,330	3,637	311	1,439	18,443
Scotland	24,065	3,822	5,683	666	2,578	35,482
Northern Ireland	5,972	1,456	1,136	157	691	9,097
Continental Shelf	0	0	6,590	66	0	6,524
Statistical discrepancy (income adjustment)	..	..	..	..	..	-634
1990						
United Kingdom	316,408	57,661	67,198	6,391	42,711	477,747
North	15,090	2,061	3,618	326	1,800	22,243
Yorkshire & Humberside	25,375	4,404	5,573	601	2,696	37,448
East Midlands	21,385	4,176	4,618	455	2,644	32,368
East Anglia	10,954	2,803	2,236	216	1,536	17,312
South East	115,206	20,803	17,748	1,826	17,467	169,398
South West	24,003	5,465	3,821	470	3,480	36,300
West Midlands	26,701	4,516	5,584	605	3,530	39,727
North West	31,756	4,965	7,395	760	4,056	47,412
England	270,472	49,193	50,592	5,259	37,210	402,207
Wales	12,462	2,554	3,592	341	1,787	20,053
Scotland	26,903	4,328	5,140	581	2,948	38,738
Northern Ireland	6,572	1,586	1,029	132	766	9,821
Continental Shelf	0	0	6,845	78	0	6,767
Statistical discrepancy (income adjustment)	..	..	..	..	..	160

1 Including imputed charge for consumption of non-trading capital.

Source: Central Statistical Office

12.9 Gross domestic fixed capital formation: by selected industry groups

£ million

	Agriculture, forestry and fishing	Energy and water supply	Manufacturing	Transport and com- munication[1]	Dwellings	Total of industries shown
1988						
United Kingdom	1,420	6,704	12,281	7,504	18,857	46,766
North	75	735	817	234	814	2,676
Yorkshire & Humberside	122	579	1,268	499	1,434	3,902
East Midlands	110	366	889	418	1,299	3,081
East Anglia	104	131	442	199	960	1,835
South East	144	1,029	3,079	3,499	6,637	14,389
South West	181	360	846	572	1,796	3,756
West Midlands	107	307	1,307	533	1,505	3,760
North West	52	493	1,473	581	1,746	4,346
England	896	4,000	10,121	6,537	16,191	37,745
Wales	119	204	846	235	820	2,223
Scotland	271	525	1,040	554	1,370	3,761
Northern Ireland	134	83	274	178	476	1,144
Continental Shelf	-	1,892	-	-	-	1,892
1989						
United Kingdom	1,485	7,960	14,260	9,029	20,076	52,810
North	79	751	903	323	918	2,974
Yorkshire & Humberside	127	567	1,325	610	1,595	4,223
East Midlands	114	443	988	507	1,520	3,573
East Anglia	107	201	497	238	901	1,944
South East	146	1,341	3,486	4,084	6,414	15,471
South West	184	491	861	776	2,076	4,389
West Midlands	111	421	1,610	720	1,681	4,542
North West	54	476	2,021	680	1,791	5,022
England	922	4,692	11,689	7,939	16,896	42,139
Wales	116	288	1,090	283	1,010	2,787
Scotland	290	385	1,198	606	1,651	4,131
Northern Ireland	157	75	286	201	517	1,237
Continental Shelf	-	2,518	-	-	-	2,518

1 Excluding sea and air transport.

Source: Central Statistical Office

12.10 Gross domestic fixed capital formation: by function of government

£ million

	General administration and defence	Education	Health and social services	Housing and community development	Economic services	Total[1]
1987						
United Kingdom	1,168	742	1,206	1,900	2,108	7,124
North	45	34	67	147	109	400
Yorkshire & Humberside	76	74	100	169	186	604
East Midlands	37	43	61	52	136	330
East Anglia	41	30	33	14	57	175
South East	410	220	362	349	548	1,892
South West	123	51	96	49	187	507
West Midlands	72	62	114	163	198	607
North West	78	71	149	306	176	776
England	880	586	982	1,248	1,595	5,291
Wales	55	62	66	130	217	530
Scotland	150	74	119	461	254	1058
Northern Ireland	46	20	39	54	42	201
1988						
United Kingdom	1,459	601	1,249	602	2,254	6,158
North	64	51	68	107	44	335
Yorkshire & Humberside	97	104	95	155	99	550
East Midlands	26	26	71	-25	89	187
East Anglia	50	28	36	-49	60	125
South East	642	80	443	-416	1,077	1,826
South West	141	22	91	-97	129	285
West Midlands	94	41	89	37	153	415
North West	96	106	133	258	78	671
England	1,209	459	1,027	-30	1,729	4,393
Wales	66	57	63	149	194	529
Scotland	132	66	126	429	288	1,040
Northern Ireland	52	20	34	46	43	196

1 The UK figures include expenditure on embassies, etc. overseas.

Source: Central Statistical Office

Notes to Chapter 12: Regional Accounts

The sources and methodology used to compile the regional accounts are given in a booklet in the *Studies in Official Statistics series (HMSO), No 31, Regional Accounts*, and more recently in the Eurostat publication *Methods used to compile Regional Accounts.*

Tables 12.1, 12.2, 12.8 and Chart 12.3 Gross Domestic Product (GDP)

Regional estimates of GDP are compiled as the sum of factor incomes, i.e. incomes earned by residents, whether corporate or individual, from the production of goods and services. This approach breaks the total down into four components: income from employment, income from self-employment, profits and surpluses and rent (including the imputed charge for consumption of non-trading capital). Stock appreciation is deducted from the sum of total domestic income to give GDP. The figures for all regions are adjusted to sum to the national totals as published in *National Income and Expenditure 1990* Edition (HMSO).

In order to accommodate the offshore oil and gas extraction industry in the regional accounts, a region known as the Continental Shelf is included. GDP for this region includes only profits and stock appreciation related to the offshore activities of United Kingdom and foreign contractors. The allocation of income from employment is not altered by the Continental Shelf region since throughout the regional accounts this is allocated according to the region of residence of the employee.

Table 12.1 GDP by industry groups

See notes to Tables 13.2-13.4 of the Standard Industrial Classification.

Table 12.4 and 12.5 Personal incomes

Total personal income is an estimate of the income of the personal sector including households, other individuals and non-profit-making bodies serving persons. Total personal incomes include the wages and salaries of employees *plus* employers' contributions; self-employment income; rent, dividends, and net interest received by the personal sector; national insurance benefits and other current grants from general government; and the imputed charge for consumption of private non-profit-making bodies. Figures are also shown of personal disposable income, which is the income remaining after deduction of taxes on income, national insurance etc. contributions and transfers abroad (net).

Tables 12.6 and 12.7 Consumers' expenditure

Consumers' expenditure measures expenditure by households and private non-profit making bodies resident in a region. Estimates are based mainly on the *Family Expenditure Survey* and are subject to sampling error and should be used with caution.

Up to date information on the data can be obtained from *Economic Trends*, No. 445, November 1990 and 450, April 1991 (HMSO).

13.1 Percentage of gross domestic product[1] derived from manufacturing and agriculture, 1990

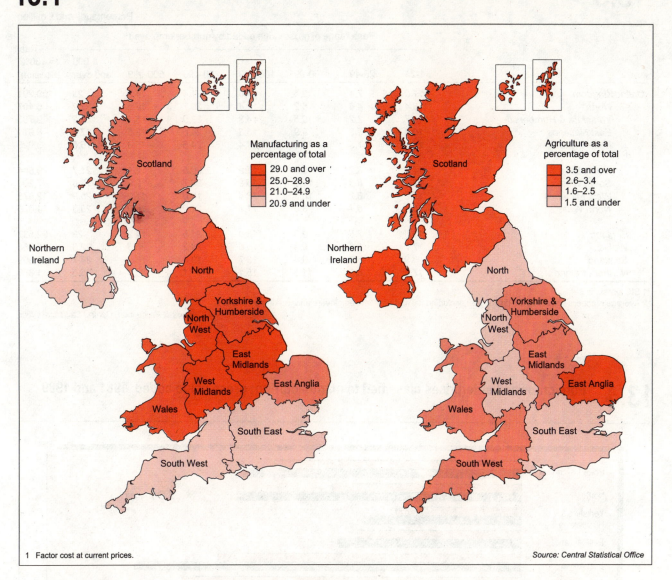

Manufacturing as a percentage of total
- 29.0 and over
- 25.0–28.9
- 21.0–24.9
- 20.9 and under

Agriculture as a percentage of total
- 3.5 and over
- 2.6–3.4
- 1.6–2.5
- 1.5 and under

1 Factor cost at current prices.

Source: Central Statistical Office

13.2 Net capital expenditure and gross value added in manufacturing[1], 1981 and 1989

| | Net capital expenditure | | | | Gross value added | | | | | |
| | £ million | | As a percentage of UK | | £ million | | As a percentage of UK | | £ per person employed | |
	1981	1989	1981	1989	1981	1989	1981	1989	1981	1989
United Kingdom	5,493.1	14,498.5	100.0	100.0	57,935.4	108,291.3	100.0	100.0	10,027	21,863
North	357.7	912.5	6.5	6.3	3,576.3	6,407.4	6.2	5.9	10,631	23,338
Yorkshire & Humberside	453.3	1,337.5	8.3	9.2	5,118.0	9,783.1	8.8	9.0	9,191	20,471
East Midlands	397.5	997.9	7.2	6.9	4,339.3	8,971.7	7.5	8.3	8,775	19,146
East Anglia	167.0	496.4	3.0	3.4	1,864.0	3,925.7	3.2	3.6	10,629	21,956
South East	1,354.8	3,536.3	24.7	24.4	16,406.4	29,544.3	28.3	27.3	10,976	24,480
South West	342.3	867.5	6.2	6.0	3,863.7	7,200.8	6.7	6.6	10,326	20,081
West Midlands	532.2	1,632.8	9.7	11.3	6,567.0	12,678.4	11.3	11.7	8,874	19,249
North West	766.3	2,070.2	14.0	14.3	7,835.5	14,026.4	13.5	13.0	10,069	22,832
England	4,371.2	11,851.1	79.6	81.7	49,570.1	92,537.7	85.6	85.5	10,014	21,834
Wales	370.9	1,114.5	6.8	7.7	2,216.4	5,558.3	3.8	5.1	9,415	24,048
Scotland	617.3	1,232.2	11.2	8.5	5,100.2	8,309.4	8.8	7.7	10,701	22,339
Northern Ireland	133.7	300.8	2.4	2.1	1,048.6	1,885.9	1.8	1.7	9,070	16,878

1 SIC Divisions 2-4.

Source: Annual Census of Production, Central Statistical Office

13.3 Gross value added in manufacturing[1]: by size of local unit, 1989

Percentages and £ million

| | Percentage of gross value added by number employed[2] | | | | | | | Total (= 100%) (£ million) |
	1-24	25-49	50-99	100-199	200-499	500-999	1,000 and over	
United Kingdom	11.0	7.4	9.5	13.0	21.4	14.8	23	108,291
North	6.4	4.6	6.2	10.4	20.7	19.5	32.2	6,407
Yorkshire & Humberside	9.7	7.2	10.5	14.3	23.0	15.1	20.2	9,783
East Midlands	10.8	8.2	9.9	15.3	24.6	13.5	17.8	8,971
East Anglia	11.2	7.5	10.2	14.4	24.5	15.8	16.5	3,925
South East	14.1	8.2	9.5	11.9	20.5	14.1	21.7	29,544
South West	12.5	8.3	11.0	15.8	23.7	9.9	18.8	7,200
West Midlands	11.2	8.2	10.3	13.4	19.0	11.9	25.9	12,678
North West	8.4	6.1	8.5	11.7	21.0	16.0	28.3	14,026
England	11.3	7.5	9.5	13.0	21.5	14.2	23	92,537
Wales	7.7	5.6	9.3	10.6	24.2	20.3	22.3	5,558
Scotland	8.9	6.8	9.4	13.7	19.6	16.9	24.7	8,309
Northern Ireland	17.9	8.5	11.0	15.1	17.1	13.9	16.5	1,885

1 SIC Divisions 2-4.
2 Average numbers employed during the year, including full and part-time employers and working proprietors.

Source: Annual Census of Production, Central Statistical Office

13.4 Foreign-owned enterprises classified to manufacturing: gross value added, 1981 and 1989

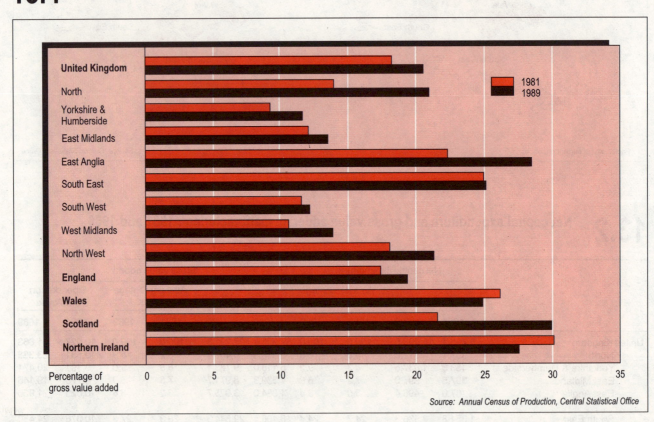

Source: Annual Census of Production, Central Statistical Office

13.5 Employment in manufacturing[1]: by size of local unit, 1989

Percentages and numbers

	Percentage in each employment size band[2]							Total number of units (= 100%)
	1-24	25-49	50-99	100-199	200-499	500-999	1,000 and over	
United Kingdom	13.6	9.0	11.3	14.6	21.3	12.8	17.3	168,256
North	8.2	6.3	7.9	13.1	23.0	16.0	25.5	5,858
Yorkshire & Humberside	11.5	8.5	12.1	16.2	24.1	13.5	14.1	14,078
East Midlands	12.4	9.6	12.2	17.2	23.3	12.8	12.6	14,494
East Anglia	13.3	8.8	11.2	14.8	22.8	15.7	13.5	6,316
South East	19.1	10.1	11.1	13.1	18.8	11.3	16.6	55,875
South West	13.8	8.9	11.4	15.4	22.5	9.8	18.3	13,223
West Midlands	12.6	9.5	11.9	14.7	19.3	11.8	20.3	20,466
North West	11.4	8.3	11.1	14.6	22.2	14.4	18.1	17,690
England	14.0	9.1	11.3	14.6	21.2	12.6	17.3	148,000
Wales	10.4	7.9	11.8	14.3	23.4	16.1	16.2	6,428
Scotland	10.7	7.8	11.3	15.1	22.0	13.5	19.7	9,720
Northern Ireland	17.5	9.8	10.9	15.9	20.6	13.0	12.3	4,108

1 SIC Divisions 2-4.
2 Average numbers employed during the year, including full and part-time employees and working proprietors.

Source: Annual Census of Production, Central Statistical Office

13.6 Construction: value at current prices of contractors' output[1], 1990

£ million

	New housing[2]		Other new work[2]			Repair and maintenance[2]			All work
			Public	Private			Other work		
	Public	Private	Public	Indus-trial	Commer-cial	Housing	Public	Private	
Great Britain	942	5,919	5,431	5,243	10,390	9,289	3,120	4,360	44,694
North	32	353	250	275	262	334	123	217	1,842
Yorkshire & Humberside	37	505	480	484	621	744	314	412	3,596
East Midlands	50	553	357	418	453	569	195	252	2,845
East Anglia	30	244	276	210	336	384	101	161	1,744
South East	341	1,508	1,869	1,874	5,799	3,439	1,193	1,657	17,678
South West	87	641	423	328	786	845	255	361	3,730
West Midlands	102	548	416	518	676	871	267	362	3,761
North West	70	622	444	542	658	868	347	440	3,991
England	750	4,971	4,514	4,648	9,592	8,053	2,799	3,863	39,189
Wales	60	352	292	239	222	395	92	161	1,812
Scotland	134	596	626	356	575	842	229	334	3,692

1 Output of contractors, including estimates of unrecorded output by small firms and self-employed workers, classified to construction in the Standard Industrial Classification (revised 1980).
2 For new work, figures are for the region in which the site is located. For repair and maintenance, figures are the region in which the reporting unit is based.

Source: Department of the Environment

13.7 Government expenditure on regional preferential assistance to industry

£ million

	1983-84	1984-85	1985-86	1986-87	1987-88	1988-89	1989-90	1990-91
Great Britain	648.9	636.8	584.1	746.2	556.2	615.7	540.1	497.2
North	130.2	125.5	96.6	137.3	109.3	134.1	117.0	85.0
Yorkshire & Humberside	36.3	44.3	36.4	41.9	38.8	50.2	32.4	29.4
East Midlands	17.5	11.4	8.8	10.7	9.4	8.8	9.5	5.5
East Anglia	0.0	0.0	0.0	0.0	0.0	0.0	0.0	0.0
South East	0.0	0.0	0.0	0.0	0.0	0.0	0.0	0.0
South West	12.1	14.6	12.3	23.0	14.8	14.7	10.7	9.0
West Midlands[1]	0.0	0.0	7.1	10.6	19.3	26.2	19.9	18.0
North West	104.2	106.4	87.5	129.6	79.0	82.3	74.3	57.5
England	300.3	302.2	248.7	353.1	270.6	316.3	263.8	204.4
Wales	120.0	147.5	138.4	150.7	132.4	148.2	131.7	133.7
Scotland	228.6	187.1	197.0	242.4	153.2	151.2	144.6	159.1

1 Certain Travel To Work Areas in the West Midlands attained assisted area status on 29 November 1984.

Source: Department of Trade and Industry

13.8 Assisted Areas [1]

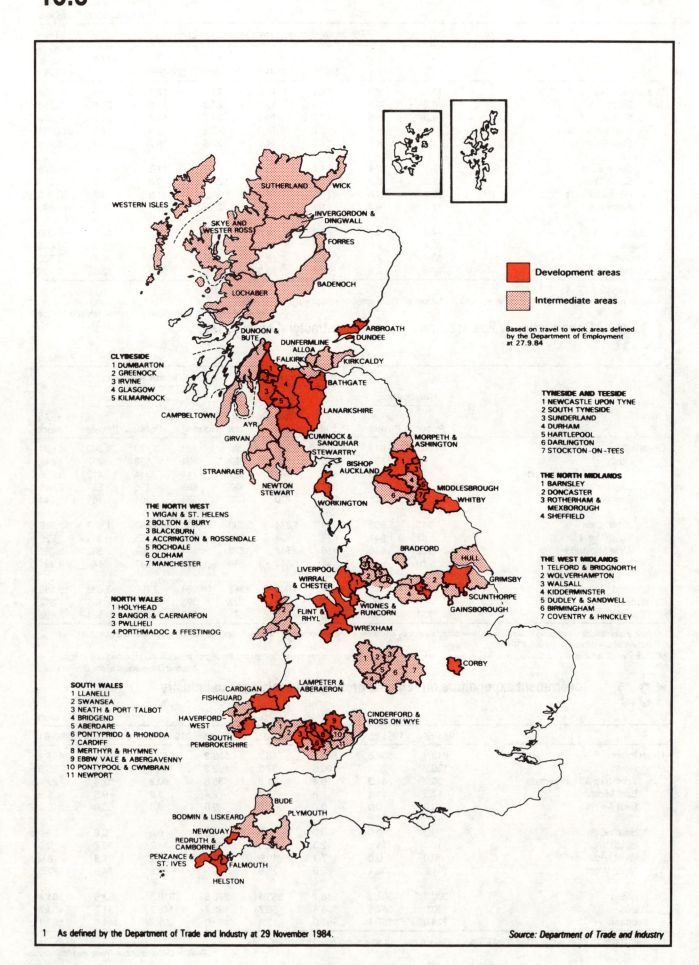

Development areas

Intermediate areas

Based on travel to work areas defined by the Department of Employment at 27.9.84

CLYDESIDE
1 DUMBARTON
2 GREENOCK
3 IRVINE
4 GLASGOW
5 KILMARNOCK

THE NORTH WEST
1 WIGAN & ST. HELENS
2 BOLTON & BURY
3 BLACKBURN
4 ACCRINGTON & ROSSENDALE
5 ROCHDALE
6 OLDHAM
7 MANCHESTER

NORTH WALES
1 HOLYHEAD
2 BANGOR & CAERNARFON
3 PWLLHELI
4 PORTHMADOC & FFESTINIOG

SOUTH WALES
1 LLANELLI
2 SWANSEA
3 NEATH & PORT TALBOT
4 BRIDGEND
5 ABERDARE
6 PONTYPRIDD & RHONDDA
7 CARDIFF
8 MERTHYR & RHYMNEY
9 EBBW VALE & ABERGAVENNY
10 PONTYPOOL & CWMBRAN
11 NEWPORT

TYNESIDE AND TEESIDE
1 NEWCASTLE UPON TYNE
2 SOUTH TYNESIDE
3 SUNDERLAND
4 DURHAM
5 HARTLEPOOL
6 DARLINGTON
7 STOCKTON-ON-TEES

THE NORTH MIDLANDS
1 BARNSLEY
2 DONCASTER
3 ROTHERHAM & MEXBOROUGH
4 SHEFFIELD

THE WEST MIDLANDS
1 TELFORD & BRIDGNORTH
2 WOLVERHAMPTON
3 WALSALL
4 KIDDERMINSTER
5 DUDLEY & SANDWELL
6 BIRMINGHAM
7 COVENTRY & HINCKLEY

Map labels: WESTERN ISLES, SUTHERLAND, WICK, SKYE AND WESTER ROSS, INVERGORDON & DINGWALL, FORRES, BADENOCH, LOCHABER, DUNOON & BUTE, ARBROATH, DUNDEE, DUNFERMLINE, ALLOA, FALKIRK, KIRKCALDY, BATHGATE, LANARKSHIRE, CAMPBELTOWN, AYR, GIRVAN, CUMNOCK & SANQUHAR, STEWARTRY, MORPETH & ASHINGTON, STRANRAER, NEWTON STEWART, BISHOP AUCKLAND, MIDDLESBROUGH, WHITBY, WORKINGTON, BRADFORD, HULL, LIVERPOOL, WIRRAL & CHESTER, GRIMSBY, SCUNTHORPE, WIDNES & RUNCORN, GAINSBOROUGH, FLINT & RHYL, WREXHAM, CORBY, CARDIGAN, FISHGUARD, LAMPETER & ABERAERON, CINDERFORD & ROSS ON WYE, HAVERFORDWEST, SOUTH PEMBROKESHIRE, BUDE, PLYMOUTH, BODMIN & LISKEARD, NEWQUAY, REDRUTH & CAMBORNE, PENZANCE & ST. IVES, FALMOUTH, HELSTON

1 As defined by the Department of Trade and Industry at 29 November 1984.

Source: Department of Trade and Industry

13.9 Business[1] registrations and deregistrations

Thousands

| | Stock end-82 | Net change (registrations less deregistrations) | | | | | | | | 1983-1990 total | | | |
		1983	1984	1985	1986	1987	1988	1989	1990	Regist-rations	De-regist-rations	Net gain	Stock end-90
United Kingdom	1,357.3	35.0	30.0	19.0	27.0	42.0	66.0	83.0	50.0	1,671.0	1,319.0	352.0	1,709.3
North	54.5	1.2	0.9	0.3	0.4	1.1	1.5	2.3	1.1	59.0	50.2	8.9	63.4
Yorkshire & Humberside	106.8	2.8	1.5	0.2	0.7	1.9	4.2	5.3	2.9	121.6	102.0	19.5	126.3
East Midlands	93.4	2.6	2.0	1.3	1.3	3.0	4.5	5.3	3.1	108.9	86.0	22.9	116.3
East Anglia	55.4	1.3	1.4	0.8	1.2	2.1	3.0	3.0	1.8	61.7	47.0	14.7	70.1
South East	447.1	13.3	13.7	12.3	15.7	21.3	30.1	38.2	25.3	669.1	499.0	170.0	617.1
South West	130.3	3.1	2.9	2.2	3.1	4.8	7.4	7.3	4.4	150.0	115.0	35.1	165.4
West Midlands	118.9	2.9	2.1	0.7	1.5	2.8	5.2	6.6	3.8	138.0	112.4	25.6	144.5
North West	133.3	2.9	1.7	-0.7	0.2	1.2	4.0	6.4	3.2	158.5	139.7	18.9	152.1
England	1,139.6	30.1	26.2	17.2	24.0	38.2	60.0	74.4	45.5	1,466.8	1,151.3	315.5	1,455.2
Wales	74.5	1.8	0.8	-0.3	0.4	1.6	3.1	3.3	1.8	70.6	58.2	12.4	86.9
Scotland	97.3	2.1	1.9	1.1	2.1	1.9	2.3	4.3	2.1	104.9	86.9	17.9	115.2
Northern Ireland	45.9	1.0	1.0	1.0	0.5	0.3	0.6	1.0	0.5	28.7	22.6	6.1	52.0

1 Businesses registered for VAT.

Source: Employment Department

13.10 Total sales by the gas supply system[1], 1981-82 and 1990-91

Million therms

| | Domestic | | Industrial | | Other | | All sectors | |
	1981-82	1990-91	1981-82	1990-91	1981-82	1990-91	1981-82	1990-91
United Kingdom[2]	8,936	10,840	5,701	5,661	2,261	3,188	16,898	19,689
Northern	494	605	294	362	143	173	931	1,140
North Western	1,292	1,458	624	699	265	370	2,181	2,528
North Eastern	569	657	223	300	139	190	931	1,147
East Midlands	963	1,095	569	649	194	247	1,726	1,991
West Midlands	891	974	520	590	185	251	1,596	1,815
Eastern	715	874	234	250	150	223	1,099	1,347
North Thames	1,024	1,249	317	301	384	521	1,725	2,070
South Eastern	1,084	1,310	180	222	247	347	1,511	1,879
Southern	587	767	146	205	165	254	898	1,226
South Western	417	578	186	252	118	187	721	1,017
England[2]	8,036	9,567	3,293	3,885	1,990	2,763	13,319	16,215
Wales	343	483	276	394	101	145	720	1,022
Scottish[2]	543	792	282	423	165	279	990	1,494
Direct sales[3]	-	-	1,847	959	-	-	1,847	959
Northern Ireland	14	-	3	-	5	-	22	-

1 Town and natural gas.
2 Includes sales by independent gas supply companies, for which a regional breakdown is not avaliable.
3 Direct sales cannot be allocated between the regions in Great Britain without disclosure relating to individual establishments.

Source: Department of Energy

13.11 Deep mined coal, 1988-89 and 1989-90

	Output of saleable coal[1] (thousand tonnes)		Average number of wage-earners on colliery books (thousands)		Output per manshift (tonnes)	
	1988-89	1989-90	1988-89	1989-90	1988-89	1989-90
Great Britain	84,464	74,975	86.9	69.9	4.14	4.41
North East	10,323	10,234	11.5	9.9	3.81	4.18
North Yorkshire	15,846	13,517	12.9	11.1	5.26	5.12
South Yorkshire	13,232	11,075	13.7	11.3	4.31	4.23
Nottinghamshire	17,146	16,814	16.4	13.9	4.35	4.79
Central	10,869	10,867	10.8	10.7	4.31	4.17
Western	9,729	6,947	10.3	6.3	3.92	4.42
Kent	443	147	0.7	0.3	2.90	2.40
England	77,588	69,601	76.2	63.6	4.34	4.50
Wales	4,980	3,435	7.4	4.5	2.88	3.09
Scotland	1,896	1,939	3.3	1.8	2.45	4.45
Percentage of GB total						
Great Britain	*100.0*	*100.0*	*100.0*	*100.0*		
North East	*12.2*	*13.6*	*13.3*	*14.2*		
North Yorkshire	*18.8*	*18.0*	*14.8*	*15.8*		
South Yorkshire	*15.7*	*14.8*	*15.7*	*16.2*		
Nottinghamshire	*20.3*	*22.4*	*18.8*	*19.9*		
Central	*12.9*	*14.5*	*12.5*	*15.3*		
Western	*11.5*	*9.3*	*11.9*	*9.1*		
Kent	*0.5*	*0.2*	*0.8*	*0.4*		
England	*91.9*	*92.8*	*87.7*	*91.0*		
Wales	*5.9*	*4.6*	*8.5*	*6.5*		
Scotland	*2.2*	*2.6*	*3.7*	*2.5*		

1 Excluding coal extracted in work on capital account for Great Britain. In 1988-89 this amounted to 571 thousand tonnes and to 597 thousand tonnes in 1989-90.

Source: Department of Trade and Industry

13.12 Agricultural holdings: by size[1], 1981 and 1990

Percentages and numbers

	1981					1990				
	Nil[2]	Under 10 hectares	10-49.9 hectares	50 hectares and over	Total holdings (= 100 %) (numbers)	Nil[2]	Under 10 hectares	10-49.9 hectares	50 hectares and over	Total holdings (= 100 %) (numbers)
United Kingdom	3.3	26.6	43.1	26.9	261,249	4.6	25.3	41.8	28.3	248,952
North	2.8	15.6	40.6	41.1	11,915	4.2	15.8	37.3	42.7	11,625
Yorkshire & Humberside	2.9	21.8	39.9	35.4	16,943	4.5	24.5	35.7	35.2	16,782
East Midlands	2.7	23.0	38.2	36.2	17,679	3.6	22.6	36.6	37.2	16,624
East Anglia	3.4	28.5	33.4	34.7	13,570	4.5	27.3	30.6	37.5	12,370
South East	4.9	32.8	30.6	31.8	26,575	7.1	32.2	30.9	29.8	26,263
South West	2.5	25.4	42.8	29.3	36,278	3.6	25.5	41.3	29.5	35,534
West Midlands	3.0	26.9	39.5	30.6	19,642	4.1	26.2	38.6	31.1	19,233
North West	3.7	30.7	46.2	19.4	12,882	5.6	30.4	42.9	21.1	12,221
England	3.2	26.1	38.7	31.9	155,484	4.7	26.1	37.0	32.2	150,652
Wales	3.2	21.8	51.4	23.5	29,567	6.0	22.7	45.9	25.4	29,646
Scotland[3]	5.7	24.3	32.3	37.7	30,974	5.9	20.7	34.7	43.5	27,166
Northern Ireland	2.1	32.9	60.3	4.7	45,224	2.6	30.0	61.0	6.3	41,488

1 Hectares of crops dead grass only at June of each year.
2 "Nil" means holdings without crops and grass (ie consisting only of rough grazing woodland or other land on agricultural holdings)
3 6,000 smaller holdings in Scotland excluded since 1986.

Source: Ministry of Agriculture, Fisheries and Food; Department of Agriculture and Fisheries for Scotland; Department of Agriculture for Northern Ireland

13.13 Agricultural land use, 1990[1,2]

Thousand hectares

	Crops and grass						
	Wheat	Barley	Oats	Potatoes	Sugar beet	Fodder crops[3]	Rape (for oilseed)
United Kingdom	2,013	1,516	105	177	194	342	390
North	66	76	6	3	-	9	21
Yorkshire & Humberside	248	161	6	22	24	26	53
East Midlands	389	152	8	26	43	46	87
East Anglia	345	179	4	29	103	50	42
South East	474	214	19	15	5	78	93
South West	191	173	12	9	1	47	18
West Midlands	147	112	13	21	17	26	24
North West	23	32	2	9	1	6	4
England[2]	1,885	1,102	70	135	194	288	343
Wales	11	39	5	4	0	7	1
Scotland	111	338	29	27	..	43	45
Northern Ireland	6	37	3	11	..	4	1

	Crops and grass (continued)				Rough grazing (sole rights)	Woodland on agricultural holdings	All other land on agricultural holdings	Total
	Horticultural	Other crops and bare fallow	All grasses under 5 years old	All grasses 5 years old and over				
United Kingdom	208	130	1,580	5,263	4,706	357	323	17,307
North	1	3	91	432	305	18	12	1,043
Yorkshire & Humberside	17	8	69	294	138	14	18	1,100
East Midlands	44	12	67	278	43	13	25	1,236
East Anglia	47	18	24	87	21	25	36	1,011
South East	44	29	143	408	46	74	68	1,709
South West	10	16	263	896	100	47	40	1,825
West Midlands	15	8	119	411	23	20	19	974
North West	8	2	53	247	54	6	7	452
England[2]	188	96	837	3,107	748	219	228	9,439
Wales	2	5	149	904	335	36	14	1,512
Scotland	15	29	409	670	3,442	89	52	5,300
Northern Ireland	3	1	185	583	181	13	28	1,055

1 At June.
2 Figures for England and Wales include minor holdings. Figures for Scotland and Northern Ireland exclude minor holdings. Figures for English regions exlude estimates for minor holdings and hence their sum is less than the England total.
3 Includes peas for human consumption and small areas of maize for threshing in England.

Source: Ministry of Agriculture, Fisheries and Food; Department of Agriculture and Fisheries for Scotland; Department of Agriculture for Northern Ireland

13.14 Agricultural investment, 1981 and 1990

£ million

	Plant and machinery		Vehicles		Buildings and work		Total	
	1981	1990	1981	1990	1981	1990	1981	1990
United Kingdom	361	431	103	211	516	540	979	1,182
North	15	23	7	18	22	26	44	67
Yorkshire & Humberside	28	36	14	28	43	42	85	107
East Midlands	39	43	10	20	41	36	90	99
East Anglia	38	38	9	18	39	32	86	89
South East	53	52	13	25	56	44	122	121
South West	44	51	9	22	61	93	114	167
West Midlands	28	32	6	14	39	57	72	102
North West	13	16	6	12	20	18	40	46
England	258	291	74	158	321	349	653	797
Wales	17	23	12	17	46	58	75	97
Scotland	59	80	10	23	79	52	149	155
Northern Ireland	27	37	7	14	70	82	103	133

Source: Ministry of Agriculture, Fisheries and Food; Department of Agriculture and Fisheries for Scotland; Department of Agriculture for Northern Ireland

13.15 Animals on agricultural holdings, 1990[1]

Thousands

	Cattle and calves			Sheep and lambs	Pigs	Poultry	
	Total	Dairy herd	Beef herd			Total fowls[2]	Total lay-ing flock[3]
United Kingdom	12,059	2,847	1,599	43,799	7,449	124,615	33,468
North	702	182	150	5,054	176	3,766	781
Yorkshire & Humberside	672	161	75	2,665	1,692	8,475	2,308
East Midlands	658	157	60	1,764	608	12,527	4,368
East Anglia	220	41	29	311	1,297	14,215	2,316
South East	828	214	79	2,304	860	18,175	5,911
South West	2,196	705	170	4,366	883	15,428	4,741
West Midlands	970	283	82	3,027	433	12,940	3,922
North West	601	255	32	1,096	343	7,344	2,451
England[4]	7,097	1,999	687	20,776	6,308	93,121	26,997
Wales	1,363	327	204	10,935	101	6,709	1,072
Scotland	2,093	244	469	9,583	449	14,670	2,533
Northern Ireland	1,506	278	239	2,505	590	10,114	2,866

1 At June.
2 Excludes ducks, geese and turkeys.
3 Excludes growing pullets (from day-old to point of lay).
4 The figures for English regions exclude estimates for minor holdings and hence their sum is slightly less than the England total.

Source: Ministry of Agriculture, Fisheries and Food; Department of Agriculture and Fisheries for Scotland; Department of Agriculture for Northern Ireland

13.16 Production and estimated yields of selected crops, 1985-1989[1] and 1990

Thousand tonnes and tonnes per hectare

	Production (thousand tonnes)						Estimated yields (tonnes per hectare)					
	Wheat		Barley		Oats		Wheat		Barley		Oats	
	1985-1989	1990	1985-1989	1990	1985-1989	1990	1985-1989	1990	1985-1989	1990	1985-1989	1990
United Kingdom	12,740	14,030	9,170	7,890	530	530	6.5	7.0	5.0	5.2	4.7	5.0
North	380	500	470	440	30	30	6.6	7.7	4.9	5.7	4.9	5.4
Yorkshire & Humberside	1,560	1,870	1,080	920	35	25	6.9	7.6	5.4	5.7	4.9	4.5
East Midlands	2,540	2,730	980	770	45	45	6.6	7.0	5.1	5.1	5.0	5.2
East Anglia	2,190	2,570	1,030	960	20	20	6.4	7.4	4.9	5.4	4.7	5.7
South East	3,070	3,060	1,370	1,070	100	100	6.2	6.5	5.1	5.0	5.0	5.2
South West	1,220	1,170	1,050	800	55	55	6.2	6.1	5.0	4.6	4.8	4.6
West Midlands	910	940	690	540	70	65	6.2	6.4	5.1	4.9	5.0	4.9
North West	100	150	200	150	5	5	5.7	6.4	4.4	4.6	4.2	3.8
England	11,970	13,010	6,880	5,670	370	350	6.4	6.9	5.1	5.1	4.9	5.0
Wales	60	70	220	170	20	15	6.0	5.8	4.4	4.4	4.2	3.7
Scotland	680	920	1,880	1,890	130	150	7.1	8.3	4.8	5.6	4.2	5.1
Northern Ireland	30	40	180	170	10	15	5.4	6.8	4.2	4.5	3.7	4.4

1 Five-year average.
2 The figures for the English regions exclude estimates for minor holdings, so ther sum may not equal the England total.

Source: Ministry of Agriculture, Fisheries and Food; Department of Agriculture and Fisheries for Scotland; Department of Agriculture for Northern Ireland

Notes to chapter 13: Industry and Agriculture

Tables 13.2, 13.3 and 13.5 Annual Census of Production

The Annual Census of Production covers United Kingdom businesses engaged in the production and construction industries, (divisions 1-5 of the Standard Industrial Classification (SIC) Revised 1980). Regional information is only available for manufacturing industry (ie Divisions 2-4 of the SIC).

Businesses often conduct their activities at more than one address (local unit) but it is not usually possible for them to provide the full range of census data for each. For this reason only employment and capital expenditure are collected for these. Gross value added (GVA) is estimated for each local unit by apportioning the total GVA for the business in proportion to the total employment at each.

Gross value added is defined as:

> The value of total sales and work done, to (from) which is added (subtracted) the value of any increase (decrease) in stocks and goods on hand for sales and work in progress.

Less: The value of purchases, from (to) which is subtracted (added) the value of any increase (decrease) in the value of stocks of material fuel etc.

Less: Payments for industrial services received.

Less The net amount of any duties, subsidies, allowances and levies payable.

Less: The cost of non-industrial services, rates and motor vehicle licences.

GVA per head is derived by dividing the estimated GVA by the total number of people employed.

The tables include estimates for businesses not responding, or not required to respond, to the census.

Employment data collected in the annual census of production for manufacturing industry may differ from those collected for manufacturing industry by the Department of Employment. This is because the reporting units to the annual census of production are mostly based on companies while those to the census of employment are based on pay points. The industrial classification of the latter may well differ from the former in many cases. Employment data collected in the annual census of production do, however, provide employment estimates consistent with the other data sought in the census.

Tables 13.2, 13.3 and 13.5 Standard Industrial Classification

The industrial classification used in Regional Trends 27 is the Standard Industrial Classification (Revised 1980). A short description of the new classification was given in the March 1983 issue of *Economic Trends*.

Table 13.7 Regional preferential assistance to industry

Details of the provisions of the *Industrial Development Act* are included in the *Annual Reports on the Industrial Development Act 1982*. The items included are: Regional Development Grants, Regional Selective Assistance and Regional Enterprise Grants; expenditure on Land and Factories by the English Industrial Estates Corporation and the Scottish and Welsh Development Agencies; and expenditure on Land and Factories and Grants by the Highlands and Islands Development Board and the Development Board for Rural Wales.

All figures are gross and include payments to nationalised industries. Data are presented in terms of the old definitions of Assisted Areas for those payments resulting from applications made up to 28.11.84, and in the terms of the new definitions for the payments resulting from applications after 2.11.84.

Table 13.9 Business registrations and deregistrations

These data were published in the article, 'VAT registrations and deregistrations in 1990,' November 1991 edition of *Employment Gazette*. This gives figures, further desegregated by industry and county. A detailed description of the data and figures for local authority districts is also available.

Table 13.10 Gas

Direct sales of natural gas by what was the British Gas Corporation and is now British Gas plc are included. Gas used by the industry in their works, offices or showrooms is excluded.

Table 13.11 Coal

Saleable output is defined as the total coal sold commercially, that is consumed by the colliery or supplied to ancillary works or disposed of free and at concessionary prices, *plus* or *minus* the change in colliery stocks. Wage earners on colliery books are the workers in industrial grades employed at collieries and in activities connected with the getting, raising, handling, preparation, and transport of coal or other minerals which are mined with coal, up to the point of despatch to consumers outside the colliery. A manshift is the normal period of attendance at the colliery by one man in one day.

Table 13.13 Agricultural area

The figures for specific crops relate to those in the ground on the date of the June census or for which the land is being prepared for sowing at that date. Any crops not specified in the return or grown in patches of less than 0.1 hectares are shown under the heading 'other crops'. All other land on agricultural holdings includes land under farm roads, yards and buildings etc.

Table 13.13, 13.14 and 13.15 Agricultural census

The figures are based on the results of the agricultural census taken at June from over 254,000 occupiers of main agricultural holdings. Except for Table 13.15, figures for the national totals include estimates for minor holdings not surveyed in the June census, in order to relate to the total national farm, whereas the individual regional figures exclude minor holdings.

Table 13.14 Agricultural investment

The figures contained in this table represent gross fixed investment in agriculture net of asset sales. As well as including investments made by farmers, *Plant and Machinery*, includes the value of new assets leased by the agricultural industry from the Banking, Insurance and Finance sector. Tractors and tractor parts are also included under this heading, but breeding livestock are excluded.

Vehicles include cars, vans and utilities used wholly or mainly in connection with the farm business. Similarly, *Building* and *Works* comprise only investments in buildings, drainage and other improvements which are wholly or mainly for agricultural purposes. More diversified investments in items such as farm shops and 'bed and breakfast' accommodation are excluded.

Table 13.16 Production and yields

In England and Wales cereal production is estimated from sample surveys held in September, November, January and April. For remaining crops, yields are estimated by technical officers in the Ministry of Agriculture. These are combined with area figures from the annual June agricultural census to produce production estimates.

Figures for England (in total) and Wales include estimates for minor holdings. The Department of Agriculture for Northern Ireland estimates of the yields for barley, wheat and oats are based on a sample survey of farms carried out in the autumn of each year. They are combined with area data from the June agriculture census to produce production estimates. The figures include estimates for minor holdings.

Chapter 14: Sub-regional statistics

STANDARD REGIONS AND COUNTIES OF ENGLAND AND WALES

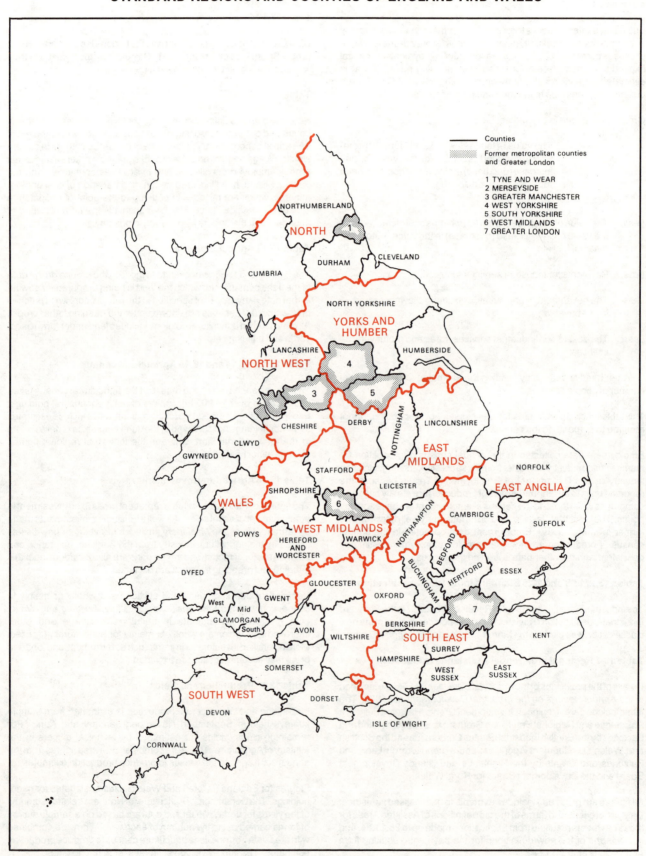

LOCAL AUTHORITY REGIONS OF SCOTLAND
AND BOARDS[1] OF NORTHERN IRELAND

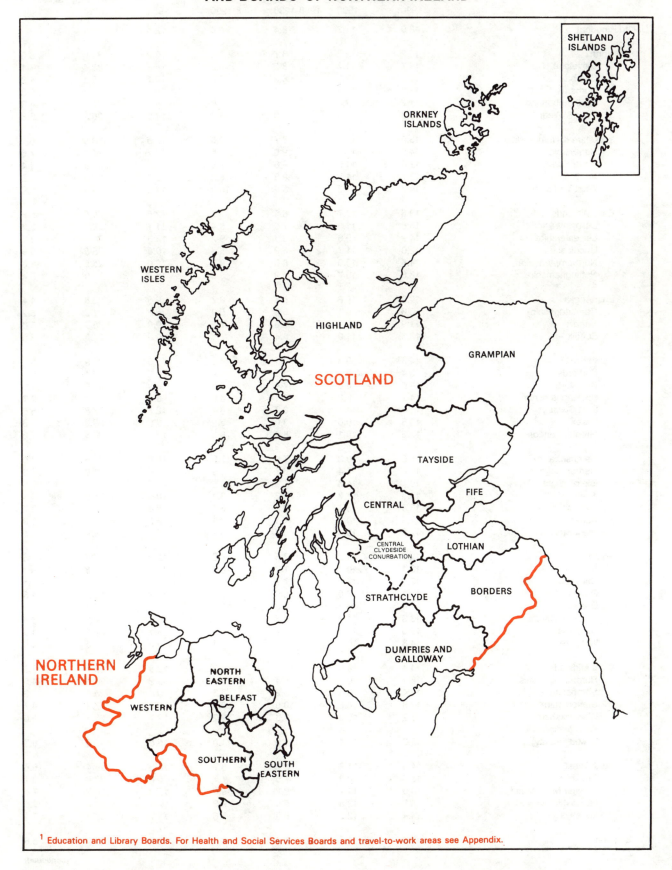

[1] Education and Library Boards. For Health and Social Services Boards and travel-to-work areas see Appendix.

14.1 Vital and social statistics

	Live births per 1,000 population 1990	Deaths per 1,000 population 1990	Perinatal mortality rate[1] 1988-1990	Infant mortality rate[2] 1988-1990	Percentage of live births outside marriage		Children in care of LA[3] (per 1,000 pop. aged under 18) 1990
					1981	1990	
United Kingdom	13.9	11.2	8.4	8.4	12.5	27.9	..
North	13.2	12.2	8.7	8.3	13.2	32.8	6.0
Cleveland	14.7	11.2	8.2	9.5	16.3	38.4	7.1
Cumbria	12.4	12.5	8.2	7.2	10.1	25.5	4.2
Durham	13.2	12.3	8.1	8.0	11.3	31.2	5.9
Northumberland	11.7	12.3	7.3	7.0	8.2	21.1	4.3
Tyne & Wear	13.3	12.5	9.8	8.4	14.9	36.3	6.8
Yorkshire & Humberside	13.9	11.5	8.7	9.0	13.5	30.6	6.1
Humberside	14.0	11.6	9.0	8.6	15.1	34.4	7.6
North Yorkshire	12.0	11.9	6.8	7.6	8.5	20.9	3.4
South Yorkshire	13.7	11.5	9.3	8.2	12.7	32.3	5.2
West Yorkshire	14.7	11.3	8.8	10.0	14.6	30.9	6.9
East Midlands	13.6	10.7	8.4	8.7	12.6	28.0	5.8
Derbyshire	13.6	11.5	7.9	8.4	11.1	26.7	5.3
Leicestershire	14.2	9.6	9.3	9.2	12.3	24.9	3.4
Lincolnshire	12.0	11.7	8.9	8.7	10.6	25.8	5.9
Northamptonshire	14.6	10.0	8.0	9.7	12.0	26.5	6.0
Nottinghamshire	13.6	10.7	7.9	8.0	15.6	33.9	8.4
East Anglia	12.9	10.8	6.4	6.7	9.5	22.8	4.4
Cambridgeshire	13.6	9.1	5.8	5.9	8.8	21.2	5.2
Norfolk	11.9	12.2	7.0	7.2	9.9	25.9	5.0
Suffolk	13.3	11.0	6.4	7.1	9.8	21.2	3.0
South East	14.3	10.3	8.1	8.0	12.6	25.9	5.2
Bedfordshire	15.4	8.9	8.6	7.9	10.2	22.1	5.5
Berkshire	14.6	8.3	7.4	7.3	8.9	20.9	4.0
Buckinghamshire	14.1	8.2	8.1	8.0	8.2	21.0	3.7
East Sussex	11.6	14.7	8.7	8.4	12.7	27.5	5.6
Essex	13.5	10.6	8.0	6.9	9.0	23.3	3.8
Greater London	15.6	10.1	8.6	8.5	17.2	30.5	7.0
Hampshire	14.0	10.3	7.5	7.9	10.0	23.5	4.6
Hertfordshire	13.6	9.4	6.7	6.5	8.4	21.0	2.6
Isle of Wight	10.7	14.3	11.3	13.3	13.2	32.4	5.5
Kent	13.8	11.2	8.2	8.4	10.4	26.0	4.9
Oxfordshire	13.4	8.4	6.1	6.5	8.4	20.4	3.7
Surrey	12.6	10.5	7.1	7.4	7.2	17.4	2.8
West Sussex	12.2	13.4	6.7	6.8	7.9	20.9	4.5
South West	12.6	11.9	7.5	8.0	10.3	24.3	4.5
Avon	13.1	10.9	7.7	8.3	11.6	25.8	5.1
Cornwall	12.0	12.4	7.9	7.7	9.6	24.3	4.1
Devon	12.1	13.0	6.9	8.8	10.7	25.8	4.8
Dorset	11.4	13.5	7.8	6.9	9.7	23.1	4.2
Gloucestershire	13.3	11.2	6.8	7.4	10.7	24.8	3.8
Somerset	12.5	11.8	7.7	6.9	9.1	22.8	4.3
Wiltshire	14.3	10.4	7.9	9.1	9.5	21.5	4.9
West Midlands	14.4	10.9	10.1	10.0	12.8	29.1	5.8
Hereford & Worcs.	13.1	10.8	8.4	8.4	9.2	23.3	4.6
Shropshire	13.4	10.5	8.2	8.3	9.6	25.1	5.3
Staffordshire	13.8	10.8	10.0	9.3	8.9	27.2	4.7
Warwickshire	13.2	10.3	8.3	9.2	9.7	23.3	5.0
West Midlands (Met. county)	15.3	11.1	11.0	11.0	16.0	32.5	6.7
North West	14.4	11.9	8.7	8.7	15.5	34.4	6.6
Cheshire	13.5	10.8	7.5	7.7	9.6	26.8	3.7
Greater Manchester	14.9	11.7	9.2	9.0	17.3	36.2	7.0
Lancashire	14.2	12.8	9.4	9.9	12.9	30.8	7.0
Merseyside	14.4	12.2	8.0	7.6	18.2	39.3	7.4
England	13.9	11.1	8.4	8.4	12.9	28.3	5.6

(continued)

14.1 *(Continued)*

	Live births per 1,000 population 1990	Deaths per 1,000 population 1990	Perinatal mortality rate[1] 1988-1990	Infant mortality rate[2] 1988-1990	Percentage of live births outside marriage		Children in care of LA[3] (per 1,000 pop. aged under 18) 1990
					1981	1990	
Wales (Counties)	13.5	11.8	8.1	7.5	11.2	29.3	4.9
Clwyd	13.0	11.8	8.0	6.9	9.3	28.0	4.1
Dyfed	11.7	12.1	9.6	7.2	9.1	23.2	3.5
Gwent	14.3	11.6	7.5	7.7	11.6	31.2	6.2
Gwynedd	12.6	12.9	7.1	7.1	11.2	27.8	4.3
Mid-Glamorgan	14.5	11.7	8.8	8.0	11.5	32.8	5.9
Powys	12.5	12.4	8.4	7.5	8.0	24.0	3.0
South Glamorgan	14.4	10.7	7.5	7.2	16.3	32.4	5.7
West Glamorgan	13.1	12.1	8.0	7.9	9.4	26.8	4.5
Scotland (LA Regions)	12.9	12.1	8.7	8.2	12.2	27.1	..
Borders	11.8	14.3	6.3	6.9	9.7	18.5	..
Central	12.7	11.4	11.3	9.7	11.2	24.7	..
Dumfries & Galloway	12.0	12.7	8.0	9.5	10.4	23.5	..
Fife	12.8	11.4	8.2	7.8	11.0	25.1	..
Grampian	13.3	10.9	8.3	7.2	10.6	20.4	..
Highland	12.7	11.8	9.1	8.0	11.3	22.6	..
Lothian	13.1	11.7	7.9	7.9	11.8	26.3	..
Strathclyde	13.1	12.3	9.0	8.5	12.9	30.1	..
Tayside	11.9	13.1	9.4	8.5	14.9	31.0	..
Islands	13.0	13.4	6.9	5.1	8.1	16.9	..
Northern Ireland (Boards)[4]	16.7	9.7	8.4	7.8	7.0	18.8	6.0
Belfast	12.0	12.1	8.2	8.3	11.6	30.9	7.4
South Eastern	15.3	9.6	8.0	7.0	4.9	16.1	7.4
Southern	18.1	9.0	7.4	7.0	4.6	12.6	4.3
North Eastern	15.9	9.0	7.9	7.5	8.0	18.2	5.5
Western	18.5	9.0	10.6	9.4	5.9	17.8	5.5

1 Stillbirths and deaths of infants under 1 week of age per 1,000 live and still births. 3 year average.
2 Deaths of infants under 1 year of age per 1,000 live births.
3 Legislation in Scotland relating to children in care is different from that in England and no comparable Scottish statistics are available.
4 Education and Library Boards. See notes in Appendix.

14.2 Education

	Day nursery places[1] per 1,000 pop. aged under 5 years[2] March 1990	Children under 5 in education[3] (percentages) Jan. 1990[4]	Pupil/teacher ratio[5] January 1990[4] Primary schools	Secondary schools[6]	Pupils aged 16 staying on in education[7] (percentages) Jan. 1981	Jan. 1990	Percentage school leavers 1989/90[5,8] with no graded results	with 5+ A-Cs[9] GCSE (no A levels)	with 1 or more A levels[10]
North	16.3	71	21.9	14.9	51	63	9.4	12.4	18.2
Cleveland	26.8	75	22.5	14.6	53	61	10.9	10.2	21.1
Cumbria	17.5	56	21.8	14.7	54	67	9.9	13.5	19.0
Durham	7.8	71	22.2	15.9	45	62	9.6	15.5	16.0
Northumberland	5.5	63	22.9	16.3	56	68	4.5	9.0	29.3
Tyne & Wear	17.0	75	21.2	14.3	51	60	9.5	12.2	14.6
Yorkshire & Humberside	25.0	59	21.3	14.9	54	64	8.7	13.1	17.6
Humberside	20.2	56	22.1	15.4	49	61	9.6	9.8	16.2
North Yorkshire	29.5	48	22.1	15.2	62	73	4.9	14.7	29.1
South Yorkshire	13.3	65	21.5	14.6	52	61	9.4	16.6	14.1
West Yorkshire	32.4	60	20.5	14.8	55	64	9.2	11.3	16.8
East Midlands	24.2	50	22.2	14.9	55	68	6.7	11.5	19.7
Derbyshire	18.1	60	21.6	14.0	56	66	5.8	12.3	15.9
Leicestershire	28.6	38	22.7	14.7	58	71	9.1	12.2	23.9
Lincolnshire	13.1	32	23.3	16.3	56	71	5.1	11.6	19.4
Northamptonshire	42.3	54	22.5	15.9	53	65	6.1	12.6	21.6
Nottinghamshire	20.4	58	21.3	14.4	52	70	6.7	9.2	19.0
East Anglia	20.4	36	22.2	15.9	51	68	6.8	15.0	19.6
Cambridgeshire	28.6	45	22.6	15.9	56	72	4.6	11.4	27.4
Norfolk	20.1	34	22.0	15.3	47	65	9.4	18.6	15.8
Suffolk	12.4	31	22.0	16.6	49	67	5.5	13.9	17.4
South East	30.4	34	21.6	15.5	61	72	8.1	14.2	22.1
Bedfordshire	33.3	38	21.5	17.0	60	78	4.4	14.4	22.4
Berkshire	22.3	26	23.5	15.5	57	74	7.0	13.2	24.0
Buckinghamshire	11.1	18	22.9	15.8	65	75	4.5	15.5	34.2
East Sussex	24.4	38	22.3	15.7	60	74	2.6	15.4	25.6
Essex	16.7	21	22.4	16.2	54	62	5.8	14.4	20.9
Greater London	46.3	48	20.6	14.9	60	71	13.3	12.8	17.9
Hampshire	3.3	21	22.1	15.6	61	72	4.5	19.4	19.6
Hertfordshire	3.7	47	21.6	15.1	69	75	6.7	15.8	26.9
Isle of Wight	25.9	43	22.9	16.8	71	88	2.1	15.2	28.1
Kent	45.6	17	23.5	16.1	57	66	6.4	9.9	21.8
Oxfordshire	24.9	18	22.7	16.2	60	77	5.9	13.7	23.6
Surrey	13.0	24	20.8	15.3	69	85	5.0	15.2	31.3
West Sussex	21.4	10	21.8	16.0	63	72	5.1	17.7	27.6
South West	17.7	35	22.5	15.9	57	71	5.1	17.6	18.6
Avon	26.3	48	22.4	16.1	58	70	6.5	12.7	21.0
Cornwall	7.7	45	23.2	15.9	58	73	5.7	16.0	21.2
Devon	10.3	28	22.3	16.1	57	72	5.1	19.0	15.9
Dorset	13.2	38	23.1	16.1	55	65	3.8	18.0	22.1
Gloucestershire	31.3	31	22.1	15.7	57	73	5.3	18.1	22.8
Somerset	31.0	33	22.2	15.5	58	76	3.7	22.7	12.4
Wiltshire	5.6	18	22.5	15.5	58	69	4.9	18.8	14.4
West Midlands	29.4	54	22.4	15.2	56	65	8.4	12.5	18.1
Hereford & Worcs.	20.5	22	23.2	16.6	61	70	7.7	15.9	21.0
Shropshire	18.4	34	21.2	14.9	57	69	4.7	13.7	21.3
Staffordshire	39.2	48	23.3	15.7	54	66	8.0	11.9	18.4
Warwickshire	18.5	50	21.8	15.5	63	73	4.7	13.3	19.7
West Midlands (Met. county)	31.0	66	22.3	14.7	53	62	9.9	11.7	16.6
North West	37.2	60	22.6	14.8	57	67	10.1	15.6	18.6
Cheshire	32.7	54	24.3	16.1	63	71	6.9	15.6	27.7
Greater Manchester	38.2	63	22.1	14.1	55	66	9.9	16.6	17.6
Lancashire	41.5	48	23.3	15.6	57	67	8.5	19.5	12.5
Merseyside	34.2	71	21.8	14.6	56	67	14.0	10.2	20.5
England	27.7	46	22.0	15.3	57	68	8.1	14.1	19.7

(continued)

14.2 *(Continued)*

	Day nursery places[1] per 1,000 pop. aged under 5 years[2] March 1990	Children under 5 in education[3] (percent- ages) Jan. 1990[4]	Pupil/teacher ratio[5] January 1990[4]		Pupils aged 16 staying on in education[7] (percentages)		Percentage school leavers 1989/90[5,8]		
			Primary schools	Secondary schools[6]	Jan. 1981	Jan. 1990	with no graded results	with 5+ A-Cs[9] GCSE (no A levels)	with 1 or more A levels[10]
Wales (Counties)	15.5	68	22.3	15.3	54	66	14.0	12.0	22.0
Clwyd	34.6	76	24.6	15.8	57	70	7.0	10.0	23.0
Dyfed	2.0	64	19.9	15.8	60	67	14.0	11.0	28.0
Gwent	12.3	69	23.1	14.9	51	63	15.0	16.0	18.0
Gwynedd	14.1	41	21.0	14.0	52	61	10.0	12.0	23.0
Mid-Glamorgan	6.1	76	23.4	15.7	47	64	24.0	10.0	18.0
Powys	12.1	51	20.0	14.4	64	76	7.0	10.0	25.0
South Glamorgan	26.5	55	22.2	15.6	54	61	15.0	8.0	26.0
West Glamorgan	13.6	90	21.4	14.7	55	73	14.0	19.0	13.0
Scotland (LA regions)	16.1	39	19.7	12.4	..	76	10.6	7.4	38.6
Borders	14.9	28	18.1	11.8	..	99	6.6	8.0	42.0
Central	23.1	50	20.2	13.2	..	72	8.5	8.1	41.1
Dumfries & Galloway	6.6	26	19.2	11.6	..	73	7.5	9.2	37.4
Fife	11.3	55	19.6	12.9	..	90	10.8	7.9	37.6
Grampian	8.6	31	19.2	12.7	..	80	8.7	9.0	39.4
Highland	2.2	18	18.2	12.0	..	75	6.9	8.5	43.0
Lothian	16.0	50	19.9	12.4	..	76	9.1	6.1	42.3
Strathclyde	18.0	39	20.3	12.5	..	72	12.7	7.0	36.0
Tayside	29.2	37	19.4	11.6	..	86	9.8	8.1	41.6
Islands	1.1	20	14.3	9.8	..	76	7.0	9.3	42.0
Northern Ireland (Boards)	5.2	45	23.2	14.9	53	68	8.6	13.0	31.7
Belfast	7.5	..	22.4	14.6	52	..	9.2	10.2	42.2
South Eastern	7.5	..	23.3	15.2	50	..	5.7	11.8	27.0
Southern	3.0	..	24.0	14.9	55	..	8.2	15.6	31.0
North Eastern	3.0	..	23.1	14.7	52	..	7.5	14.1	29.2
Western	5.8	..	23.1	15.1	54	..	13.1	12.8	29.0

1 Local authority provided and registered day nurseries only. Scotland figures are for local authority day nurseries only.

2 Population data used are mid-1989 for England, Wales and Northern Ireland, and mid-1990 for Scotland.

3 Children under 5 attending maintained nursery or primary schools as a percentage of estimated popoulation aged 3 and 4. Grant aided schools in Northern Ireland.

4 September 1989 for Scotland.

5 Maintained schools only; grant-aided schools in Northern Ireland. Excludes tertiary and further education colleges.

6 Excluding prep departments of grammar schools in Northern Ireland.

7 Pupils staying on at maintained schools or going to further education full-time or part-time day (full-time only for Northern Ireland, 1981 England data include evening only). Data for Scotland are 1990/91 estimates and are on the closest comparable basis (an estimated number of Christmas leavers). Northern Ireland figures include grant-aided and full-time further education only.

8 Includes independent schools for Scotland. Wales total includes independent schools, however, Wales county data are for maintained schools only.

9 Or equivalent grades at 'O' level, CSE, SCE ordinary, SCE standard.

10 SCE H grades in Scotland.

14.3 Economic statistics

	Unemploy-ment rate (January 1992) (percentages)	Net capital expenditure in manufacturing[1] 1989		Gross value added in manufacturing[1] 1989		Gross domestic product			
						1981		1989	
		£ million	£ per employee index UK=100	£ million	£ per employee index UK=100	£ million	Index UK=100[2]	£ million	Index UK=100[2]
United Kingdom	9.4	14,498	100.0	108,291	100.0	218,197 [3]	100.0	436,814 [3]	100.0
North	11.2	912	113.6	6,407	106.7	10,720	93.9	20,439	88.5
Cleveland	13.3	220	138.3	1,729	145.4	2,069	99.0	4,048	97.4
Cumbria	6.9	139	86.7	1,112	93.0	1,830	103.8	3,965	107.3
Durham	11.1	171	109.6	1,317	112.9	1,940	86.6	3,522	78.5
Northumberland	10.3	47	77.0	435	96.0	955	87.1	1,835	80.4
Tyne & Wear	12.6	336	125.5	1,815	90.8	3,927	92.8	7,070	83.4
Yorkshire & Humberside	9.7	1,338	95.6	9,783	93.6	16,627	92.3	33,704	90.7
Humberside	10.3	355	137.6	2,478	128.5	2,733	87.0	6,376	99.1
North Yorkshire	5.9	159	118.3	950	94.7	2,393	96.5	5,167	95.2
South Yorkshire	12.6	256	79.6	2,118	88.1	4,465	92.5	7,702	79.1
West Yorkshire	9.0	567	82.8	4,238	82.9	7,036	92.9	14,458	93.1
East Midlands	8.7	998	72.8	8,972	87.6	13,696	97.0	29,213	97.2
Derbyshire	9.1	248	73.7	2,287	91.2	3,038	90.7	6,326	90.5
Leicestershire	7.7	301	74.9	2,659	88.7	3,262	103.7	7,193	107.3
Lincolnshire	8.6	97	78.6	729	79.5	1,860	91.8	3,811	86.4
Northamptonshire	7.6	155	74.6	1,387	89.4	1,775	91.0	4,559	105.3
Nottinghamshire	10.0	198	65.2	1,909	84.1	3,762	103.3	7,324	96.0
East Anglia	7.2	496	94.8	3,926	100.4	6,706	96.6	15,578	101.3
Cambridgeshire	7.1	170	88.0	1,632	113.3	2,261	104.4	5,504	111.8
Norfolk	8.0	154	92.1	1,218	97.3	2,404	93.5	5,410	96.1
Suffolk	6.5	172	105.7	1,076	88.4	2,040	92.6	4,665	96.8
South East	8.4	3,536	100.1	29,544	112.0	72,655	116.6	155,484	119.0
Bedfordshire	8.3	126	70.4	1,359	101.8	1,768	94.6	4,147	103.9
Berkshire	5.9	170	102.1	1,558	125.2	2,928	115.2	7,099	126.2
Buckinghamshire	6.7	136	74.0	1,407	102.2	1,919	91.6	5,278	110.7
East Sussex	10.1	78	87.4	613	92.1	1,971	80.9	4,172	78.0
Essex	9.3	428	135.9	2,586	110.0	4,793	88.2	10,111	87.8
Greater London	9.4	1,171	98.0	10,328	115.8	37,080	148.7	75,156	148.0
Hampshire	7.9	406	110.6	3,048	111.2	5,812	106.6	11,849	101.9
Hertfordshire	7.3	221	78.7	2,231	106.4	3,752	106.2	7,945	107.0
Isle of Wight	11.6	8	37.7	132	80.9	328	75.9	750	76.4
Kent	9.1	403	137.2	2,572	117.3	4,776	87.8	10,556	92.2
Oxfordshire	5.9	111	89.3	982	105.7	1,859	93.6	4,495	103.5
Surrey	..	161	96.6	1,508	121.2	3,484	93.5	8,370	111.3
West Sussex	6.2	117	78.1	1,219	108.5	2,185	89.5	5,558	104.9
South West	9.1	868	82.6	7,201	91.8	14,985	93.4	32,834	93.9
Avon	9.1	185	85.6	1,513	93.7	3,494	102.7	7,384	103.1
Cornwall	12.8	58	87.6	424	85.4	1,208	77.3	2,663	76.3
Devon	9.8	168	87.7	1,228	86.0	3,130	88.5	6,438	83.1
Dorset	9.4	82	66.4	845	91.1	1,913	87.3	4,491	91.0
Gloucestershire	7.1	116	71.5	1,167	96.3	1,895	102.3	4,270	107.3
Somerset	7.9	102	78.2	900	92.8	1,445	91.6	3,247	93.7
Wiltshire	7.4	156	98.0	1,124	94.3	1,901	98.9	4,341	103.4
West Midlands	10.0	1,633	84.7	12,678	88.0	17,265	90.9	36,290	92.5
Hereford & Worcs.	8.0	152	81.4	1,217	87.4	1,893	81.2	4,306	84.8
Shropshire	7.6	150	141.2	703	88.4	1,127	80.8	2,617	86.3
Staffordshire	8.5	297	74.5	2,824	95.0	3,188	85.4	6,918	88.6
Warwickshire	7.5	152	97.3	1,175	100.6	1,541	88.2	3,585	98.7
West Midlands (Met .county)	11.7	882	81.6	6,760	83.7	9,515	97.2	18,862	95.9
North West	10.6	2,070	115.1	14,026	104.4	22,349	94.5	43,727	91.2
Cheshire	8.1	549	181.1	2,802	123.8	3,648	106.8	7,684	106.6
Greater Manchester	10.2	717	94.2	5,089	89.5	9,169	95.6	18,011	92.8
Lancashire	8.5	379	84.7	3,780	113.1	4,561	89.9	9,749	93.2
Merseyside	15.2	426	148.6	2,356	110.1	4,971	89.1	8,283	76.1
England	9.0	11,851	95.5	92,538	99.9	175,003	102.0	367,268	102.4

(continued)

14.3 (Continued)

	Unemploy-ment rate (January 1992) (percentages)	Net capital expenditure in manufacturing[1] 1989		Gross value added in manufacturing[1] 1989		Gross domestic product			
						1981		1989	
		£ million	£ per employee index UK=100	£ million	£ per employee index UK=100	£ million	Index UK=100[2]	£ million	Index UK=100[2]
Wales (Counties)	9.9	1,114	164.7	5,558	110.0	8,639	83.8	18,443	85.4
Clwyd	8.4	316	254.7	1,171	126.2	1,038	72.0	2,865	92.7
Dyfed [4]	9.6	64	160.2	233	78.2	1,368	84.1	2,745	77.8
Gwent	10.2	210	142.3	1,256	114.2	1,313	81.1	2,871	85.5
Gwynedd	11.0	26	94.0	184	87.7	662	78.1	1,467	81.1
Mid-Glamorgan	12.4	201	125.5	1,056	88.2	1,501	75.7	2,920	72.2
Powys	5.6	19	76.9	136	74.2	..	..	..	..
South Glamorgan	9.2	78	119.3	569	116.6	1,480	103.7	3,247	106.9
West Glamorgan	10.1	201	230.3	955	146.8	1,277	93.7	2,329	85.4
Scotland (LA Regions)	9.7	1,232	113.2	8,309	102.2	18,349	96.7	35,482	92.7
Borders	6.6	16	50.0	170	70.5	342	92.2	650	84.2
Central	9.8	185	291.8	650	137.0	1,040	103.8	1,925	94.4
Dumfries & Galloway	8.5	33	100.6	214	87.7	518	97.3	964	86.8
Fife	10.9	87	92.0	711	100.4	1,254	100.2	2,093	80.8
Grampian	4.3	91	101.4	657	97.9	2,131	120.0	4,560	120.5
Highland [5]	9.4	23	91.2	194	102.5	850	85.4	1,623	78.8
Lothian	8.3	4	85.1	28	84.0	2,877	104.8	5,696	102.0
Strathclyde	11.9	200	132.8	1,079	95.9	7,998	90.4	15,422	88.8
Tayside	8.7	522	101.9	4,047	105.8	1,338	92.0	2,548	86.4
Islands	..	71	85.1	559	90.2	..	..	..	..
Northern Ireland (Boards)	14.5	301	92.0	1,886	77.2	4,431	78.7	9,097	76.4
Belfast	..	..	..	..	..	..	..	..	..
South Eastern	..	..	..	..	..	..	..	..	..
Southern	..	..	..	..	..	..	..	..	..
North Eastern	..	..	..	..	..	..	..	..	..
Western	..	..	..	..	..	..	..	..	..

1 New building work plus acquisitions less disposals of land and existing buildings, vehicles and plant and machinery. Includes expenditure on establishments where production had not started before the end of the year.
2 County GDP indices are based on United Kingdom excluding continental shelf region.
3 United Kingdom data includes Continental Shelf, therefore county data do not sum to UK total.
4 GDP figures include Powys.
5 GDP figures include Islands.

14.4 Income

	Average gross full-time earnings (£) April 1991		Household income				Household disposable income			
			1986		1989		1986		1989	
	Males on adult rates	Females on adult rates	£ million	£ per head (UK=100)	£ million	£ per head (UK=100)	£ million	£ per head (UK=100)	£ million	£ per head (UK=100)
United Kingdom	318.9 [1]	222.4 [1]	310,012	100.0	414,988	100.0	248,139	100.0	333,317	100.0
North	289.3	196.4	15,277	90.8	19,445	87.3	12,428	92.3	16,126	90.1
Cleveland	297.2	188.1	2,757	90.5	3,418	85.3	2,223	91.2	2,884	89.6
Cumbria	303.4	194.4	2,699	101.6	3,598	100.9	2,169	101.9	2,949	103.0
Durham	273.5	191.0	2,770	84.6	3,597	83.1	2,212	84.4	2,939	84.5
Northumberland	281.8	185.8	1,592	96.9	1,927	87.5	1,228	93.3	1,569	88.7
Tyne & Wear	288.1	203.9	5,459	88.0	6,904	84.4	4,597	92.6	5,785	88.1
Yorkshire & Humberside	286.6	200.2	25,155	94.0	32,831	91.7	20,339	95.0	26,864	93.4
Humberside	281.8	188.2	4,220	91.1	5,623	90.6	3,392	91.4	4,517	90.6
North Yorkshire	279.7	201.0	4,228	110.6	5,398	103.1	3,386	110.7	4,377	104.0
South Yorkshire	294.7	199.6	6,338	89.4	8,196	87.3	5,279	93.0	6,770	89.8
West Yorkshire	285.7	204.1	10,369	92.5	13,614	90.9	8,282	92.3	11,200	93.1
East Midlands	292.6	199.4	20,657	96.5	27,836	96.0	16,467	96.1	22,579	97.0
Derbyshire	297.2	199.8	4,624	92.4	6,300	93.5	3,590	89.6	5,128	94.7
Leicestershire	291.9	198.6	4,797	100.4	6,310	97.6	3,805	99.5	5,003	96.3
Lincolnshire	272.2	187.6	2,950	95.2	4,179	98.2	2,399	96.7	3,465	101.4
Northamptonshire	298.3	205.2	3,001	99.1	4,161	99.6	2,395	98.8	3,335	99.4
Nottinghamshire	296.3	201.8	5,285	96.1	6,886	93.6	4,277	97.2	5,649	95.6
East Anglia	300.2	202.7	11,066	101.7	15,130	102.1	8,873	101.9	12,233	102.7
Cambridgeshire	316.4	211.3	3,672	105.9	4,986	105.0	2,911	104.8	4,010	105.1
Norfolk	288.8	197.5	4,093	103.0	5,501	101.4	3,328	104.6	4,463	102.4
Suffolk	294.6	197.3	3,301	96.2	4,642	99.9	2,634	95.9	3,761	100.7
South East	368.7	256.1	106,909	113.4	147,070	116.7	84,371	111.8	114,944	113.5
Bedfordshire	324.7	216.0	2,933	103.1	4,043	105.0	2,295	100.8	3,171	102.5
Berkshire	372.8	249.5	4,534	113.1	6,363	117.3	3,493	108.9	4,913	112.7
Buckinghamshire	351.6	236.5	3,775	112.8	5,464	118.8	2,801	104.5	4,109	111.2
East Sussex	289.2	217.9	3,949	104.8	5,352	103.7	3,196	106.0	4,261	102.8
Essex	322.7	220.1	8,890	107.6	12,110	109.0	6,787	102.7	9,575	107.3
Greater London	408.7	284.9	43,721	118.2	59,181	120.8	35,650	120.4	46,005	116.9
Hampshire	324.4	216.0	8,816	105.7	12,153	108.4	7,003	104.9	9,773	108.6
Hertfordshire	353.3	243.0	6,391	118.7	9,534	133.2	4,892	113.5	7,422	129.1
Isle of Wight	283.2	193.9	641	94.3	889	94.0	532	97.8	751	98.8
Kent	318.7	212.6	8,546	104.3	11,497	104.1	6,704	102.2	9,255	104.3
Oxfordshire	317.8	224.8	3,213	102.4	4,351	103.9	2,466	98.2	3,462	102.9
Surrey	361.2	251.4	7,275	131.7	10,263	141.6	5,274	119.3	7,791	133.8
West Sussex	324.8	230.3	4,224	111.3	5,871	114.9	3,277	107.9	4,459	108.6
South West	297.1	207.7	25,779	103.9	33,998	100.8	20,830	104.9	27,865	102.8
Avon	319.6	214.4	5,312	102.7	6,985	101.1	4,299	103.9	5,744	103.5
Cornwall	246.3	178.2	2,247	91.8	3,010	89.5	1,868	95.3	2,527	93.5
Devon	268.1	200.3	5,437	99.7	7,051	94.4	4,545	104.1	5,867	97.8
Dorset	289.2	211.9	3,872	111.1	4,925	103.4	3,092	110.8	4,078	106.6
Gloucestershire	311.3	210.5	3,161	111.9	4,345	113.2	2,389	105.7	3,347	108.6
Somerset	281.8	211.1	2,452	100.0	3,304	98.9	1,984	101.1	2,711	101.0
Wiltshire	316.5	212.1	3,298	110.8	4,378	108.1	2,652	111.3	3,592	110.5
West Midlands	291.1	202.2	25,403	89.8	34,369	90.9	20,360	89.9	27,862	91.7
Hereford & Worcs.	275.4	193.6	3,549	99.3	4,857	99.2	2,725	95.2	3,864	98.3
Shropshire	271.8	186.2	2,035	94.9	2,758	94.3	1,653	96.3	2,218	94.4
Staffordshire	281.0	196.1	4,985	89.4	6,903	91.6	4,003	89.7	5,593	92.4
Warwickshire	303.2	203.4	2,598	98.9	3,609	103.0	2,016	95.9	2,760	98.1
West Midlands (Met. county)	298.0	208.1	12,237	85.1	16,243	85.7	9,962	86.6	13,428	88.2
North West	300.3	206.8	32,111	92.2	41,924	90.6	25,606	91.9	34,267	92.2
Cheshire	319.7	212.1	5,101	98.7	6,846	98.5	3,962	95.7	5,318	95.3
Greater Manchester	300.4	206.5	12,835	91.1	16,577	88.5	10,237	90.8	13,644	90.7
Lancashire	284.1	201.9	7,150	94.8	9,436	93.6	5,653	93.7	7,685	94.9
Merseyside	299.2	208.3	7,025	87.6	9,065	86.3	5,754	89.7	7,620	90.4
England	322.8	225.2	262,358	101.7	352,603	102.9	209,274	101.3	282,740	101.8

(continued)

14.4 (Continued)

	Average gross full-time earnings (£) April 1991		Household income				Household disposable income			
			1986		1989		1986		1989	
	Males on adult rates	Females on adult rates	£ million	£ per head (UK=100)	£ million	£ per head (UK=100)	£ million	£ per head (UK=100)	£ million	£ per head (UK=100)
Wales (Counties)	280.1	199.1	13,268	86.1	17,937	86.1	10,860	88.1	14,412	86.1
Clwyd	284.8	191.7	1,965	90.0	2,717	91.2	1,545	88.4	2,141	89.4
Dyfed[2]	260.2	193.5	2,150	87.2	2,902	85.3	1,838	93.2	2,294	83.9
Gwent	275.6	188.6	2,047	84.8	2,702	83.4	1,692	87.6	2,129	81.8
Gwynedd	271.9	191.1	1,149	89.7	1,526	87.4	953	93.0	1,243	88.6
Mid-Glamorgan	277.6	207.0	2,203	75.5	3,058	78.2	1,774	75.9	2,455	78.3
Powys	250.4	..	..	..	..	..	..	..	..	..
South Glamorgan	297.4	210.7	2,008	92.9	2,643	90.2	1,629	94.2	2,140	91.3
West Glamorgan[3]	279.8	197.4	1,746	87.9	2,389	90.8	1,429	89.9	2,011	95.1
Scotland (LA regions)	299.5	206.5	27,230	97.4	34,927	94.6	22,028	98.4	28,221	95.2
Borders	..	174.5	510	91.7	684	91.9	415	93.3	552	92.3
Central	294.2	189.2	1,416	95.4	1,809	91.9	1,174	98.8	1,467	92.8
Dumfries & Galloway	268.2	183.4	764	95.3	969	90.5	659	102.7	797	92.7
Fife	285.3	196.5	1,887	100.5	2,388	95.5	1,557	103.6	1,943	96.8
Grampian	363.7	209.1	2,961	107.8	3,829	104.9	2,339	106.4	3,071	104.7
Highland[4]	293.6	206.7	1,344	89.5	1,739	87.5	1,096	91.1	1,438	90.1
Lothian	294.6	214.7	4,381	108.1	5,694	105.7	3,559	109.7	4,501	104.0
Strathclyde	291.1	209.2	11,769	91.9	14,978	89.4	9,466	92.4	12,087	89.8
Tayside	277.8	201.3	2,198	102.6	2,837	99.7	1,764	102.8	2,367	103.5
Northern Ireland (Boards)	..	..	7,157	83.6	9,521	83.0	5,979	87.3	7,942	86.2
Belfast	..	..	..	..	..	..	..	..	..	..
South Eastern	..	..	..	..	..	..	..	..	..	..
Southern	..	..	..	..	..	..	..	..	..	..
North Eastern	..	..	..	..	..	..	..	..	..	..
Western	..	..	..	..	..	..	..	..	..	..

1 Great Britain
2 Earnings figures exclude Llanelli. Income figures include Powys.
3 Earnings figures include Llanelli.
4 Includes Islands.

Notes to Chapter 14: Sub-regional

The statistics cover: counties in England and Wales; local authority regions in Scotland; education boards, area health authorities and the Belfast travel-to-work area in Northern Ireland.

Table 14.2 Education

Children under 5 in education are those aged under 5 at 31 December 1988 in England and Wales, and at September 1988 in Scotland, attending maintained nursery or primary schools at January 1989 as a percentage of estimated population aged 3 and 4 years.

Figures for *pupils aged 16 staying on in education* in England and Wales relate to all 16 year olds in full-time and part-time education at maintained secondary schools and further education establishments, expressed as a percentage of all 15 year olds at maintained secondary schools one year earlier. Figures for Northern Ireland use as the denominator pupils aged 14 two years earlier, including a small number at colleges of further education.

School leavers with no graded results are those who either did not attempt any GCSE, GCE, CSE or SCE examinations or did not achieve a sufficient standard to be awarded a grade.

Table 14.3 Economic statistics

Unemployment figures relate to claimants at Unemployment Benefit Offices - see notes to chapter 7. Unemployment rates are only calculated for broadly self-contained labour markets and rates are not calculated for Survey for this reason. Rates in these tables are calculated as a percentage of the mid-1989 estimated workforce (the sum of employees in employment, unemployed claimants, self-employed, HM Forces and participants on work-related government training programmes) in each area.

Gross Domestic Product (GDP) measures the value of production of goods and services within each county and Scottish local authority region. It does not measure the income of a county for two reasons.

Firstly, GDP excludes transfer payments such as pensions, social security, dividends and interest, which are important sources of income for residents and vary considerably between counties. Secondly, county GDP is measured on a workplace basis which means that the income from employment of commuters is attributed to the counties where they work rather than to those where they reside.

Comparisons of GDP between areas are usually in terms of GDP per head. However, in calculating GDP per head at county level, workplace estimates of GDP are divided by resident population: this results in very high estimates of GDP per head in urban counties where many workers are commuters, and low estimates for surrounding counties where these commuters reside. Thus the figures should be treated with caution.

The sources and methods used to compile county GDP are similar to those used for regional GDP although a simpler approach is sometimes necessary. A description of the methods is given in *Economic Trends*, No. 411, January 1988 (HMSO).

15.1 Area and population

	Area (sq km)	Persons per sq km 1990	Population 1990 (thousands)			Change 1981-1990 (percentages)		Percentage of 1990 population aged				
			Males	Females	Total	Total	Persons aged 75 & over	Under 5	5-14	15 to pension age	Over pension age[1]	75 and over
United Kingdom	241,807	237	28,012.4	29,397.8	57,410.2	1.9	21.4	6.7	12.3	62.7	18.3	6.9
North	15,421	199	1,499.9	1,575.5	3,075.4	-1.3	19.9	6.5	12.4	62.7	18.5	6.6
Cleveland	591	935	271.1	281.0	552.1	-3.2	21.9	7.2	13.3	63.1	16.3	5.5
Hartlepool *	94	953	43.6	46.2	89.9	-5.3	14.9	7.3	13.0	62.5	17.2	6.1
Langbaurgh *	242	594	70.9	73.1	144.0	-4.6	22.5	6.9	13.1	63.3	16.7	5.5
Middlesbrough *	54	2,626	69.6	72.0	141.6	-6.0	20.0	7.8	14.0	61.7	16.5	5.6
Stockton-on-Tees *	200	883	86.9	89.7	176.6	1.6	27.7	7.0	13.2	64.5	15.3	5.1
Cumbria	6,825	72	240.1	252.0	492.1	2.3	22.2	6.0	11.7	62.6	19.7	7.4
Allerdale	1,259	77	46.9	50.2	97.1	1.4	21.9	5.9	11.9	62.6	19.6	7.3
Barrow-in-Furness	77	908	34.4	35.5	69.9	-4.8	23.4	6.8	11.8	61.8	19.6	7.2
Carlisle	1,040	100	50.1	54.0	104.1	3.1	23.1	6.2	12.2	62.1	19.5	7.4
Copeland	737	97	36.1	35.7	71.9	-1.4	16.6	6.6	12.5	64.2	16.6	5.6
Eden	2,158	22	23.9	23.8	47.7	10.3	18.3	5.4	11.8	64.9	17.9	6.5
South Lakeland	1,553	65	48.7	52.8	101.4	6.9	25.0	5.0	10.3	61.6	23.1	9.4
Durham	2,434	246	293.0	306.4	599.4	-2.0	20.7	6.3	12.3	63.0	18.4	6.5
Chester-le-Street	68	785	26.1	27.0	53.1	1.8	26.9	6.1	12.3	65.2	16.4	5.5
Darlington	198	504	49.0	51.0	100.0	1.4	11.8	6.5	12.0	62.8	18.7	6.5
Derwentside	271	317	41.8	44.2	85.9	-2.8	23.0	6.0	12.1	61.9	20.0	7.4
Durham	187	466	42.1	45.0	87.1	-1.5	26.4	5.5	11.8	65.8	16.9	6.0
Easington	144	659	46.7	48.4	95.1	-6.2	18.2	7.1	12.8	61.5	18.6	6.6
Sedgefield	218	407	43.6	45.1	88.7	-5.2	22.9	6.5	12.4	63.3	17.8	6.0
Teesdale	843	30	12.1	12.9	25.0	0.7	12.8	5.7	11.9	61.3	21.1	7.7
Wear Valley	505	128	31.7	32.9	64.6	0.8	25.7	6.4	12.5	61.7	19.4	7.3
Northumberland	5,032	61	149.3	155.9	305.2	2.0	19.4	5.9	12.5	62.7	18.8	6.9
Alnwick	1,080	29	15.5	16.1	31.6	9.3	26.7	6.0	12.7	60.8	20.5	7.9
Berwick-upon-Tweed	975	27	12.8	13.5	26.3	0.5	17.2	5.5	12.0	59.9	22.6	9.2
Blyth Valley	70	1,132	38.5	41.1	79.6	2.4	18.6	6.5	13.6	65.1	14.8	5.1
Castle Morpeth	619	81	25.3	25.1	50.4	1.1	19.9	5.2	11.8	62.7	20.2	7.3
Tynedale	2,221	26	28.1	29.6	57.7	6.6	13.5	5.9	11.9	62.8	19.3	7.2
Wansbeck	66	898	29.1	30.5	59.6	-4.7	23.4	6.0	12.2	61.6	20.1	7.1
Tyne and Wear	540	2,086	546.5	580.1	1,126.6	-2.5	17.7	6.6	12.2	62.4	18.9	6.8
Gateshead *	143	1,431	100.2	104.8	205.0	-3.9	21.4	6.2	11.7	63.0	19.2	6.8
Newcastle upon Tyne *	112	2,483	135.0	142.8	277.8	-2.2	14.3	6.6	11.8	62.3	19.4	7.6
North Tyneside *	84	2,289	91.8	99.9	191.7	-3.4	23.2	6.4	11.8	61.4	20.4	7.3
South Tyneside *	64	2,454	76.2	79.8	156.0	-3.7	16.9	6.7	11.9	61.4	20.0	7.0
Sunderland *	138	2,151	143.2	152.9	296.1	-0.4	15.3	7.0	13.3	63.1	16.7	5.7
Yorkshire & Humberside	15,421	321	2,417.0	2,534.9	4,951.9	0.7	19.7	6.7	12.4	62.6	18.3	6.9
Humberside	3,513	245	418.1	441.1	859.2	0.2	24.2	6.8	12.7	61.9	18.6	6.8
Beverley	404	288	55.9	60.6	116.5	8.9	32.2	5.5	12.2	63.0	19.4	7.2
Boothferry	647	103	32.3	34.1	66.4	9.4	15.9	6.4	12.9	63.8	16.9	5.7
Cleethorpes	164	415	33.6	34.6	68.2	-0.7	28.5	6.6	12.1	63.6	17.7	6.1
East Yorkshire	1,044	85	43.6	45.6	89.1	18.4	16.9	5.6	11.4	62.2	20.8	7.9
Glanford	580	126	35.8	37.3	73.1	9.2	35.5	5.9	12.9	64.3	16.8	5.8
Great Grimsby	28	3,173	43.9	45.1	89.0	-3.9	27.6	8.1	13.4	60.2	18.3	6.9
Holderness	540	96	25.6	26.3	51.8	11.5	14.9	6.1	12.7	64.7	16.5	6.0
Kingston-upon-Hull *	72	3,418	118.6	126.7	245.3	-10.4	19.4	7.7	13.0	60.3	19.0	7.2
Scunthorpe	34	1,770	28.8	31.0	59.8	-9.9	40.6	8.0	13.5	59.3	19.2	7.1
North Yorkshire	8,312	87	354.3	372.1	726.4	7.3	18.8	5.9	11.4	63.3	19.4	7.6
Craven	1,180	43	24.3	26.8	51.1	7.2	18.9	5.5	11.2	61.7	21.6	8.5
Hambleton	1,312	60	39.3	39.6	78.8	5.0	32.7	5.8	11.0	64.8	18.4	7.3
Harrogate	1,334	111	70.7	76.9	147.6	5.0	10.0	5.6	11.1	63.7	19.6	7.7
Richmondshire	1,317	41	27.8	25.6	53.4	22.9	27.1	5.9	11.4	69.1	13.6	5.0
Ryedale	1,598	58	45.6	46.6	92.2	7.7	28.9	5.4	11.3	63.8	19.5	7.1
Scarborough	817	131	50.7	56.1	106.8	4.4	13.5	5.9	11.2	58.9	23.9	10.1
Selby	725	131	47.1	48.1	95.1	19.2	32.6	6.4	12.6	65.1	16.0	5.8
York	29	3,436	48.8	52.4	101.2	-0.9	12.9	6.7	11.2	62.1	20.0	8.1

15.1 *(Continued)*

	Area (sq km)	Persons per sq km 1990	Population 1990 (thousands)			Change 1981-1990 (percentages)		Percentage of 1990 population aged				
			Males	Females	Total	Total	Persons aged 75 & over	Under 5	5-14	15 to pension age	Over pension age[1]	75 and over
South Yorkshire	1,561	831	634.8	661.4	1,296.2	-1.6	22.9	6.5	12.0	63.1	18.4	6.8
Barnsley *	329	675	109.2	112.6	221.8	-1.8	26.1	6.5	12.5	62.7	18.3	6.4
Doncaster *	582	506	144.4	149.6	294.0	1.1	24.9	7.0	12.8	63.2	17.0	5.9
Rotherham *	283	900	125.4	129.1	254.5	0.7	29.4	6.9	12.9	63.4	16.8	5.8
Sheffield *	368	1,431	255.8	270.1	525.8	-4.0	18.9	6.1	10.9	63.0	20.0	7.9
West Yorkshire	2,036	1,017	1,009.8	1,060.4	2,070.1	0.2	16.4	7.0	12.8	62.4	17.8	6.8
Bradford *	367	1,279	229.4	239.4	468.8	0.8	11.3	7.9	14.2	61.0	16.9	6.5
Calderdale	364	544	96.2	101.6	197.8	2.6	12.4	6.9	12.6	62.1	18.4	7.2
Kirklees *	410	916	183.2	192.3	375.5	-0.4	12.3	6.9	13.0	62.5	17.6	6.6
Leeds *	562	1,267	346.7	365.5	712.2	-0.8	20.1	6.7	12.1	62.7	18.5	7.2
Wakefield	333	948	154.2	161.6	315.8	0.6	24.4	6.8	12.2	63.9	17.1	6.0
East Midlands	15,630	257	1,981.8	2,036.8	4,018.7	4.3	25.6	6.6	12.4	63.2	17.8	6.6
Derbyshire	2,631	355	460.9	472.2	933.0	2.1	22.5	6.4	12.2	63.1	18.4	6.8
Amber Valley	265	431	56.4	57.8	114.2	4.0	25.9	5.8	12.0	62.9	19.3	7.5
Bolsover	160	449	35.5	36.3	71.8	1.2	20.6	6.2	12.7	62.1	19.0	6.8
Chesterfield	66	1,533	49.4	51.6	101.0	4.5	26.9	5.8	11.3	63.4	19.5	7.2
Derby *	78	2,785	106.6	110.7	217.3	-0.0	21.5	7.3	12.7	61.7	18.3	6.8
Erewash	109	983	53.1	54.4	107.6	4.2	24.0	6.7	12.1	63.6	17.7	6.6
High Peak	541	157	41.8	43.3	85.1	3.2	8.9	7.0	12.7	63.9	16.3	6.3
North East Derbyshire	277	351	48.5	48.7	97.2	-0.3	34.1	5.9	12.2	64.0	17.9	6.2
South Derbyshire	339	215	36.6	36.2	72.8	6.3	12.1	5.9	12.1	65.7	16.2	5.4
Derbyshire Dales	795	83	32.9	33.1	66.0	-2.7	26.5	5.5	10.9	62.3	21.3	8.5
Leicestershire	2,553	352	443.9	453.8	897.7	4.5	25.4	6.9	12.8	63.4	16.9	6.4
Blaby	131	656	42.5	43.2	85.6	11.1	31.2	6.5	12.8	64.9	15.8	5.7
Charnwood	279	541	75.0	76.1	151.0	7.8	35.6	6.4	12.2	65.0	16.4	6.1
Harborough	593	117	35.1	34.2	69.3	12.7	32.9	6.0	11.8	65.4	16.8	6.2
Hinckley and Bosworth	297	333	49.5	49.4	98.9	12.3	44.3	6.4	12.6	64.4	16.7	6.4
Leicester *	73	3,789	135.1	142.9	278.0	-1.8	10.4	8.2	13.8	60.5	17.4	7.0
Melton	482	94	21.7	23.4	45.1	3.5	29.4	6.1	11.8	64.0	18.1	6.5
North West Leicestershire	280	289	40.1	40.9	81.0	2.3	34.3	6.3	12.3	63.4	17.9	6.6
Oadby and Wigston	24	2,205	25.4	26.5	51.9	-2.3	33.0	6.4	11.4	65.2	17.1	6.0
Rutland	394	94	19.6	17.3	36.9	11.6	26.2	5.8	13.8	66.0	14.4	5.8
Lincolnshire	5,918	100	290.5	300.8	591.3	7.0	28.8	6.0	11.8	62.8	19.4	7.1
Boston	360	145	25.3	27.1	52.4	-0.2	26.6	6.0	11.5	61.9	20.6	7.9
East Lindsey	1,762	68	59.3	60.5	119.8	13.6	27.5	5.6	11.3	61.2	21.9	8.3
Lincoln	36	2,266	40.8	40.1	80.9	5.8	15.2	7.2	11.5	63.2	18.0	6.8
North Kesteven	923	94	42.1	44.4	86.5	7.9	37.9	5.4	11.4	65.0	18.3	6.4
South Holland	737	92	33.3	34.4	67.7	8.7	47.6	5.6	11.0	61.8	21.6	8.1
South Kesteven	943	113	51.9	55.1	107.1	9.1	35.1	6.2	12.5	63.2	18.1	6.7
West Lindsey	1,156	67	37.7	39.2	76.9	-0.9	14.3	6.0	13.2	63.5	17.3	5.8
Northamptonshire	2,367	245	285.6	294.5	580.1	8.9	24.5	7.0	13.0	63.1	16.9	6.3
Corby	80	642	25.1	26.5	51.5	-2.0	79.5	8.3	13.8	61.6	16.3	5.2
Daventry	666	97	32.9	31.8	64.8	11.6	20.7	6.5	13.7	65.4	14.4	5.1
East Northamptonshire	510	133	33.9	34.1	68.1	9.1	22.3	6.4	12.5	63.3	17.8	7.1
Kettering	234	325	36.8	39.1	76.0	6.3	14.5	6.6	12.3	62.1	19.1	7.4
Northampton	81	2,295	90.7	94.4	185.1	16.5	25.1	7.6	13.2	62.1	17.2	6.4
South Northamptonshire	633	107	33.9	33.7	67.6	4.9	20.7	6.5	12.8	65.1	15.6	5.5
Wellingborough	163	411	32.3	34.8	67.1	3.7	22.8	6.6	12.7	63.7	17.0	6.3
Nottinghamshire	2,161	470	500.9	515.7	1,016.6	2.2	27.5	6.6	12.1	63.5	17.8	6.6
Ashfield	110	998	54.8	55.0	109.8	2.9	31.2	6.4	12.3	63.8	17.6	6.6
Bassetlaw	637	165	52.8	52.2	105.0	2.0	30.3	6.2	11.8	64.4	17.6	6.2
Broxtowe	81	1,363	53.7	56.8	110.5	5.8	39.9	5.9	11.3	65.0	17.8	6.7
Gedling	120	921	53.9	56.5	110.5	5.8	40.3	6.2	11.9	64.7	17.3	6.2
Mansfield	77	1,306	49.1	51.4	100.5	0.5	33.4	7.1	12.5	62.2	18.1	6.4
Newark	651	159	51.7	51.8	103.5	-1.1	18.6	6.1	12.8	63.7	17.4	6.1
Nottingham *	75	3,680	134.7	140.2	274.9	-1.2	18.7	7.5	12.3	62.1	18.2	7.0
Rushcliffe	409	249	50.2	51.7	102.0	9.6	27.1	5.8	12.0	64.4	17.9	6.5

15.1 *(Continued)*

	Area (sq km)	Persons per sq km 1990	Population 1990 (thousands)			Change 1981-1990 (percentages)		Percentage of 1990 population aged				
			Males	Females	Total	Total	Persons aged 75 & over	Under 5	5-14	15 to pension age	Over pension age[1]	75 and over
East Anglia	12,573	164	1,008.1	1,050.9	2,059.0	8.7	29.9	6.5	12.4	61.6	19.5	7.5
Cambridgeshire	3,402	195	326.6	337.9	664.5	12.4	30.9	6.9	13.0	63.6	16.5	6.2
Cambridge	41	2,462	49.5	50.7	100.2	-0.7	18.6	5.8	10.1	66.3	17.9	7.6
East Cambridgeshire	655	93	30.7	30.3	61.0	13.0	28.7	6.6	12.0	62.2	19.2	7.3
Fenland	547	136	36.1	38.1	74.2	9.7	19.3	6.1	12.1	61.4	20.4	7.2
Huntingdon	924	167	76.3	77.8	154.0	23.3	41.0	7.5	14.6	64.9	13.0	4.7
Peterborough	333	463	74.0	80.3	154.3	14.9	42.3	7.7	14.0	62.2	16.1	5.5
South Cambridgeshire	902	134	59.9	60.8	120.7	10.2	33.9	6.4	13.1	63.8	16.7	6.5
Norfolk	5,375	140	365.5	385.2	750.7	7.0	31.7	5.9	11.5	60.8	21.9	8.4
Breckland	1,310	80	51.1	53.3	104.4	7.9	44.0	6.2	11.7	60.0	22.1	8.1
Broadland	552	194	52.6	54.2	106.8	9.0	32.0	5.7	11.6	62.3	20.5	7.3
Great Yarmouth	174	517	43.4	46.4	89.9	10.4	28.3	6.4	12.6	60.1	20.8	7.8
North Norfolk	966	100	47.2	49.0	96.2	15.5	39.3	4.9	10.4	58.0	26.7	11.1
Norwich	39	3,006	54.9	62.3	117.2	-7.1	14.5	6.5	11.1	61.0	21.4	8.7
South Norfolk	907	112	49.9	51.7	101.6	6.7	39.2	5.4	11.7	61.5	21.4	8.5
West Norfolk	1,427	94	66.3	68.2	134.5	11.3	30.7	5.9	11.6	61.8	20.7	7.8
Suffolk	3,797	170	316.0	327.8	643.8	7.0	27.0	6.8	12.8	60.6	19.8	7.7
Babergh	595	131	38.6	39.0	77.7	5.0	22.2	6.2	12.1	62.0	19.6	7.2
Forest Heath	374	165	31.2	30.5	61.7	17.1	30.1	9.0	15.8	60.7	14.5	5.3
Ipswich	39	2,918	54.7	59.0	113.7	-5.6	20.2	7.3	12.3	59.7	20.7	8.3
Mid Suffolk	871	90	38.7	39.6	78.3	10.6	31.7	6.3	12.5	62.2	19.0	7.4
St Edmundsbury	657	140	44.9	47.2	92.1	5.6	34.0	6.6	12.4	62.8	18.2	6.8
Suffolk Coastal	891	127	55.7	57.4	113.1	17.1	22.4	7.0	13.6	59.2	20.2	8.1
Waveney	370	290	52.1	55.2	107.3	7.3	33.5	6.0	11.7	59.0	23.3	9.2
South East	27,227	641	8,516.0	8,942.0	17,458.0	2.6	20.5	6.8	11.9	63.3	18.0	7.1
Bedfordshire	1,235	434	267.1	268.4	535.5	4.9	26.7	7.3	13.1	64.7	14.9	5.2
Luton	43	3,953	85.4	86.0	171.4	4.0	21.8	8.7	13.6	63.9	13.8	4.9
Mid Bedfordshire	503	228	57.5	57.3	114.8	10.0	23.4	6.8	12.6	66.4	14.3	5.0
North Bedfordshire	476	292	69.4	69.7	139.0	4.2	21.7	6.5	13.2	64.0	16.3	5.8
South Bedfordshire	213	517	54.8	55.4	110.2	2.5	47.3	6.8	12.8	65.0	15.4	5.3
Berkshire	1,259	600	377.9	377.6	755.5	8.9	28.2	7.1	12.7	65.5	14.7	5.3
Bracknell	109	989	53.8	54.4	108.2	27.9	54.8	7.4	13.7	66.6	12.2	4.0
Newbury	705	201	71.2	70.2	141.5	14.4	24.9	7.2	13.0	65.5	14.3	5.0
Reading	40	3,213	63.8	66.1	129.9	-5.5	10.9	7.1	11.4	64.9	16.7	6.4
Slough	28	3,639	49.9	50.4	100.3	2.8	44.0	8.3	13.0	63.1	15.6	5.9
Windsor and Maidenhead	198	635	62.9	62.6	125.5	-6.0	23.4	6.2	11.4	64.4	17.9	6.6
Wokingham	179	839	76.3	73.9	150.1	28.3	38.0	6.8	13.4	67.9	11.8	4.0
Buckinghamshire	1,883	341	317.9	323.5	641.5	12.2	30.9	6.9	13.3	65.1	14.6	5.3
Aylesbury Vale	904	164	72.6	75.9	148.4	10.8	28.1	7.0	13.4	65.1	14.5	5.2
Chiltern	200	436	43.1	44.2	87.3	-5.9	23.3	5.7	11.5	64.1	18.7	7.1
Milton Keynes	310	596	93.2	91.9	185.0	46.9	53.1	8.1	15.0	66.5	10.4	3.6
South Buckinghamshire	144	424	30.4	30.7	61.1	-1.7	20.1	5.6	11.5	64.4	18.5	6.4
Wycombe	324	492	78.6	80.9	159.6	1.6	30.2	6.8	13.0	64.5	15.8	5.8
East Sussex	1,795	397	334.0	378.2	712.2	7.1	9.3	5.7	10.4	58.0	25.9	11.2
Brighton	58	2,418	67.1	74.1	141.2	-5.5	4.4	6.0	9.5	61.8	22.6	9.8
Eastbourne	44	1,889	37.2	46.2	83.4	7.6	12.0	5.1	9.5	54.5	30.8	14.3
Hastings	30	2,765	39.1	43.1	82.2	8.6	3.9	6.9	11.7	57.5	24.0	10.3
Hove	24	3,883	43.6	49.1	92.6	5.5	-3.7	5.6	9.4	60.0	25.0	11.5
Lewes	292	311	43.0	47.8	90.8	15.0	15.8	5.8	11.3	58.6	24.2	9.4
Rother	510	167	39.1	46.1	85.1	11.3	10.3	4.6	10.1	52.1	33.2	14.1
Wealdon	837	164	64.8	72.0	136.8	14.7	22.9	5.5	11.2	58.5	24.8	10.7

15.1 *(Continued)*

	Area (sq km)	Persons per sq km 1990	Population 1990 (thousands)			Change 1981-1990 (percentages)		Percentage of 1990 population aged				
			Males	Females	Total	Total	Persons aged 75 & over	Under 5	5-14	15 to pension age	Over pension age[1]	75 and over
Essex	3,672	418	750.1	783.5	1,533.5	3.4	28.3	6.5	12.2	62.5	18.9	7.0
Basildon	110	1,417	77.4	78.5	156.0	1.8	46.4	7.4	13.0	64.0	15.6	5.0
Braintree	612	189	56.1	59.5	115.6	2.5	30.0	6.7	12.4	63.0	18.0	7.1
Brentwood	149	459	34.0	34.3	68.3	-5.6	26.3	5.5	10.8	63.9	19.7	6.9
Castle Point	45	1,881	42.0	42.2	84.2	-2.2	23.4	6.0	12.8	64.6	16.6	6.0
Chelmsford	342	443	74.4	77.3	151.7	8.7	31.4	6.8	12.8	65.1	15.3	5.5
Colchester	334	463	76.1	78.3	154.4	11.7	30.7	6.5	12.2	64.9	16.4	6.3
Epping Forest	340	328	55.0	56.8	111.7	-4.5	32.0	6.3	11.7	62.4	19.6	6.8
Harlow	30	2,332	34.6	35.7	70.3	-11.6	46.8	7.5	12.9	63.1	16.5	4.8
Maldon	359	148	26.5	26.8	53.3	10.5	31.7	6.3	12.7	63.3	17.6	6.7
Rochford	169	436	36.3	37.4	73.6	-0.1	23.8	6.3	12.3	63.0	18.4	6.2
Southend-on-Sea	42	4,012	78.9	88.4	167.3	6.2	15.3	6.4	11.4	58.3	23.9	10.2
Tendring	337	398	63.4	70.7	134.1	16.8	28.9	5.2	10.5	54.5	29.8	12.3
Thurrock	163	778	62.6	64.3	126.8	-0.4	31.5	7.4	12.8	63.9	16.0	5.3
Uttlesford	641	103	32.9	33.4	66.3	5.6	26.4	6.3	12.7	63.6	17.3	6.8
Greater London	1,579	4,302	3,297.6	3,496.8	6,794.4	-0.2	16.3	7.1	11.6	64.2	17.1	7.0
Barking and Dagenham	34	4,316	71.1	76.5	147.6	-2.7	22.2	7.4	12.4	59.4	20.8	8.0
Barnet	90	3,462	149.5	160.5	310.0	5.0	13.3	6.6	12.3	63.4	17.7	7.3
Bexley	61	3,631	108.0	112.2	220.2	1.4	30.4	6.9	11.9	63.7	17.5	6.7
Brent *	44	5,782	125.5	130.2	255.6	0.6	17.3	7.4	12.2	65.6	14.8	5.9
Bromley	152	1,977	147.4	152.7	300.1	0.6	28.0	6.1	11.3	63.0	19.6	7.7
Camden	22	8,543	87.9	97.6	185.5	3.6	11.8	6.1	9.6	68.0	16.3	7.0
City of London	3	1,441	1.7	2.2	3.9	-26.9	6.2	1.1	3.2	84.5	11.2	4.8
City of Westminster	22	8,305	85.5	93.7	179.2	-4.8	16.6	6.0	8.3	66.8	18.9	8.0
Croydon	87	3,690	158.2	161.2	319.4	-0.5	11.3	7.1	12.2	64.7	16.0	6.3
Ealing	55	5,288	144.3	149.0	293.3	4.0	17.2	6.8	12.1	65.5	15.6	6.3
Enfield	81	3,257	128.0	136.3	264.3	1.2	20.4	6.9	12.0	63.2	18.0	7.6
Greenwich *	47	4,550	103.4	112.5	215.9	0.1	19.9	7.5	12.8	62.2	17.5	6.9
Hackney *	19	9,849	93.4	98.4	191.8	3.6	6.0	8.7	13.0	64.1	14.2	5.9
Hammersmith and Fulham *	16	9,232	69.1	80.1	149.3	-1.3	10.1	6.6	10.4	66.8	16.2	7.2
Haringey	30	6,360	94.6	98.2	192.8	-7.0	-5.3	7.8	11.8	65.7	14.7	5.9
Harrow	51	3,787	93.3	99.2	192.5	-3.3	20.3	7.0	12.4	62.5	18.1	8.0
Havering	118	1,969	113.5	118.4	231.9	-4.3	40.6	6.4	11.8	62.8	19.0	6.7
Hillingdon	110	2,135	114.2	121.5	235.7	1.0	38.9	7.0	11.7	63.7	17.5	7.1
Hounslow	59	3,373	96.9	100.4	197.4	-3.2	12.7	7.5	12.5	63.9	16.1	6.5
Islington *	15	11,661	83.4	90.3	173.6	4.6	18.5	7.2	11.1	66.0	15.7	6.4
Kensington and Chelsea *	12	10,958	61.7	69.3	130.9	-6.5	0.6	6.3	9.3	69.0	15.5	6.5
Kingston-upon-Thames	38	3,700	68.0	70.9	139.0	3.5	24.4	6.2	11.0	63.9	19.0	8.1
Lambeth *	27	8,526	114.0	118.5	232.5	-8.1	5.4	8.1	11.1	65.6	15.2	6.5
Lewisham *	35	6,516	108.1	118.2	226.3	-4.3	10.8	7.5	12.0	62.4	18.1	7.4
Merton	38	4,345	79.3	85.6	164.9	-1.6	13.5	7.0	11.7	62.4	18.8	8.2
Newham *	36	5,736	101.3	107.3	208.6	-2.0	3.7	9.1	13.4	63.1	14.4	5.6
Redbridge	56	4,158	114.1	120.7	234.8	2.4	24.4	6.4	11.5	63.4	18.6	7.7
Richmond-upon-Thames	55	3,026	80.1	87.1	167.2	3.3	21.8	6.2	10.2	63.7	19.9	8.6
Southwark *	29	7,830	109.6	115.9	225.5	3.3	18.1	8.0	11.7	63.0	17.3	7.0
Sutton	43	3,870	81.2	86.9	168.0	-1.2	13.5	6.7	11.5	62.7	19.1	8.0
Tower Hamlets *	20	8,459	83.9	83.0	166.9	14.9	17.5	8.7	12.8	63.9	14.6	6.0
Waltham Forest	40	5,382	103.1	110.3	213.4	-1.9	11.7	7.6	12.0	63.3	17.1	7.6
Wandsworth *	35	7,340	124.3	131.9	256.2	-2.2	7.0	6.7	10.4	66.4	16.6	7.1
Hampshire	3,780	409	761.5	785.5	1,547.1	3.9	25.2	6.7	12.2	63.4	17.7	6.7
Basingstoke and Deane	634	224	70.4	71.8	142.2	8.6	30.7	7.0	13.4	65.6	14.0	4.8
East Hampshire	515	199	50.9	51.8	102.7	12.1	21.1	6.7	12.6	64.2	16.5	6.1
Eastleigh	80	1,301	52.0	51.9	103.9	11.8	22.5	7.1	12.9	64.1	15.9	5.3
Fareham	74	1,382	49.8	52.7	102.4	15.1	27.8	6.5	12.6	64.8	16.1	5.4
Gosport	25	2,967	36.5	38.2	74.7	-4.0	27.2	6.9	12.6	64.0	16.4	6.7
Hart	216	372	39.3	40.8	80.1	5.0	35.9	6.5	13.0	67.2	13.2	5.2
Havant	55	2,071	54.7	59.9	114.6	-1.0	27.8	7.3	13.6	60.4	18.7	6.5
New Forest	753	217	79.7	83.7	163.4	12.3	28.3	5.9	11.7	59.3	23.1	9.2
Portsmouth	40	4,590	91.6	92.5	184.1	-3.8	13.1	6.7	10.6	62.9	19.8	8.3
Rushmoor	39	2,105	41.5	40.6	82.1	1.8	31.7	7.4	11.2	68.2	13.2	4.9
Southampton	50	3,964	96.0	101.4	197.4	-5.9	25.4	7.1	12.2	60.8	19.9	7.9
Test Valley	638	162	52.5	50.9	103.4	10.3	39.6	6.2	11.5	66.2	16.1	5.9
Winchester	661	145	46.7	49.4	96.1	3.4	21.5	5.6	12.2	63.1	19.1	7.6

15.1 (Continued)

	Area (sq km)	Persons per sq km 1990	Population 1990 (thousands)			Change 1981-1990 (percentages)		Percentage of 1990 population aged					
			Males	Females	Total	Total	Persons aged 75 & over	Under 5	5-14	15 to pension age	Over pension age[1]	75 and over
Hertfordshire	1,636	604	487.8	500.9	988.7	2.5	37.4	6.6	12.4	63.4	17.6	6.4
Broxbourne	52	1,580	40.9	41.6	82.6	3.4	58.8	6.5	12.5	65.5	15.6	5.4
Dacorum	210	628	64.6	67.4	132.0	1.0	43.5	6.9	12.9	62.4	17.8	6.2
East Hertfordshire	477	253	61.0	59.7	120.7	10.3	34.7	6.4	12.3	66.0	15.4	5.8
Hertsmere	98	898	42.1	45.8	87.8	-0.9	29.4	6.7	11.8	61.4	20.0	7.1
North Hertfordshire	376	302	55.8	57.6	113.3	5.0	24.9	6.5	12.7	63.5	17.3	6.1
St Albans	161	804	64.0	65.6	129.6	3.4	25.0	6.1	12.3	64.3	17.3	6.4
Stevenage	26	2,865	36.8	37.6	74.4	-0.4	66.0	7.8	12.7	63.1	16.4	5.6
Three Rivers	87	922	39.6	40.9	80.5	1.4	51.9	6.0	12.2	61.9	19.8	7.8
Watford	21	3,535	38.1	37.7	75.8	1.6	10.4	7.0	12.5	64.8	15.8	6.4
Welwyn Hatfield	128	721	45.0	47.0	91.9	-2.3	59.1	6.2	11.9	60.9	21.0	7.6
Isle of Wight	381	341	62.1	67.7	129.7	9.9	26.3	5.4	11.3	58.0	25.3	10.4
Medina	117	620	35.6	37.1	72.7	7.1	21.6	5.6	11.6	59.9	22.9	9.2
South Wight	264	217	26.5	30.6	57.1	13.7	31.3	5.2	11.0	55.5	28.3	11.9
Kent	3,731	409	745.5	779.9	1,525.5	2.8	17.4	6.6	12.2	62.2	19.1	7.3
Ashford	581	166	47.5	49.0	96.5	11.0	17.4	6.8	12.4	63.3	17.6	6.5
Canterbury	309	427	63.0	68.7	131.7	7.8	10.0	5.8	11.9	59.3	23.0	9.3
Dartford	73	1,076	38.3	40.1	78.4	0.2	11.0	6.9	12.2	64.1	16.8	6.0
Dover	314	340	52.6	54.1	106.7	3.2	19.0	6.3	11.7	60.8	21.1	8.2
Gillingham	32	2,936	45.9	49.3	95.1	-1.5	16.5	7.5	13.6	64.1	14.8	5.3
Gravesham	99	885	43.3	44.8	88.1	-8.5	27.0	6.8	12.0	63.1	18.1	6.6
Maidstone	393	348	67.6	69.5	137.0	4.7	26.9	6.3	12.0	64.3	17.4	6.3
Rochester-upon-Medway	160	934	73.8	75.5	149.3	3.9	37.4	7.6	12.9	64.5	15.0	5.4
Sevenoaks	369	285	53.0	51.9	104.9	-6.2	20.3	6.3	12.4	63.0	18.3	6.7
Shepway	357	248	41.8	46.7	88.5	2.8	8.5	6.1	11.2	58.4	24.3	10.1
Swale	369	318	58.8	58.4	117.2	6.4	20.8	7.0	12.5	63.2	17.3	6.4
Thanet	103	1,278	61.7	70.2	131.8	8.2	12.3	5.9	11.6	56.2	26.3	11.0
Tonbridge and Malling	240	421	50.8	50.4	101.2	3.4	27.5	6.5	11.6	65.8	16.1	5.9
Tunbridge Wells	332	298	47.5	51.5	99.0	0.5	8.1	6.0	12.0	62.3	19.7	8.1
Oxfordshire	2,608	225	290.8	295.8	586.6	8.3	33.2	6.7	12.5	64.6	16.2	6.2
Cherwell	590	219	62.9	66.0	128.9	17.9	39.9	7.9	14.7	63.1	14.3	5.0
Oxford	36	3,320	58.8	59.3	118.0	1.6	21.5	5.7	10.6	68.1	15.6	6.9
South Oxfordshire	687	189	65.0	64.8	129.8	-1.0	22.5	6.6	12.0	63.5	17.9	6.6
Vale of White Horse	580	195	55.8	57.1	113.0	9.1	51.3	6.4	12.6	63.9	17.1	6.5
West Oxfordshire	715	136	48.3	48.7	96.9	18.7	41.5	6.7	12.6	64.5	16.2	6.1
Surrey	1,679	597	487.8	515.1	1,002.9	-1.4	23.8	6.2	11.8	62.7	19.2	7.5
Elmbridge	97	1,108	51.8	55.3	107.1	-4.8	32.5	6.2	10.9	61.1	21.8	9.1
Epsom and Ewell	34	2,005	32.8	35.6	68.4	-1.4	6.6	6.1	11.5	63.2	19.2	7.9
Guildford	271	456	59.9	63.7	123.6	-1.1	30.0	6.5	12.4	62.0	19.1	7.5
Mole Valley	258	295	37.1	39.0	76.1	-1.8	17.5	5.6	11.5	62.8	20.2	8.1
Reigate and Banstead	129	894	55.1	60.3	115.4	-1.4	26.2	6.4	11.5	60.7	21.4	8.8
Runnymede	78	920	35.6	36.4	72.0	-1.6	35.0	6.2	10.5	64.1	19.1	7.3
Spelthorne	56	1,511	42.2	42.6	84.9	-8.5	37.1	6.0	10.9	63.8	19.3	6.9
Surrey Heath	97	872	41.9	42.3	84.2	8.5	29.1	6.4	13.3	67.2	13.1	4.3
Tandridge	250	301	36.4	39.0	75.3	-3.4	6.6	6.3	11.8	63.2	18.6	6.7
Waverley	345	318	52.0	57.7	109.8	-2.1	24.1	5.7	12.2	60.8	21.3	8.9
Woking	64	1,353	42.8	43.2	86.0	4.9	14.8	7.0	12.7	63.8	16.4	6.0
West Sussex	1,989	354	336.0	368.9	704.9	5.8	16.1	5.8	11.1	59.0	24.1	9.9
Adur	42	1,362	26.6	30.4	57.0	-2.7	11.0	5.7	10.3	58.1	26.0	10.2
Arun	221	586	60.2	69.3	129.5	9.2	17.0	5.2	10.0	53.7	31.1	13.1
Chichester	787	135	50.7	55.6	106.3	7.4	27.9	5.1	10.2	59.8	24.9	9.9
Crawley	44	1,920	41.4	43.2	84.7	16.3	95.5	7.2	12.5	62.6	17.7	5.8
Horsham	530	206	53.7	55.6	109.3	5.2	17.9	6.2	12.4	62.1	19.3	7.7
Mid Sussex	333	359	59.5	60.1	119.6	-1.3	6.2	6.3	12.3	64.0	17.3	6.6
Worthing	32	3,036	43.9	54.7	98.6	6.7	1.4	5.4	9.8	52.8	32.0	15.5

15.1 *(Continued)*

	Area (sq km)	Persons per sq km 1990	Population 1990 (thousands) Males	Females	Total	Change 1981-1990 (percentages) Total	Persons aged 75 & over	Percentage of 1990 population aged Under 5	5-14	15 to pension age	Over pension age[1]	75 and over
South West	23,850	196	2,254.0	2,412.5	4,666.5	6.5	25.7	6.2	11.6	61.1	21.1	8.4
Avon	1,346	707	461.9	490.1	952.0	2.5	24.2	6.3	11.7	62.6	19.4	7.6
Bath	29	2,896	39.1	44.1	83.2	-1.3	24.6	5.5	10.5	60.8	23.2	9.9
Bristol *	110	3,417	179.3	195.0	374.3	-6.7	12.0	6.9	11.2	62.1	19.8	8.0
Kingswood	48	1,857	43.5	45.4	88.9	5.1	36.2	6.3	11.9	64.1	17.6	6.2
Northavon	463	293	68.8	66.9	135.7	14.0	62.9	6.6	12.6	66.2	14.6	5.4
Wansdyke	323	256	40.4	42.2	82.6	6.9	38.7	5.7	11.8	62.5	20.0	7.6
Woodspring	374	500	90.8	96.5	187.3	15.0	27.1	5.8	12.2	61.1	20.9	8.2
Cornwall	3,564	131	223.4	244.1	467.5	9.6	29.0	6.0	11.8	60.2	22.1	8.6
Caradon	664	113	35.9	39.2	75.1	10.8	33.2	6.3	12.4	60.2	21.1	8.4
Carrick	461	173	37.5	42.1	79.5	5.1	30.4	5.7	11.1	58.6	24.5	9.6
Isles of Scilly	16	121	1.0	1.0	2.0	-0.1	44.0	5.6	11.6	60.2	22.6	8.5
Kerrier	473	185	42.9	44.8	87.7	5.0	27.8	6.3	12.0	60.6	21.1	7.9
North Cornwall	1,195	61	34.9	38.2	73.1	12.9	29.4	5.9	11.4	60.4	22.3	8.5
Penwith	303	208	29.5	33.6	63.1	16.6	26.8	5.6	11.4	59.8	23.2	9.3
Restormel	452	193	41.7	45.3	87.0	10.7	26.6	6.1	12.1	61.1	20.6	8.0
Devon	6,711	154	497.3	533.2	1,030.5	6.7	21.7	5.9	11.4	60.1	22.6	9.3
East Devon	815	146	56.4	62.4	118.8	10.1	24.3	4.8	10.5	54.5	30.2	13.1
Exeter	46	2,231	49.8	53.8	103.6	3.9	17.6	6.4	11.2	62.9	19.5	7.4
Mid Devon	915	70	31.2	32.9	64.1	9.1	26.4	6.3	12.7	60.8	20.2	8.3
North Devon	1,086	79	42.6	43.4	86.1	10.0	10.5	6.2	12.5	61.4	19.9	8.0
Plymouth *	79	3,187	124.0	128.9	252.8	-0.0	21.0	6.6	12.0	63.9	17.5	6.8
South Hams	887	88	37.4	40.6	78.1	16.1	30.7	5.8	11.9	59.6	22.8	9.3
Teignbridge	674	166	53.3	58.6	112.0	16.2	35.9	5.5	10.9	57.1	26.5	11.6
Torbay	63	1,894	54.7	64.4	119.0	5.2	13.2	5.4	10.7	56.3	27.6	12.0
Torridge	985	53	25.4	26.7	52.1	7.1	22.8	6.0	11.0	59.8	23.2	9.2
West Devon	1,160	38	22.5	21.4	43.8	2.6	12.3	5.6	10.9	61.3	22.2	8.6
Dorset	2,654	248	314.4	343.9	658.3	10.0	27.0	5.5	10.7	58.7	25.1	10.5
Bournemouth	46	3,332	71.1	82.9	154.0	7.4	8.6	5.4	9.9	56.8	27.9	12.5
Christchurch	50	779	18.1	21.2	39.3	2.7	37.1	3.9	7.7	52.9	35.5	14.8
East Dorset	355	222	38.2	40.6	78.8	14.1	42.7	5.1	11.9	57.3	25.8	10.3
North Dorset	610	91	27.1	28.2	55.3	12.9	44.4	5.8	10.8	60.9	22.4	9.4
Poole	64	2,060	64.2	68.3	132.4	10.1	28.8	6.2	11.3	59.8	22.7	9.4
Purbeck	405	118	23.4	24.2	47.6	17.5	36.9	5.5	11.2	62.7	20.7	8.3
West Dorset	1,083	80	41.2	45.1	86.2	7.8	33.4	5.2	10.3	58.8	25.7	10.5
Weymouth and Portland	42	1,555	31.2	33.4	64.6	11.3	37.4	6.1	11.5	61.7	20.7	8.5
Gloucestershire	2,643	201	256.1	275.3	531.4	5.1	31.0	6.4	11.9	62.1	19.6	7.6
Cheltenham	35	2,483	40.0	45.8	85.8	-0.3	20.4	6.6	11.7	61.0	20.8	8.6
Cotswold	1,143	66	36.3	39.1	75.4	8.1	37.9	5.6	11.2	60.7	22.4	9.1
Forest of Dean	528	150	39.2	39.8	79.0	7.9	31.2	6.0	12.8	62.7	18.6	7.3
Gloucester	33	2,759	43.8	48.2	92.0	-0.7	24.0	7.6	12.6	61.0	18.8	6.8
Stroud	454	242	53.2	57.0	110.1	7.7	32.3	6.2	12.0	62.8	19.0	7.6
Tewkesbury	450	198	43.6	45.5	89.0	8.8	45.1	6.1	11.2	64.4	18.3	6.6
Somerset	3,452	135	225.1	239.8	464.9	7.9	26.1	6.2	11.9	60.9	21.0	8.2
Mendip	740	128	46.9	47.8	94.7	5.4	24.3	6.6	11.8	62.5	19.1	7.6
Sedgemoor	564	174	47.9	50.4	98.3	9.1	26.8	6.1	12.2	61.3	20.4	8.0
Taunton Deane	462	208	46.3	49.7	96.1	8.9	23.9	6.1	11.7	61.2	21.0	8.1
West Somerset	727	45	15.0	17.6	32.6	10.5	30.1	5.4	10.7	54.2	29.8	12.8
South Somerset	959	149	69.1	74.2	143.3	7.6	26.9	6.2	12.1	61.0	20.7	7.9
Wiltshire	3,479	162	275.8	286.1	561.9	7.0	27.7	6.8	12.4	63.1	17.7	6.6
Kennet	958	72	33.5	35.1	68.6	4.4	16.2	6.7	12.9	62.7	17.7	6.9
North Wiltshire	768	149	56.2	58.1	114.3	8.9	40.2	6.6	12.1	64.0	17.3	6.8
Salisbury	1,005	101	50.0	51.6	101.6	-1.0	21.9	6.3	11.6	61.9	20.2	7.9
Thamesdown	230	743	84.8	86.2	171.1	12.8	21.0	7.6	13.0	64.2	15.2	5.2
West Wiltshire	517	206	51.4	55.1	106.4	6.2	39.0	6.5	12.2	61.6	19.6	7.4

15.1 *(Continued)*

	Area (sq km)	Persons per sq km 1990	Population 1990 (thousands)			Change 1981-1990 (percentages)		Percentage of 1990 population aged				
			Males	Females	Total	Total	Persons aged 75 & over	Under 5	5-14	15 to pension age	Over pension age[1]	75 and over
West Midlands	13,013	401	2,579.8	2,639.5	5,219.3	0.6	27.2	6.8	12.5	63.1	17.6	6.3
Hereford and Worcester	3,927	172	332.8	343.4	676.2	6.3	27.6	6.3	12.5	63.3	17.9	6.6
Bromsgrove	220	403	43.9	44.7	88.6	0.5	20.6	5.9	12.3	64.7	17.0	5.6
Hereford	20	2,409	23.8	25.3	49.0	2.3	35.8	7.1	11.7	61.0	20.2	7.7
Leominster	933	43	19.5	20.2	39.7	5.4	29.9	5.9	11.4	60.4	22.3	8.8
Malvern Hills	900	97	43.8	43.7	87.5	2.7	18.3	5.4	11.6	62.1	20.8	8.0
Redditch	54	1,453	39.6	39.3	78.8	16.5	40.7	7.7	15.4	64.8	12.0	3.8
South Herefordshire	905	58	26.4	26.0	52.5	12.4	24.7	5.9	12.1	63.0	18.9	7.2
Worcester	33	2,482	39.2	43.4	82.7	8.9	34.0	6.9	12.3	63.0	17.9	6.9
Wychavon	665	153	49.9	51.9	101.8	6.7	24.1	6.1	12.2	63.9	17.8	6.5
Wyre Forest	196	489	46.7	49.0	95.6	4.3	33.6	6.3	12.7	63.6	17.4	6.5
Shropshire	3,490	116	199.4	205.7	405.1	6.4	30.1	6.4	12.5	63.1	17.9	6.6
Bridgnorth	634	80	25.7	25.1	50.8	0.6	23.8	5.6	11.6	65.4	17.3	6.3
North Shropshire	680	84	28.2	28.6	56.8	11.0	27.2	6.1	13.0	62.7	18.2	6.9
Oswestry	256	132	16.0	17.7	33.7	6.8	40.0	6.1	10.9	61.2	21.7	9.3
Shrewsbury and Atcham	602	151	44.2	46.4	90.6	3.2	26.8	6.2	11.9	62.8	19.1	6.9
South Shropshire	1,028	35	17.5	18.3	35.8	4.8	22.2	5.5	11.0	60.9	22.6	8.8
The Wrekin *	291	473	67.8	69.6	137.4	9.5	38.2	7.4	13.8	63.8	15.1	5.1
Staffordshire	2,716	383	514.9	525.9	1,040.8	2.1	28.2	6.6	12.3	64.4	16.7	5.8
Cannock Chase	79	1,137	43.7	46.0	89.7	5.3	31.1	7.1	12.9	65.7	14.3	4.8
East Staffordshire	388	250	47.8	49.2	97.0	0.7	22.8	6.6	11.7	63.5	18.2	6.6
Lichfield	330	284	46.8	47.0	93.8	5.4	26.4	6.2	12.2	67.2	14.4	4.7
Newcastle-under-Lyme	211	562	59.0	59.7	118.7	-1.5	38.4	6.4	11.6	62.6	19.2	7.0
South Staffordshire	409	268	55.4	54.1	109.5	12.3	29.0	6.5	12.9	67.2	13.4	4.2
Stafford	599	199	58.9	60.2	119.1	1.6	33.6	6.0	11.7	64.7	17.7	6.2
Staffordshire Moorlands	576	168	47.5	49.3	96.9	1.1	20.8	5.9	12.4	64.3	17.4	6.2
Stoke-on-Trent	93	2,659	120.8	125.9	246.7	-2.2	26.6	7.0	12.1	61.9	19.0	6.8
Tamworth	31	2,242	34.9	34.5	69.4	6.3	21.3	7.6	14.2	67.1	11.1	3.3
Warwickshire	1,981	244	238.4	244.2	482.6	1.1	28.9	6.2	11.9	64.3	17.6	6.4
North Warwickshire	286	210	29.7	30.4	60.1	0.1	34.6	6.3	11.8	65.3	16.6	5.7
Nuneaton and Bedworth	79	1,470	57.6	58.4	116.1	1.9	38.6	7.1	12.1	64.3	16.5	5.8
Rugby	356	241	42.7	43.1	85.9	-1.9	21.1	6.1	12.5	64.1	17.3	6.2
Stratford-on-Avon	977	108	51.9	53.9	105.7	5.0	30.0	5.5	11.6	63.7	19.2	7.2
Warwick	283	407	56.5	58.4	114.9	-0.2	23.6	6.0	11.7	64.3	18.0	6.6
West Midlands	899	2,907	1,294.2	1,320.4	2,614.6	-2.2	25.9	7.2	12.7	62.4	17.8	6.4
Birmingham *	266	3,736	493.2	499.6	992.8	-2.7	18.5	7.7	13.2	61.5	17.6	6.6
Coventry *	97	3,146	150.8	152.8	303.7	-4.9	27.5	7.3	12.8	62.0	17.9	6.4
Dudley *	98	3,130	151.9	154.6	306.5	1.9	27.0	6.3	11.8	64.5	17.4	6.1
Sandwell *	86	3,446	144.3	150.7	295.0	-4.8	27.3	7.1	12.5	61.5	18.9	7.0
Solihull	179	1,138	99.5	103.8	203.3	2.6	53.0	6.2	12.6	64.1	17.2	6.0
Walsall*	106	2,488	131.2	132.8	263.9	-1.4	30.2	6.9	12.7	63.4	17.0	5.7
Wolverhampton *	69	3,618	123.3	126.1	249.4	-2.8	32.2	7.0	12.6	61.8	18.5	6.9

15.1 *(Continued)*

	Area (sq km)	Persons per sq km 1990	Population 1990 (thousands)			Change 1981-1990 (percentages)		Percentage of 1990 population aged				
			Males	Females	Total	Total	Persons aged 75 & over	Under 5	5-14	15 to pension age	Over pension age[1]	75 and over
North West	7,344	870	3,111.6	3,276.9	6,388.6	-1.1	16.6	6.9	12.6	62.5	18.0	6.8
Cheshire	2,333	411	470.7	488.3	959.0	2.9	25.0	6.6	12.6	63.9	17.0	6.1
Chester	448	252	54.1	59.0	113.1	-2.7	27.4	6.1	11.5	62.2	20.2	7.7
Congleton	211	410	42.3	44.3	86.7	8.3	33.2	5.8	12.0	65.4	16.8	5.9
Crewe and Nantwich	431	239	50.8	52.0	102.8	4.3	21.7	6.7	12.3	62.9	18.1	6.8
Ellesmere Port and Neston	86	911	38.7	40.0	78.7	-4.7	28.7	6.9	12.5	64.9	15.6	5.2
Halton *	74	1,672	60.9	62.6	123.5	0.3	33.2	7.9	14.5	62.9	14.6	4.9
Macclesfield	525	287	73.8	77.1	150.8	0.6	17.9	5.8	11.5	64.1	18.6	7.0
Vale Royal	381	299	56.6	57.5	114.1	1.8	24.8	6.7	13.0	63.4	16.9	5.9
Warrington	176	1,074	93.5	95.7	189.2	11.4	23.4	6.8	12.9	65.0	15.3	5.3
Greater Manchester	1,287	2,013	1,266.5	1,324.0	2,590.5	-1.1	17.4	7.1	12.6	62.9	17.4	6.6
Bolton *	140	1,910	130.6	136.3	266.9	1.8	14.9	7.2	13.2	62.8	16.8	6.3
Bury	99	1,791	86.7	90.9	177.6	0.6	16.5	6.9	12.4	63.2	17.4	6.7
Manchester *	116	3,844	219.5	227.2	446.7	-3.5	10.0	7.6	12.3	62.7	17.4	6.7
Oldham *	141	1,571	108.7	113.0	221.7	0.1	19.1	7.3	13.2	62.3	17.2	6.5
Rochdale *	160	1,305	102.2	106.3	208.5	0.1	17.3	7.5	13.8	62.4	16.3	6.0
Salford *	97	2,417	114.1	120.0	234.1	-5.2	22.2	7.0	12.3	61.4	19.3	7.6
Stockport	126	2,304	140.8	149.7	290.5	0.0	16.8	6.4	12.3	63.5	17.8	6.6
Tameside	103	2,125	107.2	112.1	219.3	0.4	25.7	7.1	12.4	62.6	17.9	6.7
Trafford	106	2,033	104.0	110.8	214.8	-3.1	23.6	6.5	12.0	62.9	18.5	7.1
Wigan *	199	1,560	152.7	157.7	310.4	0.0	16.8	6.7	12.7	64.4	16.3	5.8
Lancashire	3,070	455	678.5	716.8	1,395.3	0.7	10.6	6.8	12.5	61.5	19.2	7.4
Blackburn *	137	987	66.2	69.3	135.4	-5.0	2.8	8.1	14.4	60.5	17.0	6.5
Blackpool	35	3,978	64.8	74.3	139.1	-6.7	4.7	6.2	10.3	58.6	24.9	10.5
Burnley *	111	853	46.4	48.0	94.4	0.3	2.7	7.7	13.4	61.7	17.1	6.3
Chorley	203	480	49.0	48.3	97.3	6.9	15.6	6.7	13.1	65.5	14.8	5.2
Fylde	165	450	35.9	38.3	74.3	7.7	4.2	5.5	11.0	60.5	23.0	8.8
Hyndburn	73	1,087	38.7	40.7	79.4	-0.1	12.1	7.3	13.4	61.0	18.3	6.8
Lancaster	577	230	64.1	68.4	132.5	5.8	10.4	6.0	11.6	60.4	22.0	9.2
Pendle	170	505	42.0	43.6	85.6	-0.8	11.3	7.4	13.7	59.1	19.7	8.0
Preston *	142	903	62.2	66.4	128.5	1.7	8.7	7.6	13.2	61.4	17.8	6.8
Ribble Valley	585	89	25.5	26.3	51.8	-1.5	28.9	5.5	10.7	63.9	19.9	7.8
Rossendale	138	475	32.6	32.9	65.6	0.9	7.6	7.2	13.6	62.4	16.8	6.3
South Ribble	113	910	50.5	52.4	102.8	5.0	25.1	6.7	13.1	64.7	15.5	5.3
West Lancashire	338	309	51.1	53.2	104.3	-2.9	14.3	6.4	12.7	65.5	15.4	4.9
Wyre	283	367	49.4	54.7	104.0	4.7	22.3	5.5	10.6	59.1	24.8	9.6
Merseyside	654	2,207	695.9	747.9	1,443.7	-5.2	17.2	6.9	12.7	61.8	18.6	7.0
Knowsley *	97	1,616	76.8	80.5	157.4	-9.6	38.4	7.8	14.1	62.6	15.4	5.2
Liverpool *	113	4,100	223.6	239.3	462.9	-10.5	10.7	7.4	12.5	61.1	19.0	7.4
Sefton *	153	1,961	143.0	156.5	299.6	-0.3	19.2	6.4	12.2	61.6	19.8	7.6
St Helens *	133	1,413	91.5	97.0	188.5	-0.9	23.8	6.2	12.6	64.0	17.2	6.1
Wirral *	158	2,126	160.9	174.5	335.3	-1.5	16.0	6.7	12.6	61.2	19.5	7.5
England	130,478	367	23,368.2	24,469.1	47,837.3	2.2	21.9	6.7	12.2	62.8	18.4	7.0

15.1 *(Continued)*

	Area (sq km)	Persons per sq km 1990	Population 1990 (thousands)			Change 1981-1990 (percentages)		Percentage of 1990 population aged				
			Males	Females	Total	Total	Persons aged 75 & over	Under 5	5-14	15 to pension age	Over pension age[1]	75 and over
Wales	20,766	139	1,397.4	1,484.0	2,881.4	2.4	22.6	6.6	12.4	61.5	19.5	7.2
Clwyd	2,430	169	199.2	212.6	411.8	4.6	18.8	6.4	12.4	61.3	19.8	7.6
Alyn and Deeside	154	475	35.9	37.3	73.2	0.3	39.1	6.8	12.9	63.8	16.5	5.8
Colwyn	552	102	26.1	30.1	56.2	14.3	1.4	6.0	11.4	58.2	24.4	10.0
Delyn	281	238	32.6	34.2	66.8	2.0	30.4	6.3	12.8	62.9	17.9	6.5
Glyndwr	968	44	20.5	21.6	42.2	4.5	17.7	6.0	11.9	60.4	21.7	8.3
Rhuddlan	109	521	26.8	29.7	56.5	7.8	12.0	6.1	11.3	58.4	24.2	10.3
Wrexham Maelor	367	319	57.2	59.8	117.0	3.3	24.5	6.7	13.0	62.2	18.1	6.6
Dyfed	5,766	61	170.4	183.6	354.0	6.1	28.3	6.1	12.0	60.9	21.0	7.6
Carmarthen	1,180	49	28.2	29.1	57.3	10.3	26.5	6.0	11.9	60.4	21.6	7.5
Ceredigion	1,794	38	33.1	35.5	68.6	12.1	29.5	5.6	11.4	61.8	21.3	8.2
Dinefwr	972	40	18.9	20.0	39.0	4.9	16.9	5.8	11.9	61.0	21.4	7.9
Llanelli	233	324	36.1	39.5	75.6	-0.3	31.4	6.2	11.7	59.1	23.0	8.6
Preseli	1,151	61	33.8	36.4	70.2	1.5	30.9	6.5	12.7	61.4	19.4	6.7
South Pembrokeshire	436	100	20.4	23.0	43.4	13.3	30.9	6.3	12.7	62.4	18.6	6.7
Gwent	1,377	325	218.7	228.9	447.5	1.3	22.1	6.8	12.5	62.1	18.5	6.6
Blaenau Gwent	127	609	37.9	39.5	77.4	-3.4	20.9	6.7	12.2	60.9	20.2	7.6
Islwyn	102	673	33.7	34.9	68.6	5.5	40.2	6.7	12.4	62.1	18.8	7.0
Monmouth	831	97	40.0	41.0	81.0	13.3	29.0	5.9	12.2	63.3	18.6	6.7
Newport	190	667	61.6	65.4	127.0	-5.6	8.3	7.6	12.7	61.8	17.9	6.1
Torfaen	126	744	45.5	48.1	93.7	3.3	25.6	6.8	12.9	62.7	17.5	5.9
Gwynedd	3,863	62	115.7	125.4	241.1	4.3	19.7	6.1	12.1	59.9	21.8	8.7
Aberconwy	601	90	25.7	28.7	54.4	6.0	13.3	5.5	11.1	57.9	25.6	10.7
Arfon	410	137	27.3	28.9	56.2	2.9	20.2	6.6	12.3	62.3	18.8	7.4
Dwyfor	620	44	12.8	14.2	27.1	4.5	15.4	5.4	11.3	58.3	25.0	9.5
Meirionnydd	1,517	21	15.4	16.9	32.3	3.0	19.0	5.9	11.3	59.3	23.5	9.4
Ynys Mon	715	99	34.4	36.7	71.1	4.5	30.2	6.6	13.4	60.6	19.4	7.4
Mid Glamorgan	1,017	530	263.9	275.7	539.6	-0.3	22.8	7.0	12.9	62.2	17.9	6.3
Cynon Valley	176	366	31.4	33.2	64.6	-4.8	23.0	6.9	12.4	60.4	20.3	7.4
Merthyr Tydfil	111	540	28.9	30.8	59.7	-1.8	16.4	7.5	12.6	61.0	18.8	6.8
Ogwr	286	480	67.5	69.6	137.1	5.2	24.7	6.6	12.5	62.9	18.0	6.3
Rhondda	101	763	37.3	39.5	76.8	-7.0	20.9	7.0	12.6	59.1	21.3	8.0
Rhymney Valley	177	587	50.4	53.7	104.1	-1.3	23.5	7.4	13.7	63.1	15.8	5.3
Taff-Ely	167	583	48.4	48.9	97.3	3.3	26.7	6.9	13.1	64.6	15.4	5.1
Powys	5,077	23	58.1	59.4	117.4	6.2	21.4	6.0	11.9	61.0	21.1	7.7
Brecknock	1,791	23	20.1	21.2	41.3	1.0	19.1	5.8	11.7	60.9	21.6	7.7
Montgomery	2,059	26	26.0	26.6	52.6	8.6	21.0	6.3	12.1	61.4	20.3	7.4
Radnor	1,228	19	12.0	11.6	23.5	10.6	26.7	5.9	11.7	60.6	21.9	8.1
South Glamorgan	416	977	196.2	210.5	406.8	4.3	20.4	7.2	12.6	62.1	18.2	6.7
Cardiff	120	2,391	138.7	148.6	287.2	2.3	19.6	7.4	12.5	61.6	18.5	7.0
Vale of Glamorgan	296	404	57.6	62.0	119.5	9.5	22.7	6.7	12.7	63.3	17.3	6.2
West Glamorgan	820	443	175.3	187.9	363.2	-2.3	27.0	6.5	12.2	61.0	20.4	7.5
Afan	152	319	23.1	25.4	48.4	-11.6	33.0	6.5	12.1	59.9	21.5	7.6
Lliw Valley	218	291	30.7	32.6	63.3	4.9	35.9	6.4	12.2	61.0	20.4	7.6
Neath	204	318	31.1	33.8	64.9	-3.0	24.1	6.5	12.5	60.4	20.7	7.7
Swansea	246	759	90.5	96.1	186.6	-1.7	23.7	6.5	12.1	61.5	19.9	7.3

15.1 (Continued)

	Area (sq km)	Persons per sq km 1990	Population 1990 (thousands)			Change 1981-1990 (percentages)		Percentage of 1990 population aged				
			Males	Females	Total	Total	Persons aged 75 & over	Under 5	5-14	15 to pension age	Over pension age[1]	75 and over
Scotland	77,080	66	2,466.8	2,635.6	5,102.4	-1.5	17.0	6.4	12.4	63.5	17.7	6.4
Borders	4,670	22	49.8	53.7	103.5	2.2	18.6	5.7	11.6	60.9	21.7	8.7
Berwickshire	876	22	9.2	9.8	19.1	4.0	34.8	5.8	11.5	59.8	22.8	9.6
Ettrick and Lauderdale	1,355	25	16.5	17.8	34.3	2.9	15.9	5.9	11.9	61.1	21.1	8.1
Roxburgh	1,540	23	16.9	18.1	35.0	-1.0	12.2	5.3	11.4	61.5	21.9	8.4
Tweeddale	899	17	7.2	8.0	15.2	6.3	19.9	6.0	11.8	60.8	21.4	9.4
Central	2,627	104	131.7	140.4	272.1	-0.5	27.0	6.1	12.7	64.1	17.2	6.1
Clackmannan	160	297	23.1	24.4	47.5	-1.6	34.9	6.5	13.3	63.8	16.4	5.6
Falkirk	291	492	69.4	73.9	143.3	-1.2	26.4	6.1	12.8	63.7	17.4	6.1
Stirling	2,176	37	39.2	42.1	81.4	1.4	24.4	5.8	12.1	64.8	17.3	6.4
Dumfries and Galloway	6,370	23	71.9	76.5	148.4	2.0	24.0	6.0	12.0	61.6	20.4	7.4
Annandale and Eskdale	1,553	24	17.8	18.8	36.6	2.7	38.2	5.5	11.7	61.0	21.8	8.1
Nithsdale	1,433	40	27.9	29.9	57.8	1.9	22.0	6.3	12.2	62.2	19.3	6.9
Stewartry	1,671	14	11.4	12.1	23.5	2.8	19.3	5.6	11.9	60.3	22.2	8.4
Wigtown	1,713	18	14.8	15.7	30.5	0.7	14.8	6.1	12.2	62.1	19.6	6.7
Fife	1,308	264	168.3	177.7	345.9	1.3	23.4	6.5	12.7	62.8	18.0	6.6
Dunfermline	302	431	64.2	65.7	129.9	2.7	29.3	6.8	13.3	63.2	16.6	5.6
Kirkcaldy	248	593	71.0	76.0	147.1	-1.6	19.7	6.6	12.8	62.5	18.0	6.4
North East Fife	758	91	33.0	35.9	68.9	5.1	22.8	5.6	11.4	62.5	20.4	8.7
Grampian	8,707	58	248.5	257.6	506.1	4.4	15.0	6.4	12.5	64.3	16.8	6.3
Aberdeen City	184	1,144	102.0	109.1	211.1	-0.7	15.8	6.0	10.8	64.7	18.5	7.0
Banff and Buchan	1,528	56	42.1	43.0	85.0	2.7	17.0	6.6	13.4	63.6	16.4	6.1
Gordon	2,214	34	37.1	37.5	74.6	17.0	16.3	7.0	15.3	64.1	13.7	5.4
Kincardine and Deeside	2,550	20	25.3	25.6	50.9	20.1	10.7	6.9	13.7	64.8	14.6	5.6
Moray	2,231	38	42.1	42.4	84.5	1.2	12.4	6.5	12.9	63.8	16.7	6.2
Highland	25,304	8	100.2	104.1	204.3	4.8	21.2	6.4	13.7	62.7	17.2	6.4
Badenoch and Strathspey	2,317	5	5.4	5.7	11.2	13.5	19.6	5.6	12.3	63.4	18.7	6.9
Caithness	1,776	15	13.3	13.5	26.8	-3.1	12.8	6.6	14.0	63.0	16.5	5.8
Inverness	2,789	23	30.6	32.5	63.1	10.5	36.6	6.7	13.0	63.6	16.7	6.4
Lochaber	4,468	4	9.3	9.7	19.0	-2.4	20.0	6.7	14.1	63.1	16.1	5.9
Nairn	422	25	5.1	5.3	10.4	4.7	3.1	6.0	13.6	62.5	17.8	6.4
Ross and Cromarty	4,976	10	24.4	24.6	48.9	4.2	19.2	6.3	15.0	62.9	15.8	5.7
Skye and Lochalsh	2,691	4	5.8	6.1	11.8	11.3	14.1	6.2	13.7	59.0	21.1	8.5
Sutherland	5,865	2	6.3	6.7	13.1	-2.0	12.8	5.5	12.4	59.5	22.6	9.0
Lothian	1,756	427	361.8	387.8	749.6	0.0	16.2	6.2	11.1	65.2	17.5	6.6
East Lothian	713	120	41.6	43.9	85.5	5.9	22.4	6.0	10.9	64.7	18.4	6.9
Edinburgh City	261	1,664	207.0	227.5	434.5	-2.6	13.5	6.1	10.0	64.1	19.8	7.9
Midlothian	358	227	40.1	41.2	81.3	-2.5	22.3	6.2	12.5	66.5	14.8	4.6
West Lothian	423	350	73.0	75.3	148.3	6.4	23.2	6.8	13.6	67.7	11.9	3.9
Strathclyde	13,529	170	1,110.3	1,195.7	2,306.0	-4.5	15.1	6.6	12.6	63.6	17.3	6.0
Argyll and Bute	6,497	10	32.2	34.0	66.2	1.7	10.1	6.5	13.2	61.0	19.3	8.1
Bearsden and Milngavie	36	1,123	19.7	21.2	40.9	4.3	17.7	5.1	11.8	66.2	16.9	5.6
Clydebank	35	1,324	22.4	24.5	46.9	-11.2	16.1	5.9	12.0	63.7	18.4	5.5
Clydesdale	1,322	44	28.5	30.0	58.6	2.2	19.7	6.3	13.5	64.0	16.2	5.8
Cumbernauld and Kilsyth	103	613	30.9	32.2	63.1	1.4	31.6	6.3	14.5	68.5	10.7	3.1
Cumnock and Doon Valley	800	54	21.0	22.1	43.0	-4.2	26.4	6.9	12.5	63.1	17.5	5.6
Cunninghame	878	157	66.3	71.2	137.5	0.2	19.1	6.6	13.7	63.3	16.4	5.9
Dumbarton	472	169	38.7	41.0	79.8	1.0	22.2	7.0	14.0	63.1	15.9	5.6
East Kilbride	285	291	40.6	42.5	83.1	-0.2	24.7	6.1	12.2	67.2	14.4	3.9
Eastwood	115	530	29.4	31.6	61.0	13.4	17.5	6.2	12.0	65.6	16.2	6.0
Glasgow City	198	3,485	328.2	361.0	689.2	-11.0	7.5	6.8	11.6	62.1	19.4	7.1
Hamilton	131	814	51.7	54.8	106.6	-2.6	19.1	6.5	13.9	64.9	14.7	4.8
Inverclyde	158	593	44.9	48.6	93.5	-7.6	20.1	6.4	12.5	63.0	18.1	6.3
Kilmarnock and Loudoun	373	217	39.0	42.1	81.1	-1.6	26.0	6.8	12.9	62.5	17.8	6.3
Kyle and Carrick	1,317	86	54.2	59.6	113.7	0.5	21.6	5.8	12.0	62.1	20.1	7.4
Monklands	164	638	50.5	54.0	104.5	-6.1	18.7	6.9	13.9	64.2	15.0	4.7
Motherwell	172	853	71.3	75.5	146.8	-3.0	20.4	6.7	13.3	63.3	16.7	5.6
Renfrew	307	654	96.9	104.2	201.0	-4.2	21.1	6.5	12.3	64.8	16.4	5.5
Strathkelvin	164	547	43.9	45.8	89.7	2.6	10.3	6.4	13.5	67.1	13.0	3.9

15.1 *(Continued)*

	Area (sq km)	Persons per sq km 1990	Population 1990 (thousands)			Change 1981-1990 (percentages)		Percentage of 1990 population aged				
			Males	Females	Total	Total	Persons aged 75 & over	Under 5	5-14	15 to pension age	Over pension age[1]	75 and over
Tayside	7,502	53	188.8	205.2	394.0	-0.8	15.8	6.0	12.1	62.2	19.8	7.5
Angus	2,031	47	46.2	49.1	95.4	2.5	19.1	5.9	12.9	61.9	19.2	7.5
Dundee City	235	735	82.5	90.4	172.9	-6.4	11.4	6.4	11.8	62.1	19.8	7.3
Perth and Kinross	5,236	24	60.1	65.7	125.8	5.4	19.4	5.5	11.7	62.5	20.2	7.9
Orkney	976	20	9.6	10.0	19.6	2.0	22.9	6.6	13.0	61.5	19.0	7.7
Shetland	1,433	16	10.8	11.5	22.3	-15.5	10.3	7.3	14.9	61.6	16.2	6.7
Western Isles	2,898	11	15.2	15.4	30.7	-2.8	7.9	5.8	13.9	59.4	20.9	9.3
Northern Ireland	13,483	118	780.0	809.0	1,589.0	3.4	19.9	8.5	16.4	60.6	14.5	5.1
Antrim	405	118	..	..	48.0	..	..	..	..	..	..	..
Ards	368	118	..	..	65.0	..	..	..	..	..	..	..
Armagh	667	74	..	..	49.0	..	..	..	..	..	..	..
Ballymena	634	90	..	..	57.0	..	..	..	..	..	..	..
Ballymoney	417	58	..	..	24.0	..	..	..	..	..	..	..
Banbridge	441	73	..	..	32.0	..	..	..	..	..	..	..
Belfast	130	2,270	..	..	295.0	..	..	..	..	..	..	..
Carrickfergus	85	365	..	..	31.0	..	..	..	..	..	..	..
Castlereagh	84	692	..	..	58.0	..	..	..	..	..	..	..
Coleraine	478	102	..	..	49.0	..	..	..	..	..	..	..
Cookstown	512	54	..	..	28.0	..	..	..	..	..	..	..
Craigavon	280	279	..	..	78.0	..	..	..	..	..	..	..
Derry	373	269	..	..	101.0	..	..	..	..	..	..	..
Down	638	90	..	..	58.0	..	..	..	..	..	..	..
Dungannon	763	57	..	..	44.0	..	..	..	..	..	..	..
Fermanagh	1,700	30	..	..	51.0	..	..	..	..	..	..	..
Larne	337	86	..	..	29.0	..	..	..	..	..	..	..
Limavady	585	51	..	..	30.0	..	..	..	..	..	..	..
Lisburn	436	226	..	..	99.0	..	..	..	..	..	..	..
Magherafelt	562	59	..	..	33.0	..	..	..	..	..	..	..
Moyle	494	30	..	..	15.0	..	..	..	..	..	..	..
Newry and Mourne	886	101	..	..	90.0	..	..	..	..	..	..	..
Newtownabbey	151	483	..	..	73.0	..	..	..	..	..	..	..
North Down	72	1,008	..	..	73.0	..	..	..	..	..	..	..
Omagh	1,124	41	..	..	46.0	..	..	..	..	..	..	..
Strabane	861	42	..	..	36.0	..	..	..	..	..	..	..

* Urban Programme authorities.
1 Women aged 60 and over, men aged 65 and over.

Source: Office of Population Censuses and Surveys; Welsh Office; General Register Offices for Scotland and Northern Ireland

15.2 Housing and households

	Housing starts (numbers)		Local authority tenants				Households 1990		
	Private enterprise 1990	Housing associations, local authorities etc. 1990	Total number of tenancies April 1991	Average weekly unrebated rent per dwelling (£) April 1991	Community charge[1] (£) April 1991	Stock of dwellings (thousands) 1990[2]	All households (thousands)	Average size	Lone parent households as a % of all households
United Kingdom	140,674	28,152	4,947,088	..	.	23,355.5	22,440.4	2.52	..
North	7,781	1,256	354,626	22.96	265.87	1,277.9	1,204.8	2.52	10.2
Cleveland	1,140	422	55,166	26.70	310.55	221.1	211.2	2.60	11.7
Hartlepool *	344	108	9,481	25.78	297.00	36.4	33.7	2.65	12.8
Langbaurgh *	265	70	13,794	25.45	331.80	58.1	56.1	2.55	10.6
Middlesbrough *	198	170	15,678	29.90	309.42	56.6	53.2	2.63	13.2
Stockton-on-Tees *	333	74	16,213	25.20	300.28	69.9	68.2	2.57	10.9
Cumbria	1,751	219	30,667	25.62	255.14	207.0	190.7	2.54	9.1
Allerdale	343	19	5,455	24.15	211.63	40.2	37.2	2.57	9.9
Barrow-in-Furness	377	23	3,914	29.78	276.35	30.7	27.8	2.49	8.3
Carlisle	240	84	9,530	24.55	298.50	42.2	40.4	2.53	10.1
Copeland	249	0	5,050	25.98	228.62	29.0	27.1	2.62	9.8
Eden	245	18	2,005	24.50	217.40	20.0	18.1	2.61	8.9
South Lakeland	297	75	4,713	26.09	273.57	44.9	40.2	2.45	7.3
Durham	1,592	188	71,797	23.72	248.08	250.2	235.8	2.51	9.8
Chester-le-Street	235	24	6,904	24.15	268.93	21.6	21.2	2.49	8.9
Darlington	284	55	7,578	20.31	275.63	41.4	40.1	2.45	10.9
Derwentside	209	0	10,921	27.33	276.44	36.4	33.6	2.53	9.5
Durham	204	42	9,672	22.23	278.87	33.8	33.7	2.54	8.8
Easington	87	0	15,530	24.11	214.90	40.9	37.2	2.54	9.9
Sedgefield	242	51	13,071	22.76	229.92	38.7	34.7	2.51	10.4
Teesdale	120	16	1,202	19.40	172.54	10.6	9.8	2.53	7.9
Wear Valley	211	0	6,919	25.10	216.26	26.9	25.5	2.51	9.9
Northumberland	..	..	30,565	21.39	279.30	128.7	116.9	2.55	8.9
Alnwick	142	-	2,594	22.66	256.68	13.6	12.2	2.54	10.1
Berwick-upon-Tweed	110	7	3,231	17.39	219.34	12.8	10.6	2.43	10.8
Blyth Valley	..	..	8,825	21.77	295.00	32.2	30.8	2.58	8.9
Castle Morpeth	133	0	3,564	25.41	304.34	20.2	18.3	2.58	7.7
Tynedale	148	0	4,204	18.46	302.70	23.9	21.6	2.58	8.4
Wansbeck	261	21	8,147	21.91	255.00	26.1	23.3	2.55	8.9
Tyne and Wear	2,176	385	166,431	21.22	254.80	470.9	450.3	2.48	10.6
Gateshead *	239	108	30,965	23.81	227.18	85.0	82.5	2.47	9.6
Newcastle upon Tyne *	348	59	40,238	25.34	316.32	120.0	113.9	2.40	11.0
North Tyneside *	726	53	24,236	19.59	284.50	82.7	78.0	2.44	10.8
South Tyneside *	325	112	26,142	19.04	220.00	65.6	61.7	2.51	10.9
Sunderland *	538	53	44,850	17.90	215.05	117.6	114.3	2.57	10.7
Yorkshire & Humberside	9,857	2,056	469,603	21.64	228.43	2,012.1	1,963.8	2.49	9.8
Humberside	2,368	328	77,120	22.37	257.86	353.1	336.5	2.53	10.0
Beverley	393	0	4,966	19.26	286.00	45.5	45.2	2.54	8.3
Boothferry	324	0	4,082	21.81	220.13	26.1	25.4	2.60	8.5
Cleethorpes	121	0	3,030	22.70	293.91	27.9	26.8	2.52	8.0
East Yorkshire	476	40	4,285	23.15	247.18	36.4	35.5	2.48	8.8
Glanford	371	0	3,377	17.43	254.11	29.0	28.4	2.56	9.0
Great Grimsby	130	44	7,236	23.23	291.00	36.4	34.5	2.55	12.6
Holderness	204	0	2,180	22.65	287.50	20.3	19.8	2.58	8.4
Kingston-upon-Hull *	281	244	40,177	23.00	230.00	106.3	97.6	2.49	11.3
Scunthorpe	68	0	7,787	22.06	269.00	25.0	23.4	2.53	12.5
North Yorkshire	2,001	310	34,895	24.35	203.69	298.6	286.6	2.47	8.0
Craven	77	66	1,936	26.03	171.41	21.8	20.3	2.46	8.9
Hambleton	362	22	4,307	23.83	190.39	32.2	30.1	2.56	8.3
Harrogate	261	0	5,308	25.75	253.90	60.4	59.3	2.42	7.6
Richmondshire	144	0	2,347	27.44	189.30	18.8	19.2	2.64	8.9
Ryedale	325	44	0	.	207.19	37.5	35.8	2.53	6.3
Scarborough	228	42	6,587	23.95	183.05	49.0	44.3	2.35	7.8
Selby	468	55	4,791	23.95	204.99	35.4	36.2	2.59	7.1
York	136	81	9,619	23.19	184.00	43.5	41.6	2.39	9.9

15.2 (Continued)

	Housing starts (numbers)		Local authority tenants				Households 1990		
	Private enterprise 1990	Housing associations, local authorities etc. 1990	Total number of tenancies April 1991	Average weekly unrebated rent per dwelling (£) April 1991	Community charge[1] (£) April 1991	Stock of dwellings (thousands) 1990[2]	All households (thousands)	Average size	Lone parent households as a % of all households
South Yorkshire	1,903	718	160,942	20.90	210.45	525.5	515.4	2.49	9.7
Barnsley *	708	66	27,316	20.44	182.20	90.7	86.3	2.56	9.9
Doncaster *	432	67	29,881	18.63	200.34	115.3	113.3	2.57	10.6
Rotherham *	403	171	30,433	15.36	232.46	99.7	98.3	2.58	10.0
Sheffield *	360	414	73,312	24.29	217.42	219.7	217.6	2.39	8.9
West Yorkshire	..	..	196,646	21.48	236.21	835.0	825.2	2.48	10.4
Bradford *	566	133	31,008	25.98	223.00	182.2	180.9	2.57	11.1
Calderdale	309	92	13,668	24.93	177.62	80.5	79.5	2.46	10.8
Kirklees *	661	97	30,651	24.36	239.61	154.0	149.6	2.48	10.1
Leeds *	1,138	247	80,855	18.70	269.45	291.4	290.8	2.42	10.4
Wakefield	770	89	40,464	20.22	213.05	126.9	124.4	2.51	9.6
East Midlands	12,459	1,218	309,882	23.33	255.82	1,628.5	1,576.6	2.52	9.3
Derbyshire	2,984	277	73,637	21.10	266.66	383.0	365.4	2.53	9.1
Amber Valley	436	5	6,855	19.82	257.25	46.6	44.7	2.54	8.4
Bolsover	340	0	6,881	20.72	212.49	29.5	27.5	2.60	9.0
Chesterfield	301	32	12,065	20.38	264.63	41.3	41.9	2.38	8.8
Derby *	451	132	17,394	20.90	270.00	90.6	86.6	2.48	10.3
Erewash	266	32	7,144	21.47	274.45	43.6	42.1	2.54	9.3
High Peak	203	0	5,322	24.32	260.79	33.9	31.9	2.63	9.8
North East Derbyshire	334	0	10,092	20.75	278.62	39.9	37.8	2.56	8.7
South Derbyshire	506	73	4,183	23.21	296.89	28.8	26.9	2.65	8.0
Derbyshire Dales	147	3	3,701	20.77	277.03	28.7	26.0	2.50	7.0
Leicestershire	2,450	329	58,238	25.51	273.90	349.5	346.8	2.56	9.4
Blaby	543	4	2,781	15.50	227.85	31.8	32.9	2.58	7.9
Charnwood	309	69	7,369	20.46	257.08	56.5	58.5	2.56	8.2
Harborough	354	71	2,940	26.39	264.78	26.8	26.9	2.55	7.1
Hinckley and Bosworth	351	0	4,478	24.33	238.25	39.0	38.1	2.57	8.0
Leicester *	259	143	29,554	29.15	319.00	111.5	108.4	2.53	12.1
Melton	143	0	2,301	22.30	250.49	17.6	17.8	2.51	9.7
North West Leicestershire	273	20	5,548	21.26	267.15	32.9	31.4	2.57	7.8
Oadby and Wigston	106	22	1,597	20.80	287.00	20.5	20.0	2.57	9.0
Rutland	112	0	1,670	24.61	254.04	12.9	12.8	2.80	7.5
Lincolnshire	2,774	140	42,577	24.23	212.31	249.4	233.1	2.49	8.4
Boston	273	7	5,357	22.58	215.00	22.4	21.1	2.45	7.5
East Lindsey	562	66	5,457	27.42	217.59	53.1	47.7	2.47	7.9
Lincoln	201	50	9,500	23.20	224.00	35.6	33.8	2.34	10.5
North Kesteven	724	16	4,778	26.12	204.96	33.6	32.7	2.53	9.1
South Holland	186	0	4,916	22.81	217.21	27.8	27.2	2.46	8.4
South Kesteven	538	0	8,176	25.09	199.72	45.2	41.9	2.54	8.0
West Lindsey	290	1	4,393	22.42	210.11	31.8	28.7	2.62	7.0
Northamptonshire	..	..	47,847	23.46	219.23	233.2	225.6	2.54	9.6
Corby	209	-	8,070	20.32	250.00	20.6	19.1	2.69	12.9
Daventry	217	16	4,094	22.74	249.05	25.0	24.2	2.64	8.0
East Northamptonshire	215	30	4,761	22.30	219.50	27.3	26.3	2.58	8.4
Kettering	..	..	4,915	24.50	229.50	31.7	29.8	2.53	8.8
Northampton	654	14	16,111	25.07	226.46	73.3	74.2	2.46	10.7
South Northamptonshire	219	9	3,839	25.66	226.45	27.6	26.0	2.58	8.1
Wellingborough	201	58	6,057	22.51	129.00	27.8	26.1	2.55	9.4
Nottinghamshire	2,033	361	87,583	23.26	276.70	413.4	405.6	2.48	9.8
Ashfield	285	0	9,594	19.30	245.49	44.0	43.2	2.53	8.2
Bassetlaw	380	29	9,172	20.15	281.25	42.2	40.9	2.53	9.4
Broxtowe	244	31	5,737	24.93	265.00	44.1	44.3	2.48	8.5
Gedling	168	44	4,622	21.23	266.58	43.8	44.5	2.47	7.9
Mansfield	270	0	9,153	22.92	295.00	41.7	40.0	2.50	8.9
Newark	126	0	7,121	21.47	274.22	42.8	40.3	2.54	9.0
Nottingham *	302	209	38,045	25.46	295.00	115.8	111.6	2.42	13.1
Rushcliffe	258	48	4,139	22.99	265.11	39.1	40.9	2.46	7.0

15.2 *(Continued)*

	Housing starts (numbers)		Local authority tenants				Households 1990		
	Private enterprise 1990	Housing associations, local authorities etc. 1990	Total number of tenancies April 1991	Average weekly unrebated rent per dwelling (£) April 1991	Community charge[1] (£) April 1991	Stock of dwellings (thousands) 1990[2]	All households (thousands)	Average size	Lone parent households as a % of all households
East Anglia	7,751	849	143,320	27.74	240.45	863.7	805.4	2.52	8.1
Cambridgeshire	2,447	310	46,791	26.23	241.85	268.7	256.0	2.56	8.4
Cambridge	242	0	9,760	26.56	329.00	41.5	41.9	2.34	8.8
East Cambridgeshire	223	41	4,280	26.32	215.20	25.2	23.7	2.56	6.6
Fenland	565	39	4,620	24.51	232.15	32.5	29.0	2.54	7.5
Huntingdon	612	77	7,753	24.63	196.28	56.2	56.4	2.69	9.2
Peterborough	470	121	13,045	26.12	266.73	65.0	60.0	2.55	9.6
South Cambridgeshire	335	32	7,333	28.68	204.56	48.4	45.1	2.62	7.0
Norfolk	2,727	344	54,378	24.72	231.47	327.1	301.9	2.45	7.9
Breckland	601	100	6,818	26.80	234.80	45.2	41.2	2.51	7.4
Broadland	467	22	2	20.53	228.37	44.1	41.2	2.54	6.6
Great Yarmouth	312	47	7,374	23.29	259.74	37.8	35.6	2.48	8.4
North Norfolk	427	53	5,842	24.21	184.69	45.0	39.2	2.39	7.1
Norwich	149	15	20,326	25.05	276.91	54.7	51.2	2.25	9.5
South Norfolk	375	106	5,272	27.12	230.33	42.6	40.3	2.49	7.3
West Norfolk	396	1	8,744	22.41	203.83	57.6	53.2	2.50	8.7
Suffolk	2,577	195	42,151	26.26	249.99	268.0	247.6	2.55	8.0
Babergh	264	34	4,750	33.00	234.88	33.3	29.8	2.57	7.5
Forest Heath	302	7	3,765	26.96	217.00	22.1	22.2	2.69	7.3
Ipswich	32	49	10,245	27.96	309.47	49.6	45.4	2.46	9.9
Mid Suffolk	313	42	4,453	26.43	230.25	32.5	29.6	2.62	8.0
St Edmundsbury	307	45	7,859	23.40	239.22	36.8	34.9	2.58	8.0
Suffolk Coastal	993	0	5,173	23.84	230.41	46.8	42.7	2.59	7.3
Waveney	366	18	5,906	23.22	252.09	46.8	43.0	2.46	7.4
South East	32,935	6,694	1,277,537	31.49	236.81	7,137.0	6,923.1	2.47	9.7
Bedfordshire	1,617	368	24,520	28.30	262.58	207.5	204.9	2.59	9.5
Luton	524	215	10,528	30.01	249.75	67.3	64.9	2.63	11.0
Mid Bedfordshire	499	127	7,092	24.28	265.93	43.2	42.4	2.66	8.5
North Bedfordshire	153	26	109	32.41	263.74	53.9	54.3	2.53	8.7
South Bedfordshire	441	0	6,791	29.79	277.87	43.1	43.3	2.53	9.2
Berkshire	..	..	37,057	30.20	253.23	289.6	286.5	2.60	8.6
Bracknell	.	.	8,496	27.18	228.04	..	41.6	2.55	7.7
Bracknell Forest	228	54	.	.	..	37.4	.	.	.
Newbury	..	..	142	25.92	245.67	52.3	51.7	2.70	8.1
Reading	342	205	9,250	31.04	323.68	54.6	51.4	2.49	10.6
Slough	..	..	9,018	31.11	190.30	39.0	38.0	2.62	11.8
Windsor and Maidenhead	92	32	6,780	30.04	286.96	53.9	48.9	2.51	7.7
Wokingham	520	1	3,371	33.62	262.77	52.5	54.9	2.70	6.4
Buckinghamshire	2,558	1,054	24,804	26.20	269.73	249.0	241.1	2.63	8.6
Aylesbury Vale	540	20	9,848	26.37	213.13	55.5	55.1	2.62	8.4
Chiltern	181	47	0	.	251.08	35.8	33.6	2.56	7.5
Milton Keynes	615	866	6,150	23.73	299.42	71.2	69.9	2.64	9.3
Milton Keynes (New Town)	505	0	.	.	..	.	.	.	.
South Buckinghamshire	214	60	215	27.27	220.89	25.6	23.1	2.60	8.2
Wycombe	503	61	8,591	27.75	268.11	60.9	59.4	2.66	8.7
East Sussex	1,527	354	36,032	29.76	246.44	313.2	306.2	2.26	8.2
Brighton	176	48	10,810	32.66	255.60	66.7	62.1	2.21	9.1
Eastbourne	227	45	5,221	28.93	274.00	38.1	36.7	2.19	7.6
Hastings	160	43	4,817	27.90	274.00	35.4	35.1	2.26	8.8
Hove	55	103	3,729	28.24	196.97	40.4	43.3	2.09	7.9
Lewes	279	51	4,060	27.54	245.09	38.1	38.1	2.34	8.5
Rother	177	0	3,473	28.64	232.08	39.2	36.5	2.27	7.9
Wealdon	453	64	3,922	29.93	246.66	55.3	54.5	2.46	7.3

15.2 (Continued)

	Housing starts (numbers)		Local authority tenants				Households 1990		
	Private enterprise 1990	Housing associations, local authorities etc. 1990	Total number of tenancies April 1991	Average weekly unrebated rent per dwelling (£) April 1991	Community charge[1] (£) April 1991	Stock of dwellings (thousands) 1990[2]	All households (thousands)	Average size	Lone parent households as a % of all households
Essex	4,431	548	92,838	29.76	236.61	633.5	601.5	2.52	8.5
Basildon	274	66	5,637	31.04	316.10	68.5	60.7	2.56	10.1
Basildon (New Town)	19	0	.	.	..	.	.	.	.
Braintree	772	53	10,445	28.13	214.66	49.5	44.7	2.55	8.3
Brentwood	81	0	3,157	38.20	229.44	28.9	26.9	2.47	8.6
Castle Point	189	0	1,980	32.65	215.00	34.0	33.0	2.54	7.9
Chelmsford	328	159	8,731	27.47	228.10	61.2	58.2	2.58	7.6
Colchester	614	29	8,347	26.98	208.18	58.1	59.3	2.54	9.4
Epping Forest	279	78	8,142	32.10	248.28	47.7	43.5	2.55	7.6
Harlow	50	91	14,025	25.65	319.00	30.0	27.6	2.53	10.1
Maldon	142	7	2,209	29.57	203.23	21.5	20.8	2.54	9.0
Rochford	188	0	2,185	30.60	217.14	30.0	28.5	2.57	7.9
Southend-on-Sea	155	0	7,599	37.79	208.00	69.0	68.9	2.38	8.3
Tendring	409	37	4,031	28.68	205.62	58.3	57.0	2.32	6.3
Thurrock	779	0	12,751	29.90	268.10	51.1	47.1	2.66	10.0
Uttlesford	152	28	3,599	29.54	208.15	26.0	25.2	2.60	8.5
Greater London	7,392	2,589	701,159	35.81	240.48	2,820.3	2,762.7	2.41	11.4
Barking and Dagenham	56	7	26,185	23.64	170.00	60.1	57.1	2.56	11.5
Barnet	337	22	14,410	35.64	247.00	118.7	120.7	2.52	9.9
Bexley	58	0	9,390	25.65	202.00	85.9	86.3	2.54	9.0
Brent *	193	173	19,637	33.50	328.00	93.5	102.3	2.47	13.2
Bromley	301	81	12,835	41.15	190.00	122.7	123.0	2.41	8.7
Camden	2	187	32,074	31.48	300.00	79.0	81.7	2.15	11.7
City of London	3	0	2,299	37.26	175.00	3.4	1.8	1.91	11.5
City of Westminster	63	20	18,345	42.90	36.00	101.0	79.2	2.10	10.1
Croydon	155	93	17,710	41.95	180.00	126.7	125.0	2.51	10.1
Ealing	127	114	19,512	56.46	255.00	106.8	116.9	2.47	10.5
Enfield	842	429	16,330	43.57	248.00	103.5	104.2	2.51	9.7
Greenwich *	31	0	33,913	31.90	242.00	87.5	85.4	2.49	12.5
Hackney *	12	0	43,823	32.31	322.00	76.5	79.5	2.37	18.3
Hammersmith and Fulham *	105	0	16,685	40.79	247.00	67.4	67.8	2.14	14.0
Haringey	11	226	22,642	41.81	419.81	82.0	80.0	2.38	12.8
Harrow	244	32	7,017	43.80	253.00	78.6	73.2	2.61	8.8
Havering	229	0	13,699	30.43	229.00	92.2	90.1	2.55	8.4
Hillingdon	..	..	15,001	38.76	215.00	94.8	89.9	2.58	9.1
Hounslow	266	26	17,979	29.50	285.00	80.4	76.7	2.54	10.2
Islington *	174	61	38,309	39.23	376.19	74.2	76.2	2.23	14.9
Kensington and Chelsea *	203	24	7,896	45.22	189.29	77.4	59.3	2.06	9.6
Kingston-upon-Thames	280	20	6,180	50.86	239.12	55.8	58.3	2.36	8.0
Lambeth *	50	0	46,163	29.43	424.89	107.6	99.5	2.28	16.1
Lewisham *	..	..	36,694	33.22	168.00	98.2	93.3	2.40	13.6
Merton	117	0	10,086	44.84	269.00	72.9	67.9	2.41	9.3
Newham *	63	129	28,947	30.58	304.00	81.0	78.3	2.65	13.1
Redbridge	232	0	8,924	56.88	255.00	89.0	91.7	2.52	8.5
Richmond-upon-Thames	..	..	8,631	39.80	279.00	70.8	72.8	2.26	8.0
Southwark *	5	35	55,775	34.07	188.27	100.7	93.3	2.37	15.5
Sutton	371	18	10,483	35.09	259.50	71.4	68.7	2.41	9.4
Tower Hamlets *	..	..	39,802	30.02	147.00	67.1	65.9	2.47	14.8
Waltham Forest	302	55	19,615	32.51	296.50	86.8	86.1	2.45	11.3
Wandsworth *	86	49	24,168	45.95	0.00	106.8	110.6	2.26	13.3
Hampshire	..	..	97,565	30.63	215.63	622.1	600.8	2.52	9.2
Basingstoke and Deane	..	..	10,112	29.98	186.98	55.4	54.5	2.58	8.4
East Hampshire	212	29	4,428	32.15	223.27	40.4	38.3	2.62	8.7
Eastleigh	543	7	4,856	28.04	245.11	41.6	39.6	2.61	8.4
Fareham	275	101	3,214	28.16	225.00	39.8	38.7	2.61	9.4
Gosport	83	38	5,270	30.00	246.00	31.6	27.6	2.60	10.4
Hart	502	36	2,503	30.49	225.41	32.1	29.1	2.67	10.3
Havant	67	21	3,759	34.00	229.30	48.4	44.5	2.56	11.5
New Forest	572	0	6,495	36.72	199.13	70.2	65.7	2.44	7.9
Portsmouth	90	108	18,940	30.87	179.00	74.6	75.9	2.34	9.7
Rushmoor	71	0	5,463	29.99	218.00	29.8	30.5	2.55	9.0
Southampton	165	31	19,929	28.17	255.00	78.7	80.4	2.42	9.7
Test Valley	415	24	6,584	32.92	180.40	40.4	39.7	2.54	8.8
Winchester	288	39	6,012	31.13	211.94	39.2	36.1	2.57	7.9

15.2 (Continued)

	Housing starts (numbers)		Local authority tenants				Households 1990		
	Private enterprise 1990	Housing associations, local authorities etc. 1990	Total number of tenancies April 1991	Average weekly unrebated rent per dwelling (£) April 1991	Community charge[1] (£) April 1991	Stock of dwellings (thousands) 1990[2]	All households (thousands)	Average size	Lone parent households as a % of all households
Hertfordshire	..	..	85,546	24.46	251.53	390.3	382.4	2.54	8.7
Broxbourne	304	29	4,415	36.67	220.51	32.3	31.7	2.60	9.1
Dacorum	57	16	13,832	26.30	226.75	53.1	52.3	2.50	8.3
East Hertfordshire	251	0	7,586	33.71	229.24	46.4	46.1	2.58	8.3
Hertsmere	111	43	6,571	32.17	228.71	36.2	33.2	2.57	8.5
North Hertfordshire	209	13	10,512	27.52	228.92	46.1	43.6	2.57	8.7
St Albans	..	..	6,865	35.51	243.15	48.0	49.5	2.52	8.0
Stevenage	94	51	11,976	26.87	293.20	29.7	29.5	2.50	10.4
Three Rivers	37	0	5,807	29.87	275.21	30.6	29.8	2.62	8.9
Watford	182	0	5,929	26.88	294.00	29.7	29.6	2.52	8.6
Welwyn Hatfield	112	0	12,053	26.77	313.90	38.2	37.0	2.46	9.3
Isle of Wight	144	0	59	37.74	214.36	54.1	52.8	2.38	7.7
Medina	22	0	0	.	195.46	23.1	29.3	2.42	7.6
South Wight	122	0	59	37.74	237.94	31.0	23.5	2.33	7.8
Kent	2,838	556	61,523	33.42	178.84	621.0	593.9	2.52	8.8
Ashford	164	33	7,470	38.82	175.86	38.0	37.2	2.57	8.7
Canterbury	122	98	6,227	41.62	194.00	53.7	52.2	2.46	9.1
Dartford	376	11	5,734	32.54	205.69	30.9	28.3	2.67	9.6
Dover	163	0	6,223	38.41	192.69	44.4	42.7	2.45	8.1
Gillingham	126	83	3,844	30.55	172.96	37.6	35.5	2.64	10.3
Gravesham	88	9	7,378	32.48	153.82	36.8	33.9	2.58	7.8
Maidstone	334	19	8,097	27.21	218.28	54.0	53.2	2.53	9.0
Rochester-upon-Medway	448	151	0	.	50.93	58.5	57.1	2.59	9.8
Sevenoaks	160	35	57	18.63	190.90	44.6	39.6	2.62	8.4
Shepway	130	-	4,213	29.96	203.45	41.0	36.9	2.34	8.0
Swale	190	40	6	27.50	194.43	46.5	45.2	2.57	8.3
Thanet	151	33	6,671	27.83	174.63	54.9	54.1	2.36	9.2
Tonbridge and Malling	239	14	85	27.45	208.42	40.5	38.6	2.58	8.0
Tunbridge Wells	147	30	5,518	34.13	208.27	39.8	39.4	2.45	8.3
Oxfordshire	1,563	157	33,505	28.56	282.73	218.0	218.8	2.63	8.7
Cherwell	398	82	7,287	27.73	249.21	46.1	46.6	2.72	9.7
Oxford	121	2	10,297	27.40	344.46	39.6	44.3	2.58	10.0
South Oxfordshire	291	66	6,055	35.20	309.14	52.7	49.6	2.56	8.2
Vale of White Horse	446	7	5,447	25.97	265.39	42.9	41.8	2.67	7.8
West Oxfordshire	307	0	4,419	26.69	240.04	36.7	36.6	2.60	7.4
Surrey	2,104	278	48,833	34.32	266.94	417.0	384.6	2.54	8.5
Elmbridge	364	11	5,183	36.33	338.54	48.6	42.8	2.46	7.8
Epsom and Ewell	34	0	1,851	33.12	327.00	26.6	24.5	2.60	8.7
Guildford	348	6	6,484	35.07	250.50	50.1	48.0	2.53	8.7
Mole Valley	89	38	4,245	26.75	254.91	32.9	29.5	2.53	7.1
Reigate and Banstead	351	12	6,264	36.92	270.82	48.2	45.0	2.47	9.1
Runnymede	155	0	3,929	38.46	198.00	30.4	27.0	2.58	8.8
Spelthorne	31	100	3,756	40.98	247.00	38.0	34.6	2.42	7.7
Surrey Heath	294	0	3,048	28.33	252.50	31.2	30.7	2.71	10.4
Tandrige	128	0	3,495	27.05	273.35	30.3	27.4	2.64	8.0
Waverley	185	71	6,125	34.69	256.17	45.9	42.4	2.53	8.8
Woking	125	40	4,453	35.00	259.68	34.8	32.8	2.57	8.8
West Sussex	1,726	230	34,096	32.55	208.99	301.5	287.0	2.40	7.6
Adur	20	19	3,407	31.16	266.13	25.8	23.7	2.37	8.6
Arun	452	0	4,795	3,545.00	220.17	60.1	55.8	2.27	6.0
Chichester	277	10	6,645	32.41	170.25	45.0	43.4	2.37	9.0
Crawley	310	54	10,704	30.22	235.00	30.9	32.9	2.55	10.7
Horsham	358	61	5,715	35.34	196.83	46.5	42.3	2.55	7.1
Mid Sussex	257	49	0	.	205.10	50.0	45.7	2.57	6.6
Worthing	52	37	2,830	32.84	195.00	43.3	43.2	2.21	7.0

15.2 *(Continued)*

	Housing starts (numbers)		Local authority tenants				Households 1990		
	Private enterprise 1990	Housing associations, local authorities etc. 1990	Total number of tenancies April 1991	Average weekly unrebated rent per dwelling (£) April 1991	Community charge[1] (£) April 1991	Stock of dwellings (thousands) 1990[2]	All households (thousands)	Average size	Lone parent households as a % of all households
South West	12,476	2,351	270,891	27.18	255.59	1,945.0	1,846.3	2.47	8.5
Avon	..	..	64,977	26.87	314.85	392.3	382.6	2.45	8.9
Bath	21	94	6,417	27.06	244.67	36.0	35.5	2.30	9.0
Bristol *	..	..	36,352	25.74	369.06	160.6	154.4	2.38	10.4
Kingswood	407	70	4,649	24.22	258.50	35.9	35.2	2.51	8.5
Northavon	627	8	5,073	36.45	267.00	52.7	50.4	2.65	7.6
Wansdyke	211	9	4,576	24.07	284.01	32.8	32.0	2.56	7.0
Woodspring	239	8	7,910	28.94	304.00	74.3	75.3	2.44	7.7
Cornwall	1,640	351	24,406	25.59	233.19	205.8	183.6	2.49	8.5
Caradon	464	124	4,176	24.91	235.66	33.2	29.0	2.50	8.6
Carrick	167	2	4,620	25.83	250.54	36.4	32.8	2.38	7.4
Isles of Scilly	6	0	142	29.19	105.00	1.1	0.8	2.35	10.7
Kerrier	195	35	3,910	25.89	247.40	37.1	33.6	2.57	8.1
North Cornwall	342	139	4,072	27.65	213.92	34.2	28.3	2.52	9.2
Penwith	91	10	3,455	26.59	225.18	27.6	25.8	2.40	9.8
Restormel	375	41	4,031	22.67	224.95	36.2	33.2	2.55	8.3
Devon	..	..	54,455	26.14	242.31	424.7	407.0	2.46	8.4
East Devon	240	113	5,122	22.81	242.34	52.3	49.0	2.36	6.9
Exeter	..	..	6,699	21.73	237.00	37.3	42.2	2.41	8.9
Mid Devon	281	22	4,240	25.86	254.30	26.0	24.9	2.55	8.3
North Devon	202	0	3,784	28.21	243.74	35.5	32.5	2.58	7.5
Plymouth *	200	168	19,594	24.00	240.00	96.9	96.3	2.55	9.7
South Hams	392	25	3,592	34.86	239.88	36.1	30.8	2.45	8.4
Teignbridge	549	75	4,393	29.30	265.09	46.1	44.7	2.41	8.0
Torbay	284	0	3,260	36.41	240.00	53.1	49.0	2.31	8.7
Torridge	238	40	2,163	26.86	206.17	22.4	20.7	2.49	7.8
West Devon	161	0	1,608	25.92	244.35	18.6	17.0	2.50	6.1
Dorset	..	..	25,729	32.09	212.60	285.2	270.5	2.37	7.6
Bournemouth	290	102	5,900	38.92	208.00	68.2	65.7	2.25	8.2
Christchurch	152	4	0	.	216.14	20.0	18.1	2.14	7.7
East Dorset	161	15	108	40.57	245.33	33.8	31.9	2.44	6.0
North Dorset	178	22	3,110	29.12	199.72	22.0	21.7	2.51	6.9
Poole	..	..	5,545	31.17	200.00	57.3	53.7	2.43	8.0
Purbeck	94	60	2,022	30.65	177.52	19.3	18.5	2.48	8.4
West Dorset	275	16	5,461	30.33	214.87	38.9	35.1	2.40	7.4
Weymouth and Portland	154	35	3,583	28.05	240.00	25.6	25.8	2.42	7.3
Gloucestershire	1,789	214	32,240	29.06	270.62	216.5	207.9	2.52	8.7
Cheltenham	160	89	6,328	28.17	276.40	37.5	35.3	2.38	9.9
Cotswold	372	39	4,810	34.73	254.12	32.2	30.1	2.47	6.9
Forest of Dean	73	64	4,815	27.11	271.68	30.3	29.8	2.63	7.6
Gloucester	426	0	6,174	31.25	261.23	36.1	35.0	2.58	10.8
Stroud	396	22	6,585	24.73	304.99	45.0	43.2	2.53	8.4
Tewkesbury	362	0	3,528	29.87	245.42	35.4	34.6	2.55	8.2
Somerset	1,132	138	31,456	25.32	254.32	191.3	181.7	2.51	8.3
Mendip	183	1	5,532	27.42	268.13	37.9	36.5	2.55	7.8
Sedgemoor	117	16	5,831	26.06	241.26	39.4	37.8	2.57	9.0
Taunton Deane	206	37	7,596	23.22	239.96	39.5	38.1	2.46	8.2
West Somerset	105	84	2,014	26.94	250.22	14.4	13.5	2.35	8.6
South Somerset	521	0	10,483	25.02	264.79	60.0	55.8	2.53	8.3
Wiltshire	1,566	263	37,628	26.91	236.86	229.2	213.0	2.59	8.7
Kennet	229	74	5,223	27.97	212.67	27.9	24.9	2.67	9.2
North Wiltshire	496	49	6,560	27.70	242.15	44.8	42.9	2.61	8.1
Salisbury	211	17	7,356	29.84	208.49	42.8	38.4	2.57	8.2
Thamesdown	298	115	12,423	22.85	259.45	70.1	65.4	2.59	9.2
West Wiltshire	332	8	6,066	29.90	238.71	43.6	41.5	2.53	8.9

15.2 *(Continued)*

	Housing starts (numbers)		Local authority tenants				Households 1990		
	Private enterprise 1990	Housing associations, local authorities etc. 1990	Total number of tenancies April 1991	Average weekly unrebated rent per dwelling (£) April 1991	Community charge[1] (£) April 1991	Stock of dwellings (thousands) 1990[2]	All households (thousands)	Average size	Lone parent households as a % of all households
West Midlands	13,234	2,615	471,195	26.70	265.28	2,078.7	2,022.2	2.55	9.7
Hereford and Worcester	2,552	509	46,398	24.46	231.92	271.1	259.4	2.57	9.1
Bromsgrove	431	91	3,863	20.49	222.09	35.4	33.9	2.58	8.9
Hereford	88	31	4,917	20.96	211.00	20.7	19.5	2.48	8.9
Leominster	82	8	1,881	22.06	201.37	16.6	15.4	2.54	10.0
Malvern Hills	47	9	4,941	29.96	239.07	35.8	33.8	2.53	7.6
Redditch	126	140	8,728	24.23	261.54	29.7	29.9	2.62	9.5
South Herefordshire	487	43	2,147	23.34	186.68	20.6	19.5	2.63	10.1
Worcester	604	78	5,903	25.15	257.07	33.0	32.3	2.53	9.4
Wychavon	337	34	7,125	24.62	217.60	41.2	38.3	2.63	8.3
Wyre Forest	350	75	6,893	25.80	253.24	38.0	36.9	2.56	9.8
Shropshire	..	..	27,085	24.68	257.00	160.5	154.0	2.59	8.8
Bridgnorth	108	20	3,194	25.08	210.73	19.7	19.2	2.57	8.1
North Shropshire	331	0	3,104	21.67	226.25	20.7	20.7	2.69	8.1
Oswestry	155	0	2,507	22.73	263.32	13.6	13.1	2.53	8.3
Shrewsbury and Atcham	181	90	6,378	22.14	263.35	36.1	34.8	2.56	7.9
South Shropshire	171	0	1,733	26.18	232.06	15.5	13.4	2.64	8.4
Telford	634	0	.	.	..	.	.	.	.
The Wrekin *	564	43	10,169	27.28	287.89	54.9	52.7	2.59	10.1
Staffordshire	3,085	351	77,962	23.06	247.51	412.7	401.6	2.56	8.7
Cannock Chase	504	0	7,767	24.28	269.42	34.1	33.5	2.66	9.0
East Staffordshire	272	18	6,246	24.34	243.85	39.8	37.3	2.57	9.1
Lichfield	266	28	5,583	19.67	236.23	36.0	35.3	2.61	8.9
Newcastle-under-Lyme	401	34	10,421	17.65	268.64	49.3	47.0	2.51	8.1
South Staffordshire	289	61	5,673	24.67	208.88	40.5	45.7	2.54	7.8
Stafford	410	30	7,346	22.29	236.29	47.3	41.4	2.62	7.5
Staffordshire Moorlands	239	0	3,648	19.19	237.25	38.3	36.6	2.60	7.7
Stoke-on-Trent	456	172	24,973	23.98	260.58	101.2	98.2	2.49	9.3
Tamworth	248	8	6,305	30.27	246.00	26.2	26.6	2.61	10.7
Warwickshire	1,549	251	30,594	24.42	287.19	195.5	187.0	2.55	8.4
North Warwickshire	334	39	4,246	20.57	309.81	23.8	23.1	2.58	6.5
Nuneaton and Bedworth	319	17	7,913	23.47	327.26	45.9	44.0	2.61	9.3
Rugby	266	107	4,911	25.85	279.41	34.4	33.5	2.54	8.3
Stratford-on-Avon	435	70	6,484	25.79	265.73	43.5	40.6	2.56	7.9
Warwick	195	18	7,040	25.55	260.21	47.9	45.9	2.45	9.1
West Midlands	3,917	1,332	289,156	25.61	278.66	1,039.0	1,020.2	2.54	10.7
Birmingham *	864	903	108,359	28.05	266.00	395.5	389.0	2.52	12.1
Coventry *	223	39	21,626	26.81	294.00	122.5	119.3	2.52	10.8
Dudley *	635	32	31,628	23.35	275.00	122.4	120.0	2.54	7.7
Sandwell *	770	179	47,358	29.70	319.00	119.0	114.1	2.57	10.2
Solihull	380	55	13,536	28.41	256.11	78.4	79.1	2.54	10.0
Walsall*	746	50	32,737	21.82	285.00	102.1	101.5	2.58	10.2
Wolverhampton *	299	74	33,912	25.29	275.00	99.1	97.1	2.54	10.9

15.2 (Continued)

	Housing starts (numbers)		Local authority tenants				Households 1990		
	Private enterprise 1990	Housing associations, local authorities etc. 1990	Total number of tenancies April 1991	Average weekly unrebated rent per dwelling (£) April 1991	Community charge[1] (£) April 1991	Stock of dwellings (thousands) 1990[2]	All households (thousands)	Average size	Lone parent households as a % of all households
North West	13,937	2,977	537,188	24.57	284.38	2,579.1	2,477.7	2.54	10.6
Cheshire	..	..	62,270	20.00	301.68	385.1	366.5	2.59	9.2
Chester	162	74	7,507	22.28	309.35	48.5	45.1	2.46	8.8
Congleton	483	14	4,402	18.50	295.56	33.9	33.9	2.52	8.0
Crewe and Nantwich	402	6	7,249	21.02	312.49	42.5	40.3	2.53	8.8
Ellesmere Port and Neston	..	..	7,678	14.94	309.36	31.9	30.0	2.61	10.2
Halton *	39	0	8,305	24.20	325.00	45.9	45.1	2.72	11.1
Macclesfield	337	26	7,192	19.28	282.51	63.3	59.6	2.49	8.9
Vale Royal	475	11	8,429	19.11	292.01	44.8	43.0	2.63	8.8
Warrington	624	42	11,508	19.90	296.58	74.3	69.5	2.68	9.3
Greater Manchester	..	..	269,709	24.20	274.63	1,046.0	1,016.3	2.52	11.2
Bolton *	927	127	23,447	22.89	265.87	103.5	104.4	2.54	10.5
Bury	540	35	10,297	20.72	295.92	71.2	68.3	2.56	9.8
Manchester *	986	540	87,292	25.61	291.88	186.4	177.4	2.47	14.6
Oldham *	487	149	21,482	24.61	268.90	89.3	86.9	2.53	10.7
Rochdale *	407	108	18,352	25.57	249.00	82.6	80.5	2.57	11.9
Salford *	589	101	33,984	24.58	300.00	98.4	93.5	2.47	12.2
Stockport	386	106	14,269	23.76	310.18	117.6	115.2	2.50	10.1
Tameside	..	..	18,914	23.64	270.00	86.8	85.9	2.54	10.3
Trafford	159	67	11,824	23.30	205.00	87.1	85.8	2.48	9.9
Wigan *	880	124	29,848	21.68	267.61	123.2	118.5	2.61	8.9
Lancashire	..	..	75,825	26.50	271.59	569.7	545.9	2.51	9.7
Blackburn *	427	67	11,935	31.52	287.23	54.4	51.2	2.61	10.9
Blackpool	112	26	6,605	24.63	294.00	63.7	57.8	2.28	9.3
Burnley *	207	114	6,019	27.16	209.00	39.3	36.3	2.57	11.4
Chorley	..	..	3,658	20.57	293.76	36.7	37.3	2.59	8.8
Fylde	168	26	2,096	24.00	268.47	31.2	30.4	2.38	7.5
Hyndburn	199	112	4,107	30.01	243.00	32.0	31.3	2.52	11.1
Lancaster	219	36	4,612	24.41	279.00	52.0	52.2	2.46	8.0
Pendle	81	26	4,486	26.75	218.00	35.4	34.0	2.51	9.3
Preston *	287	40	9,428	28.72	314.14	54.0	49.4	2.55	11.3
Ribble Valley	165	1	1,591	23.14	273.46	20.2	19.0	2.55	8.0
Rossendale	113	6	5,118	27.19	260.57	26.7	25.5	2.56	10.8
South Ribble	285	0	3,614	23.04	286.51	39.9	39.1	2.62	9.6
West Lancashire	367	4	9,381	23.79	260.27	41.1	39.9	2.58	11.4
Wyre	311	24	3,175	22.86	259.29	43.2	42.5	2.43	7.8
Merseyside	..	..	129,384	26.17	302.47	578.3	548.9	2.59	11.5
Knowsley *	209	80	22,229	29.06	291.43	59.2	56.2	2.78	14.8
Liverpool *	1,138	323	53,302	26.09	333.95	197.0	177.6	2.56	12.6
Sefton *	150	59	15,661	25.08	283.48	115.4	71.4	2.61	10.5
St Helens *	324	215	17,769	23.39	260.97	70.9	113.5	2.60	10.0
Wirral *	519	188	20,423	26.47	304.00	135.8	130.2	2.55	10.4
England	110,430	20,016	3,834,242	27.26	250.76	19,522.1	18,820.0	2.50	9.7

15.2 (Continued)

	Housing starts (numbers)		Local authority tenants				Households 1990		
	Private enterprise 1990	Housing associations, local authorities etc. 1990	Total number of tenancies April 1991	Average weekly unrebated rent per dwelling (£) April 1991	Community charge[1] (£) April 1991	Stock of dwellings (thousands) 1990[2]	All households (thousands)	Average size	Lone parent households as a % of all households
Wales	7,643	2,537	215,435	26.68	121.25	1,162.4	1,085.0	2.63	9.8
Clwyd	1,608	467	31,433	21.61	146.26	165.0	157.0	2.60	9.0
Alyn and Deeside	541	91	4,767	20.72	135.17	28.3	28.0	2.76	..
Colwyn	235	29	2,402	24.94	137.19	23.8	21.0	2.35	..
Delyn	401	74	4,435	25.08	143.92	25.7	25.0	2.76	..
Glyndwr	22	56	2,734	23.40	154.30	17.8	16.0	2.60	..
Rhuddlan	58	70	2,572	20.76	167.95	23.3	23.0	2.39	..
Wrexham Maelor	351	147	14,523	20.10	146.61	46.0	45.0	2.65	..
Dyfed	1,258	297	22,936	25.35	97.17	144.3	134.0	2.62	8.8
Carmarthen	.. 196	28	3,300	25.24	89.02	22.9	21.0	2.64	..
Ceredigion	235	42	3,100	26.39	85.19	27.8	24.0	2.51	..
Dinefwr	174	8	2,404	21.71	98.54	16.0	15.0	2.61	..
Llanelli	124	124	6,467	27.46	112.14	30.9	32.0	2.58	..
Preseli	236	62	5,056	23.72	85.18	29.2	27.0	2.70	..
South Pembrokeshire	293	33	2,609	25.51	82.75	17.6	15.0	2.69	..
Gwent	818	365	44,485	29.68	123.90	178.9	168.0	2.63	10.3
Blaenau Gwent	108	48	9,601	29.20	128.52	31.8	31.0	2.61	..
Islwyn	55	112	5,611	27.77	121.99	25.4	25.0	2.67	..
Monmouth	203	37	4,531	27.99	108.65	30.1	26.0	2.66	..
Newport	241	0	12,481	28.94	135.59	54.9	51.0	2.63	..
Torfaen	211	168	12,261	32.31	123.60	36.6	35.0	2.61	..
Gwynedd	559	195	15,533	25.02	120.94	107.3	92.0	2.56	9.7
Aberconwy	197	49	2,421	26.08	114.69	23.8	21.0	2.42	..
Arfon	65	28	4,710	23.15	105.20	23.1	21.0	2.57	..
Dwyfor	71	8	1,371	23.12	115.71	13.9	11.0	2.55	..
Meirionnydd	55	35	1,904	25.89	122.41	16.7	13.0	2.51	..
Ynys Mon	171	75	5,127	26.42	129.80	29.8	26.0	2.70	..
Mid Glamorgan	1,355	288	40,221	27.26	118.48	212.1	197.0	2.71	10.3
Cynon Valley	214	12	4,698	26.48	112.69	27.3	25.0	2.64	..
Merthyr Tydfil	156	0	6,323	23.92	105.21	24.1	23.0	2.65	..
Ogwr	402	74	8,820	26.04	117.06	51.7	47.0	2.73	..
Rhondda	37	87	4,450	28.95	108.00	32.2	31.0	2.64	..
Rhymney Valley	251	22	9,330	30.23	131.07	39.5	38.0	2.79	..
Taff-Ely	295	93	6,600	27.31	118.50	37.3	34.0	2.74	..
Powys	497	125	6,297	25.72	92.00	49.8	45.0	2.60	8.5
Brecknock	105	43	2,564	24.43	102.74	17.2	16.0	2.58	..
Montgomery	277	51	2,682	26.16	83.51	22.4	16.0	2.62	..
Newtown	24	0	.	.	.	..	4.0	2.64	..
Radnor	91	31	1,051	27.74	92.32	10.2	9.0	2.56	..
South Glamorgan	707	606	23,637	27.74	129.96	158.0	153.0	2.62	11.2
Cardiff	512	464	17,984	28.57	137.73	114.0	110.0	2.60	..
Vale of Glamorgan	195	142	5,653	25.09	111.03	44.0	42.0	2.66	..
West Glamorgan	841	194	30,893	28.01	125.23	146.9	138.0	2.60	9.5
Lliw Valley	237	58	4,673	26.36	108.46	25.2	23.0	2.59	..
Neath	235	15	5,124	27.22	117.01	26.7	25.0	2.57	..
Port Talbot	84	85	5,261	29.36	117.65	20.7	20.0	2.68	..
Swansea	285	36	15,835	28.30	136.13	74.2	70.0	2.59	..

15.2 (Continued)

	Housing starts (numbers)		Local authority tenants				Households 1990		
	Private enterprise 1990	Housing associations, local authorities etc. 1990	Total number of tenancies April 1991	Average weekly unrebated rent per dwelling (£) April 1991	Community charge[1] (£) April 1991	Stock of dwellings (thousands) 1990[2]	All households (thousands)	Average size	Lone parent households as a % of all households
Scotland	16,897 [3]	3,776 [4]	735,506	22.31	247.00	2,103.3	1,996.4	2.50	..
Borders	541	52	12,314	21.11	125.00	46.5	41.8	2.43	
Berwickshire	37	38	2,276	20.62	134.00	8.7	7.6	2.51	
Ettrick and Lauderdale	212	0	3,705	18.84	148.00	14.9	13.7	2.42	
Roxburgh	154	0	4,977	23.93	145.00	16.1	14.4	2.39	
Tweeddale	138	14	1,356	17.81	141.00	6.8	6.1	2.43	
Central	947	227	44,854	21.28	187.00	108.4	105.3	2.54	
Clackmannan	198	22	7,894	23.77	277.00	18.8	18.4	2.55	..
Falkirk	488	115	26,347	19.73	201.00	57.7	56.2	2.51	..
Stirling	261	90	10,613	23.26	272.00	31.9	30.7	2.58	..
Dumfries and Galloway	576	88	17,390	22.92	132.00	61.1	56.0	2.62	
Annandale and Eskdale	149	40	4,506	24.14	172.00	15.1	13.9	2.60	..
Nithsdale	272	43	6,672	21.18	172.00	23.1	21.9	2.59	..
Stewartry	75	0	2,187	24.42	153.00	10.3	8.8	2.65	..
Wigtown	80	5	4,025	23.63	165.00	12.6	11.3	2.67	..
Fife	1,137	388	44,048	22.15	198.00	139.5	131.7	2.58	
Dunfermline	342	42	17,160	21.33	244.00	49.6	47.6	2.72	..
Kirkcaldy	451	271	21,088	22.62	245.00	61.6	58.2	2.52	..
North East Fife	344	75	5,800	22.89	256.00	28.3	25.9	2.47	..
Grampian	2,005	422	64,290	20.97	136.00	209.3	195.7	2.50	
City of Aberdeen	738	202	35,264	20.76	227.00	91.9	88.3	2.27	..
Banff and Buchan	224	21	10,766	21.29	176.00	34.2	31.1	2.68	..
Gordon	378	76	5,433	23.44	159.00	28.7	26.7	2.78	..
Kincardine and Deeside	451	76	3,522	19.03	140.00	20.1	18.3	2.69	..
Moray	214	47	9,305	20.70	152.00	34.5	31.3	2.62	..
Highlands	797	251	22,935	23.64	132.00	86.8	75.6	2.64	
Badenoch and Strathspey	122	10	990	18.82	142.00	5.3	4.2	2.56	..
Caithness	56	8	3,687	22.21	137.00	11.2	9.9	2.65	..
Inverness	339	156	6,237	23.91	137.00	24.9	23.2	2.62	..
Lochaber	71	6	2,576	23.59	167.00	8.5	7.2	2.62	..
Nairn	74	20	1,046	23.53	140.00	4.2	3.9	2.64	..
Ross and Cromarty	32	9	5,867	25.10	164.00	20.2	17.5	2.76	..
Skye and Lochalsh	57	20	826	24.02	145.00	5.7	4.3	2.67	..
Sutherland	46	22	1,706	23.43	149.00	6.8	5.4	2.37	..
Lothian	1,821	405	82,767	24.18	273.00	316.1	304.0	2.38	
East Lothian	273	46	12,516	21.95	339.00	34.7	33.0	2.52	..
City of Edinburgh	98	124	42,600	28.88	381.00	196.7	188.5	2.20	..
Midlothian	215	67	9,643	15.93	327.00	30.1	29.3	2.71	..
West Lothian	1,235	168	18,008	19.03	306.00	54.6	53.2	2.72	..
Strathclyde	7,465	1,365	383,643	23.54	173.00	935.3	899.9	2.52	
Argyll and Bute	156	61	7,349	23.60	238.00	30.8	25.1	2.55	..
Bearsden and Milngavie	174	0	1,588	24.62	226.00	14.7	14.5	2.84	..
Clydebank	136	42	9,436	26.70	273.00	19.3	18.7	2.47	..
Clydesdale	259	1	8,418	20.68	242.00	22.2	21.6	2.63	..
Cumbernauld and Kilsyth	289	101	3,664	22.95	211.00	22.6	22.3	2.83	..
Cumnock and Doon Valley	119	6	8,864	20.32	214.00	16.7	16.2	2.65	..
Cunninghame	335	153	19,342	20.27	253.00	56.3	52.4	2.60	..
Dumbarton	333	32	10,493	25.95	291.00	31.2	29.6	2.65	..
East Kilbride	315	188	1,119	22.53	261.00	31.0	31.4	2.63	..
Eastwood	241	23	1,654	18.15	192.00	22.0	21.9	2.78	..
City of Glasgow	1,962	679	147,009	26.92	266.00	306.4	292.6	2.29	..
Hamilton	260	0	18,971	21.63	248.00	40.2	39.5	2.69	..
Inverclyde	282	0	17,095	22.10	232.00	37.8	36.5	2.52	..
Kilmarnock and Loudoun	211	12	14,473	19.38	224.00	32.6	31.6	2.54	..
Kyle and Carrick	353	31	14,320	20.46	262.50	45.9	44.5	2.52	..
Monklands	137	0	24,650	22.39	249.00	38.3	38.0	2.72	..
Motherwell	640	0	34,388	19.80	227.00	55.2	54.3	2.65	..
Renfrew	893	0	32,254	20.90	262.00	81.3	79.1	2.49	..
Strathkelvin	370	36	8,556	21.51	250.00	30.6	30.2	2.87	..

15.2 *(Continued)*

	Housing starts (numbers)		Local authority tenants				Households 1990		
	Private enterprise 1990	Housing associations, local authorities etc. 1990	Total number of tenancies April 1991	Average weekly unrebated rent per dwelling (£) April 1991	Community charge[1] (£) April 1991	Stock of dwellings (thousands) 1990[2]	All households (thousands)	Average size	Lone parent households as a % of all households
Tayside	1,179	459	57,067	24.20	189.00	170.2	159.6	2.40	..
Angus	253	96	11,903	17.90	219.00	39.7	37.2	2.53	..
City of Dundee	346	238	32,417	28.18	269.00	78.1	73.4	2.27	..
Perth and Kinross	580	125	12,747	19.94	227.00	52.4	49.0	2.49	..
Orkney	68	35	1,312	25.60	191.00	8.2	7.2	2.69	..
Shetland	76	16	2,542	24.12	189.93	9.8	8.6	2.53	..
Western Isles	99	0	2,344	29.12	215.00	13.0	11.0	2.75	..
Northern Ireland	5,704	1,823	161,905	22.86	.	567.7	539.0	2.91	11.7
Antrim	154	1	4,975	..	.	14.7	..	..	..
Ards	284	177	6,093	..	.	24.7	..	..	..
Armagh	172	43	4,065	..	.	17.1	..	..	..
Ballymena	219	2	5,620	..	.	20.4	..	..	..
Ballymoney	96	0	2,906	..	.	8.2	..	..	..
Banbridge	154	64	3,187	..	.	11.8	..	..	..
Belfast	403	882	36,452	..	.	117.3	..	..	..
Carrickfergus	295	15	3,663	..	.	12.3	..	..	..
Castlereagh	352	21	6,480	..	.	23.5	..	..	..
Coleraine	361	32	5,570	..	.	19.8	..	..	..
Cookstown	99	0	2,203	..	.	10.0	..	..	..
Craigavon	313	20	7,940	..	.	26.6	..	..	..
Derry	235	231	12,364	..	.	29.6	..	..	..
Down	283	2	4,539	..	.	19.6	..	..	..
Dungannon	56	12	3,613	..	.	14.9	..	..	..
Fermanagh	230	29	4,143	..	.	18.5	..	..	..
Larne	126	7	2,742	..	.	11.5	..	..	..
Limavady	112	18	2,939	..	.	8.7	..	..	..
Lisburn	408	17	10,844	..	.	34.1	..	..	..
Magherafelt	116	41	2,794	..	.	11.3	..	..	..
Moyle	77	6	1,580	..	.	5.5	..	..	..
Newry and Mourne	306	66	7,532	..	.	26.6	..	..	..
Newtownabbey	379	48	7,797	..	.	27.6	..	..	..
North Down	241	5	4,215	..	.	28.1	..	..	..
Omagh	180	50	3,523	..	.	14.0	..	..	..
Strabane	53	34	4,126	..	.	11.4	..	..	..

* Urban Programme Authorities.
1 After the £140 budget reduction and capping.
2 Scottish data are for 1989.
3 Includes estimates for outstanding returns for which no further breakdown is available.
4 Includes estimates for Scottish Homes for which no further breakdown is available.

15.3 Unemployment and economic statistics

	Unemployment January 1992				Gross value added in manufacturing (£ million) 1989	Net capital expenditure in manufacturing (£ million) 1989
	Males (numbers)	Females (numbers)	Total (numbers)	Percentage long-term[1] unemployed		
United Kingdom	2,045,371	628,493	2,673,864	27.9	108,291	14,499
North	123,461	34,535	157,996	31.6	6,407	912
Cleveland	27,018	6,956	33,974	34.7	1,729	220
Hartlepool *	4,826	1,169	5,995	29.6	220	49
Langbaurgh *	6,596	1,616	8,212	34.1	762	..
Middlesbrough * [2]	7,893	2,027	9,920	37.8	111	109
Stockton-on-Tees *	7,703	2,144	9,847	35.2	636	62
Cumbria	13,188	4,469	17,657	22.9	1,112	139
Allerdale	2,942	1,114	4,056	27.4	192	25
Barrow-in-Furness	2,879	905	3,784	19.3	339	23
Carlisle	2,791	923	3,714	25.3	233	33
Copeland	2,389	711	3,100	30.6	91	12
Eden	658	243	901	13.3	76	8
South Lakeland	1,529	573	2,102	9.3	180	39
Durham	20,869	6,118	26,987	26.4	1,317	171
Chester-le-Street	1,629	528	2,157	26.3	42	8
Darlington	3,668	1,017	4,685	27.7	165	14
Derwentside	3,477	967	4,444	30.0	94	11
Durham	2,519	872	3,391	29.1	128	19
Easington	3,273	821	4,094	23.6	153	37
Sedgefield	2,952	904	3,856	20.3	382	58
Teesdale	561	228	789	23.8	..	9
Wear Valley[3]	2,790	781	3,571	27.9	352	15
Northumberland	9,394	3,121	12,515	25.9	435	47
Alnwick	844	324	1,168	24.7	15	2
Berwick-upon-Tweed	797	280	1,077	13.0	35	3
Blyth Valley	2,922	911	3,833	28.3	131	12
Castle Morpeth	1,171	430	1,601	25.8	51	9
Tynedale	1,083	426	1,509	21.1	79	11
Wansbeck	2,577	750	3,327	29.8	125	9
Tyne and Wear	52,992	13,871	66,863	35.5	1,815	336
Gateshead *	8,825	2,363	11,188	34.1	444	47
Newcastle upon Tyne *	14,260	3,778	18,038	40.0	438	40
North Tyneside *	7,372	2,036	9,408	29.9	359	31
South Tyneside *	8,172	2,227	10,399	34.2	186	31
Sunderland *	14,363	3,467	17,830	35.7	387	186
Yorkshire & Humberside	180,725	52,365	233,090	29.4	9,783	1,338
Humberside	34,305	9,643	43,948	28.9	2,478	355
Beverley	2,180	822	3,002	20.1	439	35
Boothferry	1,888	607	2,495	21.5	119	18
Cleethorpes	2,534	699	3,233	25.3	189	11
East Yorkshire	2,327	846	3,173	21.7	102	12
Glanford	1,778	610	2,388	21.5	82	17
Great Grimsby[4]	4,586	1,025	5,611	30.2	321	79
Holderness	1,386	530	1,916	21.9	193	..
Kingston-upon-Hull *	14,982	3,826	18,808	35.0	619	90
Scunthorpe	2,644	678	3,322	25.6	415	92
North Yorkshire	14,757	5,528	20,285	20.2	950	159
Craven	832	320	1,152	16.7	96	8
Hambleton	1,385	512	1,897	19.5	55	7
Harrogate	2,265	839	3,104	18.5	139	27
Richmondshire	634	333	967	13.5	19	2
Ryedale	1,187	476	1,663	19.2	149	33
Scarborough	3,507	1,308	4,815	21.3	122	26
Selby	1,705	782	2,487	16.1	115	20
York	3,242	958	4,200	26.0	256	36

15.3 *(Continued)*

	Unemployment January 1992				Gross value added in manufacturing (£ million) 1989	Net capital expenditure in manufacturing (£ million) 1989
	Males (numbers)	Females (numbers)	Total (numbers)	Percentage long-term[1] unemployed		
South Yorkshire	58,147	16,058	74,205	32.5	2,118	256
Barnsley *	9,314	2,489	11,803	30.7	270	29
Doncaster *	13,460	3,857	17,317	30.6	430	47
Rotherham *	10,958	3,157	14,115	31.7	541	81
Sheffield *	24,415	6,555	30,970	34.6	877	99
West Yorkshire	73,516	21,136	94,652	29.3	4,238	567
Bradford *	18,587	4,881	23,468	32.3	959	116
Calderdale	6,396	2,126	8,522	25.8	542	67
Kirklees *	11,982	3,609	15,591	25.7	904	118
Leeds *	25,430	7,291	32,721	31.0	1,342	159
Wakefield	11,121	3,229	14,350	26.1	491	107
East Midlands	128,208	40,264	168,472	26.4	8,972	998
Derbyshire	29,951	9,675	39,626	26.6	2,287	248
Amber Valley	2,928	1,070	3,998	22.3	415	50
Bolsover	2,660	755	3,415	26.7	85	13
Chesterfield	3,747	1,146	4,893	32.0	197	22
Derby *	9,548	2,735	12,283	29.2	761	69
Erewash	3,250	1,022	4,272	23.5	209	21
High Peak	1,973	794	2,767	19.8	255	27
North East Derbyshire	3,017	1,041	4,058	31.3	115	11
South Derbyshire	1,641	616	2,257	20.1	98	19
Derbyshire Dales	1,187	496	1,683	19.5	152	16
Leicestershire	25,808	8,303	34,111	25.4	2,659	301
Blaby	1,700	583	2,283	16.9	147	14
Charnwood	3,148	1,170	4,318	20.6	419	74
Harborough	1,186	378	1,564	13.7	119	22
Hinckley and Bosworth	1,999	730	2,729	17.7	286	27
Leicester *	13,295	3,841	17,136	31.9	892	74
Melton	835	311	1,146	16.5	214	18
North West Leicestershire	2,116	717	2,833	23.0	385	34
Oadby and Wigston	1,078	380	1,458	17.8	121	27
Rutland	451	193	644	16.9	76	10
Lincolnshire	16,868	5,863	22,731	22.5	729	97
Boston	1,565	472	2,037	23.2	47	9
East Lindsey	4,209	1,546	5,755	18.8	89	17
Lincoln	3,797	1,082	4,879	34.3	161	19
North Kesteven	1,618	656	2,274	21.7	56	6
South Holland	1,356	561	1,917	12.8	77	9
South Kesteven	2,323	821	3,144	15.0	199	24
West Lindsey	2,000	725	2,725	24.6	100	12
Northamptonshire	16,563	5,489	22,052	21.1	1,387	155
Corby	2,352	768	3,120	21.7	249	56
Daventry	1,303	532	1,835	15.5	116	10
East Northamptonshire	1,474	557	2,031	13.7	102	12
Kettering	2,166	631	2,797	22.7	151	12
Northampton	6,067	1,863	7,930	25.7	508	39
South Northamptonshire	1,235	438	1,673	14.8	92	11
Wellingborough	1,966	700	2,666	18.8	169	15
Nottinghamshire	39,018	10,934	49,952	31.1	1,909	198
Ashfield	4,117	1,059	5,176	30.4	315	26
Bassetlaw	3,490	1,139	4,629	26.8	197	21
Broxtowe	2,826	921	3,747	23.0	300	35
Gedling	2,901	1,061	3,962	25.0	122	14
Mansfield	4,043	1,050	5,093	30.0	96	14
Newark	3,283	947	4,230	24.5	151	18
Nottingham *	16,082	3,987	20,069	37.3	622	59
Rushcliffe	2,276	770	3,046	27.7	105	11

15.3 *(Continued)*

	Unemployment January 1992				Gross value added in manufacturing (£ million) 1989	Net capital expenditure in manufacturing (£ million) 1989
	Males (numbers)	Females (numbers)	Total (numbers)	Percentage long-term[1] unemployed		
East Anglia	54,899	18,208	73,107	22.0	3,926	496
Cambridgeshire	17,773	5,886	23,659	21.7	1,632	170
Cambridge	2,774	838	3,612	23.0	154	18
East Cambridgeshire	1,184	420	1,604	17.0	48	4
Fenland	2,554	867	3,421	23.7	128	16
Huntingdon	3,297	1,263	4,560	17.4	252	38
Peterborough	6,130	1,828	7,958	25.7	699	59
South Cambridgeshire	1,834	670	2,504	14.9	351	35
Norfolk	21,683	7,041	28,724	22.9	1,218	154
Breckland	2,739	1,026	3,765	18.2	177	17
Broadland	1,775	611	2,386	19.9	156	23
Great Yarmouth	3,942	1,447	5,389	23.3	71	10
North Norfolk	2,231	668	2,899	19.1	75	11
Norwich	5,402	1,436	6,838	29.2	329	34
South Norfolk	1,899	682	2,581	19.5	105	17
West Norfolk	3,695	1,171	4,866	22.6	305	43
Suffolk	15,443	5,281	20,724	21.2	1,076	172
Babergh	1,772	577	2,349	19.6	144	27
Forest Heath	1,005	388	1,393	19.5	87	15
Ipswich	4,005	1,054	5,059	25.0	206	20
Mid Suffolk	1,365	554	1,919	21.5	138	21
St Edmundsbury	2,163	759	2,922	19.9	228	47
Suffolk Coastal	1,928	664	2,592	17.9	73	14
Waveney	3,205	1,285	4,490	20.9	201	28
South East	592,310	191,914	784,224	23.7	29,544	3,536
Bedfordshire	16,820	5,019	21,839	22.4	1,359	126
Luton	7,507	1,972	9,479	24.7	547	32
Mid Bedfordshire	2,209	886	3,095	17.0	219	28
North Bedfordshire	3,981	1,196	5,177	24.5	284	31
South Bedfordshire	3,123	965	4,088	18.3	309	35
Berkshire	18,526	5,752	24,278	17.4	1,558	170
Bracknell	2,304	767	3,071	16.0	124	29
Newbury	2,846	934	3,780	14.3	160	18
Reading	4,740	1,115	5,855	20.5	336	26
Slough	3,838	1,259	5,097	21.3	579	69
Windsor and Maidenhead	2,446	904	3,350	15.8	222	16
Wokingham	2,352	773	3,125	12.4	137	11
Buckinghamshire	16,059	5,078	21,137	17.3	1,407	136
Aylesbury Vale	3,733	1,259	4,992	18.3	348	29
Chiltern	1,504	494	1,998	15.6	144	-
Milton Keynes	6,054	1,824	7,878	16.8	379	59
South Buckinghamshire	1,067	394	1,461	15.9	135	23
Wycombe	3,701	1,107	4,808	18.4	401	26
East Sussex	24,331	7,306	31,637	24.8	613	78
Brighton	7,746	2,365	10,111	27.6	101	8
Eastbourne	2,727	761	3,488	23.0	112	9
Hastings	3,805	956	4,761	26.8	96	9
Hove	3,578	1,238	4,816	26.2	61	6
Lewes	2,257	681	2,938	23.0	105	7
Rother	1,919	596	2,515	22.7	46	25
Wealdon	2,299	709	3,008	15.8	92	12

15.3 *(Continued)*

	Unemployment January 1992				Gross value added in manufacturing (£ million) 1989	Net capital expenditure in manufacturing (£ million) 1989
	Males (numbers)	Females (numbers)	Total (numbers)	Percentage long-term[1] unemployed		
Essex	47,215	14,714	61,929	21.0	2,586	428
Basildon	5,943	1,837	7,780	21.0	400	57
Braintree[5]	3,413	1,136	4,549	19.2	762	193
Brentwood	1,508	499	2,007	14.9	..	..
Castle Point	2,644	838	3,482	18.1	45	4
Chelmsford	3,618	1,253	4,871	19.2	143	22
Colchester	4,144	1,389	5,533	21.0	186	11
Epping Forest	2,948	1,104	4,052	21.2	140	16
Harlow	2,829	1,062	3,891	22.7	211	38
Maldon	1,456	416	1,872	21.4	69	7
Rochford	2,003	607	2,610	16.8	62	4
Southend-on-Sea	6,390	1,745	8,135	24.9	231	16
Tendring	4,296	1,127	5,423	23.8	76	8
Thurrock	4,706	1,242	5,948	21.6	180	40
Uttlesford	1,317	459	1,776	15.1	80	10
Greater London	292,679	101,365	394,044	27.5	10,328	1,171
Barking and Dagenham	6,056	1,665	7,721	23.2	828	156
Barnet	8,243	3,255	11,498	20.7	161	19
Bexley	6,684	2,286	8,970	21.7	204	40
Brent *	12,818	4,656	17,474	25.1	584	83
Bromley	7,346	2,498	9,844	20.5	223	20
Camden	8,908	3,621	12,529	27.4	369	25
City of London	89	24	113	27.4	496	49
City of Westminster	6,741	2,729	9,470	22.6	602	40
Croydon	10,672	3,473	14,145	21.9	294	33
Ealing	10,519	3,793	14,312	24.4	774	54
Enfield	9,653	3,131	12,784	25.1	455	93
Greenwich *	10,991	3,325	14,316	30.9	245	25
Hackney *	14,377	4,715	19,092	36.2	274	19
Hammersmith and Fulham *	8,224	3,169	11,393	31.7	159	13
Haringey	13,623	4,812	18,435	33.0	142	14
Harrow	5,150	2,063	7,213	17.3	225	37
Havering	6,476	1,987	8,463	17.5	153	27
Hillingdon	6,322	2,076	8,398	17.6	423	44
Hounslow	6,810	2,560	9,370	20.3	458	52
Islington *	11,264	4,335	15,599	34.6	435	34
Kensington and Chelsea *	4,760	2,246	7,006	29.6	101	6
Kingston-upon-Thames	3,356	1,197	4,553	14.8	283	18
Lambeth *	17,106	5,990	23,096	33.3	155	16
Lewisham *	13,698	4,619	18,317	33.1	85	7
Merton	5,513	1,910	7,423	21.1	256	27
Newham *	13,611	3,918	17,529	31.6	250	29
Redbridge	7,024	2,523	9,547	21.2	126	8
Richmond-upon-Thames	3,754	1,623	5,377	17.6	169	27
Southwark *	14,746	4,800	19,546	32.2	325	41
Sutton	4,575	1,430	6,005	20.0	159	23
Tower Hamlets *	11,595	3,181	14,776	37.9	509	51
Waltham Forest	10,437	3,430	13,867	27.4	215	20
Wandsworth *	11,538	4,325	15,863	28.0	191	23
Hampshire	46,754	13,068	59,822	20.8	3,048	406
Basingstoke and Deane	3,643	1,055	4,698	16.1	417	100
East Hampshire	2,078	656	2,734	15.1	115	26
Eastleigh	2,569	671	3,240	16.5	248	30
Fareham	2,221	701	2,922	15.9	120	25
Gosport	2,361	870	3,231	21.1	95	11
Hart	1,424	496	1,920	13.6	49	6
Havant	4,699	1,162	5,861	22.6	351	41
New Forest	4,025	1,082	5,107	20.3	286	58
Portsmouth	8,096	2,281	10,377	25.5	480	26
Rushmoor	2,014	687	2,701	17.4	105	12
Southampton	9,632	2,256	11,888	25.6	565	38
Test Valley	2,179	612	2,791	15.3	162	24
Winchester	1,813	539	2,352	15.6	57	9

15.3 *(Continued)*

	Unemployment January 1992				Gross value added in manufacturing (£ million) 1989	Net capital expenditure in manufacturing (£ million) 1989
	Males (numbers)	Females (numbers)	Total (numbers)	Percentage long-term[1] unemployed		
Hertfordshire	26,629	8,758	35,387	17.3	2,231	221
Broxbourne	2,505	1,012	3,517	21.9	188	19
Dacorum	3,309	1,066	4,375	16.0	243	21
East Hertfordshire	2,575	905	3,480	16.4	307	31
Hertsmere	2,224	757	2,981	17.5	126	11
North Hertfordshire	3,237	1,111	4,348	18.8	289	18
St Albans	2,679	878	3,557	13.3	158	14
Stevenage	3,117	900	4,017	18.8	408	34
Three Rivers	1,695	488	2,183	15.8	137	13
Watford	2,535	807	3,342	18.0	121	13
Welwyn Hatfield	2,753	834	3,587	15.7	255	47
Isle of Wight	4,895	1,750	6,645	24.7	132	8
Medina	2,714	898	3,612	25.8	106	6
South Wight	2,181	852	3,033	23.3	26	2
Kent	48,496	14,203	62,699	21.6	2,572	403
Ashford	2,578	759	3,337	21.4	161	25
Canterbury	3,840	994	4,834	23.0	106	14
Dartford	2,374	686	3,060	21.9	259	48
Dover	3,517	1,019	4,536	17.9	138	42
Gillingham	3,429	1,048	4,477	20.8	102	10
Gravesham	3,656	1,118	4,774	22.4	181	20
Maidstone	3,409	1,081	4,490	17.3	411	22
Rochester-upon-Medway	6,130	1,852	7,982	22.5	234	26
Sevenoaks	2,361	709	3,070	18.5	121	32
Shepway	3,149	764	3,913	22.1	76	12
Swale	4,302	1,319	5,621	25.3	290	74
Thanet	5,234	1,440	6,674	27.2	110	13
Tonbridge and Malling	2,495	769	3,264	16.1	299	49
Tunbridge Wells	2,022	645	2,667	16.8	86	17
Oxfordshire	13,568	3,987	17,555	18.6	982	111
Cherwell	3,001	958	3,959	18.5	268	38
Oxford	3,753	1,012	4,765	23.3	378	31
South Oxfordshire	2,878	779	3,657	15.9	117	27
Vale of White Horse	2,141	584	2,725	15.9	124	11
West Oxfordshire	1,795	654	2,449	16.3	94	4
Surrey	19,426	5,996	25,422	13.5	1,508	161
Elmbridge	2,135	672	2,807	13.0	517	51
Epsom and Ewell	1,250	376	1,626	12.1	13	1
Guildford	2,469	725	3,194	13.7	102	9
Mole Valley	1,266	378	1,644	12.6	87	7
Reigate and Banstead	2,297	673	2,970	14.6	121	19
Runnymede	1,559	504	2,063	13.3	98	5
Spelthorne	1,988	689	2,677	13.4	129	23
Surrey Heath	1,510	470	1,980	11.5	128	19
Tandrige	1,272	432	1,704	14.8	44	7
Waverley	2,030	577	2,607	14.2	143	9
Woking	1,650	500	2,150	13.8	124	11
West Sussex	16,912	4,918	21,830	15.7	1,219	117
Adur	1,650	468	2,118	18.0	131	9
Arun	3,636	917	4,553	15.9	129	16
Chichester	2,215	585	2,800	17.0	112	10
Crawley	2,248	782	3,030	14.3	364	24
Horsham	2,297	725	3,022	13.4	156	33
Mid Sussex	2,186	703	2,889	12.5	158	1
Worthing	2,680	738	3,418	18.9	169	24

15.3 *(Continued)*

	Unemployment January 1992				Gross value added in manufacturing (£ million) 1989	Net capital expenditure in manufacturing (£ million) 1989
	Males (numbers)	Females (numbers)	Total (numbers)	Percentage long-term[1] unemployed		
South West	152,408	48,921	201,329	22.6	7,201	868
Avon	34,753	10,876	45,629	26.5	1,513	185
Bath	2,951	1,002	3,953	29.2	99	6
Bristol *	19,216	5,775	24,991	31.0	640	63
Kingswood	2,525	749	3,274	18.9	134	13
Northavon	3,450	1,171	4,621	16.9	282	29
Wansdyke	1,761	585	2,346	20.9	157	26
Woodspring	4,850	1,594	6,444	20.6	201	48
Cornwall	19,158	6,693	25,851	20.0	424	58
Caradon	2,464	886	3,350	19.8	41	6
Carrick	3,245	1,005	4,250	19.9	63	7
Isles of Scilly	34	30	64	7.8	-	-
Kerrier	3,840	1,185	5,025	25.8	67	9
North Cornwall	2,512	970	3,482	22.5	63	8
Penwith	3,108	1,090	4,198	19.1	28	3
Restormel	3,955	1,527	5,482	14.0	163	26
Devon	35,424	11,175	46,599	22.3	1,228	168
East Devon	2,526	838	3,364	15.7	99	14
Exeter	3,573	988	4,561	21.5	80	9
Mid Devon	1,485	473	1,958	16.6	102	20
North Devon	3,065	1,074	4,139	21.0	116	14
Plymouth *	11,701	3,476	15,177	28.8	447	29
South Hams	1,963	739	2,702	17.7	106	35
Teignbridge	3,082	884	3,966	16.7	95	17
Torbay	5,277	1,623	6,900	20.4	76	14
Torridge	1,621	626	2,247	19.7	60	9
West Devon	1,131	454	1,585	20.1	46	8
Dorset	20,914	6,312	27,226	21.2	845	82
Bournemouth	6,997	1,949	8,946	23.2	106	7
Christchurch	1,142	327	1,469	15.5	115	7
North Dorset	979	351	1,330	15.6	50	9
Poole	4,775	1,256	6,031	22.1	290	29
Purbeck	1,150	412	1,562	15.8	45	5
West Dorset	1,855	681	2,536	20.2	95	11
Weymouth and Portland	2,318	809	3,127	24.0	24	1
Wimbourne	1,698	527	2,225	18.2	120	13
Gloucestershire	14,445	4,397	18,842	22.3	1,167	116
Cheltenham	2,919	748	3,667	27.5	200	20
Cotswold	1,392	496	1,888	15.9	78	12
Forest of Dean	1,955	694	2,649	20.0	152	15
Gloucester	3,637	918	4,555	25.8	148	19
Stroud	2,788	966	3,754	19.2	191	15
Tewkesbury	1,754	575	2,329	20.3	399	35
Somerset	12,852	4,367	17,219	23.5	900	102
Mendip	2,784	887	3,671	23.7	280	42
Sedgemoor	3,117	1,055	4,172	22.2	141	14
Taunton Deane	2,515	782	3,297	26.5	109	13
West Somerset	909	357	1,266	21.5	19	2
Yeovil	3,527	1,286	4,813	22.8	351	31
Wiltshire	14,862	5,101	19,963	19.1	1,124	156
Kennet	1,393	508	1,901	17.7	55	12
North Wiltshire	2,537	988	3,525	16.0	187	24
Salisbury	2,477	828	3,305	17.7	121	11
Thamesdown	5,784	1,798	7,582	22.0	525	71
West Wiltshire	2,671	979	3,650	18.2	236	39

15.3 *(Continued)*

	Unemployment January 1992				Gross value added in manufacturing (£ million) 1989	Net capital expenditure in manufacturing (£ million) 1989
	Males (numbers)	Females (numbers)	Total (numbers)	Percentage long-term[1] unemployed		
West Midlands	197,400	61,392	258,792	28.3	12,678	1,633
Hereford and Worcester	18,217	6,272	24,489	20.0	1,217	152
Bromsgrove	2,363	803	3,166	21.4	53	6
Hereford	1,730	637	2,367	19.3	195	18
Leominster	858	290	1,148	15.8	34	8
Malvern Hills	1,872	603	2,475	18.8	76	9
Redditch	2,520	854	3,374	20.3	214	25
South Herefordshire	993	419	1,412	18.5	64	6
Worcester	2,773	803	3,576	23.8	179	22
Wychavon	2,251	853	3,104	15.0	191	37
Wyre Forest	2,857	1,010	3,867	22.0	211	19
Shropshire	10,552	3,739	14,291	21.2	703	150
Bridgnorth	1,045	431	1,476	16.0	60	30
North Shropshire	1,000	380	1,380	19.0	45	4
Oswestry	829	287	1,116	25.0	46	5
Shrewsbury and Atcham	2,211	724	2,935	21.7	81	12
South Shropshire	810	318	1,128	21.1	61	14
The Wrekin *	4,657	1,599	6,256	21.9	410	84
Staffordshire	30,822	10,158	40,980	21.2	2,824	297
Cannock Chase	3,191	965	4,156	19.0	164	19
East Staffordshire	3,061	1,028	4,089	21.6	444	61
Lichfield	2,383	843	3,226	19.1	154	21
Newcastle-under-Lyme	3,296	1,144	4,440	21.6	553	27
South Staffordshire	2,856	971	3,827	23.0	132	23
Stafford	2,709	956	3,665	19.6	344	33
Staffordshire Moorlands	1,826	746	2,572	16.2	178	23
Stoke-on-Trent	8,677	2,532	11,209	22.8	733	75
Tamworth	2,823	973	3,796	23.2	122	14
Warwickshire	13,211	4,762	17,973	19.0	1,175	152
North Warwickshire	1,695	609	2,304	18.7	122	11
Nuneaton and Bedworth	4,177	1,279	5,456	21.6	169	30
Rugby	2,280	1,008	3,288	19.3	449	66
Stratford-on-Avon	2,049	805	2,854	15.2	151	20
Warwick	3,010	1,061	4,071	18.2	284	24
West Midlands	124,598	36,461	161,059	33.1	6,760	882
Birmingham *	54,362	15,493	69,855	36.0	2,443	401
Coventry *	14,770	4,393	19,163	30.2	1,013	127
Dudley *	10,921	3,423	14,344	28.3	554	53
Sandwell *	14,408	4,274	18,682	34.4	934	120
Solihull	6,399	2,208	8,607	24.0	377	37
Walsall*	11,316	3,182	14,498	30.3	733	81
Wolverhampton *	12,422	3,488	15,910	33.6	706	63

15.3 *(Continued)*

	Unemployment January 1992				Gross value added in manufacturing (£ million) 1989	Net capital expenditure in manufacturing (£ million) 1989
	Males (numbers)	Females (numbers)	Total (numbers)	Percentage long-term[1] unemployed		
North West	249,966	71,990	321,956	31.5	14,026	2,070
Cheshire	28,538	8,797	37,335	24.7	2,802	549
Chester	3,416	975	4,391	29.1	124	27
Congleton	1,764	722	2,486	20.1	284	23
Crewe and Nantwich	3,180	1,078	4,258	22.1	294	22
Ellesmere Port and Neston	2,791	813	3,604	24.6	517	99
Halton *	5,923	1,662	7,585	30.8	543	205
Macclesfield	2,794	964	3,758	17.8	467	73
Vale Royal	3,031	1,007	4,038	23.8	218	38
Warrington	5,639	1,576	7,215	22.9	356	61
Greater Manchester	101,630	29,395	131,025	30.0	5,089	717
Bolton *	9,601	2,654	12,255	28.6	546	59
Bury	4,583	1,463	6,046	22.0	297	36
Manchester *	26,889	7,082	33,971	37.0	759	95
Oldham *	8,273	2,713	10,986	26.3	366	65
Rochdale *	7,892	2,188	10,080	27.8	405	45
Salford *	10,459	2,579	13,038	33.9	401	62
Stockport	7,723	2,382	10,105	24.6	475	39
Tameside	8,015	2,498	10,513	25.3	750	60
Trafford	6,940	2,124	9,064	28.0	652	151
Wigan *	11,255	3,712	14,967	27.0	437	106
Lancashire	43,143	12,669	55,812	22.5	3,780	379
Blackburn *	5,425	1,335	6,760	26.1	445	67
Blackpool	6,393	1,753	8,146	19.4	100	13
Burnley *	2,906	914	3,820	25.9	270	33
Chorley	2,365	876	3,241	18.0	116	14
Fylde	1,106	302	1,408	13.6	467	33
Hyndburn	2,292	719	3,011	17.8	171	27
Lancaster	4,189	1,260	5,449	24.5	117	18
Pendle	2,278	723	3,001	18.8	271	34
Preston *	5,306	1,295	6,601	28.5	412	19
Ribble Valley	658	271	929	16.7	84	10
Rossendale	1,786	495	2,281	19.2	152	16
South Ribble	2,420	766	3,186	19.8	853	59
West Lancashire	3,759	1,348	5,107	26.4	216	27
Wyre	2,260	612	2,872	19.9	107	9
Merseyside	76,655	21,129	97,784	41.3	2,356	426
Knowsley *	10,393	2,569	12,962	45.8	794	175
Liverpool *	31,624	8,542	40,166	45.9	668	104
Sefton *	12,243	3,499	15,742	36.0	206	20
St Helens *	7,487	2,190	9,677	36.4	355	82
Wirral *	14,908	4,329	19,237	35.4	331	46
England	1,679,377	519,589	2,198,966	..	92,538	11,851

15.3 *(Continued)*

	Unemployment January 1992				Gross value added in manufacturing (£ million) 1989	Net capital expenditure in manufacturing (£ million) 1989
	Males (numbers)	Females (numbers)	Total (numbers)	Percentage long-term[1] unemployed		
Wales	101,149	27,606	128,755	27.9	5,558	1,114
Clwyd	11,964	3,562	15,526	21.9	1,171	316
Alyn and Deeside	2,005	617	2,622	19.1	444	172
Colwyn	1,595	508	2,103	23.5	51	5
Delyn	1,712	477	2,189	19.2	106	32
Glyndwr	953	367	1,320	21.1	50	12
Rhuddlan	1,903	552	2,455	23.4	34	4
Wrexham Maelor	3,796	1,041	4,837	23.4	486	92
Dyfed	11,007	3,599	14,606	23.0	233	64
Carmarthen	1,355	449	1,804	21.6	24	8
Ceredigion	1,603	562	2,165	16.8	16	2
Dinefwr	1,143	379	1,522	24.7	34	3
Llanelli	2,476	797	3,273	24.0	120	47
Preseli	2,568	766	3,334	27.0	27	2
South Pembrokeshire	1,862	646	2,508	21.9	12	1
Gwent	16,063	4,180	20,243	30.4	1,256	210
Blaenau Gwent	2,965	583	3,548	33.9	220	26
Islwyn	1,998	479	2,477	26.9	113	11
Monmouth	1,826	611	2,437	23.5	158	11
Newport	5,712	1,503	7,215	32.7	496	128
Torfaen	3,562	1,004	4,566	29.4	269	34
Gwynedd	9,093	3,119	12,212	26.5	184	26
Aberconwy	1,689	585	2,274	21.3	35	7
Arfon	2,411	733	3,144	30.9	46	4
Dwyfor	994	380	1,374	20.8	6	1
Meirionnydd	1,136	463	1,599	21.0	17	2
Ynys Mon	2,863	958	3,821	30.3	81	13
Mid Glamorgan	21,368	5,200	26,568	31.7	1,056	201
Cynon Valley	2,942	681	3,623	31.8	87	14
Merthyr Tydfil	2,537	592	3,129	36.7	68	9
Ogwr	4,771	1,431	6,202	27.9	358	88
Rhondda	3,437	719	4,156	33.5	75	9
Rhymney Valley	4,463	940	5,403	34.5	199	27
Taff-Ely	3,218	837	4,055	28.0	269	53
Powys	2,409	939	3,348	19.4	136	19
Brecknock	950	336	1,286	22.7	22	2
Montgomery	1,080	410	1,490	17.4	82	11
Radnor	379	193	572	16.8	32	6
South Glamorgan	16,324	3,843	20,167	30.4	569	78
Cardiff	12,417	2,854	15,271	32.2	460	61
Vale of Glamorgan	3,907	989	4,896	24.8	109	16
West Glamorgan	12,921	3,164	16,085	28.3	955	201
Port Talbot	1,581	371	1,952	25.0	497	97
Lliw Valley	1,894	478	2,372	21.8	155	18
Neath	2,155	583	2,738	24.6	57	11
Swansea	7,291	1,732	9,023	31.8	246	75

15.3 (Continued)

	Unemployment January 1992				Gross value added in manufacturing (£ million) 1989	Net capital expenditure in manufacturing (£ million) 1989
	Males (numbers)	Females (numbers)	Total (numbers)	Percentage long-term[1] unemployed		
Scotland	184,108	57,243	241,351	30.6	8,309	1,232
Borders	2,241	856	3,097	17.3	170	16
Berwick	361	136	497	12.3	24	2
Ettrick and Lauderdale	656	266	922	20.1	48	5
Roxburgh	858	310	1,168	16.4	81	8
Tweedale	366	144	510	19.2	17	2
Central	9,066	2,968	12,034	29.1	650	185
Clackmannan	1,742	519	2,261	32.7	113	11
Falkirk	4,989	1,637	6,626	29.0	477	144
Stirling	2,335	812	3,147	26.9	60	30
Dumfries and Galloway	4,191	1,757	5,948	20.4	214	33
Annandale and Eskdale	863	418	1,281	16.5	63	6
Nithsdale	1,668	628	2,296	22.0	109	24
Stewartry	491	232	723	17.0	21	2
Wigtown	1,169	479	1,648	22.6	21	1
Fife	11,692	3,927	15,619	27.3	711	87
Dunfermline	4,502	1,355	5,857	26.8	353	22
Kirkcaldy	5,961	1,999	7,960	29.0	309	58
North East Fife	1,229	573	1,802	21.8	48	8
Grampian	8,525	3,318	11,843	20.8	657	91
Aberdeen City	4,199	1,199	5,398	21.8	320	62
Banff & Buchan	1,435	554	1,989	19.5	101	10
Gordon	681	372	1,053	16.8	79	6
Kincardine and Deeside	485	266	751	16.4	24	5
Moray	1,725	927	2,652	22.7	133	7
Highlands	6,770	2,831	9,601	23.2	194	23
Badenoch and Strathspey	307	167	474	14.1	10	0
Caithness	985	310	1,295	29.2	15	3
Inverness[6]	1,960	664	2,624	23.5	48	14
Lochaber	697	394	1,091	17.8	42	..
Nairn	248	103	351	23.1	6	-
Ross and Cromarty	1,690	668	2,358	21.6	66	4
Skye and Lochalsh	445	268	713	23.0	2	-
Sutherland	438	257	695	31.2	6	1
Lothian	25,096	7,623	32,719	28.0	1,079	200
East Lothian	2,466	664	3,130	28.8	58	7
Edinburgh City	15,179	4,637	19,816	29.3	600	118
Midlothian	2,444	752	3,196	25.8	102	12
West Lothian	5,007	1,570	6,577	24.9	319	63
Strathclyde	102,325	28,944	131,269	33.9	4,047	522
Argyll and Bute	2,047	910	2,957	26.6	45	10
Bearsden and Milngavie	683	251	934	23.0	8	1
Clydebank	2,387	554	2,941	33.6	85	6
Clydesdale	1,832	578	2,410	27.3	31	4
Cumbernauld and Kilsyth	2,190	664	2,854	24.2	278	123
Cumnock and Doon Valley	2,422	633	3,055	35.1	39	1
Cunninghame	6,044	1,943	7,987	27.1	62	13
Dumbarton	3,103	943	4,046	31.8	162	9
East Kilbride	2,604	943	3,547	21.8	187	22
Eastwood	899	367	1,266	19.4	17	1
Glasgow City	41,438	10,789	52,227	38.7	1,045	93
Hamilton	4,306	1,115	5,421	35.7	128	15
Inverclyde	4,670	1,212	5,882	33.4	388	35
Kilmarnock and Loudoun	3,421	1,077	4,498	32.6	136	15
Kyle and Carrick	3,782	1,332	5,114	27.4	122	20
Monklands	4,481	1,111	5,592	35.9	150	15
Motherwell	6,168	1,575	7,743	35.8	444	49
Renfrew	7,597	2,196	9,793	30.8	669	81
Strathkelvin	2,251	751	3,002	27.4	51	8

15.3 *(Continued)*

	Unemployment January 1992				Gross value added in manufacturing (£ million) 1989	Net capital expenditure in manufacturing (£ million) 1989
	Males (numbers)	Females (numbers)	Total (numbers)	Percentage long-term[1] unemployed		
Tayside	12,159	4,345	16,504	31.9	559	71
Angus	2,330	1,060	3,390	26.3	140	27
Dundee City	7,061	2,263	9,324	37.5	320	35
Perth and Kinross	2,768	1,022	3,790	23.2	98	9
Orkney Islands	364	154	518	21.8	8	1
Shetland Islands	292	111	403	15.4	10	1
Western Isles	1,387	409	1,796	28.5	10	1
Northern Ireland	80,737	24,055	104,792	49.7	1,886	301
Antrim	1,748	652	2,400	39.6	..	..
Ards	1,997	739	2,736	41.3	..	..
Armagh	2,341	752	3,093	50.3	..	..
Ballymena	1,943	691	2,634	45.6	..	..
Ballymoney	1,271	314	1,585	55.0	..	..
Banbridge	1,135	408	1,543	41.5	..	..
Belfast	19,875	5,420	25,295	53.7	..	..
Carrickfergus	1,259	511	1,770	37.7	..	..
Castlereagh	1,708	765	2,473	41.6	..	..
Coleraine	2,554	781	3,335	46.7	..	..
Cookstown	1,679	491	2,170	54.3	..	..
Craigavon	3,351	1,033	4,384	49.8	..	..
Derry	7,241	1,486	8,727	55.0	..	..
Down	2,359	872	3,231	39.8	..	..
Dungannon	2,635	742	3,377	53.0	..	..
Fermanagh	2,767	683	3,450	56.7	..	..
Larne	1,493	449	1,942	38.9	..	..
Limavady	1,817	457	2,274	52.6	..	..
Lisburn	3,649	1,272	4,921	47.3	..	..
Magherafelt	1,840	539	2,379	51.5	..	..
Moyle	941	243	1,184	51.1	..	..
Newry and Mourne	5,288	1,453	6,741	50.9	..	..
Newtownabbey	2,754	1,054	3,808	40.1	..	..
North Down	1,780	881	2,661	35.3	..	..
Omagh	2,495	781	3,276	51.4	..	..
Strabane	2,817	586	3,403	58.7	..	..

* Urban programme authorities.
1 Persons claiming benefit for more than 52 weeks as a percentage of all claimants.
2 Net capital expenditure figure includes Langhbaugh.
3 Gross value added figure includes Teesdale.
4 Net capital expenditure figure includes Holderness.
5 Net capital expenditure and gross value added figures includes Brentwood.
6 Net capital expenditure figure includes Lochaber.

Source: Employment Department; Central Statistical Office

Notes to Chapter 15: Districts

Tables 15.1-15.3, show selected statistics for individual districts. Regional Trends 24 included a chapter on urban statistics, which presented a range of data for a sub-set of districts which were regarded as urban. Previous editions have included tables showing statistics for London boroughs, metropolitan districts of England and a selection of urban areas in Scotland and Wales.

These tables complement the data shown sub-regionally in Chapter 14 and regionally in Chapters 3 to 13. A wide range of data are presented, covering population in Table 15.1, housing and households in Table 15.2, unemployment and economic statistics in Table 15.3. In the vast majority of cases, all the districts in Great Britain are included, and in some cases coverage is extended to the whole of the United Kingdom. Many of the points made in the notes to Chapter 14 also apply to Chapter 15 tables.

Where data can be easily combined, county, local authority region, regional and national totals are given to make comparison easier. However, it is sometimes the case that different sources of data or methodologies are used when desegregating data to lower and lower geographical levels, therefore it is not necessarily the case that data in this chapter are strictly comparable with data in other chapters. These data identify local as well as regional trends and because of the level of desegregation more caution in interpretation is necessary.

There are specific and known problems in comparing population, and unemployment data. Primarily these are brought about the fact that people will not always work or claim at an unemployment benefit office in the district where they live.

At national and regional level, unemployment is often expressed as a rate of the estimated total workforce. Such rates are only calculated for broadly self-contained labour markets and it is entirely inappropriate to calculate rates for individual districts. Table 15.3 excludes unemployment rates for the above reason.

Allowing for the difficulties in interpreting such geographically disaggregated data, the figures in the Chapter 15 can be used to give a broad picture of a particular district and how it compares with other districts.

The tables are intended to take a reasonably broad sweep across a range of subjects. More detailed statistics on specific topics may be readily available elsewhere. For example:

> Key population and vital statistics (local and health authority areas of England and Wales)
>
> The Registrar General's Annual Report for Scotland
>
> The Registrar General's Annual Report for Northern Ireland
>
> Housebuilding in England by Local Authority area
>
> Employment Gazette (unemployment by local authority districts and parliamentary constituency).

Appendix: Regional Classification

Standard Regions

Most of the statistics in *Regional Trends* are for the 11 standard regions of the United Kingdom. These coincide with the Economic Planning Regions and are illustrated on pages 5, 152 and 153.

Counties of England and Wales

The 46 counties of England and the 8 counties of Wales are listed in the selected sub-regional statistics in Chapter 14.

Metropolitan Counties and Districts

Selected statistics are given for the former metropolitan counties in Chapters 14 and 15 and in some tables in other chapters.

Greater London

Greater London was not a metropolitan county, but statistics for Greater London are shown wherever figures for the metropolitan counties appear and in a number of additional tables.

Local Authority Regions of Scotland

The 10 LA regions of Scotland are listed in the selected statistics in Chapter 14. The Islands area comprises Orkney, Shetland and the Western Isles.

Northern Ireland

In Chapter 14 the 26 districts of Northern Ireland have been grouped into 5 Education and Library Boards. Some data are, however, only available for Health and Social Services Boards or for travel-to-work areas. In the latter case, data are only shown for the Belfast travel-to-work area. The districts comprising the Education and Library Boards are as follows:-

Board	Districts
Belfast	Belfast
South Eastern	Ards, Castlereagh, Down, Lisburn, North Down.
Southern	Armagh, Banbridge, Cookstown, Craigavon, Dungannon, Newry and Mourne.
North Eastern	Antrim, Ballymena, Ballymoney, Carrickfergus, Coleraine, Larne, Magherafelt, Moyle, Newtownabbey.
Western	Fermanagh, Limavady, Londonderry, Omagh, Strabane.

Health and Social Services Boards are as follows:-

Northern	as North Eastern Education and Library Board but including Cookstown.
Eastern	as South Eastern Education and Library Board but including Belfast.
Southern	as Southern Education and Library Board but excluding Cookstown.
Western	as Western Education and Library Board.

All travel-to-work areas in the United Kingdom were revised in September 1984.

Other Regional Classifications

Regional Health Authorities are used in Chapter 6.

Regional figures for *unemployment* up to 1983 are built up by aggregating the appropriate local employment office areas. The boundaries, however, do not in all cases agree precisely with county or regional boundaries. From 1984, the data are based on electoral wards - see supplement to the September 1984 edition of *Employment Gazette*.

MSC Vocational and Educational Training Group regions are used in Charts 7.21 and 7.22. The regions in this table are comparable with the standard statistical regions except that East and West Midlands are combined into one Midlands region, and the South East region includes East Anglia, but excludes Greater London, which is a separate region. Cumbria is included in the North West region. On 1 July 1986 certain MSC regions were changed. Midlands region was divided to form the West Midlands region and the East Midlands and Eastern region. Luton and Ipswich areas became part of East Midlands and Eastern.

The *United Kingdom Continental Shelf* is treated as a separate region in Tables 12.1 and 12.2.

REGIONAL HEALTH AUTHORITY AREAS

Health authority boundary

SCOTLAND

NORTHERN

YORKSHIRE

NORTH WESTERN

1

TRENT

WEST MIDLANDS

EAST ANGLIA

WALES

OX-FORD

2

NORTH EAST THAMES

WESSEX

3

SOUTH EAST THAMES

SOUTH WESTERN

1. MERSEY
2. NORTH WEST THAMES
3. SOUTH WEST THAMES

ENTERPRISE ZONES

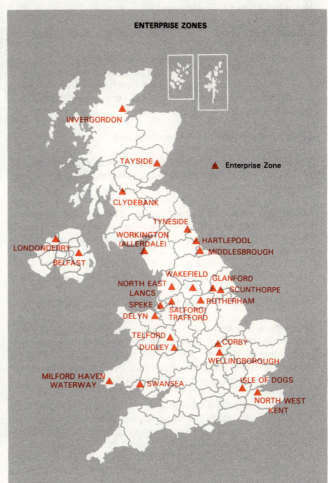

▲ Enterprise Zone

INVERGORDON

TAYSIDE

CLYDEBANK

TYNESIDE

LONDONDERRY

WORKINGTON (ALLERDALE)

HARTLEPOOL

MIDDLESBROUGH

BELFAST

WAKEFIELD

GLANFORD

NORTH EAST LANCS

SCUNTHORPE

SPEKE

ROTHERHAM

DELYN

SALFORD/TRAFFORD

TELFORD

CORBY

DUDLEY

WELLINGBOROUGH

MILFORD HAVEN WATERWAY

ISLE OF DOGS

SWANSEA

NORTH WEST KENT

GAS REGIONS

ISLAND AREA

Gas regional boundary

SCOTTISH

NORTHERN

NORTH EASTERN

NORTH WESTERN

EAST MIDLANDS

WEST MIDLANDS

EASTERN

WALES

NORTH THAMES

SOUTH WESTERN

SOUTH EASTERN

SOUTHERN

ELECTRICITY BOARD REGIONS

Central Electricity Generating Board regional boundary

NORTH OF SCOTLAND

SOUTH OF SCOTLAND

NORTH EASTERN

NORTH WESTERN

YORKSHIRE

MERSEYSIDE & NORTH WALES

EAST MIDLANDS

MID-LANDS

EASTERN

SOUTH WALES

SOUTHERN

SOUTH EASTERN

SOUTH WESTERN

1. LONDON

Notes to Chapter 7: Employment

Chart 7.1 and Tables 7.3 and 7.7 Employees in employment

Numbers of employees in employment are based on the Census of Employment which is held periodically. Estimates are from quarterly series derived from sample surveys benchmarked on the latest census. Figures exclude HM Forces, the self-employed and employees in private domestic service.

Chart 7.1 and Table 7.3 Civilian workforce

The civilian workforce comprises employees in employment, the self employed, the unemployed and participants in work related government training programmes.

Estimates of the numbers of self-employed persons, with or without employees, are based on the Census of Population with estimates for other dates obtained by using Labour Force Surveys and, before 1975, national insurance card counts.

See notes to Tables and Charts 7.13-7.16 for unemployment data.

Tables 7.2, 7.4 and 7.10 The labour force and activity rates

The *civilian labour force* includes people aged 16 or over who are either in employment (whether employed, self-employed or on work-related government employment and training programmes, but excluding those in the armed forces) or unemployed. Two different definitions of the unemployed are used for the figures in these Tables.

Estimates up to 1984 are on the former *'Great Britain Labour Force definition'*, which counted as unemployed people without a job and seeking work in a reference week (or prevented from seeking work by temporary sickness or holiday, or waiting for the results of a job application, or waiting to start a job they had already obtained), whether or not they were available to start (except students not able to start because they must complete their education).

From 1984, estimates and projections, are based on a different definition, which follows the guidelines of the International Labour Office (ILO) and is used by the Organisation for Economic Co-operation and Development (OECD). The 'ILO definition', counts as unemployed people without a job who were available to start work within two weeks and had either looked for work in the past four weeks or were waiting to start a job they had already obtained. Estimates on the ILO definition are not available before 1984, as the Labour Force Survey did not then collect information on job search over a four-week period.

The *civilian activity* rate in a given age/sex category is the civilian labour force expressed as a percentage of the population in that category.

These estimates are consistent with the national (Great Britain) labour force figures published in the April 1992 issue of *Employment Gazette*.

Estimates of the civilian labour force and activity rates for 1971 are based mainly on data from the Census of Population. Estimates for later years incorporate survey estimates from the Labour Force Survey (see note below) supplemented by data from the Census of Population on the economic activity of those not in private households. Further details of sources and methods appear in *Employment Gazette, April 1992 and June 1992*.

The *civilian workforce* (Chart 7.1 and Table 7.3) is broadly similar in concept to the civilian labour force (Tables 7.2, 7.4 and 7.10). There are however numerous differences in definition and coverage between the two series. For example, employees in employment with two jobs will be counted twice in the workforce but once in the labour force; while persons seeking work but not claiming benefits are in the labour force but are not covered by the working population. This can lead the two series to exhibit different short-term movements, over the longer term the paths followed are similar.

Tables 7.2, 7.4, 7.8 and 7.10 Labour Force Survey

The 1991 Labour Force Survey was a sample survey of private households covering about half a per cent of private households. Results of this survey are grossed up to an estimate of the private household population.

Table 7.5 Economic characteristics of head of household

The full-time/part-time categories are classified according to survey respondents' own assessment. The unemployed, are identified using the ILO definition, (see earlier definition).

Table 7.7 Industrial distribution of employees

This table is based on the Census of Employment for all industries except agriculture. A more detailed industry breakdown appears in the *Employment Gazette*. The estimates of employment in agriculture are based on June Censuses of Agriculture. They exclude a small number of employees of agricultural machinery contractors but include seasonal and temporary workers. Paid family workers are included in the figures for Great Britain but not for Northern Ireland.

See notes to Tables 13.2-13.6 of the Standard Industrial Classification.

Table 7.8 Educational qualifications

Degree or equivalent includes graduate membership of a professional institute.

Other higher education includes: Business and Technology Education Council (Higher National Certificate and Diploma) and their Scottish equivalents and teaching and nursing qualifications.

GCE 'A' level or equivalent includes: Business and Technology Education Council (National Certificate and Diploma) and their Scottish equivalents and City and Guilds qualifications.

GCE 'O' level equivalent includes CSE grade 1.

Further information on educational qualification classifications can be found in *Employment Gazette*, 7 March 1992, pages 119-120.

Table 7.9 Occupational grouping

The occupation groupings used are based on major groups in the new *Standard Occupational Classification*, (HMSO), first published February 1990.

Table 7.12 Industrial disputes

The table shows working days lost and rates per 1,000 employees for various years by Standard region for all industries and services and, as the number of stoppages can vary considerably from year to year, an annual average for the years 1978-1988. The statistics relate only to disputes connected with terms and conditions of employment. Stoppages involving fewer than 10 workers or lasting less than one day are excluded except where the aggregate of working days lost exceeded 100. When interpreting the figures the following points should be borne in mind:

> 1. Geographical variations in industrial structure affect overall regional comparisons.
>
> 2. A few large stoppages affecting a small number of firms many have a significant effect.
>
> 3. The number of working days lost and workers involved relate to persons both directly and indirectly involved at the establishments where the disputes occurred. This relationship varies between industries and, therefore, between regions.

4. The regional figures involve a greater degree of estimation than the national figures owing to the need to allocate large national stoppages to particular regions, sometimes using incomplete information.

See notes to Tables 13.2-13.6 of the Standard Industrial Classification.

Tables and Charts 7.13-7.16 Unemployment statistics

Figures relate to persons claiming benefit (that is, unemployment benefit, income support or national insurance credits) at an unemployment benefit office on the day of the monthly count, who on that day were unemployed and satisfied the conditions for claiming benefit. Students claiming benefit during a vacation but who intend to return to full-time education, and temporarily stopped workers, are excluded. Figures for the claimant basis for Great Britain prior to May 1982 and for Northern Ireland prior to November 1982 are estimates - see the article in *Employment Gazette*, December 1982.

National and regional unemployment rates are calculated by expressing the number of unemployed as a percentage of the estimated total workforce (the sum of the unemployed claimants, employees in employment, self-employed, HM Forces and participants on work-related government training Programmes). These rates are shown in Table 7.16.

Table 7.18 Restart Interviews, definitions

People contacted:

The number of people who are invited to a Restart interview, (Nb. all people are contacted every 6 months).

Given an offer:

The aim of a Restart interview is to assess an individual's circumstances and make the most appropriate offer of help to meet their needs.

Taking up an offer:

The number of clients who accept (ie. agree to pursue) the offer of help made at their interview.

Everyone who has been unemployed for 6 months or more is invited to attend an advisory interview.

The aim of the interview is to establish contact with longer term unemployed people, review their situation with them, give advice about opportunities available to them and how they could be used, and to help them decide on the best route to return to work.

18-24 year olds who have been unemployed for 6-12 months are guaranteed an offer of a place in a jobclub, on one of the JIG options, on Employment Training or on an Enterprise Awareness day at either their main Restart interview or at a follow up interview.

Employment Training (ET)

ET is a programme for the long term unemployed, locally planned and delivered to help people find and stay in employment. Training and Enterprise Councils are responsible for the planning and delivery of ET.

Destination figures for leavers who left ET before January 1991 relate to the leaver's activity at the time of the survey, which was conducted three months after they had left the programme. Leavers who left in January 1991 or later were followed up six months after they left ET, they were asked about their status three months after leaving.

Table 7.23 Youth Training (YT)

YT aims to provide broad based training mainly for 16 and 17 year olds and to provide better qualified young entrants into the labour market. Training and Enterprise Councils are responsible for the planning and delivery of YT.

Destination figures relate to the leaver's activities at the time of the survey. Those who left the scheme before October 1990 were surveyed three months after leaving; leavers between October and December 1990 were followed up in June 1991; and those leaving after December 1990 were followed up six months after leaving.

Notes to Chapter 8: Income and spending

Comparability of earnings statistics

Earnings statistics shown in this section are not comparable owing to differences in the coverage of the surveys, differences in classifying individuals to regions and different levels of reliability of the regional data. The basis of the surveys differ, in that the Survey of Personal Incomes is a sample of administrative records, the Family Expenditure Survey is a sample of households and the New Earnings Survey is a sample of employees. The administrative and household surveys are classified according to regions of residence while the surveys of employees and firms are classified to the region of work place. The reliability depends partly upon the size of the sample and response rates. Different surveys will have their own sources of bias which will affect the reliability of their results.

Table 8.1 and 8.2 Household income

The 1980-1981 and 1989-1990 figures for income (Table 8.1) cannot be directly compared, following the introduction in 1982 of the Housing Benefit Scheme, as changes were made to the way household income and household expenditure were calculated.

These tables contain results from the Family Expenditure Survey. The survey covers all types of private households in the United Kingdom. A sample of around 12,000 addresses is selected annually giving an effective sample of about 1 in 2,000 households, of which about seventy per cent co-operate. The available evidence suggests that co operation in older households, households where the head is self-employed, those without children and higher income households is less likely. In Greater London response is noticeably lower than in other areas.

Results of this survey are published in the annual *Family Spending* (HMSO), together with a full list of definitions and items on which information is collected. A full description of sampling and fieldwork procedure is provided by the technical handbook *Family Expenditure Survey Handbook* (HMSO).

A *household* comprises one person living alone or a group of people living at the same address having meals prepared together and with common housekeeping. The members of a household thus defined are not necessarily related by blood or marriage. The survey covers private households, people living in hostels, hotels, boarding houses or institutions are excluded.

Household income is the aggregate of the gross incomes of the individual members of the household before deduction of income tax, national insurance contributions and any other deductions at source. Income thus defined excludes housing benefit; money received by one member from another member of the household; proceeds from the sale of cars, income in kind, furniture or other capital assets; and receipts from legacies, maturing insurance policies and windfalls, the exceptions are luncheon vouchers and an imputed amount for owner-occupied and rent-free accommodation.

Tables 8.3-8.5 New Earnings Survey

These contain some of the regional results of the New Earnings Survey 1991, fuller details of which are given in part E of the report *New Earnings Survey 1991* (HMSO), published in November 1991. Results for Northern Ireland are published separately by the Department of Economic Development, Northern Ireland. The survey measured gross earnings of a one per cent sample of employees, most of whom were members of Pay-As-You-Earn (PAYE) schemes for a pay-period which included 10 April 1991. The earnings information collected was converted to a weekly basis where necessary, and to an hourly basis where normal basic hours were reported.

Figures for Great Britain regions are only given where the number of employees reporting in the survey were 50 or more and the standard error of average weekly earnings was 5 per cent or less. Gross earnings are measured before tax, national insurance or other deductions. They include overtime pay, bonuses and other additions to basic pay but exclude any payments for earlier periods (eg. back pay), most income in kind, tips and gratuities. All the results in this volume relate to full time men and women on adult rates whose pay for the survey pay period was not affected by absence. Employees were classified to the region in which they worked (or were based if mobile), and to manual or non-manual occupations on the basis of the Standard Occupational Classification (SOC). Part A of the report gives full details of definitions used in the survey.

Full-time employees are defined as those normally expected to work more than 30 hours per week, excluding overtime and main meal breaks (but 25 hours or more in the case of teachers) or, if their normal hours were not specified, as those regarded as full-time by the employer.

Table 8.5 Average weekly earnings

See notes to Tables 13.2-13.6 of the Standard Industrial Classification.

Table 8.6 The Survey of Personal Incomes

The survey covers all individuals for whom income tax records are held by the Inland Revenue: not all are taxpayers - about eight per cent do not pay tax because the operation of personal reliefs and allowances removes them from liability. The data in Table 8.6 relate to tax units (single persons and married couples) whose income over the year amounted £3,000 or more. This is a little higher than the threshold for operation of Pay-As-You-Earn, which was around £2,780 in 1989-90. Below this threshold, coverage of incomes is incomplete in tax records.

The income shown is that liable to assessment in each tax year. For most incomes this is the amount earned or receivable in that year, but for business profits and professional earnings the assessments are normally based on the amount of income arising in the trading account ending in the previous year. Those types of income that were specifically exempt from tax eg. certain social security benefits are excluded.

Incomes are allocated to regions according to the place of residence of the recipient.

The table classifies incomes by range of *Total Income*. This is defined as gross income, whether earned or unearned, before deducting employees' superannuation contributions, but after deducting employment expenses, losses, capital allowances, stock relief, and any expenses allowable as a deduction from gross income from lettings. Superannuation contributions have been estimated and distributed among earners in the Survey of Personal Incomes consistently with information about numbers contracted in or out of the State Earnings Related Pension Scheme and the proportion of their earnings contribution. The coverage of unearned income also includes estimates of that part of the investment income (whose liability to tax at basic rate has been satisfied at source) not known to tax offices.

Table 8.7 Expenditure on cash benefits.

Retirement pension took the place of the former contributory old age pension. The table excludes non-contributory retirement pension (formerly Old Persons Pension) which is payable to all persons aged 80 or over who did not qualify for a retirement pension, or qualified for one at a lower rate than the rate of non-contributory pension.

Sickness and Invalidity benefit, these benefits are generally paid to claimants who are certified incapable of work and satisfy the contribution conditions for the benefits. The figures do not include expenditure for Statutory Sick Pay (SSP). Invalidity Benefit is payable after there has been entitlement to SSP or sickness benefit for 28 weeks in a period of interruption of employment.

Disablement benefit also includes Reduced Earnings Allowance and is payable to a claimant who is disabled as a result of an industrial accident or prescribed disease. This does not include Industrial Death Benefit or other industrial injury benefits.

Income Support replaced Supplementary Benefit in April 1988. It is a non-contributory benefit payable to people working less than 24 hours a week, whose incomes are below the levels (called 'applicable amounts') laid down by parliament. The applicable amounts generally consist of personal allowances for members of the family, premiums for particular groups (eg pensioners or disabled) and, where appropriate, amounts for certain housing costs.

Figures in the tables do not include Social Fund payments or loans, which replaced single payments for specific requirements under the former Supplementary Benefit scheme.

Child benefit is payable usually for all children, including the first or only child below the specified age-limits. It replaced Family Allowance in April 1977.

War pensions, allowances or other payments may be awarded for disablement or death due to service in HM Forces. Benefit can also be paid for injury incurred in the course of war service in the Naval Auxiliary Service, or in the Mercantile Marine or in a fishing fleet, or in the Civil Defence services.

A brief description of the main features of the various benefits paid in Great Britain is set out in *Social Security Statistics* (published annually by HMSO). Detailed information on benefits paid in Northern Ireland is contained in *Northern Ireland Annual Abstract of Statistics* and *Northern Ireland Social Security Statistics*.

The estimates of regional distribution in Great Britain have been based on regional analyses of population or claimants combined with Post Office encashment returns for England, Scotland and Wales. The resulting percentages were applied to the Great Britain annual expenditure to obtain regional expenditure. Because of changes in method, the estimates may not be entirely consistent with those published for previous years. Particular components may differ from estimates published elsewhere. The figures for Northern Ireland are actuals for the province. Calculations of supplementary benefits are based on net supplementary benefit payments.

Table 8.8 Income tax payable

Income tax is calculated as the liability for the income tax year, regardless of when the tax may have been paid or how it was collected. Where a tax unit consists of a married couple, the tax liability of the couple is calculated according to whether a wife's earning election is beneficial, regardless of whether an election was made.

The income tax liability is calculated from the total income of the tax unit, including tax credits on dividends, and interest subject to the composite rate of tax grossed up at the basic rate of tax. From total income is deducted allowable reliefs etc, including relief at the basic rate given at source on mortgage interest, and personal allowances.

The estimate of the total number of tax units with income tax records is shown under the "Basic Rate" heading as all tax payers (including those liable at higher rate) pay some tax at basic rate. For definition of total income see the notes to Table 8.6. Only tax units with incomes in excess of the thresholds for the operation of Pay-As-You-Earn, (around £2,780 in 1989-90) are included in the figures for total income.

Table 8.9 Family Expenditure Surveys

This table contains results from the Family Expenditure Surveys for 1989 and 1990. Some details of the survey are given in the notes to Tables 8.1 and 8.2.

Expenditure excludes savings or investments (eg life assurance premiums), income tax payments, national insurance contributions, housing benefit and mortgage and other payments for the purchase of, or major additions to, dwellings.

Expenditure of households living in their own dwellings consists of the payments by these households for rates, water, ground rent and insurance of the structure, together with imputed rent (the weekly equivalent of the rateable value of the dwelling) less receipts (if any) from letting.

Housing estimates of expenditure on a few items are below those which might be expected by comparison with other sources eg. alcoholic drink, tobacco and, to a lesser extent, confectionery and ice cream.

Table 8.10 and 8.11 The National Food Survey

This is a continuing sample enquiry of about 14,000 addresses selected annually in Great Britain. An effective sample of some 13,600 households is obtained, of whom about fifty five per cent voluntarily co-operate by keeping a record of food obtained for consumption in the home during one week.

Detailed results of the Survey and definitions are published in the Annual Reports of the *National Food Survey Committee 'Household Food Consumption and Expenditure'* (HMSO).

Table 8.12 Durable goods

Figures for Great Britain are taken from the General Household Survey (GHS), which is a continuous survey of about 13,000 addresses per year. An effective sample of some 12,000 private households is obtained, of which eighty four per cent co-operated for 1989 and eighty one per cent for 1990.

Results for Northern Ireland for 1980-1981 are taken from the expanded sample of households taken for the Family Expenditure Survey (FES). Data for 1989-1990 are derived from the Continuous Household Survey.

Until 1981 the GHS and FES used the same definition of a household (see notes to Tables 8.1-8.2). In 1981 a new definition was adopted in the GHS in order to improve comparability with the Census of Population. From 1981 a household is 'a single person or a group of people who have the address as their only or main residence and who either share one meal a day or share the living accommodation' (not just a kitchen or bathroom).

Subject Index

Figures in the index refer to table or chart numbers, page numbers refer to maps. Explanatory notes and definitions and the appendix and regional profiles are not indexed.

employment 2.1, 7.1-7.23
    see also economic activity, employees and
          unemployment
    civilian labour force 7.2, 7.4
    income from 12.4, 12.5
    manufacturing 13.5
        foreign enterprises 13.4
    occupational grouping 7.9
    training and employment measures 7.18-7.23
    vacancies 7.17
    workforce 7.1, 7.3, 7.8
    working population 7.1-7.3
Employment Training 7.21
energy and water supply industry
    coal 13.11
    earnings 8.5
    employees 7.7, 15.3
    gas 13.10
    Gross Domestic Fixed Capital Formation (GDFCF) 12.9
    Gross Domestic Product (GDP) 12.2
    water see water authorities
ethnic origin 3.15
European Agricultural Guidance and Guarantee Fund 2.1
European Communities 2.1, 3.9-3.11, p30
European Regional Development Fund 2.1
examinations see qualifications
expenditure
    assistance to industry 13.7
    capital 14.3, 15.3
    cash benefits 8.7
    consumers' 12.6, 12.7
    education 5.15, 5.17
    health authorities 6.18
    household 8.9
    manufacturing 13.2, 13.7, 14.3, 15.3
    roads 10.6

firearms 9.5
food 8.10, 8.11
food, drink and tobacco 8.9, 12.6
foreign enterprises in manufacturing 13.4
freight
        air 10.10
        rail 10.8
        road 10.7
        sea 10.9
further education 5.4-5.6, 5.12, 5.16

gas sales 13.10
general practitioners (GPs) 6.3, 6.19
Gross Domestic Fixed Capital Formation (GDFCF) 12.9, 12.10
Gross Domestic Product (GDP) 2.1, 12.1, 12.3, 12.8, 13.1, 14.3
Gross Value Added (GVA)
    manufacturing 13.2, 13.3, 14.3, 15.3
    foreign enterprises 13.4

health 6.1-6.21
    see also National Health Service
Health Authority Areas 6.1
health visitors 6.20
heart disease 6.4
high court (Scotland) 9.10
HIV-I antibody positive reports 6.7
    Aids 6.8
homeless households 4.11, 4.12
hospital services see National Health Service
hours worked 8.3, 8.4

households
    economic characteristics of heads 7.5
    ethnic origin of population in 3.15
    expenditure 8.9, 8.10
    income 8.1, 8.2, 14.4
    lone parent 15.2
    size 15.2
    with car 10.1
    with selected durables 8.12
housing 4.1-4.12, 15.2
    completions 4.5
    expenditure on 8.9, 12.6
    land 4.7, 11.9
    local authority 4.2, 4.10-4.12, 15.2
        allocation 4.11
        sales 4.10
    mortgages 4.9
    prices 4.7, 4.8
    provision for homeless 4.11, 4.12
    renovations 4.4
    starts 15.2
    stock 4.1-4.3, 4.6
        age 4.3
        tenure 4.2
        values 4.6

immunisation 6.12
income 8.1-8.6, 12.4, 12.5, 14.4
    from employment 12.8
    household 8.1, 8.2, 14.4
    personal 8.6, 12.4
    personal disposable 12.5
    tax payable 8.8
Income Support 8.7
industrial distribution
    employees 7.7
    Gross Domestic Product (GDP) 12.2
industrial stoppages 7.12
industry, assistance to 13.7, 13.8
infant mortality 6.1, 6.2, 14.1
infectious diseases 6.6
in-patients 6.14
international migration 3.9-3.11
inter-regional movements 3.7
    by age 3.8

jobcentre vacancies 7.17

labour force 7.2, 7.4
land use 11.8, 11.9
law enforcement 9.1-9.14
    see also crime
    indictable and summary offences 9.4, 9.6, 9.9
    motoring offences 9.11, 9.12
    police 9.1-9.6
live births see births
livestock 13.15
local authority homelessness action 4.12
local authority housing see housing

magistrates' courts 9.9, 11.7
manpower
    coal industry 13.11
    health services 6.19-6.21
    police 9.14
    teachers 5.1